D1238577

For Jack & Suzie,
Hope you enjoy this production of mine! Would love to see you!
Happy Holidays,
[signature]
12/17/04

COLLEGE RODEO

NUMBER NINETY-NINE

Centennial Series of the Association of Former Students

Texas A&M University

COLLEGE RODEO

From Show to Sport

Sylvia Gann Mahoney

Foreword by Tuff Hedeman

Texas A&M University Press · College Station

The paper used in this book
meets the minimum requirements
of the American National Standard for Permanence
of Paper for Printed Library Materials, z39.48-1984.
Binding materials have been chosen for durability.

LIBRARY OF CONGRESS CATALOGING-IN-PUBLICATION DATA

Mahoney, Sylvia Gann, 1939–
        College rodeo : from show to sport / Sylvia Gann Mahoney ;
    foreword by Tuff Hedeman.—1st ed.
            p. cm.—(Centennial series of the Association of Former
    Students, Texas A&M University ; no. 99)
        Includes bibliographical references (p.   ) and index.
        ISBN 1-58544-331-X
        1. Rodeos—United States—History.   2. College sports—Unites States—
    History.   3. National Intercollegiate Rodeo Association—History.
    I. Title.   II. Series.
    GV1834.5M35   2004
    791.8'4—dc22   2003018575

*The author and the publisher gratefully acknowledge
a generous grant from Wrangler—Division of VF Corp
in support of publication of this volume.
Special thanks to Bill "Mr. Wrangler" and Hoppy Hervey.*

To

Gordon and Evelyn Macha Gann

Contents

Illustrations

Foreword

It's about time someone put together a comprehensive account of the history of college rodeo, and with more than a quarter century of experience in the sport, Sylvia Mahoney is the perfect person to do it. A former rodeo coach and the wife of my college rodeo coach, John Mahoney, Sylvia knows this sport top to bottom, from every angle. This book is the first of its kind and is long overdue. I expect it to set and maintain the industry standard on this subject for many years to come.

College rodeo is an important stepping stone, and it plays a vital role in every participant's life, whether that individual pursues a career in professional rodeo or not. For me, it was not just a training ground that helped me gain the skills and strength that led to a rewarding career in professional rodeo, it was also my only shot at a college education. Without scholarship support afforded me by college rodeo, my education would have ended after high school. Instead, I had some great years at Sul Ross State University in Alpine, Texas, where I learned a ton, books to bulls.

I am not alone in college rodeo's pivotal role in my career and life. Countless ProRodeo Hall of Famers have roots in the college rodeo ranks. Like me, they all say college rodeo played a vital role in their development, both in the arena and out. And college rodeo is not just for the superstar types. For others, it is a great social sideline to their college years, serving as a fun, healthy after-school activity that supplements their studies. Diplomas in hand and with life-long friends made through college rodeo, they go on to become successful professionals in every imaginable field. College rodeo builds character for life, and this book acknowledges that fact.

Tuff Hedeman, PBR and three-time World Champion Bull Rider

Preface

Seldom does a college sport exist for more than eighty years without having a book written about it, but college rodeo has. The extent of available information for research consisted of brief references in college yearbooks, rodeo history books, and museums. The National Intercollegiate Rodeo Association's (NIRA) home page on the Internet had a limited amount of background information. For this reason, erroneous information, which slowed research, had found its way into obituaries, college rodeo programs, awards ceremonies, and biographies. A need was evident for a documented, detailed history of college rodeo supplemented with the records of national champions and the schools that won them. Most schools did not have an accurate record of their own champions because the national records were incomplete and had several early-day errors. Also, a list of the persons who were at the organizational meetings was needed to give credit to those who actually helped start the NIRA.

Prior to starting my seventeen years of research on the history of college rodeo, I spent an initiation period of about eight years. When I was hired to teach English at New Mexico Junior College (NMJC), it was a young, robust institution in an oil-rich county one hundred miles long and forty miles wide, with most of the county being ranch country. Under the strong leadership of John Sheppard, vice president for instruction, NMJC provided the environment for creative ideas and supported them with wise direction and encouragement.

So that NMJC could have a rodeo program, the ranchers and area rodeo groups built an arena and gave it to the college. I replaced the English instructor and rodeo club sponsor, so I was asked to do both, also. Since they assured me that there was no one else available, I, after making calls to recruit help, agreed to do it. The fall of 1977, when I became the rodeo club sponsor, attorney and NMJC board member Ray Potter, who twenty years later became my brother-in-law, directed the idea of moving the NMJC rodeo program into the athletic department so that it could be funded, resulting in my acquiring the title of rodeo coach.

While I was a rodeo coach and an English instructor at New Mexico Junior College, NIRA commissioner Tim Corfield initiated me into the field of writing rodeo articles, illustrated with photos, for the national college rodeo newspaper as well as for other national magazines, such as *Western Horseman*. Tim recommended me to Randy Witte, *Western Horseman* publisher, who offered me writing opportunities and enthusiastically promoted the NIRA alumni association and the writing of this book. After I presented several papers on college rodeo to the Texas Folklore Society (TFS), Dr. Francis Abernethy, TFS secretary and editor, asked me to write the entry on rodeo for *The New Handbook of Texas*, an encyclopedia.

The research and writing for this book about college rodeo started when I became the executive director of the Lea County Cowboy Hall of Fame (LCCHF) and Western Heritage Center on the NMJC campus at Hobbs, New Mexico. When the interim college president, R. N. Tydings, remarked to me after a coaches' meeting to plan a $4 million addition to the gym that he didn't see anything in the plans for rodeo, I presented a proposal to him to showcase some of the world champions from Lea County—approximately fifty-seven championships had been won at that time. President Tydings called county rancher Tuffy Cooper, whose talks to my Southwest literature classes about the fact that the county had spawned so many rodeo world champions had led to my proposal to President Tydings. After the three of us talked, the LCCHF resulted, with a thirteen-member talented, visionary board of directors from area ranches, especially inspired by rancher Daisy Clayton, seven hundred charter members, an annual induction dinner, and five thousand square feet of space to fill.

As the executive director with museum displays to create, I called on Museum of New Mexico curators for advice, and they welcomed me for a week to learn some basics. Then, I started research on ranchers and county rodeo champions. While doing research on a former college cowgirl who said that she had won an NIRA all-around championship (she had), I found that the NIRA had limited records on early-day NIRA cowgirls. In fact, the cowgirl national champions were not listed in the national records prior to 1956. During the first few years, the nomadic national office, run by college students, winnowed the files down to almost nothing, leaving them incomplete. No records existed on the twenty-nine years of college rodeo history prior to the organization of the National Intercollegiate Rodeo Association, which is the only college rodeo association.

I discovered that the only sources of information on college rodeo before the founding of the NIRA were from the cowboys and cowgirls and their scrapbooks with newspaper clippings and rodeo programs. As I called people, they started expressing a desire to have an NIRA alumni association, so in 1992 one of the alumni, Betty Sims Solt, and I organized the NIRA Alumni (NIRAA), which meets annually at the College National Finals Rodeo (CNFR). The members of this group helped verify that some national records were incorrect or incomplete. The alumni also filled in many history blanks, information that could not be found in printed material.

As a coach, I started attending college rodeos in 1977 in the Southwest Region, which included the colleges and universities from Fort Worth to San Angelo down to the Big Bend country up to the Texas Panhandle, and at that time, all of New Mexico. Along the way, I married a rodeo coach, John Mahoney from Sul Ross State University, who took a coaching job at Vernon Regional Junior College. After I quit coaching, I continued going to the Southwest Region rodeos with my coach husband and to every CNFR since 1979, making it easy to connect with present and past cowboys and cowgirls since rodeo people have an intricate networking.

I started my research by collecting every book on rodeo that I could find. There are no books on the history of college rodeo and few on professional rodeo. In my search, I started recording interviews with former NIRA members and champions; many of those more than 150 people are now deceased. Without them, countless questions would have gone unanswered.

To establish where and when the first intercollegiate rodeo was held, I started contacting people at land-grant universities for information. Charlie Rankin provided Texas A&M history that led to the 1920 date for the first college rodeo on a campus. Then, everything came together when John Bascom of Victorville, California, who made copies of all the information at the *Victor Press* on the first intercollegiate rodeo produced by Cal Godshall, called to tell me that he had located Jeanne Godshall, Cal's daughter. The turning point in my research came when I talked to Jeanne Godshall, who initially said that she wasn't well and didn't feel like talking. However, forty-five minutes later she had given me valuable, previously unavailable information and insight that helped tie my research together.

A surprising fact found during my research was that college rodeo had run parallel with professional rodeo while both were in their infancy, but college rodeo remained relatively unknown. With this fact, the effects of the new breed of cowboy and cowgirl on professional rodeo became a part of my research. With rodeo originating in the daily work of cowboys on ranches, the cultural aspect of a college education on ranch rodeo cowboys, and the spread of rodeo internationally by college rodeo networking and new careers contributed to the research. My research became more than a record of college championships, it became a project to gain insight into rodeo in a collegiate atmosphere and the perpetuation of a sense of the Spirit of the West by educated college rodeo people who moved beyond ranches. It illuminated the reason that college rodeo athletes are hard working, independent, fun, down-to-earth people. Cowboys and cowgirls, who are responsible for the feeding and care of their horses every day, are kept honest by their horses, as horses kick champions as fast as they kick anyone. These attributes along with persistence in taking what they love—their horse and their competition—wherever they go, successfully transplanted rodeo to the college campus and changed it from a show to a college sport, resulting in educated rodeo people who perpetuated the Western way of life as they moved into numerous new professions in new geographical areas while maintaining a strong network of friendships and a love for the sport of rodeo.

Acknowledgments

The history of the writing of this book is a trail of people who gave me their time, their expertise, their treasures, their college rodeo knowledge, their history, and their friendship.

Dr. Jim Harris, NMJC English instructor, inspired me to write with his prolific, creative writing talent, his interest in things Western, and his encouragement. He introduced me to the Texas Folklore Society, a constant source of inspiration with member writers such as Elmer Kelton and Dr. Lawrence Clayton, who said to me one day, "Quit doing research and get your book published. Put the rest of it in the next book." Dr. Lou Rodenberger's professional advice about writing and publishing served me well. Henry DeVillers helped with photography.

The NIRA office staff, Donna Maiden, Shelly Hill, and Sarah Neely, provided numerous copies of minutes, lists, and other information from the national records. Twice being the CNFR media director gave me ready access to the media, current champions, coaches, and knowledge of NIRA politics. Editing the Vernon College history book at the request of Dr. Wade Kirk when I went to work there as the marketing director gave insight.

NIRA Alumni members, especially Charlie Rankin and Jack and Evelyn Bruce Kingsbery provided first-hand knowledge, stacks of letters, newspaper articles, and photos that documented the beginning of the NIRA. A major primary source was Sonny and Joanne Sikes, whose knowledge of NIRA history spanned the years because they helped make it. Bob Clore, Kansas State art professor, NIRA alumnus, and photographer, provided numerous photos, information, and ideas. Clara Wilson's collection of letters and newspaper articles provided the key to understanding the split in the NIRA. National Cowboy Symposium executive director Alvin G. Davis, who helped create early NIRA history, also provided me an opportunity to appear on panels about rodeo and helped make my first contact with a publisher.

Mentor and friend Barbara Houston, Hobbs High School English department head, and life-time friend Peggy Rice Kenyon read my manuscript with a critical eye for content, style, and form. Friends from Lovington, New Mexico, Robert and Susie Brown, with their expertise helped me purchase my first computer. My niece Rhonda Nance provided computer instructions. Ten years later, Chris Slosser of Vernon College rescued much of my writing from defective discs when my computer's hard drive crashed. Susie Crowson, NMJC Humanities Division secretary, transcribed numerous taped interviews for me. Jackye Berry, Eunice, New Mexico; Gail Samberson, Lovington, New Mexico; Frances Marie Owens, Quanah, Texas; and Anna Wright and Susan Couch, Vernon, Texas, encouraged me by believing that my project would be completed. My mother Evelyn Gann, my sister Susie Potter, and my children Lesli Laughter and John R. Benge, were constant cheerleaders for my project. My husband John, a valuable rodeo resource, started rodeoing in the 1950s and helped with his phenomenal recall of names and details. Thanks to my Texas A&M editors and Dawn Hall for their wise direction and dedication to achieving excellence.

Thanks to Professional Rodeo Cowboys Association (PRCA) commissioner Steve Hatchell and NIRA commissioner John Smith for acknowledging the contribution of this history of college rodeo to the broad scope of rodeo.

Wrangler—Division of VF Corp, continuing with its longstanding, successful partnership with rodeo, gave a generous grant in support of publishing this first history of college rodeo. Thanks to Wrangler president Phil McAdams, and to Bill "Mr. Wrangler" and Hoppy Hervey for recognizing the book's contribution to rodeo history.

Thanks also to the many unnamed friends I acquired along the way who graciously helped me succeed at preserving some of the history of college rodeo.

COLLEGE RODEO

College Rodeo

Produces a

New Breed of Cowboy

"Look at that cowboy. He's wearing a college ring!" said a city visitor at a branding on the McElroy Ranch near Crane, Texas, in the 1930s.[1] Some seventy years later, many cowboys and cowgirls wore college rings and trophy buckles. A new breed of rodeo cowboy and cowgirl developed on college campuses and intertwined with the development of professional rodeo. Rodeo, which had originated in the daily chores of the working cowboy, rode onto campus in the 1920s with college cowboys competing on campus and in any other rodeo available. Competing both places satisfied many a rancher's son and daughter until a California entrepreneur recognized the entertainment potential in creating intercollegiate rodeo competition. However, World War II stopped college rodeo production in many places, while at the same time it helped to internationalize rodeo and expand competition for women. The number of cowgirl contestants grew as they learned riding and roping skills while filling vacancies left on the ranches by brothers who answered Uncle Sam's call. With the opportunity to attend college provided by a prosperous economy and the GI Bill, numerous veteran cowboys, not just the sons of ranchers, grabbed the chance to get an education. As the number of college rodeos grew, the contestants recognized the need to have a national intercollegiate rodeo organization.

Education had moved west following in the dust of the Civil War veterans turned cattle drovers, farmers, and ranchers. Almost simultaneously, one-room schoolhouses and shotgun rodeo chutes dotted the western prairies and rolling hills. Education settled comfortably side-by-side in the West with America's only original sport, rodeo. However, the comfort level evaporated when cowboys and cowgirls, bred and reared in an atmosphere of independence, with a love for equality and rodeo competition, expected to find these same traits on college campuses. As Owen Wister depicted in his novel *The Virginian,* when East met West, when tradition met independence and originality, conflict and compromise created something new and uniquely American. The same was true when cowboys and cowgirls took rodeo to college.

Ranch cowboy riding and roping competition resulted in the development of rodeo events in the late nineteenth century. The cowboy competitive spirit often turned a pasture into an arena. By the late 1800s, four states had cowboy competitions in such places as Deer Trail, Colorado; Pecos, Texas; Prescott, Arizona; and North Platte, Nebraska. The daily work of the cowboy moved to the competitive level and the arena.[2]

Frequent rodeo competition demanded standardized rules administered by a national organization. The Rodeo Association of America (RAA), organized in 1928 by rodeo producers, attempted to standardize rules and to stop a proposal to ban rodeo competition by the California legislature. Rodeo producers were businessmen; cowboys competed for the love of competition and a paycheck. Cowboys never stayed anywhere long enough to organize. Problems finally forced the cowboys to confront the rodeo producers. On November 6, 1936, in New York City, the cowboys organized the Cowboys Turtle Association (CTA), a union of rodeo cowboys to look after their own interests. Some say that the CTA used the word *turtle* due to their slowness to organize. The CTA set goals, a first for American rodeo cowboys, for better working conditions, regulations for the amount of prize money, entrance fees added to the prize money, and experienced, qualified judges.

Strict rules of conduct helped to polish the tarnished image of the early rodeo cowboy, a ranch cowboy who left his legitimate work to compete and ultimately to party. Early contestants viewed rodeo as entertainment. When the seasonal work gave way to some time off from the ranch, cowboys often gathered together for roping and riding competition. Afterward, they celebrated their win or loss, much to the chagrin of the ranch owners. Their celebrations often disturbed the quiet communities, thus the cowboys' tarnished image. City people perceived cowboys to be "an ignorant lot of illiterates, uncouth in every respect."[3] The CTA included a blacklist rule for objectionable conduct. The RAA and the CTA each included a rule to improve the cowboys' image for proper dress and for proper equipment. With these guidelines, the rodeo cowboy had a framework of rules much like that his counterpart the working cowboy followed on the big ranches.

Professional rodeo gained its focus when the media defined the professional rodeo cowboy while the new rodeo cowboy organization worked to discipline its members. With standard rules, more rodeos, and assurance that entry fees would be included in the payoff, some rodeo cowboys tried to make rodeo a profession. The cowboy began "taking himself and his efforts more seriously."[4] In 1936 an article in *Western Horseman* burnished the rodeo cowboy's image with words that echoed the promise of rodeo as a respectable profession. In 1940 a regular contributor to *Hoofs and Horns,* the official publication of the RAA, and later to *Western Horseman,* Bruce Clinton, possibly the first, used the term *professional* in regard to the rodeo cowboy. Clinton "was possibly the first writer to recognize that rodeo was emerging as a bona fide sport and that its participants were athletes, not circus performers."[5]

Rodeo advanced as a profession, a business, in the 1940s when rodeo associations established national offices and demanded fair splits of the entry fees. In 1942 the CTA established a national office and hired a salaried secretary. In 1945 the CTA moved its headquarters to Fort Worth, Texas, changed its name from Turtles to Rodeo Cowboys Association (RCA), reorganized its management structure, and worked for better pay for cowboys. The RCA elected as its president Toots Mansfield, the 1943 RCA calf roping champion from Bandera, Texas, who later won a total of seven world calf roping championships. Earl Lindsey, a Texas businessman, became the business manager and public relations agent bringing experience as a former representative for Gene Autry's rodeo organization.

Professional rodeo competition led to a system of recognizing national champions and to the solicitation of corporate sponsors. In 1929 the Rodeo Association of America (RAA) started keeping cumulative records to determine annual national champions. Before then, many cowboys, called national or world champions, based their titles on winning major rodeos. On January 1, 1945, the RCA also started a point-award system. Each association proclaimed its own world champions until 1955 when the RCA became the sole source for naming national champions. In 1946 the RAA combined with the National Rodeo Association to form the International Rodeo Association (IRA), which named its national champions at a national finals at the Grand National Rodeo at San Francisco's Cow Palace.[6] Later, the IRA discontinued awards to the top contestants and aligned itself more with management and other activities such as the sponsorship of the Miss Rodeo America pageant.[7] The IRA also sought corporate sponsors for rodeos, which helped to offset the costs of production.

Professional rodeo experimented with various rodeo publications to inform contestants of rodeo entry information and to increase rodeo audiences. In 1910 "Corral," a column in *Billboard,* a weekly show and theatrical magazine, carried rodeo news, the first publication to do so. In 1917 Homer Wilson, a cowboy and rodeo promoter, started a short-lived publication known as *The Wild Bunch.* In 1936 Ethel A. Hopkins' publication *Hoofs and Horns* began a longtime run as the official publication for the RAA. In 1945 the RCA started publishing its own publication *The Buckboard* in Fort Worth, Texas.[8]

As professional rodeo expanded, related businesses resulted. The production of rodeos evolved into a full-time business. The names of major rodeo producers became as familiar as the names of the champions. Everett Colborn managed the World's Championship Rodeo Corporation and the Gene Autry and Associates in Dublin, Texas. Colonel Jim Eskew and his JE Ranch Rodeo headquartered in Waverly, New York. Elliot and Nesbitt worked out of Plattsville, Colorado. Harry Rowell of Hayward, California, produced rodeos on the west coast. Big Timber, Montana, had Leo F. Cremer's company. Beutler Brothers of Elk City, Oklahoma, became a familiar and respected name in rodeo.

World War II helped polish the image of rodeo. President Franklin D. Roosevelt declared that baseball should continue as a morale builder. Following suit in the West, many people felt that they owed it to the cowboys serving their country to keep rodeo alive. Associations even allowed nonmember working cowboys to enter to have adequate contestants at a rodeo. Membership in professional rodeo associations took a leap as well as did audience support.[9]

Wartime rodeos, promoting patriotism and raising funds, aided in maintaining a pool of experienced rodeo hands. The first major wartime rodeo, the 1942 National Western Rodeo in Denver, Colorado, focused on courage in the arena, patriotism, and the importance of the livestock industry to the country in wartime. A grand entry with 150 mounted cowboys and cowgirls stirred patriotism in the spectators. Many producers staged rodeos for the sole purpose of raising funds for wartime causes.[10] However, 28 percent of the regularly scheduled rodeos had been canceled by 1941, so the RAA encouraged smaller rodeos to support the wartime efforts.[11]

World War II spread rodeo competition and gained international fans. Often soldiers in the army camps, needing respite from the war, organized rodeos. By 1942 the CTA reported about one hundred members serving in the armed services. In the fall of 1942, Camp Roberts, California, staged its first successful all-soldier rodeo. By 1944 rodeos had spread to overseas military installations in France, Australia, Italy, and even India, creating an international audience.[12]

Wartime rodeos also added new audiences worldwide by sending rodeo publications and broadcasts to the troops. In 1944 California stock contractor Harry Rowell donated $200 that Sears, Roebuck and Company matched to make *Hoofs and Horns* available for the servicemen. The Office of War Information recorded the 1944 Madison Square Garden Rodeo for broadcast to U.S. armed forces overseas.[13]

A review of women in professional rodeo showed them scarce but often treated as celebrities until the 1940s when they almost disappeared. The first record of a cowgirl bronc rider appeared in 1896 in Fort Smith, Arkansas.[14] At the first Cheyenne Frontier Days Celebration in 1897, Bertha Blancett gave an exhibition ride in a water-filled arena to placate the audience and to keep from having to reimburse the gate money. The cowboys decided to ride after Blancett rode. By 1901 many rodeos featured lady bronc riding. By the 1920s three cowgirl events had become regularly featured at the rodeos: bronc riding, trick riding, and relay races, and some entered the steer roping. Many rodeo contract acts featured women in trick riding and trick roping. World War II affected professional cowgirl competition. With the shortage of gasoline and with limited numbers of rodeo stock, rodeo promoters eliminated women's events except barrel racing.[15] The belief that women should not compete in dangerous events could also have been an influence.[16] During that time, women, not associated with rodeo, received "little encouragement to develop their athletic or career aptitudes, and no one had even given voice to the concept of gender equity in sport."[17] One rodeo promoter marginalized cowgirls with his promotion of singers and entertainment, which averted the focus from the contestants.[18] In response to the lack of cowgirl events at professional rodeos, cowgirls in 1948 founded the Girls Rodeo Association, now Women's Professional Rodeo Association, to produce their own rodeos with rough-stock and roping events as well as barrel racing.[19] However, between 1947 and 1955 only about 160 cowgirls won money in professional rodeo.

Some college rodeo cowboys competed on the professional rodeo circuit before college rodeos became available on many campuses. Earl Bascom, a 1940 Brigham Young University graduate, said, "In order to finance my tuition, board and room, and art supplies, I competed in rodeos all summer between school years." He earned the title of BYU's First Collegiate Rodeo Cowboy to "finance his way through college solely by riding in professional rodeos."[20] However, Bascom did not compete in college rodeos.

At the same time, some cowgirls challenged barriers on college campuses although they were not competing in campus rodeos. One early cowgirl, the late Fern Sawyer of Crossroads, New Mexico, said, "Colleges frowned on coeds entering any kind of rodeo during the 1930s." Sawyer, a National Cowgirl Hall of Fame honoree, said that during her first semester at Texas Tech at Lubbock, "They were going to kick me out because I went to a rodeo." She said that she had to sneak out to enter a rodeo, so she finally quit college, but she added, "Since then, I have gone back to Texas Tech to judge their college rodeos."[21]

By the end of World War II, college rodeos had flourished for twenty-five years, especially at land-grant colleges. Rodeo developed quietly and almost unnoticed on college campuses starting as early as 1920 in Texas. As land-grant colleges, named agricultural and mechanical colleges, opened in the West, ranch families, recognizing the need for more education, enrolled their children in these colleges with farm and ranch programs. Young cowboys naturally satisfied their competitive spirit by transplanting their riding and roping skills to college campus competition. Furthermore, when the college cowboys returned with more knowledge to run the farms and ranches, they also returned with newly honed riding and roping skills, a knowledge of rodeo production, and an expanded network of people of like kind.

An agricultural and mechanical college in the Lone Star State proved to be a natural place to start college rodeo competition. A type of campus rodeo competition, not intercollegiate rodeo, started November 5, 1920, when Texas A&M had a parade at 8:00 A.M. led by a Duchess with "sixteen of her most royal attendants" who were "selected by a committee and consisted of the most popular and most beautiful debutantes of College Station and Bryan."[22] "The program consisted of a broncho [*sic*] busting, goat roping, saddle racing, mounted wrestling, polo, greased pig contest, and cow ballards [*sic*] by the Cast Iron Quartet." This competition, initiated by the need to raise funds to send the livestock judging team to Chicago, grew from the First Agricultural Show held on November 27, 1919. The agricultural show opened with a parade of cattle owned by the institution, followed by horses, and a chariot race with mules. They had muleback races, potato races, chair races, and a quartet.[23] Texas A&M's annual college rodeo resulted from new events being added each year.

With livestock shows and rodeos being combined in Texas to meet the needs of the cattlemen and ranchers, colleges transplanted the new idea to their campuses. The Southwestern Exposition & Livestock Show & Rodeo at Fort Worth possibly influenced the Texas A&M campus rodeo events. In 1896 the first Fort Worth Stock Show was held "when purebred livestock was the new trend, and Fort Worth was in its infancy."[24] The first indoor rodeo was held in Fort Worth in 1918 at Cowtown Coliseum, also known as Northside Coliseum. In 1917 a stock-show booster, Ray McKinley, editor and publisher of the *Daily Reporter* and *Sunday North Fort Worth News,* suggested having a competitive event featuring cowboys.[25] So the future Southwestern Exposition & Livestock Show & Rodeo began in 1918, only two years before Texas A&M held its first cowboy contest on campus to raise traveling funds for the Aggie livestock judging team.

During the 1920s, rodeo on the Texas A&M campus flourished. In 1922 it drew a crowd estimated at fifteen hundred with a gate receipt of more than $600, which was used to send a stock judging team to Chicago.[26] In 1924 "a float carried the Queen of the Rodeo, Miss Myrtle Astin representing 'Miss America' and her escort Colonel Frank Stubbs as 'Uncle Sam' to their throne." The gate was $1,200.[27] By 1927 the Texas A&M rodeo events included bulldogging, roping, wild cow milking, mounted wrestling, jumping, and steer and bronco riding. An article stated, "No other activity seems more characteristic of the spirit of the College and the State than this annual show."[28]

Another land-grant school, Colorado A&M (Colorado State) at Fort Collins, followed the Texas A&M model of producing a rodeo on campus to raise travel funds for its livestock judging team. Two years after Texas A&M produced its first campus rodeo, the Colorado A&M livestock judging team needed $400 to get to the International Livestock Show held in Chicago, so the Colorado A&M Livestock Club held a "Kow College Karnival" in 1922. The Aggie students raised the money with events such as bronc riding, greased pig catching, wild cow milking, and dancing. It continued each year as a collegiate show until 1940 when Colorado A&M invited the University of Wyoming and Colorado State Teachers College to compete in its first intercollegiate rodeo.[29] Possibly the Colorado A&M cowboys learned of the Texas Aggie's successful college rodeo fund-raiser at the livestock show in Chicago where both schools sent teams annually. Both Aggie schools continued campus rodeos until intercollegiate rodeos became the vogue about twenty years later.

College rodeo competition, especially at land-grant colleges, had spread rapidly by the late 1930s. William "Bill" Felts, while a sophomore at the University of Arizona, a land-grant school, said, "In 1937 I had an idea of a student rodeo. I took this idea to our student body president Lee Lowery, so the first UA college rodeo was born."[30] On April 30, 1938, at 2:00 P.M. at the Tucson Rodeo grounds, UA had its first college rodeo. They had seven events: wild steer riding, calf roping, bronc riding, team tying, quarter-mile cow-horse race, wild steer riding, three-quarter mile relay, and wild cow milking. The 1939 UA rodeo included three rodeo contestants from another college: Occidental College. The first official intercollegiate rodeo at UA, when they sent invitations to other schools to join in their rodeo, was in 1940.[31]

A California entrepreneur, a natural promoter with experience, clout, and financing, produced the first intercollegiate rodeo. Cal Godshall, a Victorville, California, promoter, friend of movie stars, and guest-ranch owner, recognized the potential of producing a rodeo limited to college contestants because of his college daughter, Jeanne Godshall. The Godshall's were a media-savvy family. In 1919 the famous media mogul William Randolph Hearst moved Jeanne's maternal grandfather, Maximilian F. Ihmsen, from New York where he had promoted Hearst's political career to Los Angeles to work at the *Los Angeles Examiner*.[32] Jeanne's grandmother had been an actress on the New York stage before marrying Mr. Ihmsen. Jeanne's mother wrote for the newspaper for seventeen years. With these media connections and Cal Godshall's natural talent for promotion, the idea of a rodeo with teams strictly limited to college students came naturally to Godshall's creative mind.[33]

The state of the economy played a role in initiating Cal Godshall's interest in producing the first intercollegiate rodeo. Jean Campbell DeBlasis, who grew up with Jeanne Godshall and lives on the North Verde Guest Ranch at Victorville, California, said, "Cal was always promoting Jeanne."[34] Another friend, Ann Rivers, reared on the Loma Yucca Guest Ranch, said that in 1938 Godshall held a Queen's Contest with girls elected from surrounding counties. All the girls then competed at Salinas with Jeanne Godshall being elected as the queen. "It was the depression years, and Cal was trying to bring some business into the area because we all lived on and ran guest ranches," said Rivers.[35]

Cal Godshall possibly picked up the idea of producing an intercollegiate rodeo while at a Tucson, Arizona, rodeo. Cal often took Jeanne to trick ride at rodeos to advertise his amateur annual Victorville rodeo. In the spring of 1938, the University of Arizona had produced its first college rodeo. Six months later, in the fall of 1938, Cal displayed Jeanne's riding skills at Tucson.

After Cal Godshall returned from Tucson, he started planning an intercollegiate rodeo. He contacted world champion professional cowboys to help with the rodeo, and he sent out numerous news releases announcing their appearance at the rodeo. The 1940 professional all-around cowboy from Long Beach, California, Fritz Truan, a frequent guest at the Godshall ranch, helped Godshall connect with the cowboys. Godshall listed Burl Mulkey, world all-around champion from Salmon, Idaho, as judge; Andy Juaregui, three-time world roping champion, as stock contractor; and making appearances were Johnny Bowman, 1936 world champion from Oakdale; Smoky Snyder, world champion bull rider; Mike McCrory, world champion bulldogger from Deadwood, South Dakota; Canada Kid, all-around cowboy from Calgary; Clay Carr, twice all-around cowboy champion from Visalia, California; Jackie Cooper, champion from Canada; and Dave Campbell, a Las Vegas bulldogging record holder.[36]

Along with the list of world champion cowboys slated to appear at Godshall's intercollegiate rodeo, five movie stars, Harry Carey, Dick Foran, Curley Fletcher, Tex Ritter, and Errol Flynn, made the list as well as some of the best acts available. Rodeo clown Brahma Bill and his trained Brahma bull, world's champion trick rider Lloyd McBee, and a cowboy's stock horse performance completed the list of attractions.[37]

To promote the intercollegiate rodeo, Cal Godshall also used the local newspaper to publish a steady stream of rodeo articles. A columnist, "Desert Sage Says," spotlighted the Godshall family in the *Victor Press*. "Jeanne Godshall's pa an' ma has a ranch near here where they still tries [*sic*] to make a honest livin' with cattle, stead of the WPA. They has did [*sic*] it an' now the best way they knowed [*sic*] to entertain their gal's high-toned college friends was to throw an' old fashioned wingding right out back of the ranch in the corral." He commented on the background of some of the entrants: "many of these collegiate waddies has ben brung [*sic*] up in cow country." He also commented on the ability of the cowgirls. He said that if a cowboy "gits bucked off, his gal friend most likely kin jump into the saddle an' show him how it really should have ben did [*sic*]."[38]

With a team trophy and the idea of intercollegiate competition, Cal Godshall enticed college cowboys and cowgirls to enter his rodeo. Godshall "sweetened the pot with a silver cup standing three feet high with a bucking horse and rider surmounting" to be awarded as a perpetual intercollegiate trophy to the college or university with the most points. This was done with the idea of making it an annual event.[39]

A marketing professional, the father of a college cowgirl, produced the first full-fledged intercollegiate rodeo on his ranch at Victorville, California, on April 8, 1939. The *Victor Press* billed Cal Godshall's rodeo at the C Bar G Ranch (Ihmsen Ranch) as the first intercollegiate rodeo. Further supporting the premise that Godshall connected with the idea of an intercollegiate rodeo in Arizona is the fact that a picture of University of Arizona cowboy Bill Felts on a bronc captioned "champion bronc rider" dominated the front page of the Victorville newspaper that promoted the rodeo.[40]

College cowboys entered traditional rodeo events that remained basically the same through the years; however, the women's events spanned the gamut from rodeo events to games. Entries included forty-four men and eighteen women from ten California colleges and universities and one Arizona university. The rodeo had a grand entry of celebrities and wild steer riding, calf roping, wild cow milking, saddle bronc riding, and team roping and tying for men. Girls entered the rescue race, potato race, bareback and saddling race, wild cow milking, and pipe and needle race.

Some novice college students entered the first intercollegiate rodeo. Jim Lau from the University of California at Los Angeles noticed a poster on the school's bulletin board advertising the rodeo and decided to enter his first rodeo. Lau and some friends made the hundred-mile trip from Los Angeles to Victorville. The newspaper noted the starting time as 1:30 P.M., but Lau said that they started earlier. He entered the bull riding (steer riding) and rode a borrowed calf roping horse. No entry fee was required. Lau said that Universal Films made a newsreel of the rodeo that was shown in theaters.[41]

Cal Godshall's rodeo proved to be a success, so the contestants at Godshall's rodeo left determined to produce an intercollegiate rodeo on their campuses. Lougher of the University of California-Davis won the championship trophy and was crowned "king of college cowboys" with second going to UA's Bill Felts. Five Pomona cowgirls won four of the five women's events.[42] Soon, the University of Arizona sent invitations to their first intercollegiate, "which was inspired by the California rodeo."[43] On March 2, 1940, eighty students from four other colleges accepted invitations to compete.[44] Contestants entered from UA, Arizona State, Flagstaff State Teachers College, Colorado A&M, and University of New Mexico.[45] Arizona governor Bob Jones rode in the parade.[46] Approximately four thousand fans saw UA's Tom Finley, and Cherrie Osborne, Flagstaff State Teachers College, win the all-around titles and win the mixed team roping. Osborne also won the cowpony race, a quarter-mile race. Rodeo committee chairman Bill Felts, the Victorville saddle bronc champion, won the 1940 UA rodeo bronc championship.[47]

The contestants who entered University of Arizona rodeos spread the idea of intercollegiate rodeo to all parts of the country. In 1940 Colorado A&M, after having collegiate rodeos for approximately twenty years, invited UA, qualifying it as an intercollegiate rodeo. Hyde Merritt and three other University of Wyoming students won second among nine schools at the 1941 UA rodeo. In 1941 UW produced its first intercollegiate rodeo after Merritt helped organize a UW rodeo club. Merritt said, "With the Laramie Chamber of Commerce underwriting us, we built a rodeo arena in ten days. The day following the show, we had to tear it down, return all the lumber . . . and leave the grounds in the condition we found it." In 1942 the UW students built a permanent arena. Club members with the help of an attorney wrote bylaws and rules for a rodeo association and presented them to UW president Morrill who approved it.[48]

To increase the number of contestants and fans at college rodeos, cowboys included cowgirl events. For the first time, in 1940 or possibly 1941, Texas A&M, an all-male school, included an event for females and had a rodeo king and queen, Aggie bronc rider King J. R. "Shorty" Fuller and Queen Annabelle Edwards, Big Spring, Texas. F. C. "Caddo" Wright, the Aggies' rodeo director, used rodeo equipment furnished by the Texas Prison System at Huntsville,

Members of the first Texas A&M intercollegiate rodeo team, formed in 1942, are
(left to right) *F. C. "Caddo" Wright, J. R. "Shorty" Fuller, Fred Dalby, and John Hardin.*
Photo courtesy of John Hardin, Marion, Arkansas, and NIRA Alumni archives.

which had produced a rodeo for approximately ten years. The seventy-two contestants hailed from Texas, Oklahoma, Arizona, Montana, and New Mexico. The women's event, goat tying, had seven contestants and was called a Sponsor Contest; originally, different towns sponsored girls.[49] Sponsor Events, held at professional rodeos, such as Madison Square Garden in New York City, and Boston Garden, used cowgirls to ride in the parade and the grand entry to advertise the rodeos.

College rodeos proliferated during the 1940s. In New Mexico in 1940, Eastern New Mexico Junior College (now ENMU) at Portales, New Mexico, invited Lovington High School seniors to compete in bareback riding, calf roping, steer riding, and wild cow milking with merchandise as prizes. "I remember that Bill Spires and I won the wild cow milking, and we each won two pair of socks and two ties," said Giles Lee, a Lovington, New Mexico, rancher.[50]

Schools started designating their entries as rodeo teams and requiring sponsors. In 1942 New Mexico A&M organized a rodeo club, sponsored by the athletic department in name only. To be college sanctioned, the club had to be affiliated with the college even though no school funds were allocated. Local businesses helped the cowboys with travel expenses for their first college rodeo trip in March 1942 to the University of Arizona. The Dona Ana Sheriff's Posse donated expense money, and Claude Everett's Chevrolet garage furnished two pickups and paid the bills on them. An A&M cowboy, Giles Lee, said, "We stayed in the gym. We just rolled our bedrolls out in the gym and stayed there while we were in Tucson. About thirteen New Mexico Aggies and our sponsor Kermit Laabs, a coach at New Mexico A&M, attended."[51]

Land-grant schools, typically all male, rapidly implemented the idea of intercollegiate rodeo competition, which included women's events. The New Mexico Aggies, at their first rodeo on May 1, 1942, at the Salt Cedar arena, invited the University of Arizona and New Mexico high school seniors to enter bareback riding, saddle bronc riding, steer riding, calf roping, and double mugging. The cowgirls competed in a cigar race and a stake race. In the cigar race, a girl on horseback started at one end of the arena while a cowboy waited with a cigar and a match at the other end. The girl raced to the cowboy, dismounted,

Members of the first New Mexico A&M Rodeo Club, organized in 1942, are (standing, left to right) *Bud Prather, Giles Lee, Jim Rush, El Ray Fort, Smoky Nunn;* (seated, left to right) *Bob White, Bob Malcolm, Pat Patterson, Bill Maxwell. Other active members not present were Lewis Cain, F. C. Stover, Buster Miller, and Pee Wee Smith. Photo courtesy of Giles Lee, Lovington, New Mexico, and NIRA Alumni archives.*

lit the cigar, remounted, than raced back across the finish line. In the stake race, a cowgirl ran a figure-eight barrel race, instead of the cloverleaf pattern used today. They also crowned a rodeo queen, Jean Isaacks.[52]

Growing up on a ranch in southeastern New Mexico, Giles Lee, typical of many of the prewar ranch cowboys who went to college, rode and roped and worked cattle as an everyday part of his life. Rodeos had long been his family's entertainment. Giles remembers the Lee family attending a rodeo when he was seven or eight: "Cars parked in a circle made the arena in a pasture west of Lovington. Shotgun chutes were used for the bucking stock and set-up pens for the rest of the stock. People brought in one or two old horses, and they got stock rounded up and rode steers."[53]

Pair the small hometown-rodeo experience for a ranch cowboy with a trip to a major rodeo, such as the Southwestern Exposition & Livestock Show & Rodeo at Fort Worth, and a rodeo cowboy was born, a cowboy who insisted on taking his event to college. Ranch cowboy Lee said, "I saw my first coliseum rodeo in 1936 or '37. That impressed me. I thought, now this is the life for me." That never changed for Lee, typical of many early-day college rodeo cowboys who left the ranch, went to college, competed in college rodeos and other rodeos, earned a degree, returned to run the ranch, continued to rodeo in the area, and raised a family that went to rodeos for entertainment. Eventually, Lee joined the Old Timers Steer Roping Association for ropers over fifty, and his three daughters married ranchers who competed in rodeos. Lee watched the third generation of his family become NIRA contestants when Jeff Hilton and Jessica Berry Hilton followed Danny Berry, Jessica's dad, into college rodeo.[54]

College rodeo also filled the social needs of ranch cowboys and cowgirls. Some rodeo freshmen "got a little too much grape one night and decided to redo their room, so they painted the inside of it red. It didn't go over too good," said Lee. Fun and adventure going down the road together bonded the college rodeo contestants. Lee said, "On one of our trips to Tucson, we were pulling two horses in a homemade two-horse trailer that stood about two feet off the ground. There were six of us in the '46 Chevrolet pulling it. As we started down this long hill, the trailer started jack-knifing on us and trying to pass us. Harley May and a bunch were behind us. They said that at times when we would go to one side of the road and back to the other, the dual trailer wheels would get two or three feet off the ground and almost turn over. It never did. When we got to the bottom, we had to stop and rest."[55]

Forced by economic necessity, college cowboys and cowgirls shared horses, trailers, and equipment, which added an element of bonding and networking. Some of the college students owned horses, but many borrowed good horses from professional ropers in the area. Lee said, "At the time we were rodeoing in college, there wasn't much money in it. It was just more or less for glory. You just tried to ride a bucking horse or rope a calf or something, and if the girls were watching, that made it a lot of fun."[56]

Initially, colleges often used pasture-gathered stock and borrowed old-spoiled horses. In the early 1940s, cowboys used a loose rope and bell in the bareback riding. "When you came out on one of those old wild mares with a bell under her belly, well, be ready for anything," said Lee.[57]

Early college cowboy graduates streamed into many different professions other than ranching. Members of the 1942 New Mexico A&M team illustrated the diversity of college degrees. The White Sands Missile Range in New Mexico hired Jim Rush. Pat Patterson became a real estate partner in California with NIRA champion Harley May. Bud Prather worked as a head chemist for Hunt's Ketchup. El Ray Fort went to Alaska. Bill Maxwell chose the Indian Service in Albuquerque, New Mexico. Bob White, a businessman and rancher, died in a plane crash. Three became ranchers: Giles Lee, Lewis Cain, and Smoky Nunn.

World War II halted rodeo activity on most college campuses from 1942 to 1945 as cowboys went to defend their country. Ranchers felt the void left by their sons—working cowboys—going to war. Their daughters, of whom Mary Ellen Chandler Kimball of Alpine, Texas, is typical, replaced their brothers on the ranches. "Riding and working cattle daily changed the interests of many young women," said Ms. Kimball.[58] Arriving home, the veteran cowboys found that many women had learned to ride, rope, compete, and they enjoyed it, just as the men did.

In spite of the hiatus for rodeo during the war, college rodeo experience helped cowboys spread rodeo to foreign soil. In 1945 a Texas A&M student from Lufkin, Texas, Bob Frazer, a contestant in three events at the 1940 Texas A&M rodeo, was stationed at an airbase near Karachi, India (Pakistan). As managing director of a Fourth of July rodeo in India for GI cowboys, Frazer used cowboy ingenuity to produce the international rodeo. Frazer, mounted on a South African horse and saddle, wore a shirt made of "parachute silk, and his leggins [*sic*] were made from tanned cowhide purchased at the local market."[59] They "rode very rank mules with a loose rope (bull rope). The first rodeo was so successful that the commanding general ordered me to put on a second one."[60]

During the war, many cowboy-soldiers gained rodeo production experience, using it later to produce college and professional rodeos. One cowboy-soldier, Cecil Jones, the 1949 NIRA Invitational Championship Rodeo secretary, competed on the 1940 U.S.A. rodeo team in Sydney, Australia, and returned with all-around and bull riding championships. He helped produce a GI rodeo in Tokyo. After World War II, Jones joined Harry Rowell as manager and secretary of the Rowell Ranch Rodeo and served for more than thirty years as the secretary for the Grand National Rodeo at the Cow Palace. Jones later used his NIRA national finals experience as the secretary for the first professional National Finals Rodeo in Dallas in 1959.[61]

After the war, the GI Bill created a major surge in college rodeo contestants. The cowboy-veterans entered college more mature, more experienced, and more aware of the need to further their education in a changing, technological world. Also, they had taken rodeo to war, so taking rodeo to college was a natural. The cowboy veterans headed for college ready to fight another battle if necessary to continue their favorite sport while earning an education.

Reorganization of college rodeo clubs started; however, some schools had managed to continue their annual intercollegiate rodeos during the war. In March, 1947, when the University of Arizona sent invitations to its eighth annual intercollegiate rodeo, 226 contestants from nine other schools responded. The 1947 UA rodeo program listed the following schools: Arizona State College at Flagstaff, Arizona State College at Tempe, California Aggies at Davis, CalPoly at San Luis Obispo, New Mexico A&M, University of New Mexico, Texas A&M, University of Utah, and University of Wyoming. TAMU won the team championship with Prince Wood winning all-around.[62]

Many schools had intercollegiate rodeos for the first time. On April 18–19, 1947, Hardin-Simmons University at Abilene, Texas, sponsored its first. Invitations went to forty-five schools to participate in bareback riding, bull riding, calf roping, team tying, and wild cow milking for the men and goat tying and cow milking for the women. Only six Texas schools entered: Texas Tech, Abilene Christian College, McMurray College (Abilene), Texas A&M, Howard County Junior College, and John Tarleton Agricultural College. Competing on Cullen Robinson's stock with judges Johnny Down and Jack Stricklin making the marks, Texas Tech's team tallied the most points. Hardin-Simmons'

Jessie Myers won the women's all-around, and McMurray's Jimmy Bird, the men's. They used the Western Intercollegiate Rodeo Association's rules, an earlier attempt to organize a national organization in Arizona.[63]

College rodeo spread into Big Sky country. In 1947 Montana State College in Bozeman had its first collegiate rodeo. MSC cowboys elected Gene Pedersen to organize the rodeo. MSC students Stuart Hauptmann, Ralph Nichols, and Bob Chambers, all attending on the GI Bill, helped produce the MSC rodeo at the old Bozeman Fairgrounds.[64] In 1948 MSC produced its first intercollegiate rodeo with the University of Montana and North Dakota Teachers College competing, which introduced college rodeo to Montana and the Northwest.[65]

As intercollegiate rodeo spread, contestants recognized the importance of standardized eligibility rules as well as college sponsors/advisers. By 1946 rodeo rules became similar to the current NIRA requirements: a 2.0 GPA, sanctioned by their college or university, and a college-appointed sponsor, usually a faculty member. However, most sponsors had no rodeo experience, and many functioned in name only. A few early sponsors tried to go to the rodeos, but other sponsors saw their home rodeo only. One cowboy recalled that the team forgot their sponsor when they left, but "he showed up a day later all smiles. He didn't know anything about rodeo, but he was willing and ready to try."[66] Many college rodeo sponsors through the years proved to be invaluable in helping college rodeo gain acceptance, funding, and scholarships on their campuses. The greenhorn sponsor, often a faculty member or an administrator, bridged the gap between having a rodeo program and not having one.

By 1947 contestants wanted an organization to standardize rules, name champions, and guard their right to compete simultaneously at both college and professional rodeos. In November 1947 at the John Tarleton Agricultural College rodeo at Stephenville, Texas, contestant Jack Longbotham said that "the idea of creating a national association of college cowboys and cowgirls to award national titles was bantered about."[67] Sul Ross State Teachers College sent its rodeo team. Sul Ross won the team trophy with Buster Lindley taking the all-around, adding to their desire to create a national organization. President Joe Lane of the Bar SR Bar Rodeo Association, organized in the fall of 1947, and sponsor E. E. Turner, associate agriculture professor, played major roles in the initiation of a meeting at the Sul Ross rodeo to plan a national organization.

New Mexico A&M cowboy F. C. Stover, shown roping a calf in 1947 on his big gray horse, later won the 1951 and 1952 NIRA calf roping championships. Photo courtesy of Giles Lee, Lovington, New Mexico, and NIRA Alumni archives.

Americans' general fascination with things western after the war, especially between 1945 and 1955, supported the growing interest in college rodeo. Western tourism, film, television, music, and dress expounded on America's continuing interest in cowboys and rodeo. Advertisers used the mystique of the rodeo cowboy to promote their products. In 1947 Wrangler created a special design of jeans created for and endorsed by rodeo cowboys. The cut of the Wrangler 13MWZ Cowboy Cut Jeans fit the needs of the rodeo cowboys, who faithfully wore them. The partnership between Wrangler and rodeo has been a continuing American success story.[68]

Quietly, rodeo competition on college campuses starting in 1920 had intertwined with the development of professional rodeo. Intercollegiate competition started in 1939 when a California entrepreneur recognized the marketability of college rodeo-team competition, resulting in the first rodeo competition among schools. Once cowboys and cowgirls experienced intercollegiate competition, it spread. Although World War II caused a hiatus on campus, it contributed to college rodeo's growth afterward. The GI Bill stimulated college rodeo's growth along with the growing economy, the cowgirl, who had filled in at the ranch during the war, and the maturity of the cowboy-veterans. With the leadership of cowboy veterans on many campuses, the idea of a national organization gained momentum. Cowboys and cowgirls competed in a new college sport on campus almost unnoticed by the academic world.

NIRA Creates

a New Vision

and a National Finals

In the late 1940s the number of annual invitational intercollegiate rodeos grew as did the desire to establish a national organization to determine national champions. This organization could also standardize rules and set eligibility, contestants' conduct, prizes, and lead to recognition as a college sport. The idea had been bantered around at many college rodeos. Finally, in the fall of 1948 with the GI Bill providing college financing for an influx of mature World War II veteran-cowboys, they organized the National Intercollegiate Rodeo Association (NIRA) and produced the first college national finals rodeo, resulting in a new type of rodeo cowboy and cowgirl.

In 1948, twenty-eight years after the first collegiate rodeo (one college competing) at Texas A&M and ten years after the first intercollegiate rodeo (several colleges competing) in California, the contestants at Sul Ross State Teachers College's first intercollegiate rodeo on November 4 to 6 in Alpine, Texas, decided to plan an organizational meeting. One of the visionary organizers, Hank Finger, Sul Ross Rodeo Association president, had transferred to Sul Ross from Texas A&M along with another cowboy, Jim Watts. In the spring of 1948, SR cowboy Buster Lindley and Finger, returning from a University of Arizona rodeo, had discussed some rule changes that they disliked.[1] An attempt to organize a Western Intercollegiate Rodeo Association had occurred in 1946 or 1947 at the University of Arizona.[2] Apparently, it failed, for unknown reasons. Lindley and Finger, along with Watts and others, continued to discuss the need for an organization until it materialized at the Sul Ross rodeo.

The meeting to begin organizational plans occurred in part because of the strong leadership talent, motivation, and maturity of many of the college students. Hank Finger's election as president of the Bar SR Bar Rodeo Association attested to his leadership ability and charisma, attributes that helped direct the organizing of the NIRA. However, at the time of his election, Finger's major concern was producing a successful first intercollegiate rodeo at Sul Ross. On December 8, 1947, sixty-one Sul Ross students entered their first home rodeo.[3] In 1948 they invited other schools to compete at Sul Ross.

Rodeo production success followed strong leadership and motivation. Hank Finger's promotional and public relations talent showed with the numerous prize-solicitation letters and news releases he sent to promote the Sul Ross rodeo. Along with the prizes and publicity, a rodeo arena had to be completed. In the fall of 1947, the Sul Ross administration appropriated $3,000 for arena materials, and the rodeo members supplied the labor.[4] The cowboys borrowed knocked-down bleachers from the Odessa Independent School District, a distance of approximately 150 miles, and returned them immediately after the rodeo.[5]

Headed for a historical rodeo event, eleven teams from Texas, New Mexico, Colorado, and Oklahoma, of the twenty-four invited, arrived at the little Texas town of Alpine in the mountains in Big Bend country. On November 6, 1948, after the three-day rodeo, Sul Ross had won most of the titles. Both all-around championships remained at Sul Ross. Mary Ellen Chandler Kimball's second in goat tying and first in barrel racing cinched for her Sul Ross's first intercollegiate rodeo women's all-around title and prizes of a hat, a pair of boots, head stall, and a buckle set. Chandler Kimball borrowed Charlie Hall's roping horse for her events.[6] Sul Ross freshman Bob King won the all-around saddle with a first in ribbon roping and a second place in calf roping.

The historical event centered on more than just the action in the arena. The presence of twelve schools (including SR) on a campus whose administration strongly supported intercollegiate rodeo along with cowboys matured by their war years and individuals with charismatic personalities and talent for promotion provided the perfect combination to pursue the idea of creating a national organization. "Ham Scott of New Mexico A&M and I were talking over our troubles at producing college rodeos. We agreed that we should get all those interested together to discuss the problems of rodeoing on other campuses. I called a meeting for that night at the Range Animal Husbandry building," said Hank Finger.[7]

The representatives of twelve schools from four states met to elect some officers. On November 6, 1948, they elected Hank Finger as chairman of the constitutional committee and Charlie Rankin of Texas A&M as organizational publicity director. They planned to contact junior and senior colleges to send representatives to a meeting at Fort Worth in January, 1949, during the Southwestern Exposition & Livestock Show & Rodeo. They requested sample constitutions so that they could consolidate the ideas and create a constitution and bylaws.[8]

After the initial Sul Ross meeting, Hank Finger and Charlie Rankin dedicated a major amount of time to promoting the idea of a national organization. With the approval and support of administrators at both schools, Finger and Rankin started to work immediately, sending out information about the January meeting. Sul Ross subsidized Finger's correspondence. Bar SR Bar secretary Evelyn Bruce Kingsbery joined Finger in sending reams of invitational letters. The Texas A&M Animal Husbandry Department picked up the tab for Rankin's publicity releases. Finger received guidance and support from Sul Ross president Dr. R. M. Hawkins and the Sul Ross rodeo team sponsor Range and Animal Science professor E. E. Turner. Likewise, Dr. J. C. Miller, head of the Texas A&M Animal Husbandry Department, and Ike Dahlberg, faculty advisor of the Texas A&M Saddle and Sirloin Club, guided and supported Rankin.[9]

A news release that compared college rodeo to other campus sports caught the attention of newspaper editors. Charlie Rankin's first article made headlines in the *Bi-Weekly Rodeo News,* where he quoted Hank Finger: "The boy from the country coming to college needs an extra-curricular activity to coincide with his classroom work the same as a city boy has his tennis, golf, or football."[10] In January, 1949, *The Buckboard* used it, and numerous promotional articles repeated it.[11] Another article in *The Buckboard* extended the idea: "With the right kind of organization, we think rodeos can become one of the major scholastic sports along with football, basketball, track, and baseball. In later years all major sports have looked to colleges for talent, and there is no reason why the same thing would not hold true for rodeos. This move has the blessing of the RCA, and they plan to work in close harmony with the colleges to see that this new organization has every opportunity to succeed."[12]

People in positions of power with experience, insight, and resources can speed up the organizational process. That person for the NIRA was Hyde Merritt, then associate editor of the *Bi-Weekly Rodeo News,* who emphasized in an editorial the merits of a college rodeo organization. Merritt, while a student at the University of Wyoming, had roped at the 1942 University of Arizona intercollegiate rodeo and other college rodeos. Merritt had also helped to produce UW's first two intercollegiate rodeos in 1941 and 1942 and helped to organize and write the bylaws for the University of Wyoming's rodeo club, so with his college rodeo experience and his use of the power of the pen, he helped the NIRA.[13] Merritt sent his editorial to Carl L. Garrison, secretary-manager of the Cow Palace, and suggested that it would be "a natural arena show" for the Grand National Junior Livestock Exposition in San Francisco.[14] Recognizing the potential after having the successful IRA finals rodeo at the Cow Palace in 1946, Garrison immediately contacted Hank Finger, who flew to Denver during the National Western Stock Show and Rodeo, to discuss having the first national intercollegiate championship rodeo in April, 1949, at the Cow Palace.

The prospect of having a championship NIRA rodeo forced the student organizers to move rapidly without thinking about the magnitude of their responsibilities in establishing a college sport outside of the athletic system. Even the first obstacle did not slow them down. Lack of motel rooms in Fort Worth during the 1949 Southwestern Exposition & Livestock Show & Rodeo forced the delegates to meet in Dallas. On January 28, 1949, in spite of a blizzard that coated the roads with ice and snow, thirty-three delegates from thirteen schools arrived in Dallas. Colorado A&M's Dr. R. S. Jackson served as the official faculty adviser to delegates from eight Texas schools and one each from Wyoming, Colorado, Oklahoma, Arizona, and New Mexico.[15]

In two days the students created an organization that has basically remained the same with only minor updates, revisions, refinements, and expansions. The delegates adopted a constitution, bylaws, rules, and then elected interim officers to serve until the organization could have a convention. The delegates spent the two busy days consolidating and revising two sample constitutions submitted by Sul Ross and Texas A&M. Aggie Charlie Rankin said that the one he submitted was a slightly revised version of the National Future Farmers of

America (FFA) Constitution. When the delegation adjourned on January 30, 1949, they had officially organized the National Intercollegiate Rodeo Association. Since Hank Finger was scheduled to graduate in May, delegates elected Rankin as president pro tem.

After organizing, the students immediately faced opposition to the idea, opposition framed by administrative apathy. President pro tem Charlie Rankin said, "As no one had any experience at starting an organization of this kind, we had to go by trial and error, which was rather expensive and time wasting. We had the blessings of both rodeo unions and some of the colleges, but no one actually helped us by sitting down and making their valuable experience available to us in the form of actual material or mental help. Sure, congratulations were passed on, but they were of no help in organizing. I condemn the actions of the schools more than anyone else. Their attitude is 'Sure, it's fine, but do it yourself.' The schools' publicity departments could have grabbed the idea and helped tremendously. Attitudes that also had to be worked out among the schools were that we were hogging the show and trying to railroad our ideas in."[16]

The student-leaders faced yet other problems, complex major financial and professional problems. The financial problems stemmed from start-up expenses and no income. The team members needed compensation for travel expenses. The required amateur status for college athletes caused jackpotted entry fees to be questioned. The professional problems came from the unique nature of rodeo competition. For most sports, college competition is considered amateur; however, many college cowboys rejected relinquishing their professional Rodeo Cowboys Association (RCA) cards for college rodeo cards. The NIRA proposed dual competition for college contestants. This was difficult to explain to college administrators, familiar with the National Collegiate Athletic Association's (NCAA) emphasis on amateur status for college athletes.

NIRA membership hinged on approval of dual college and professional competition for NIRA contestants. In fact, the cowboys wanted documented proof that they could still compete in professional rodeos. On February 21, 1949, Hank Finger wrote to RCA president Toots Mansfield, "When Hyde [Merritt] talked to you, an agreement was worked out whereby these men might officially resign from the RCA and join the NIRA. The NIRA would issue them a membership card which would also serve as credentials for their eligibility to enter an RCA approved show. . . . We need an official written document from the RCA approving this plan."[17] Mansfield said that college students could resign from

The first NIRA student president Charlie Rankin of Texas A&M rode Black Hills to a first place win at the Aggie rodeo in 1949. Photo by James Cathey, Fort Worth, and courtesy of NIRA Alumni archives.

the RCA and use their NIRA cards to enter RCA rodeos. With the stroke of a pen, RCA president Mansfield recognized and approved a new type of cowboy, the college cowboy. From that point on, membership in the NIRA grew rapidly.

With dual competition approved, the new organization faced another concern. Some worried that professional cowboys might enroll in college just to compete in college rodeos. An NIRA rule addressed this potential problem. A student had to attend school one quarter or one semester before becoming an NIRA contestant. The older NIRA veteran members did not consider an age limit for college rodeo. Later, an eligibility rule gave college contestants four years of eligibility to be used within six years after high school graduation.

Professional rodeo's early-day rowdy image led NIRA founders to promote a new image acceptable to college administrators. They incorporated strict conduct and high academic standards into the NIRA's eligibility rules. Charlie Rankin said, "the Rules of Conduct are strict, and the punishment is severe;

therefore, the conduct in the arena is so far above other rodeos that the spectators notice it and comment on it."[18] The 1949 Constitution stated that if an individual was guilty of unbecoming conduct at a rodeo that individual would be expelled from that rodeo and warned to refrain from that type of conduct or the individual would be blacklisted. A two-thirds majority vote of the clubs present at that rodeo would enforce the rule of conduct. The academic standards required that a student pass twelve hours with a minimum grade point average of C, which exceeded the requirements of other college sports.[19]

The young NIRA officers learned business practices rapidly as school administrators confronted them. Initially, agriculture departments at the land-grant schools accepted the NIRA because students in their programs belonged to it. The framers of the 1949 Constitution debated the issue of classifying rodeo but decided that it was to be an organized and standard college activity. However, some agriculture departments rejected it as a dangerous activity. For example, the animal husbandry department of Oklahoma A&M "flatly refused" to sponsor the rodeo team as it was "too dangerous for college participation, and they will accept no part of the responsibility." However, Bill Brady, an Oklahoma A&M student, wrote the Sul Ross Rodeo Club that the Dean of Men had requested information so that he could "impress him [the school president] with the interest the other schools are taking in these clubs."[20] The possible hazards of the sport continued to obstruct the formation of rodeo programs on many campuses until recruiting and safety data of successful rodeo programs convinced administrators otherwise.

Many administrators considered funding to be the problem, more so than the potential danger. Administrators and athletic directors rejected adding another sport to share in tight budgets or that threatened the territory of traditional sports. They used the element of danger to fog their territorial sport biases. Classifying rodeo often stalled its acceptance into any department. Was it a sport or an activity in the agriculture department? At universities, rodeo usually remained in agriculture departments.

Rodeo's recognition as a college sport benefited from the proliferation of two-year schools in the 1960s. Unhindered by universities' sports traditions, many community college administrators recognized the recruiting power of a sport with unlimited numbers of contestants. Later, a government regulation helped rodeo move into the sports category. With the movement for sports equality for women, the passing of Title IX by the federal government required athletic departments to provide women with the same opportunities in sports as men. College rodeo, being coed and not limited by numbers of contestants, afforded schools easy access to compliance with the law by moving rodeo into the athletic departments. However, rodeo was often the first to be cut in sports departments when budgets had to be trimmed.

Fluctuating between being an activity or a sport plagued funding for college rodeo programs through the years. For example, Montana State University started its rodeo program in 1947 but changed it in 1982 to a varsity sport equal to football, basketball, and other sports. Faced with the loss of funding for the rodeo program by the Associated Students of Montana State University (ASMSU), which started funding it in 1955, MSU Dean of Agriculture James Welsh, rodeo adviser Sandy Gagnon, athletic director Tom Parac, and MSU President Tietz moved rodeo from under the jurisdiction of the College of Agriculture into the Department of Athletics.[21] They hired John Larick, an educated, experienced rodeo cowboy and coach. By the late 1990s, MSU rodeo contestants had brought national recognition to the university by winning thirty-five team and event championships, ranking them third in the nation in national championships. In spite of this, MSU administrators, because of budget cuts, ruled that the rodeo program must raise money to fund itself. This would be unthinkable applied to a university sport, such as football, basketball, or baseball. With the fund-raising and political expertise of Larick, the rodeo program survived that year and was shifted back to athletic funding.

Cultural aspects hindered rodeos' acceptance into college athletic departments. The word *show,* a carry-over from the Wild West Show days, continued in the contestants' daily references to college rodeos. Recognizing this problem, NIRA leaders and rodeo coaches made an effort to replace rodeo's vaudeville show image as they promoted rodeo as a college sport in athletic departments. At the 1950 convention, the delegates replaced the word *show* with the word *rodeo* in the 1949 NIRA Constitution. However, it faded slowly from use by contestants. On occasion, it is still used today.

NIRA officers showed motivation and business ability as they encountered a myriad of organizational details and a testing of the new rules. First, the NIRA needed a logo, so George Harley, a Sul Ross student, designed it. Sanctioned college rodeos encouraged NIRA membership, yet some schools did not join. However, Hank Finger cautioned the University of Texas Varsity Rodeo Club in March 1949, "your show is not NIRA approved so we are not permitted to attend."[22] Charlie Rankin wrote about eligibility problems to Finger: "That 'C' average has hit us a little and evidently has hit a few others harder; I have been called a SOB more than once (never to my face though) for carrying out the constitution to the letter."[23]

College rodeo contestants moved from the competitive arena to the administrative arena, which is unique to a college sport. Five days after the first finals rodeo, the NIRA held its first convention April 15 and 16, 1949, at the Shirley-Savoy Hotel in Denver, Colorado. President pro tem Charlie Rankin presided while the delegates, after considerable discussion, adopted the constitution, bylaws, rules and regulations, and then elected officers. The NIRA national officers, elected by the membership to be the executive committee, included a president, vice president, publicity director, three regional direc-

Delegates to the first NIRA convention on April 15–16, 1949, in Denver, Colorado, are (front, left to right) Dr. R. S. Jackson, Colorado A&M; next two are unknown; Bill Jones, University of Wyoming; Frank Lilley, Colorado A&M; Clint Josey, University of Texas; next one unknown; Pete Burns, University of Wyoming; Hank Finger, Sul Ross State; Sid Lanier, Texas A&M; Mac McArthur, Cameron Agricultural College; Eldon Dudley, Oklahoma A&M; Rocky Mountain Region director Perry Clay, University of Wyoming; (back, left to right) unknown; Buster Lindley, Sul Ross State; unknown; Pacific Northwest Region director J. H. "Pokey" Foss, State College of Washington; president Charlie Rankin, Texas A&M; unknown; Southern Region director Dick Kelley, New Mexico A&M; vice president Joe Forney, Colorado A&M; unknown; Tommie Bell, Texas Tech; Paul Kramer, Texas A&M; NIRA secretary Timi Kramer; two unknown. Photo courtesy of Joe Crockett, La Belle, Florida, and NIRA Alumni archives.

tors, and the faculty advisers of the three directors. The president would appoint a secretary-treasurer, who would not have a vote or be required to be enrolled in a college. The secretary-treasurer was paid one dollar per hour.[24] The first NIRA student officers were president, Charlie Rankin of Texas A&M; vice president, Joe W. Forney of Colorado A&M; and publicity director, Evelyn Bruce Kingsbery of Sul Ross State. The three regional directors were Pacific Northwest Region, J. H. Foss of State College of Washington; Southern Region, R. S. "Dick" Kelley of New Mexico A&M; and Rocky Mountain Region, Perry W. Clay of University of Wyoming. Kelley, one of the many veterans, was appointed chairman of the committee to design the stationery. Mrs. Paul (Timi) Kramer of Texas A&M, hired as the secretary-treasurer, was not a student.

The NIRA was officially incorporated a few months later as a nonprofit corporation. Twenty-nine years after Texas A&M held the first college rodeo on its campus, the NIRA was officially approved as a nonprofit corporation at College Station, Brazos County, Texas, on August 5, 1949.

The student leaders defined regions, with elected student directors from each region, that later proved to be an integral part of the NIRA. The states of Washington, Idaho, California, Nevada, and Oregon comprised the Pacific Northwest Region. The states of Colorado, Kansas, Utah, Wyoming, Montana, North and South Dakota, and Nebraska set the Rocky Mountain Region. Texas, Oklahoma, New Mexico, Arizona, and Louisiana defined the Southern Region.

Selecting delegates to the annual national convention emphasized the importance of maintaining a student-led board. The bylaws defined delegates as being the national officers and past presidents of the NIRA and two delegates from each active member club. Any member in good standing could attend the convention and participate in all discussion and business of the convention but could not vote. Travel expenses were the responsibility of each collegiate club.[25]

The NIRA cowboy competition, governed by the professional event rules, reflected the traditional professional rodeo events. The 1949 Constitution defined six events with five being required at each NIRA rodeo: bareback riding, saddle bronc riding, bull riding, steer wrestling (included steer decorating), tie-down calf roping, and team roping, which could be ribbon roping, wild cow milking, or team tying. The April 18, 1948, official RCA and IRA rodeo rules adopted at Red Bluff, California, governed the NIRA cowboys events, unless an exception was stated in the NIRA Rules and Regulations. Each NIRA event awarded three hundred points at each rodeo. These three hundred points were divided into equal parts, the number of parts being one more than the number of go-rounds held in that event. The points were divided 40, 30, 20, 10 percent among the top four men in a go-round. If a rodeo had one go-round, the points were split six ways: 29, 24, 19, 14, 9, and 5 percent.[26]

The NIRA board members debated the dual nature of one event, team roping, which created continuous problems because it required two contestants. Team roping partners split the points fifty-fifty between the header and the heeler. Each contestant could enter twice, but not with the same partner. When a winning contestant's partner was from another school, half the points went to the other school. Therefore, coaches seldom chose team ropers as team members and seldom gave them scholarships. However, correcting this problem failed through the years because team ropers voted on their event rules, and they preferred having a chance to win twice as much prize money as contestants in other events.

Rules for teams and unlimited numbers of contestants from each school reflected the nontraditional aspects of college rodeo. At a regional college rodeo, a team could consist of from one to six men; at the national championship rodeo, a team had to have six men—no more, no less. Having a team and having an unlimited number of individuals from the same school competing at the same rodeos required some creative thinking for the officers and delegates. Contestants challenged a rule to limit the number of contestants. Initially, only team members were assured an entry in a rodeo. Later, any NIRA-eligible student could enter a regional rodeo.

Even with NIRA regions, originally, contestants could compete in any NIRA rodeo in the nation. The rule stated that schools must invite all member clubs of the association to participate. The freedom to compete in any college rodeo initially appeared to be fair. However, at year's end, when a championship race had developed, some cowboys and cowgirls dashed to all the regional rodeos pursuing points and missing many days of classes, which defeated the basic reason for college rodeo. Also, numerous college rodeos in the southwest created discontented contestants from the northern and western states because of distances. Eventually, the NIRA limited students to competition in one region only.

Matching uniforms for team members reflected another nontraditional aspect of college rodeo. Uniforms for all teams were compulsory at a national rodeo and the color schemes of all teams had to be submitted to the Executive Committee for approval.[27] The uniforms evolved into vests for all contestants with their school's name on the front and the back. Contestants later individualized their vests with the use of various types of fabric, leather, fringe, feathers, silver conchos, religious symbols, designs, state shapes, and glitter.

The NIRA officers soon realized that the NIRA, a business, required a permanent, stable national office. However, the mobility and transitory nature of the college-student officers created instability. The first year illustrated this problem. President Charlie Rankin said, "Texas A&M gave us [NIRA] office space, and Mrs. Timi Kramer, whose husband was in veterinarian school, had consented to work as office manager and secretary,"[28] Mrs. Kramer said, "We lost our office this year, so we have set up a makeshift one in my home while Charlie is out scouting around for another one."[29] For many years, from the dorm room of the outgoing president, the new NIRA president would receive the NIRA records, usually kept in a cardboard box serving as a filing cabinet. Rankin wrote Hank Finger, "To assure everyone that all money will be used correctly, I have made arrangements with Mr. C. G. White, Texas A&M director of student activities, to open an account in the name of the NIRA in the student activities book."[30]

Lacking a means for frequent communication and being at different schools, the NIRA officers deferred the decisions to the president. Hyde Merritt, associate editor of the *Bi-Weekly Rodeo News*, wrote Rankin about the need for the new organization to have a newspaper to use for communication with its members. Merritt suggested that if a person was a subscriber at the time of joining the NIRA, he would extend their subscription free to the end of the fiscal year, February 1, 1950.[31] This generous offer, as so many new ideas in an organization often do, had critics. Rankin wrote H. G. Bedford, president of the Texas Tech Rodeo Association, that "someone accused him [Merritt] of using the college students for the paper's benefit, so he suggested for the welfare of all concerned that we make the subscription optional."[32]

College rodeo contestants never considered it a problem to produce their own rodeo and compete in it, as it was second nature to their lifestyle. They did not complain that football and basketball players did not have to raise money, sell tickets, hire judges, and run the concession at their games while playing in them. Schools scheduled student-produced college rodeos every weekend after the convention until the spring semester ended in 1949. Kansas State and Hardin-Simmons University in Texas had rodeos in April. Five schools held May rodeos: Oklahoma A&M, New Mexico A&M, Cameron College in Oklahoma, Trinidad Junior College in Colorado, and the University of Wyoming, its seventh annual intercollegiate rodeo.

With the NIRA being a business, colleges added a new career: rodeo coach. After earning a degree, many college rodeo alumni returned from the professional ranks to become college rodeo coaches, often hired by their alma maters. A *Western Horseman* writer in 1949 predicted that "one day soon, past and present big name professional rodeo cowboys will be pressed into service as rodeo team coaches."[33] Two of the 1949 UW contestants, Pete Burns and Bill Laycock, later returned to coach the UW rodeo in the 1990s. Another 1949 UW contestant and NIRA national champion, Dale Stiles, coached many years at Casper College.

The NIRA founders offered a college scholarship to a high school student. The NIRA awarded its first scholarship of $150 to the all-around cowboy at the 1949 high school finals. The scholarship could be used at any of the twenty-eight NIRA member schools.[34] Awarding this scholarship gave media exposure to the NIRA. A picture of Rankin presenting the scholarship at Halletsville, Texas, on August 27, 1949, to the all-around winner, R. W. Nixon of Breckenridge, Texas, appeared in the *Houston Chronicle Magazine* on October 9, 1949. Earlier, Rankin had written Rocky Mountain Region director Joe Fornay that the Texas A&M club planned to send someone to recruit each year at the Texas Championship High School Rodeo. Other member schools would benefit by doing this.[35] Scholarships became a major recruiting tool for schools.

Publicity for the first NIRA finals rodeo benefited the new organization. The students also gained rodeo production and media experience working with the professionals. However, media coverage suffered because of the students themselves. Cow Palace general manager Carl L. Garrison requested information and pictures from each school for advance publicity, which brought membership requests and aided students' presentations seeking to establish rodeo programs. President Charlie Rankin worked with Garrison on the rodeo promotional materials and with the NIRA board making convention plans. The publicity information from the schools trickled in. Rankin wrote to Red Clark, secretary of Pierce College of Agriculture Rodeo Club in California, "To date only the University of Wyoming has responded to Mr. Garrison's request for pictures and publicity material."[36] The student-led NIRA was responsible for its own publicity, but the students lacked the skills and the time to prepare news releases, so the NIRA remained unknown to the media and to the public for many years.

With the national finals invitational rodeo approaching at the Cow Palace, the student officers faced the issue of rodeo prize money. Rankin wrote Ham Scott, New Mexico Aggie Rodeo Association president, "Mr. Garrison cannot officially charge entry fees as schools do not recognize such awards; that's why the phrase 'not for cash awards' is in Clause 9. But as he said, if we want to get up a jackpot among ourselves, that is up to us."[37]

Of the fifteen schools invited to send a six-man team to the first finals rodeo, only one declined. The University of California at Davis, the school closest to San Francisco, would not give approval for six of their Roping Club members to compete. An article in the California Aggie College of Agriculture paper gave reasons: "The NIRA is a group of clubs, and it is not an association of colleges. Members of the team would have to be cleared through the recorder's office and such clearance, it is felt by the administration, would amount to official recognition by the University of California. . . . The matter is still pending, and Dean Ryerson has promised to carry through with the investigation, but appearance of the Roping Club at the Cow Palace in April is out."[38]

Contestants gained rodeo business experience making arrangements to compete at the NIRA finals that ten years later would be used by some to help produce the first professional rodeo finals. The Cow Palace negotiated a contract with each school for its team's travel expenses. Garrison signed fourteen contracts, which specified that each school could send a team of six men and one faculty representative. The contract included five cents per mile for two cars only and hotel accommodations with $250 cash for the NIRA. The five-performance rodeo at San Francisco would have a matinee and evening performance on April 9 and 10 and an evening performance on April 11. The number of entries in the six events required an added performance on Friday evening, April 8. No mention was made of funding the extra night. The school's faculty adviser had to certify their entries. The 1949 NIRA finals experience helped Harley May, president of the RCA in 1959, when he chaired the NFR Commission, which planned and produced the first professional National Finals Rodeo.[39]

Fourteen schools from nine states sent teams to the historic 1949 national championship rodeo. California and Texas each sent teams from three schools. California's entries were California State Polytechnic College at San Luis Obispo, Pierce College of Agriculture at Canoga Park, and Fresno State College. Texas entries were from Texas A&M at College Station, Texas Tech at Lubbock, and Sul Ross State College at Alpine. New Mexico A&M at Las Cruces and University of New Mexico at Albuquerque sent teams. University of Wyoming at Laramie, Colorado A&M at Fort Collins, Oklahoma A&M at Stillwater, Montana State College at Bozeman, Arizona State College at Tempe, and Kansas State at Manhattan each sent a team.

With limited time for selecting six team members and preparing for the trip to San Francisco, mini-dramas unfolded at several schools. Sul Ross State student Harley May recalled the events leading up to his team's trip to San Francisco: "Two boys that weren't on the team took the two horses and left a couple of days ahead of time. We used Gene Newman's roping horse, and another boy going to school there had a stud horse that we roped cows on. At first, I wasn't chosen to go on the team. I wasn't that well acquainted. (May had just enrolled at Sul Ross in January, 1949, after attending New Mexico A&M for a year and a half in 1946 and 1947.) The boy that they elected to go as the steer wrestler, about a week before the team left, admitted that he had never competed in the steer wrestling. They started looking for an alternate. They chose me to go in his place." Sul Ross sent Range Animal Science professor E. E. Turner along as the sponsor. "He went as a chaperon more than anything else," said May.[40]

Today, rodeo cowboys traverse the country frequently, but in 1949, the new experience for many of the contestants needed cowboy ingenuity to make it. The cowboys arrived in San Francisco by jeep, car, and plane. Three Oklahoma A&M cowboys made the 1,700-mile trip in a jeep pulling a horse trailer.[41] University of Wyoming's Dale Stiles recounted his team's trip: "We were having finals, and they wouldn't let us off to go to the finals rodeo, so we raffled off a saddle at the bar where I worked. Roy Barnes from Denver donated the saddle. We chartered a private twin-engine plane with the money. The woman who owned the bar/brothel added enough money to cover the cost. We flew out of San Francisco at 2:00 A.M. so that we could be back in Laramie to take our finals at 8:00 A.M. We gave our third-place trophy to the woman who helped finance our trip. That caused an uproar at the University when the administrators found out that the trophy was on display at her place of business."[42]

The Texas Tech rodeo team members were loaded and ready to head for San Francisco to the Cow Palace in 1949 for the first NIRA rodeo finals. Photo courtesy of Texas Tech 1940s–1950s Alumni/Harley Shannon & Mozelle Montana, and NIRA Alumni archives.

Another school did some creative planning to make it to the Cow Palace. The Kansas State team had to change its plans to represent the college when they found that two of the team's best riders failed to meet college eligibility requirements because they had not attended the Manhattan school long enough. To circumvent this, they decided to represent the Chaparajos Club instead. Riding for the club instead of the college meant no college funds for the trip. The club helped with part of the expense, but the men had to pay the rest.[43]

The first national championship finals set a standard for quality of personnel that has continued to be a benchmark for finals productions. The audience

The 1949 University of Wyoming rodeo team stands in front of the plane that they used to fly to the first finals at the Cow Palace in San Francisco, where they placed third. Team members are (left to right) *Fran Marsh; Bob Laramore; Pete Dalzell; saddle bronc champion Dale Stiles; Bill Whitney, and John Gammon. Photo courtesy of Jaune Miller, Wheatland, Wyoming, and NIRA Alumni archives.*

at the rodeo watched the top professional announcer, clown, judges, and rodeo producers. Along with the expertise of the manager Carl L. Garrison and rodeo secretary Cecil Jones, Cy Taillon of Denver, Colorado, using his legendary style at the microphone, highlighted the contestants and the events. The popular clown Slim Pickens kept the audience's eyes tracking his every move. Two judges, Buster Ivory of Modesto, California, and Cecil Henley of Hayward, California, used their professional standards on the college cowboys. The eighty-four contestants "challenged Harry Rowell's stock that had grounded many a professional cowboy." Each rodeo team dressed in identical uniforms in colors representing their schools. The Montana State cowboys had the "prettiest uniforms . . . blue silk jackets with gold sateen sleeves."[44]

The newspapers, while heralding the history-making competition, highlighted the extra activities. Along with the six rodeo events, the rodeo featured ten other attractions. The Liberty Horse Act ("twelve of the most perfectly trained horses of the circus world"), a Bareback Duo, a calf-riding contest, a calf scramble, a Roman Chariot Race, High School Horses ("six beautiful girls, six gorgeous horses in matchless precision routines"), a greased pig scramble, and a stock horse class contest had been held. The *San Francisco Examiner* featured Jone Pederson, Santa Rosa (California) High School senior, dressed in shorts and an off-the-shoulder peasant blouse, being crowned Queen of the Cow Palace NIRA Rodeo by Charlie Rankin, NIRA student president.[45]

The 1949 finals set a benchmark in competition to match the quality of the production. Two of the most talented young cowboys battled it out for the number one spot. One was from Texas and the other from California. They both made the professional cowboys take a look at the quality of college competition. Sul Ross's Harley May won a record three individual NIRA championships that has been matched only twice in fifty years. He won the all-around,

The Queen of the Cow Palace NIRA Rodeo, Miss Jone Pederson, was admired by 1949 NIRA finals contestants (left to right) *Boog Trainham of New Mexico A&M; J. R. "Bubba" Day; Harry Hopson of New Mexico A&M; looking over saddle, Hank Finger, Sul Ross State; Queen Jone; unknown; squatting, plaid jacket, "Bo" Damuth of Texas A&M; leaning over, volunteer driver with car, Jack Shugart, Texas A&M; with rope, Buster Lindley of Sul Ross State; unknown. Photo by The Photo Shop, Hot Springs, New Mexico, and courtesy Charlie Rankin, McAllen, Texas, and NIRA Alumni archives.*

bareback riding, and bull riding. Both May and Cal Poly's Cotton Rosser placed in four events, but May had 225 points while Rosser had 165. May claimed eighty points in the bareback riding, seventy-five in the bull riding, fifty in the saddle bronc riding, and twenty in the steer wrestling. Rosser earned forty points in the bull riding, forty in the saddle bronc riding, fifty in the wild cow milking, and thirty-five in the calf roping. Both went on to become legends in college and professional rodeo.

Winning the first national team championship put the little Texas teacher's college, Sul Ross State College, on the national map, identifying it as a rodeo college. Other winning colleges also established an identity and a tradition as a favorite for rodeo cowboys, such as Cal Poly at San Luis Obispo, University of Wyoming, Colorado A&M, and New Mexico A&M. Sul Ross's six team members—Harley May of Deming, New Mexico; Texas cowboys Hank Finger of Alvin, Bub Hull of Seminole, Gene Newman of San Angelo, Charles Hall of Iraan, and Buster Lindley of Mertzon—captured the first national championship with 345 points. Cal Poly took second with three hundred points.

The 1949 Cow Palace teams became a model for well-balanced championship teams. Of the fourteen schools that sent teams, eleven had team members who placed in the top four in an event. All six men on Cal Poly's team placed, a standard that coaches continue to strive for but seldom match. Sul Ross and Texas A&M had four men place in the top four. Three men on four other teams placed in the top four. Sul Ross's Harley May placed nine times in the top four with team members placing fourteen times. Cal Poly's Cotton Rosser placed eight times in the top four with his team members placing thirteen times.

The professional cowboys watching the college action recognized a challenge headed their direction with this new cowboy competition. Carl L. Garrison saw team competition at a rodeo prove to be a success.[46] The Friday matinee crowd numbered 5,474 fans, while 6,990 witnessed both performances on Saturday.[47] University of Wyoming saddle bronc rider Dale Stiles spurred Sad Sam to a first round win followed by a second round win on Big Ben, giving him the champion bronc riding saddle, gold and silver belt buckle, two hats, and a pair of levis. In the bull riding, Colorado A&M's Billy Bashor won a round, and Texas A&M's Bubba Day took the other round, but May's aggregate points gave him the championship. Montana State's Bob Sauke won the only wild cow milking NIRA championship ever awarded. New Mexico A&M steer wrestler Tom Hadley turfed his first steer in a 10.9 and his second in 10.5

The Sul Ross State men's team, displaying their first place 1949 NIRA trophy, won at the first finals rodeo at the San Francisco Cow Palace, are (left to right) *Buster Lindley; Harley May, all-around, bareback, and bull riding champion; Hank Finger; sponsor Professor E. E. Turner. Team members not pictured are Charles Hall, Bub Hull, and Gene Newman. Photo courtesy of Harley May, Alpine, Texas, and NIRA Alumni archives.*

earning the championship. Oklahoma A&M calf roper Eldon Dudley carried home the gold with a total of 41.7 seconds on three head.

Many of the finals contestants went on to emblazon their names in professional rodeo history and remain active in the field of rodeo. Most earned degrees and became successful businessmen, stock contractors, rodeo announcers, or ranchers. One contestant added glitter and glamor by using his talent for handling livestock to create a career in Hollywood. Pierce College's Buford "Corky" Randall, in his forty-year career, fulfilled Hollywood film directors' requests for livestock and fowl, such as seven hundred head of cattle, fourteen buzzards, and three hundred horses.[48]

When the eighty-four finals rodeo contestants reported back to their rodeo clubs about the success of the rodeo, the stock, and the prizes, it motivated their clubs to promote the new organization. Texas Tech Rodeo Club secretary-treasurer Tibba McMullan said that their team "convinced our club that the show was a success and that we should help in every way we can to promote another show this year."[49] In October, 1949, Texas Tech reported having twenty-six members, eighteen roping calves, eighteen bucking horses, and a new arena.[50] West Texas State's WT Anchor Rodeo Association agreed to "pay our gas and oil expenses to and from rodeos."[51] James Mickler, president of Hardin-Simmons Rodeo Association, said that they were "building a rodeo arena at school and plan to have a small weekly rodeo between our students to create an interest and for practice." HSU had 130 paid members of their club.[52] Maxie Overstreet, Texas A&M Rodeo Association president, said that they had forty NIRA members and sixty-five in the rodeo club.[53]

College cowgirls helped develop the NIRA while increasing the numbers of cowgirl contestants. In fact, students elected a cowgirl, Evelyn Bruce Kingsbery of Sul Ross State College, to serve as NIRA publicity director. Bruce Kingsbery, the first woman elected to the NIRA board, did not attend the first convention, but she was elected to office anyway. She found out about her election five days later. She said, "The announcement was made in assembly Tuesday that I had been elected publicity director for the NIRA. It is still hard for me to believe because I know much less than I should."[54] Bruce Kingsbery, who served as secretary-treasurer of the Bar SR Bar Rodeo Association while Hank Finger served as president, had been unanimously elected on the recommendation of Sul Ross delegates Buster Lindley and Finger.[55]

After the organizational meeting, along with being a contestant and a full-time student, Bruce Kingsbery started a stream of correspondence and articles to publicize the NIRA. She had a flare for writing news releases that caught the attention of editors. After attending the September, 1949, NIRA Executive Committee meeting, Bruce Kingsbery wrote to two rodeo papers seeking space for NIRA news. Chuck King, editor of *Bi-Weekly Rodeo News,* in Billings, Montana, said, "We'll have the necessary cut made and set the section up and get it rolling for the NIRA. All I ask in helping promote the NIRA is that you furnish new and interesting material for each issue of the paper."[56] Ethel "Ma" Hopkins, editor of *Hoofs and Horns,* complimented Bruce Kingsbery on the excellent article that she sent about the NIRA. She said, "We shall plan to print the article in this month's issue . . ." and "your officers and members are to be congratulated on the work they have accomplished in such a short time."[57]

Most of the student-leaders brought a wealth of experience as they had been involved in many other activities and organizations. Confidence in Bruce Kingsbery's ability was earned as she went through a two-year school and on to a four-year school. She attended John Tarleton Agricultural College and went to Sul Ross State College to finish her degree. She had been elected agriculture editor of the JTAC school paper and FFA sweetheart. Later, she won the Sul Ross Rodeo Queen title. Bruce Kingsbery was elected to the national NIRA board as a junior. She later married the 1948–49 president of the Texas A&M Saddle and Sirloin Club, Jack Kingsbery, who also helped to organize the NIRA. As did so many early day contestants, they both stayed close to education and rodeo while they ranched at Crystal City, Texas, and reared four children. Along with running the ranch, Evelyn worked for many years as the Southwest Texas Junior College librarian at Uvalde, and Jack ran a successful gun safe business and penned several books on rodeo.[58]

A few cowgirls, along with a drove of cowboys, sent in their membership fees to the NIRA the first year. The cowgirls created their own events and tried to convince the administrators and the outside world that they had a legitimate right to rodeo with the cowboys. NIRA president Charlie Rankin reported before the first finals in 1949 that Sul Ross had twenty-four members, two of whom were women: Evelyn Bruce Kingsbery and Jo Gregory Knox. However, women were not invited to the first college finals as the promoters were familiar with traditional professional rodeo where cowgirl competition had practically disappeared. Two years (1951) passed before the NIRA named a national women's all-around champion and twelve years (1961) before naming a national champion women's team due in part to the small number of women competing in college rodeos. The 1949 NIRA Constitution Rules and Regulations Number 10 included criteria for the cowgirl all-around and team titles. Women were limited to two events per show governed by the Girls Rodeo Association (GRA). Their events were approved, but undefined. The rules did not specify the number for women's teams. Women's team points were separate from the men's team points.

Many NIRA member schools were A&M schools that had no females, but college cowboys understood the merit of cowgirls competing at the same rodeo with them. Sponsor events, usually goat tying, had been used at Texas A&M as early as 1941 or 1942. The female entries had been sponsored by area towns around Texas A&M. Since sponsorships had worked for them, the idea of sponsor and cowgirl events was approved. The 1949 NIRA Constitution stated that sponsor and cowgirl events for approved NIRA rodeos were to be recommended by the regional director subject to the approval of the executive committee. Sponsorships of the cowgirl events were optional to each sponsor of approved NIRA shows.

With the scarcity of college cowgirls and events undefined, cowgirl contestants were like shadows with their names in rodeo programs, but seldom in rodeo articles in newspapers. Mixed team roping had been a consistent part of college rodeos during the late 1930s. Beginning with the first intercollegiate rodeo in 1939, cowgirls had at least one event but usually two and sometimes as many as four. In fact, almost half of the contestants at the first intercollegiate rodeo were cowgirls. In 1940 the University of Arizona, at its first intercollegiate rodeo, included mixed team roping. College rodeos usually included barrel racing and an optional event, either goat tying or calf roping, which could be breakaway roping or tie-down calf roping. Barrel racing had grown in popularity using both the figure eight and cloverleaf patterns while relay racing, trick riding, and steer riding had become events of the past.

Early cowgirls struggled with stereotypical thinking of administrators and the public. Hank Finger, who became the Alpine Chamber of Commerce executive director, knew that events or activities sponsored by public institutions must conform to the public's mores to succeed. Finger said that no women entries for the wild cow riding had been sent to the Sul Ross rodeo. "This is not because none of the girls want to enter, but because of a policy of the administration. Mr. Turner and I are of the opinion that any girls' event which requires the riding of bucking stock and is approved by the NIRA is leaving the school producing the show and the NIRA liable for a great deal of detrimental criticism." Finger said that the chance of injury and the "un-lady like nature" of cow riding or horse riding would stimulate criticism.[59] A letter from cowgirl Jo Gregory Knox, Sul Ross Bar SR Bar Rodeo Association secretary, explained the girls' position: "I want to, and also the other girls, but we are afraid to go ahead and enter because we might not get to rodeo next spring." She also said, "Hank said we could stay in town if we all could stay in the same hotel or courts; otherwise, it was no soap."[60] The eight girls planned to take three horses among them. Fifty years later, one girl might take three horses just for her events.

Cowgirls' hard work and dedication influenced the new organization in schools from north to south. Cowgirls often led the fund-raising events for their college rodeo clubs. Gwen Burke, Montana State Rodeo Club secretary, said, "We anticipate the drawing for a saddle to finance a rodeo trip to some southern NIRA rodeo." Cowgirls accepted the responsibility of publicity and communication for the NIRA. Janice K. Grey, Washington State Hackamore Club secretary/publicity director, which had thirty-two club members and three NIRA members, wrote that they would hold a rodeo in the spring jointly with the University of Idaho. The administrative ability of the cowgirls did not go unnoticed by the cowboys. In 1949 J. H. Foss, Pacific Northwest regional director and member of the Washington State club, said, "In December we will elect a new rodeo chairman. I would like to see Miss Grey get the job. That would be an innovation, but the girls in our Hackmore Club are at the moment far more active than the men."[61]

Reporters also noted the importance of cowgirls in the new organization, but they reflected the idea of the beauty queen rather than the image of the athlete. Joe Koller, a freelance writer from Belle Fouche, South Dakota, wrote, "I have every confidence that rodeo will make the grade in the colleges. The IRA has approved a plan to promote a rodeo queen of the year. Most big shows have queens, and many will be college girls."[62]

With strong leaders, the success of the first finals, and the combined efforts of cowboys and cowgirls, the NIRA grew rapidly. During the first membership year, 373 individuals from twenty-nine colleges and universities in ten states had joined the NIRA. Texas had fifteen member rodeo clubs; California had three. Arizona, New Mexico, and Oklahoma each had two. Five states had one: Colorado, Kansas, Montana, Wyoming, and Washington. Seventeen cowgirls from seven schools belonged: Arlington State College, Oklahoma A&M, Sul Ross State, Texas Christian University, Texas Tech, University of Texas, and Texas A&I.[63] Large rodeo clubs supported the NIRA members, which attested to the strong interest on college campuses in things Western.

As with any organization, life's realities often give pause for the group to consider the effects of circumstance and change. Along with efforts to support their NIRA members and nurture their rodeo club, Hardin-Simmons University Rodeo Club members had to deal with change brought by the tragic death of their rodeo club president, Carl Meyers, killed August 4, 1949, at a professional rodeo at Big Spring, Texas, when he was hit by a stray bullet that killed the rodeo judge Buck Jones.

The officers tried to stabilize the NIRA in various ways. President Charlie Rankin contacted several public relations agencies seeking ways to help promote the NIRA. One PR consultant, J. Ben Dow of Fort Worth, gave Rankin four points of advice that had the NIRA been able to follow it, success would have been achieved much earlier. The first point emphasized that the NIRA needed national publicity and that a constant stream of news releases and articles would help achieve this. The second point, sponsors for the regions or for the national organization should be found. The third point, local sponsors were needed to buy uniforms and equipment. The final point, the NIRA should work through the American Medical Association to get doctors and hospitals to give care to any member who received injuries. Even with the marketing advice, the student officers fell prey to doing the most immediate task, which was finding a location and producing the finals rodeo along with maintaining the membership and business of the NIRA.[64]

The officers considered expanding the NIRA into an international college rodeo organization. Regarding the question of opening NIRA membership to Canadians, Mexicans, and Australians, J. H. Foss said, "All the ties this organization can make and keep during its infant years will be of inestimable value to the officers of the future for all will not be clear sailing with the NIRA throughout the coming years." He encouraged a flow of correspondence with anyone who was interested in college rodeo. Foss said, "We have everything to gain and nothing to lose but postage. This old world is in need of some good old good-neighbor policy."[65]

From this point, the NIRA standardized rules, named national champions, and guided college rodeo. It promoted college rodeo as an organized sport on college campuses governed by the students themselves on the national level. To achieve this, many NIRA members while maintaining a full load of college courses contributed an endless flow of volunteer work to establish the national organization with member clubs on campuses. A belief in meeting the need for the country-reared students to have a campus sport motivated the student-leaders in the organization. The milestone year 1949 gave the sport of rodeo a new organization that created a new direction for rodeo, resulting in a new image, a new way to network, a new recruiting field for professional rodeo, new fans, a new type of college coach, and college-educated rodeo contestants. As always with the young and inexperienced, the NIRA would face some serious growing pains in the next decade.

1950s—Rodeo Tested

on College Campuses

The National Intercollegiate Rodeo Association moved rodeo onto college campuses promoting it as a sport, but without institutional funding. During the 1950s the NIRA student officers struggled with financial instability and rapid change in leadership caused by graduation. The loss of the older, experienced war veterans, the constant change in leadership, and the lack of communication and cohesion between the national office and the membership resulted in organizational instability. Problems surfaced, such as a location for the annual national finals rodeo, the need to limit competition to regions, and the status of cowgirls. However, the NIRA continued to grow. An executive secretary was hired, rules were refined, champions set records, regional rodeos proliferated, and cowgirls established their events during the decade; however, management disagreements caused the 1950s to end with a split in the young organization, which threatened to destroy it.

As the NIRA officers wrangled with problems, a rodeo magazine columnist highlighted the major problems addressed at the convention; some would take at least a decade to solve. In 1950 Hyde Merritt, of the *Western Horseman,* noted problems such as hiring a paid executive secretary, the revision of contest rules, the point-award system, too many contestants, governing by regions, the status of cowgirls, location of the 1950 championship rodeo, entry qualifications, and forming an advisory board. Emphasizing the image of rodeo, Merritt wrote, "Too often rodeo has been referred to as a show, associating it

47

with a circus by our larger newspapers and magazines." Rodeo needs to be seen as "keen competition between top athletes of the sport" and be placed "on the sport page of every newspaper."[1]

Student leadership succeeded than failed due to constant change. In 1950 the convention delegates at Denver, Colorado, addressed the student leadership problem. They would hire a business manager/executive secretary, a paid employee not a student transacting business out of a dorm room, to establish a permanent national office. A student would still be elected to serve as NIRA president but would be relieved of the management of the office.[2]

NIRA organizational stability progressed during the second year with an executive secretary and a permanent headquarters. The Executive Committee voted to employ Charlie Rankin, the NIRA president who had just graduated. Evelyn Bruce Kingsbery, NIRA publicity director, said, "I can't praise Charlie and the work he has done too highly. I think he has been the factor in getting the NIRA where it is today, and he deserves every bit of credit he receives and more, too. It was the good fortune of the association to have him as its first president."[3] Rankin, who had earned his degree in January, 1950, in animal husbandry from Texas A&M, moved to Alpine, Texas, in February to set up the NIRA office. After five months, Rankin was called in June, 1950, to active duty on an Navy aircraft carrier during the Korean War.

The NIRA lost a well-qualified first executive secretary. Charlie Rankin, later the well-known "Voice of Agriculture" in South Texas at Radio KURV, Edinburg, was born in Dallas in 1925. Rankin grew up early when at age thirteen his father died, so he moved with his mother to Corsicana. The 1943 Corsicana High graduate served on a Navy aircraft carrier during World War II. In 1946 Rankin entered Texas A&M University. In 1949 the twenty-four-year-old war veteran stepped into history when he proved willing to expend the time and effort to help start an organization to bring rodeo to college campuses. When Rankin returned stateside in 1954, he began his lifetime career in radio broadcasting, which earned many awards, such as 1983 Man of the Year in Texas Agriculture.[4]

With continuing financial instability, the second year the NIRA returned to its original management format of a student president, instead of a hired executive secretary. The second-year officers had no funds to hire an executive secretary, so the student president Harley May, for January 1950 to 1951, added the executive secretary's responsibilities to his office. Garnet Rose Kotkin, NIRA

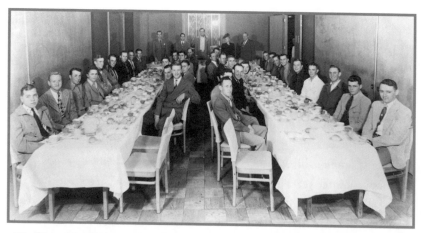

The thirty-eight delegates and guests at the 1950 NIRA Convention, held in Denver, Colorado, on January 2 are (back, head table, left) *Bob Denhardt,* Western Horseman; *Hyde Merritt,* Bi-Weekly Rodeo News; *NIRA president Charlie Rankin, Texas A&M; Mrs. & Mr. J. T. Caine, general manager of the National Western Stock Show and Rodeo;* (left, row 1, back to front) *Sul Ross adviser E. E. Turner; Tommie Bell, Texas Tech; Bill Caperton, West Texas State College; unidentified; Earl Reynolds, West Texas State College; Frank Lilley, Colorado A&M; unidentified; Dick Kelley, New Mexico A&M; J. H. Foss, State College of Washington;* (row 2, back) *Charlie Wampler, Texas A&M; George Masek, University of Arizona; B. F. Yeates, Texas Tech; John Finley, Kansas State; Dr. R. S. Jackson, Colorado A&M; unidentified; James Cathey, Ft. Worth;* (back, row 3) *Harley May, Sul Ross; Hank Finger, Sul Ross; Gene Frazier, Hardin-Simmons; James Mickler, Hardin-Simmons; Evelyn Bruce Kingsbery, Sul Ross; Jack Cargill, University of New Mexico; unidentified; Ham Scott, New Mexico A&M* (row 4, right back) *unidentified; Eldon Dudley, Oklahoma A&M; Buddy Reger, Oklahoma A&M; Bill Hogg, Texas A&M; Pete Burns, University of Wyoming; Clay Cade, Sul Ross; unidentified; Bill Gray, Hardin-Simmons; Bill Brown, University of Wyoming. Photo courtesy of Evelyn Bruce Kingsbery, Crystal City, Texas, and NIRA Alumni archives.*

publicity director from Washington State College, said, "I would lot rather pay for insurance than around five hundred a month for a National Secretary."[5] The first executive secretary in 1950 had actually been paid $250 per month.[6]

The NIRA felt the loss of a constant supporter. Twenty-four-year-old Hank Finger, a founder and moving force in the NIRA, died in a car accident on December 17, 1950, near Del Rio, Texas. Raised in Alvin, Texas, Finger had become the Alpine Chamber of Commerce manager after his graduation from Sul Ross State College. Although no longer an NIRA member, Finger had continued as a vocal advocate, a friend, and a consultant to the officers and members.[7]

Following Harley May, three more cowboy students served as NIRA president before the NIRA hired another executive secretary. Even with the workload of having responsibility for the regions and memberships, management of the national office and records, producing a national finals rodeo, and resolving the daily problems of the national organization, the student presidents won national championships and earned degrees. The 1951 NIRA president Bill Guest, thirty-three years old, was known as the "old man" of college rodeo, or "Old Folks." Guest's college career at John Tarleton Agricultural College had been interrupted in 1941 when he joined the Army Air Corps. After serving for five years, he returned to his home in Abilene, Texas, where he and his gray dogging horse Sam became a familiar sight at all the major rodeos, even Madison Square Garden in New York City.[8] Then, he decided to finish his degree. Having military veterans like Guest in the NIRA led to the 1951 NIRA Convention's delegates agreeing that "if a national emergency were declared, the NIRA would voluntarily become inactive until it was declared over and that the Board of Directors that were in office when the emergency was declared would be expected to reactivate the NIRA to its original position."[9]

Keeping the records current and distributing the NIRA standings created a constant source of problems for the NIRA student presidents. With the U.S. mail being the primary method of communication, students were slow to send the results, which complicated the president's job. A reporter, after trying unsuccessfully to get the current standings to promote the 1952 college finals in Oregon, wrote "that is why Bill Guest, the unpresent [*sic*] expected guest was sought so much Monday and Tuesday. He is the only guy who knows how everybody stands up to now. When last heard from, he was somewhere in Wyoming." Sul Ross cowboy Ross May said, "Last we heard five weeks ago, we were in the lead."[10] After Guest's arrival in Portland, detailed information was still missing. The top twelve were available, but when Oregon State requested its standing, Guest answered, "We've got 'em somewhere."[11]

The fourth NIRA student president, Dick Barrett, served for two years, 1952 and 1953. Barrett attended Oklahoma A&M then Hardin-Simmons University, won the 1952 all-around and ribbon roping championships along with the 1952 and 1953 bareback riding championships while president of the NIRA. During his tenure, the board changed the rodeo point year to coincide with the school year. NIRA business required Barrett to travel, often conflicting with his class schedule. In 1952 Barrett met in Fort Worth with representatives of the Rodeo Cowboys Association to reaffirm an agreement that allowed college cowboys to compete at RCA rodeos. College cowboys could use their NIRA cards to enter RCA rodeos if they would not compete in non-RCA rodeos. The two groups also agreed to honor each other's blacklists and allow RCA stock contractors to produce college rodeos.[12]

The final student president with full responsibility for NIRA business, recognizing the disaster caused by the student president's limited time, encouraged the board members to hire a part-time secretary-manager. After five years, the NIRA returned to the management plan that the original board had initiated with one exception—the secretary-manager was a part-time employee. President Bill Teague of Hardin-Simmons University "brought the records and materials of the NIRA to my home in Brownfield when I took over the work. These materials were all contained in two filing cabinets," said Alvin G. Davis, hired as secretary-manager October 1, 1955. He took over working with the membership of approximately fifty schools and more than five hundred student members. Davis had founded and served as secretary-manager and announcer for the American Junior Rodeo Association (AJRA), an organization for elementary through high school students. Davis, a banker at Brownfield, Texas, later became a rodeo announcer, artist, poet, general manager of the Ranching Heritage Center and founder and chairman of the National Cowboy Symposium and Celebration in Lubbock, Texas.[13]

The new secretary-manager changed financial and management methods to create efficiency and encourage communication. Davis, who served from 1955 to 1958, established a bookkeeping method and changed the membership renewal date from December 31 to October 15. The office stamped the NIRA cards either amateur rodeo or RCA, valid for one year. Club membership included a subscription to the official publication *Rodeo Sports News* and a newsletter from the NIRA office. To disseminate current rodeo points, the NIRA office mailed rodeo results to the regional directors, the NIRA officers, and all member clubs. The office mailed rules and applications to club sponsors, but many students said they did not know about them. Davis encouraged the faculty sponsors to meet with the clubs regularly.[14] Davis organized and stabilized the national office while working to solve communication problems.

After Davis resigned, the board hired Hoss Inman of Lamar, Colorado, noted

Officers of the 1956 NIRA board, who met in Lubbock, Texas, on March 3, 1956, are (left to right) Alvin G. Davis, Brownfield, Texas, secretary-manager; Dick Hecker, Montana State, Rocky Mountain Region; Perry Still, Cal Poly-San Luis Obispo, West Coast Region; Howard Samuell, Texas Tech, Southwest Region; Sonny Sikes, Sam Houston State, Southern Region; and President John Gee, Colorado A&M. Photo courtesy of Alvin G. Davis, Lubbock, Texas, and NIRA Alumni archives.

stock contractor and later a thoroughbred breeder and trainer. Inman, who served as the third secretary-manager from November 19, 1958, to June 18, 1960, brought business and rodeo production experience. Inman, born in Canyon, Texas, in 1929, moved to Lamar in 1949 to work on his parents' ranch until he established his own ranch, the Flying I Ranch, and stock contracting business. In 1979 Inman sold his rodeo business and focused on Thoroughbred racing. In 1992 he was inducted into the Nebraska Racing Hall of Fame. A horse-drawn hearse carried him in 1993 to his final resting place in the Lamar Pioneers Cemetery next to his Flying I Ranch. His success in several careers reflected his adept management and business skills that helped him successfully negotiate a reconciliation with the student leaders when the NIRA had erupted, resulting in two college rodeo organizations.[15]

The RCA had always supported the NIRA, but in 1950, they had a problem. The RCA protested the NIRA's moving their finals to San Antonio. NIRA secretary-manager Charlie Rankin and president Harley May negotiated with the San Antonio Junior Chamber of Commerce to add the five-day college finals rodeo to the Fiesta San Jacinto, April 18 to 22, 1950.[16] The RCA protested it because of its rodeo only two months before that date. Rankin said, "Earl Lindsey, RCA manager, is reported to have threatened the San Antonio Livestock Show and Rodeo Board of Directors, if they allowed the NIRA finals in the coliseum, the RCA would not approve the regular stock-show rodeo held in February. The NIRA had to release the San Antonio Chamber of Commerce from the agreement."[17]

Refusal to allow RCA contract acts to be used at NIRA rodeos caused another disagreement. University of Idaho's Howard Harris protested this in a letter to the RCA newspaper, *The Buckboard:* "Too many people have the idea that rodeo is an exhibition or a pseudo-vaudeville performance of the cowboy. We believe that the stimulation of rodeo as a sport on a national basis through college participation would follow through with greater attendance and greater interest in all rodeo. And we can't see how that would hurt the RCA."[18] Nothing changed.

The officers stressed image by encouraging members to follow the NIRA rules or face discipline. Blacklist rules provided a method of discipline. Contestants involved in "unbecoming conduct at rodeos such that he brings discredit to his school, club, NIRA, or works a non-approved rodeo could be blacklisted for six months enrolled school time and fined $25."[19]

The officers considered international expansion of the NIRA. Former NIRA president Harley May wrote to Guy Weadick, who originated, produced, and managed The Stampede at Calgary from 1912 through 1932.[20] May asked Weadick to promote the NIRA to Canadian cowboys. On May 12, 1951, Weadick wrote, "By return mail send me what is required of member colleges to join your organization so I can write intelligently on it when I suggest Western Canadian Colleges should be represented in your set up to give it an international flavor."[21] Through the years, attempts at adding Canadian colleges to the NIRA membership have not succeeded.

Novice college rodeo advisers struggled to produce smooth-running, fast-paced college rodeos. In 1958 Mike Cervi of Colorado State University, later a major PRCA stock contractor, wrote a twenty-five-page booklet, "How to

Produce a Collegiate Rodeo," in which he thanked the Cal Poly Rodeo Club, Lex Connelly of the RCA, and Mike Swift of the Rodeo Information Commission, Inc., for supplying information. He suggested that each college should have a rodeo manager and assistant manager, who would be enrolled in school the following year and be the manager. The well-organized booklet featured checklists for each aspect of the planning and production of a rodeo, including the entry blanks, publicity, and record of the rodeo results.[22]

To improve college rodeos, the NIRA rules required a unified appearance for team members and contracts with reputable stock contractors. Uniforms, which could be any type of clothing in school colors, had to be approved by the president. Most of the teams obtained shirts, hats, neckerchiefs, and warm-up jackets for their uniform. The NIRA also warned the clubs to contract reliable stock producers. "Some contractors in the past have failed to fulfill their promises and have broken contracts because they were producing college rodeos."[23]

The NIRA lacked regional and national publicity, so it remained unknown to the general public. The publicity director position disappeared from the NIRA board instead of becoming a full-time position as suggested by the first directors. The first publicity director, Evelyn Bruce Kingsbery, said, "James Cathey, a writer and photographer for western and rodeo publications, attended the convention at Denver in January 1950 and offered to take the job for a fee or salary. I voted to employ him, as I thought the job was too demanding for a college student. Since a majority voted to continue to have an NIRA member handle the job, I felt a sense of defeat at this time. On reflection, I decided that I must have done a satisfactory job or the NIRA would have made a change."[24] Attempts at generating constant publicity faltered through the years. Various types of NIRA publications for the membership perished quickly.

Without a publicity director, publication of NIRA news moved from place to place through the years. In May 1950 the *Bi-Weekly Rodeo News,* which published NIRA news, combined with the new publication, *Quarter Horse News,* which was scheduled to be published twenty-six times annually. Former University of Wyoming rodeo contestant Hyde Merritt became the managing editor.[25] Once again, the NIRA had an advocate in the media world.

The second year, the NIRA attempted to publish a magazine. President Harley May edited and published a quarterly magazine, *The Rigging,* with the help of Jack Ruttle, who drew the cartoons. They published only four issues of the magazine. The membership welcomed the new magazine, but Mary Ann Reed, treasurer of the University of Wyoming Rodeo Association, said, "I have been wondering if you could use some help with the magazine in the nature of a column or so an issue about the northern half of the NIRA organization. There are a good many times when we up here feel left out of things about the northern schools."[26] Regional news was scarce because of students' lack of time and journalistic training.

Seven years passed before another short-lived attempt was made to publish an NIRA newspaper. In 1957 NIRA executive secretary Alvin G. Davis and his wife Barbara, working as editor and publisher, started a semi-annual newspaper that sold for $1.50 each. The *Rodeo Roundup* covered news of the NIRA, the American Junior Rodeo Association, and the National High School Rodeo Association. Davis wrote, "There is an apparent need for a publication that is able to carry most of the junior, high school, and college rodeo news."[27] However, this publication soon went out of print.

The NIRA found its way into the national news and caught the attention of an international audience mesmerized by the cowboy. In 1951 *Saturday Evening Post* writer Jean Muir said, "Sports writers prophesy that western colleges may someday offer the same inducements to likely cowpokes as to promising football material. It delights leathery souls to see rodeo horning its way into the colleges." Muir charted some support found on college campuses. "Hardin-Simmons and Texas A&I have built handsome new arenas." Attendance at Sul Ross State's rodeo "was three times the size of the football crowd." University of New Mexico president Tom L. Popejoy "gives letters and provides a coach." "When a rancher gave $500 to the rodeo team at Oklahoma A&M, President Henry G. Bennett matched the sum out of his own pocket. The rodeo club has grown from 16 to 200 members."[28] The article caught the eye of official Washington. Jean Muir wrote NIRA president Harley May that she "heard from the State Department the other day. They asked permission to translate and distribute the college rodeo article to magazines all over continental Europe, Latin America, and Africa."[29]

Even with the recognition and growing membership of the NIRA, the college athletic conferences were not interested in adding rodeo to their sports lists. Jean Muir's article in the *Saturday Evening Post* noted the resistance: "Last spring a move got under way in the Skyline Conference to authorize letter awards for rodeo teams. The strongest talking point is the sportsmanship of the cowboys. The boys haze for each other, lend saddles and horses, and exchange tips on the tricks of the calves and steers." However, "the Border Conference in May flatly turned down a motion to make rodeo a standard college sport."[30]

In 1951 the NIRA changed the point year. The 1949–50 president, Harry Hopson, and 1950–51 president, Don Driggers of the New Mexico A&M Rodeo Club, submitted a proposal at the January, 1951, convention in Albuquerque to shift the point year from the spring and fall semesters to the fall and spring semesters with the finals following the spring semester. The system based on January through December caused first year students and graduating seniors to be ineligible for half a year. Initially, eligibility after one semester was designed to discourage professional cowboys from college competition. Dr. R. A. Nichols, New Mexico A&M adviser, proposed that the point year coincide with the school year "to put collegiate rodeos on the same basis as other collegiate sports and thus chances of recognition. Rodeo trips at some colleges are considered cuts. The Veterans Administration has been jumping on various colleges for this. If rodeos were recognized as collegiate sports, this would not happen."[31] At the 1952 finals the points for three semesters were combined, the spring and fall semesters of 1951 and spring semester of 1952, to determine the champions. Beginning with the fall of 1952, all points were accrued in the fall and spring semesters of each school year with the finals following the spring semester.

The change in the point year corrected the problem of accruing points in two separate school years; however, as the change faded into history, confusion with understanding the awarding of championships prior to 1953 created inaccuracies in the records. The 1949 national champions earned their titles with the points won at the invitational Cow Palace rodeo. All the points won during the 1949 spring and fall semesters and at the finals held in the spring of 1950 went into the NIRA records as the 1950 champions; however, during that time, the contestants considered themselves the 1949 champions. The pattern continued in 1950 with the 1951 champions earning their points in 1950. Actually, there were no champions based on the 1951 point year as those points were combined with the spring 1952 points.

Qualifying teams, individuals, and women for competition at the national finals rodeo was a factor that had to be determined. In 1951, the top ten teams were invited. "If a man is sitting in the top five in any particular event, and his team is not one of the top ten, he will also receive five cents per mile, providing the high point individuals from the same section of the country make the trip together (four or five in the same car)." Lodging was to be furnished for all the contestants. Each of the ten schools could choose "a girl to represent them in the girls' events. Her expenses will be paid the same as the boys, provided the girl brings her own horse." Each school that belonged to the NIRA could "send one girl to represent their school, providing her expenses are defrayed by her respective school or individually."[32]

The differences among the northern, eastern, and southern states in climate, population, and the number of schools with rodeo programs caused insurmountable problems for the NIRA. The board struggled with equalizing regions, points, and distances to rodeos. Bill Brock, Pacific Region director from Washington State College, proposed cosponsoring a rodeo with the University of Idaho after the spring thaw and before the end of the semester and issue double points. Brock said that with two schools close together, it is difficult to get prizes for one rodeo and almost impossible for two. With two schools, they could move the rodeo to Lewiston, Idaho, thirty-five miles south, 1,400 feet lower in elevation. Other schools had reserved all of the weekends in May, but teams might travel farther for double points. The schools nearest to WSC were Montana State College, 350 miles, and Oregon State, five hundred miles with others being over one thousand miles.[33]

Fairness and equality of rodeo competition while earning an education proved to be a complex problem for the NIRA. Limiting rodeo competition to regions seemed to be a solution. Students who saw the gleam of gold buckles crisscrossed the western states trying to add points. Delegates at the 1955 convention in Denver, Colorado, voted for contestants to compete in regions. They also tried to relieve the workload of the president by assigning jobs to regional officers for a small salary. The four regional vice presidents would figure the regional points and provide regional publicity. They would be compensated for actual expenses and $20 a month. The national president would correlate the publicity for the four regions and receive $30 a month and actual expenses.[34]

In 1955, for the first time, students were required to enter college rodeos in their home regions only. The West Coast Region consisted of California, Oregon, Washington, Arizona, Nevada, and Idaho. The Rocky Mountain Region included North Dakota, South Dakota, Montana, Utah, Wyoming, Iowa, Colorado, Nebraska, and Kansas. The Southwest Region encompassed New Mexico and West Texas, all the clubs west of Brownsville, Austin, Waco, Fort Worth, and Denton. The Southern Region consisted of Oklahoma, East Texas, and Louisiana. To increase the number of contestants at a rodeo, the West Coast Region was combined with the Rocky Mountain Region into one region for rodeo competition and known as the Northwest Region, but the vice presidents took care of their regions as if not combined.

With the new eligibility rule, NIRA competition spanning a decade became a thing of the past. For example, in 1940 calf roping champion F. C. Stover competed for New Mexico A&M. World War II interrupted his college years. After the war, he competed in eighteen matched ropings in 1946 and 1947. Stover roped his way north in 1947. "I won the calf roping, cow milking and hazed for every position in steer undecorating at the Calgary Stampede in 1948." In 1950 Stover enrolled at New Mexico A&M again and competed at the 1950 Cow Palace finals. Stover won the 1951 and 1952 NIRA calf roping championships while winning the 1950 and 1951 Calgary Stampede calf roping championships.[35]

By the mid-1950s, the NIRA board revised eligibility and competition rules. In 1955 the board set a 5-and-a-half-year eligibility limit after high school graduation. Points for contestants or teams were limited to their top five rodeos. The three high-point individuals in each event in each region qualified for the finals and the two high-point teams. The national finals rodeo had three go-rounds. Finals entry fees for each event were set at $30. Judges would draw timed-event stock thirty minutes prior to the rodeo. They would draw one complete go-round for the riding events and post the draw time. Each three hundred–point event required five contestants before points were given. For men, the events were bareback riding, saddle bronc riding, bull riding, calf roping, steer wrestling (or steer decorating), and team roping with four variations: wild cow milking, ribbon roping, team tying, and dally team roping.[36] In 1957 wild cow milking and team tying were eliminated.

College rodeo grew on many campuses in spite of occasional setbacks. The Texas A&I East Campus rodeo arena at Kingsville was torn down because the Navy reclaimed the auxiliary airfield. Rodeo club members led by Kemp Janecek, club president and bareback rider, used the material to build another one. Another setback occurred when Jim Deutsch was leading the 1953 bull riding standings. Late entry fees disqualified the team for the West Texas State College rodeo, forcing Deutsch to cancel his plans to compete at Oklahoma A&M and ruining his chance to win the championship.[37]

On the west coast, college rodeo grew, especially at California State Polytechnic College at San Luis Obispo. Cal Poly held its first NIRA rodeo, a two-day rodeo, on May 18 and 19, 1951. Cotton Rosser set the pace for Cal Poly's record forty-one national championships won by the turn of the century. Rosser, who later added flare and professionalism to rodeos with his Flying U Rodeo Company, won the all-around title at the first Cal Poly rodeo. Teammate Dan Rogers won the "bareback riding with a thrilling ride that had the crowd of 4,000 on its feet." Other team members adding team points were Manfred Sander, Bill Stroud, Don Koester, and Wade Orchard. Andy Juaregui's stock challenged the cowboys from four colleges and Camp Roberts. The soldier-cowboys could not compete for college awards. The famous rodeo clowns Bob and Gene Clark entertained while judges Gene Rambo and Andy Juaregui, along with producer Gordon Davis, added professionalism to the college rodeo.[38]

Cowgirls sought more contestants and more events. At the April, 1950, Hardin-Simmons University rodeo, Jo Gregory Knox of Sul Ross State College chaired a meeting to discuss recruiting cowgirl contestants and which events they preferred. The 1951 rule book used GRA rules and set options for two events required at each rodeo: goat tying, cow milking, flag race, cloverleaf barrel race, straight figure-eight barrel race, calf roping, or cutting-horse contest. The all-around, the only championship for women, averaged the first go-round points for the two events and repeated for the second go-round. The entry fee was $10 for each event. The ladies qualified for the 1951 finals with points from their best five rodeos in the spring and fall of 1950.

Cowgirls challenged the lack of cowgirl events at the finals rodeo. They tried to persuade the men to include them in the finals. In 1951 Garnet Rose Kotkin, the NIRA publicity director, wrote Harley May, past NIRA president and current editor of *The Rigging*, to remind him that at the convention it had been mentioned that "they should try to have one or two girls' events at the Cow Palace show. I wonder if you and Bill Guest happened to remember that when talking with Mr. Garrison." Kotkin closed with the following statement: "Like most women, I talk too much, just hope you can understand what I am trying to put across."[39] Kotkin, in another letter to May, said, "Do you think the girls' event at the championship show could be an action event? And I don't mean barrel racing. That is all right for a gymkhana, but not for a rodeo. I will try to find out as many girl ropers as they have in the schools."[40]

In the 1950s the cowgirls started with one championship and eventually had three. The winners were not included in the NIRA records until 1956. In 1951 and 1953, the two events were averaged for the all-around championship. No record for 1952 all-around champion exists. In 1954 the optional racing championship for goat tying, flag race, or cow milking was added. In 1955 barrel racing gained a separate championship award. The 1955 rule book stated: "Points from each NIRA rodeo within the region must be sent to the regional office along with the boys' points and a complete record of all girls' points will be maintained in that office for determining girls' regional champions." A regional vice president, elected by the girls at the first rodeo, was responsible for the girls' event points at each rodeo. The girls' prizes had to be comparable to the ones given for the boys' events.

The first women's championship coincided with the finals move to Texas in 1951. At the Third National Intercollegiate Championship Rodeo in Fort Worth, seven women from six colleges competed in two events: the barrel racing and flag racing. Sul Ross State College's Jo Gregory Knox won the national all-around championship. Gregory Knox, who won the flag race and placed third in the barrel race, started goat tying and flag racing at Sul Ross in February, 1949. Born in Colorado City, Texas, where her dad brought security to the town for sixteen years as sheriff, Gregory Knox said, "My early years I grew up in town, but I always had a pony to ride. I went as a Sponsor Girl to different rodeos where we were judged, not timed." She married New Mexico A&M cowboy Tee Knox, who had helped organize the NIRA. They ranched at Tarzan, Texas, near Midland until her death in 1993.[41]

At the 1951 finals, Texas Western College cowgirl Beverly Thorn Weyerts, known as Beverly Bonnet for her pioneer bonnets preference rather than hats, settled for second in the all-around. Mary Lee Bridges of Texas Christian University, riding her palomino champion stallion, Booger Bear, finished third. Other cowgirl contestants were Mary Lou Echols of Hardin-Simmons University, who won the barrel race, Sally DeGroot of the University of New Mexico, June Pritchard of TCU, and Berva Dawn Sorenson Taylor of John Tarleton Agricultural College.[42]

At the 1953 finals, a couple won two championships, and one cowgirl came in leading the all-around standings while another one left with the title. The first championships to a couple went to Sul Ross State's Charlotte Martin, the first goat tying champion, and Tex Martin, the 1953 all-around and 1954 bull

The first NIRA all-around cowgirl Jo Gregory Knox accepts her trophy saddle at the finals rodeo held in Fort Worth in 1951. Photo courtesy of Jo Gregory Knox, Tarzan, Texas, and NIRA Alumni archives.

riding champion.[43] For the second year, Texas Western cowgirl Beverly Thorn Weyerts finished second, and a Sul Ross cowgirl wore the buckle. The all-around cowgirl Elisabeth Prude Longbotham grew up on the Prude Ranch, near Fort Davis, Texas, and married Jack Longbotham, an NIRA officer who earned a Ph.D. at Texas A&M and was a professor of education at Hardin-Simmons

University for twenty-five years. Elisabeth, with a master's degree in reading from Texas A&M, taught in the public schools and at McMurray University in Abilene, Texas. The couple wrote a series of books, which included children's stories about buffalo, such as *The Adventures of Buffalo Bill and Cody*. On their ranch near Abilene along with cattle and Quarter Horses, they raised buffalo to show at elementary schools to educate children about the Old West.[44]

One cowgirl starting in 1955 often won two of the three events. The 1954 all-around champion from Hardin-Simmons University, Becky Jo Smith Doom, won the 1955 all-around and the goat tying titles. In 1955 Kathlyn "Chickie" Younger Knox of McNeese State University won the first barrel racing championship. After transferring to Colorado A&M, she won the 1956 all-around and the barrel racing titles, the first recorded in the NIRA records. At Penrose Stadium in Colorado Springs, Colorado, Betty Sims Solt, on a stud called Sonny and a mare named Dusty, won the 1957 all-around and the barrel racing titles and the 1958 barrels again.

Sims Solt, a 1990 National Cowgirl Hall of Fame honoree, grew up with five brothers on a New Mexico ranch near Santa Rosa. Her paternal grandparents arrived by railroad immigrant car to homestead at Vaughn. In 1923 her dad George Sims won the bronc riding at the Teddy Roosevelt Rough Riders Reunion at Las Vegas, New Mexico, and her mother Wahlecia Sims occasionally entered the wild cow milking. Later, Sims Solt immortalized her mother in a poem often requested at Cowboy Poetry gatherings. In 1992 Sims Solt and Sylvia Mahoney of Vernon, Texas, paired up to organize the NIRA Alumni (NIRAA) association. After retiring from teaching, Sims Solt bought and operated a New Mexico ranch.[45]

By the end of the 1950s, one cowgirl won a record four championships and another won a record three consecutive titles. New Mexico State University's Pat Dunigan Marr, a city girl turned cowgirl, won the 1956 goat tying, the 1958 and 1959 all-around, and 1959 calf tying. The calf tying title has only been awarded twice. Dunigan Marr said, "We had tied goats all year, but when we arrived in Klamath, they had 250-pound calves to tie. I used a piggin' string and legged my calves."[46] Dunigan Marr, whose father was an El Paso attorney, was not the typical ranch-raised cowgirl. She had entered her first college rodeo in 1956 without knowing what horse she might ride. Going to a San Angelo rodeo, Betty Sims Solt, her father, and Dunigan Marr stopped to eat where a man asked Mr. Sims if he knew someone who could use a good barrel horse because his daughter had eloped. Dunigan Marr and the horse Toni began winning barrel races. She, later, qualified for the Women's Professional Rodeo Association barrel racing national finals several times and was the 1966 WPRA reserve champion. In 1959 West Texas State's Mike Reid Settle started a winning streak in barrel racing that finished with a record three consecutive wins.

Crowning a rodeo queen started in the 1920s, but the first Miss College Rodeo wore the crown in 1956–57. NIRA secretary-manager Alvin G. Davis sent a flyer to winners of NIRA-approved rodeo queen contests seeking national entries. The Colorado Springs Chamber of Commerce agreed to name the winner at the finals. Judged 75 percent on beauty, 15 percent scholarship, and 10 percent horsemanship, the trophy winner received an all-expense eight-day stay in Colorado Springs as a guest of the Broadmoor Hotel. The finals grand entry each night and appearances at service clubs and on television helped the winner advertise the rodeo. One of sixteen contestants, 1957 Queen Karna Jean Thorson of Cal Poly and Weiser, Idaho, won the 1957 Cal Poly contest, the 1956 Miss Rodeo Idaho, and the 1956 Miss Rodeo America third runner-up. Her brother Freeland Thorson, the 1957 West Coast Region director, supported her.[47]

Many NIRA queen contestants competed in college rodeo and belonged to sororities. One of twelve entries, 1958 Queen Patricia Louise McDaniel from Texas Christian University belonged to Delta Delta Delta sorority, the TCU Rodeo Club, and qualified for the 1958 finals. In 1957 she placed third in the Texas Barrel Racing Association and was Fort Worth Fat Stock Show Sweetheart.[48]

In the early 1950s, college administrators and dorm assistants often questioned cowgirls' traveling alone. Hardin-Simmons' Becky Jo Smith Doom had to leave the dorm by the back door when she had her jeans on.[49] However, the independent cowgirls placated administrators and handled road problems including wrecks. In April, 1951, traveling to Abilene, Texas, to the Hardin-Simmons rodeo, Sul Ross cowgirls Audrea Cox and Mary Green on the five-hour trip rolled their pickup and trailer loaded with two horses. Although their pickup was almost a total loss, they hitched a ride for themselves and their horses and made it in time to compete, with Green winning third in the women's events and first in the goat tying average.[50]

Although the finals roamed, the champions continued to set records. In the 1950s, the finals traveled to five states and were held in major metropolitan areas, in coliseums initially, but later moved outside. Some of the 1950s records included the first NIRA champion to win a world championship, the first champion to have a son and a daughter win championships followed by world titles, the first champion to be blacklisted, the first individuals other than team members to earn a berth at the finals, the champion to win the most consecutive championships, and a record eight event championships.

The second finals returned to a major metropolitan area with a record number of fans cheering the teams on and a first, individuals who qualified. The promoters at the coliseum offered incentives of mileage and rooms for the teams and a premier rodeo with a top PRCA rodeo producer and personnel. The board gave the Cow Palace in San Francisco the nod for a return engagement in April, 1950. With Harry Rowell producing the rodeo, Cecil Jones keeping the books, Buster Ivory and Sonny Tureman marking the rides, the top seven teams competed under the eyes of professionals. For the first time, three high-point individuals, Earl Reynolds of West Texas State College and James Mickler and Bill Guest of Hardin-Simmons University, qualified to compete along with teams from Sul Ross State College, the University of New Mexico, University of Wyoming, and A&M schools from Colorado, Texas, New Mexico, and Oklahoma.[51]

In 1950 the champions won using combined annual and finals points giving some the first consecutive championships. Sul Ross State College had consecutive team, bull riding, and all-around championships. Members of the Sul Ross team, Bob Burkholder, Clay Cade, Buster Lindley, Harley May, Ross May, and Gene Newman, carried the three-foot sterling silver trophy donated by Levi Strauss & Co. back to Texas. Harley May claimed his second all-around and bull riding championships along with the saddle bronc riding title, winning a record eight titles by 1951. University of New Mexico's Tuffy Cooper, the 1950 calf roping champ, saw his daughter Betty Gayle Cooper Ratliff win the 1972 breakaway roping championship, a first. Twenty-five years later his son Roy Cooper won the calf roping title, a first.[52]

The first champion to be blacklisted happened in 1950. After returning home, the University of Wyoming faculty adviser E. K. Faulkner learned that Les Gore, a UW team member, was ineligible. Gore had won the bareback riding and placed in saddle bronc and bull riding giving him the all-around title.[53] Faulkner reported it to the NIRA, which "established the Wyoming teams and club's good faith."[54] The NIRA recalculated the results. The NIRA placed Gore on the non-contesting blacklist for six months enrolled school time.[55]

Sul Ross State College men's team added their second championship in 1950 at the return engagement at the Cow Palace in San Francisco. (Left to right) Cow Palace manager Carl Garrison; announcer Cy Taillon; (front) Levi Strauss manager A. J. Cronin; (team, left to right) Clay Cade, Ross May, Harley May, Gene Newman, Buster Lindley, Bob Burkholder. Photo courtesy of Harley May, Alpine, Texas, and NIRA Alumni archives.

Controversy caused the finals to move to Texas the third year. Conflicting dates eliminated the Cow Palace, so the finals accepted Fort Worth's offer. However, Carl L. Garrison invited seven teams to an invitational Cow Palace rodeo with six making it. With Cy Taillon at the mike, Slim Pickens clowning, Cecil Jones keeping books, and Bob Barmby producing the rodeo, Garrison used top professionals in spite of losing the finals contract. The Cal Poly cowboys flew with pilot/cowboy Cotton Rosser to the rodeo,[56] where Rosser took the all-around title with team members Manfred Sander, second, and Curtis Beach, third. Dan Rogers, Bill Stroud, and Lem Boughner added enough points to earn the two-foot silver team trophy.[57]

The finals at historic Fort Worth with its flamboyant production of the college competition garnered national publicity. "Thousands of Fort Worth rodeo fans had come to watch the educated cowboys. Before the competition began, the Hardin-Simmons College Cowboy Band came whooping into the coliseum, and a 34-girl marching and dancing group [Rangerettes] from Kilgore Junior College, dressed in abbreviated white satin outfits and Indian headdresses started the five-day competition, which had seventy-three contestants,"

The 1950 NIRA calf roping champion Tuffy Cooper of the University of New Mexico shows his roping style at a college rodeo in 1951. He later trained his daughter Betty Gayle Cooper Ratliff and son Roy Cooper, who became NIRA and world champions.
Photo by James Cathey, Fort Worth, Texas, and courtesy of NIRA Alumni archives.

competing on the stock of Earl Sellers of Del Rio, Texas.[58] Over 3,763 fans attended seven performances. Doak Walker and DeWitt Coulter, former all-American football players, presented the trophies.[59]

The first cowgirl champion and the cowboy with eight championships took the 1951 Fort Worth awards along with some firsts for other champions. Sul Ross cowgirl Jo Gregory Knox won the first all-around championship, renewing cowgirls' interest. Sul Ross State College began a rodeo dynasty with its third national team championship, permanently possessing the Levi Strauss traveling trophy won by team members Harley May, Jimmy Dyer, Clay Cade, Gene Newman, Johnny Ackel, and Ross May. Adviser E. E. Turner watched May add his third all-around and second saddle bronc titles, totaling eight overall. May added the 1952 professional steer wrestling championship, the first for an NIRA champion. Clowns Gene Newman of Sul Ross and Bo Damuth of Texas A&M deflected the bulls while Texas A&M's Maxie Overstreet, the only bull rider to cover three bulls, stopped May from making it three bull riding titles.[60] Roy Reynolds of West Texas State collected the first ribbon roping championship. Thirty-year-old calf roping champion F. C. Stover of New Mexico A&M and thirty-three-year-old steer wrestling champion Bill Guest of Hardin-Simmons established a record for age. HSU bareback rider James Mickler added his second consecutive title, the first of four cowboys to achieve two consecutive bareback riding championships.

The fourth finals used points from three semesters, a first and only, along with being at an outdoor arena in a metropolitan area. The 1952 finals, held during the Festival of Roses, went to Multnomah Stadium in Portland, Oregon. With a crowd of 11,868 fans and in spite of the rain-soaked turf, the fourth team championship and a bull riding title went to Sul Ross State team members James Ward, Jimmy Calvert, Tex Martin, Ross May, Clyde May (brothers of Harley May), and Johnny Ackel, the bull riding champ. Harley Tucker's stock tested the sixty-three contestants while University of Idaho cowboy Howard Harris ran clowning interference. Seven schools sent six-man teams, and five others had four or fewer.[61] Six schools had one or two women entered. Texas entries were Mary Lee Bridges from Texas Christian University and Sul Ross's Mary Green and Charlotte Cox along with University of Idaho's Virginia Fox, Colorado A&M's Joyce Zeeck and Virginia Painter, Washington State's Lorraine Rich, and Montana State's Kay Nash and Carol Mosher, who won the all-around and the barrel race at the rodeo.[62] No records for women's national all-around could be found.

Rain soaked the fifth finals, the first held on a college campus. Students competed in a "sea of mud" during the five-day performance at the Carl Myers Memorial Arena at Hardin-Simmons University in Abilene, Texas. Austin, Texas, stock contractor Tommy Steiner provided the stock with Nat Fleming of Wichita Falls, Texas, announcing and Billy LeBlanc of New Mexico A&M clowning.[63] Sul Ross's Tex Martin and Elisabeth Prude Longbotham won the all-around titles, but the team champion was HSU along with two event championships. Lee Cockrell, Gip Lovejoy, Bill Teague, Gene Frazier, James Mickler, Joe Chase, saddle bronc champ, and Dick Barrett, bareback champ, stopped Sul Ross's domination of the team title; HSU had 2,879.5 to Sul Ross's 2,692. Sam Houston State roper Sonny Sikes won two roping events while Sul Ross bull rider Ira Akers won his first of eight titles and had the winning ticket for a horse trailer.[64]

Two cowboys met head on at the 1954 finals. University of Idaho cowboy

The 1953 NIRA champions are (left to right) *Tex Martin, all-around; Dick Barrett, bareback; Ira Akers, bull riding; Sonny Sikes, calf roping and ribbon roping; Don Fedderson, steer wrestling; Joe Chase, saddle bronc; and Elisabeth Prude Longbotham, all-around. Photo courtesy of Sonny Sikes, Huntsville, Texas, and NIRA Alumni archives.*

Howard Harris placed in six events to beat Colorado A&M's Bob Schild for the all-around by eleven and a half points at Lake Charles, Louisiana. Schild, twice reserve all-around, won the bareback and saddle bronc riding. He helped Colorado A&M's team of Marion Stanley, Ted Thomas, Don Yates, and John Gee, the steer wrestling champ, win A&M's first team championship. After earning a bachelor of science degree, Schild rode saddle broncs, barebacks, and bulls from San Francisco to Madison Square Garden in New York for eighteen years, going full-time for eight of those years. As a cowboy poet, Schild said, "Cinch your riggin's boys, the money's in their manes," and it was for Schild. Later, Schild spent thirty-three years running his saddle shop in Blackfoot, Idaho, where he captured rodeo memories in *Spur Tracks and Buffalo Chips,* followed by *Pure Bull—Well Organized.* He presented his poem, "College Cowboy," a first, to an NIRA alumni reunion.[65]

A six-event cowboy was unusual, and one from the east coast was rare in any era. Howard Harris, the 1954 all-around champion, came from New Jersey, but the Harris family had owned cattle there for twelve generations. When the Miller 101 Ranch Wild West Show disbanded, Harris's father and grandfather bought them out. At age four, Harris and his little black pony with the white tail performed from New England to Ohio. The Harris family bought a ranch in Wyoming and started shipping cattle out of Idaho. In 1950 Floyd Skelton, an Idaho cattleman, enrolled Harris at the University of Idaho. Stock contractor Harley Tucker greatly influenced Harris with his knowledge of stock and his management style. Harris said, "Stockman Harley Tucker became my

Hardin-Simmons cowboy Joe Chase won the 1952 and 1953 NIRA saddle bronc riding championships. Photo courtesy of Betty Sims Solt, Roswell, New Mexico, and NIRA Alumni archives.

hero and still is today. Harley told me to get in the bronc riding. That became one of my best events." In 1958 Harris took over the Cowtown Rodeo in New Jersey, which his father had started in 1954. Harris, now living in Claremore, Oklahoma, has produced rodeos in twenty states, had stock in thirty states, four provinces in Canada, Italy, Switzerland, and Argentina. Harris became a stockman who knew the family trees for many generations of the bucking stock that he raised as well as where they went and how they bucked.[66]

Occasionally, a combination of winners occurs that can never be equaled. At the 1955 finals at Lake Charles, Louisiana, two Sam Houston State cowboys won the men's all-around championship and five of the six men's event titles with four to one cowboy. Hardin-Simmons's Gene Frazier won the steer wrestling championship. Ira Akers, who had transferred to Sam Houston State University, won all three bucking events: bareback riding, saddle bronc riding,

Former NIRA champion Harley May (standing, left to right) presents awards to the 1954 NIRA champions: goat tying, Charlotte Martin, Sul Ross; calf roping, Lee Cockrell, Hardin-Simmons; bull riding, Tex Martin, Sul Ross; team roping, Bill Teague, Hardin-Simmons; all-around, Becky Jo Smith Doom, Hardin-Simmons; University of Idaho Howard Harris's father accepting all-around. (Front, left to right) unidentified; bareback and saddle bronc riding, Bob Schild, Colorado A&M; steer wrestling, John Gee, Colorado A&M. Photo courtesy of Bob Schild, Blackfoot, Idaho, and NIRA Alumni archives.

and bull riding, cinching the all-around championship. With his 1953 bull riding championship, Akers had five buckles. Sam Houston State cowboy Sonny Sikes roped two more: team roping and calf roping. Sikes, a four-time champion, later became the NIRA secretary-manager for many years. Ironically, Sikes, not designated as a team member, could not count his points as team points. Texas Tech University won with team members who became well known in the professional ranks: Dave Hopper, Johnny Leonard, Neal Love, B. F. Yeates, Lee Cockrell, and Gene Graham.

Sam Houston State's phenomenal victory in 1955 set a course that placed it in the winner's circle thirty-eight times, second only to one other school. At the 1956 finals at Spencer Penrose Stadium in Colorado Springs, Colorado, Sam Houston State won its first of three men's team championships with team members Ira Akers, Sonny Sikes, Bill Latham, Jim Greene, E. M Holt Jr., and Melbourn Shillings. Akers won all-around, saddle bronc riding, and bull riding, making a total of eight, tying the record of Sul Ross's Harley May. Akers's and May's record eight still stands.

International fame came to a 1956 champion for his book on horse training skills. The 1956 team roping and 1957 steer wrestling champ Monty Roberts captured his life in his book *The Man Who Listens to Horses,* published in England in 1996, and it became a best-seller in the United States. He even demonstrated his horse training skills for Her Majesty Queen Elizabeth II of England. Monty and his wife Pat, a noted sculptor, raised some world champions on their Flag is Up Farms at Salinas, California. One horse, Jonny Tivio, won four world titles in the Western division. Monty and Pat also appeared in the film *East of Eden* with James Dean.[67]

Cowboys set new records at the 1957 finals. McNeese State University at Lake Charles, Louisiana, with seventy-five NIRA men and sixteen women had a record number of students competing during the years for them. With this pool of contestants, McNeese won its first team and event championships at Colorado Springs, Colorado, with team members: Jim Miller, Warren Frey, Rudy Trahan, Cotton Kinney, Carl Martin, and Clyde May under the leadership of Coach Ken Sweeny. Clyde May's all-around championship, the first event championship for McNeese, made him and Harley May the first brother combo to win all-around titles. The saddle bronc champ Bill Duffy, a Klamath tribal member and Modoc Indian who attended Oregon Technical Institute, had his lost buckle returned to him forty years later when a person heard about

Eight-time NIRA champion Ira Akers, who attended Sul Ross State and Sam Houston State, started his winning streak in 1953 as the bull riding champion and finished in 1956 with eight championships. His four event titles in 1955 set a prevailing record. Photo courtesy of Mrs. Ira Akers, Clyde, Texas, and NIRA Alumni archives.

The 1955 NIRA champions are (left to right) *calf roping and team roping, Sonny Sikes,
Sam Houston State; barrel racing, Kathlyn "Chickie" Younger Knox, McNeese State;
all-around and goat tying, Becky Jo Smith Doom, Hardin-Simmons; steer wrestling,
Gene Frazier, Hardin-Simmons; Sam Houston State Ira Akers with his four saddles for
all-around, bareback, saddle bronc, and bull riding by Lake Charles sponsor
Kenneth Swinney. Photo courtesy of NIRA Alumni archives.*

the NIRA Alumni association and called the first chairperson. The bull riding
champ, Arizona State University's Kenneth Adams, the second NIRA Alumni
chairman, diversified but stayed close to the sport of rodeo by operating a vet
supply business in the Phoenix area while writing about his riding experiences in the book *Rodeos, Pig Races & Other Cowboy Stories.*

One cowboy set a record in the final years of the 1950s that still stands, four
consecutive calf roping championships. Overall, Texas A&I cowboy Jack
Burkholder won six titles. In 1957 Burkholder and Grady Allen won the first
NIRA championships for Texas A&I, now Texas A&M at Kingsville. Allen beat
Burkholder for the team roping title by seventeen points; however, Burkholder's
calf roping championship started a record four-year winning streak for him.
Burkholder, raised on a dairy near San Antonio, won his first saddle at age
eleven. Burkholder, the 1953 president of the National High School Rodeo

The 1957 NIRA champions are (left to right): *calf roping, Jack Burkholder; bull riding, Ken Adams; saddle bronc riding, Bill Duffy; team roping, Grady Allen; all-around Clyde May; bareback riding, Dave Hopper; steer wrestling, Monty Roberts; all-around and barrel racing, Betty Sims Solt; and goat tying, Teresa Sully. Photo courtesy of Betty Sims Solt, Roswell, New Mexico, and NIRA Alumni archives.*

Association, won the 1954 high school all-around and steer wrestling championships. Burkholder roped professionally while teaching typing at South San Antonio High School. He won many professional rodeos including the 1965 Cheyenne Frontier Days Rodeo co-championship in calf roping.[68]

McNeese State University, with one returning team member, Jim Miller, beat the other seven teams, two from each region at the 1958 finals at Colorado Springs, Colorado. Miller won the bareback riding, helping sponsor D. D. Spivey's team win the second of three consecutive team trophies with members Tommy Flenniken, Jim Wynn, Ron McMullan, Greg Bollich, and Robert Penny.

Forty years after the 1959 bareback riding champion was named at the finals at Klamath, Oregon, on the Fourth of July, the NIRA named co-champions. Except for Texas A&I's Jack Burkholder's third national calf roping championship, all of the other event titles went to cowboys in the West Coast or Rocky Mountain Regions. Cal Poly's Jack Roddy started his legendary rodeo career by winning the NIRA all-around and steer wrestling titles on his way to being the 1966 and 1968 world steer wrestling champion and a major fund-raiser for Cal Poly's rodeo team. The bareback riding championship, pending for forty years, was resolved when Dick Henson of Idaho State University and Larry O'Neill of the University of Texas attended the NIRA Alumni 50th Anniversary celebration in 1999. In 1959 O'Neill won the championship, beating Henson by four and a half points. Then, the NIRA notified O'Neill that an error was made, and Henson beat O'Neill by four and a half points. For forty years, Henson was the champion. Neither Henson nor O'Neill knew the other would be at the 1999 NIRA Alumni reunion nor that Sonny Sikes, retired NIRA executive secretary, would bring the old record books to the reunion. Henson and O'Neill reviewed the records with some of the other 1959 cowboys, who agreed that Henson and O'Neill were co-champions. The NIRA approved this decision.[69]

Controversy grew among the regions, so the 1958 NIRA Convention held at Colorado Springs, Colorado, during the finals had a full agenda. For the first time, the NIRA had a legal adviser in attendance, attorney J. Woodson Railey, Hoss Inman's attorney. Railey's job was to help with updating the NIRA rules. The regional directors or a spokesman discussed the lack of a vote for the school advisers and sponsors with the northern state representatives insisting that they be given voting privileges. The secretary-manager and office staff salaries, funded by individuals and club membership fees, financially drained the organization. A suggestion for a percent of net receipts of college rodeos to go to the NIRA caused concern in the organization. Rumors circulated that two regions might form a new college rodeo organization. The NIRA board proposed that new NIRA sub-organizations, such as an advisers' conference and an alumni association, be created. NIRA president Mickey McCarty said that this would give advisers input and encourage graduates to continue to help. Another problem was the lack of regional information being sent to the national headquarters. Yet another unresolved issue was the right of individual members from nonmember schools to vote on issues. Only member schools had the privilege of sending two voting delegates to the convention. The board voted to enforce the use of schools' emblems and colors at all NIRA rodeos.

In the spring of 1959 the controversy escalated to the point of causing a split in the NIRA. Students and advisers in the Rocky Mountain Region searched for solutions to the unequal number of rodeos in a region and the vast distances between rodeos. In June, 1959, University of Wyoming adviser C. O. Schoonover voiced his opinion in a letter to Montana State College adviser

Charles Bowman after Schoonover and Red Heath, Lamar College adviser, had met at the Rocky Mountain Regional Finals rodeo at Lamar College, Colorado. Schoonover said, "The one thing that seems to be quite important was the proposal that perhaps the Rocky Mountain Region would be split this year." He said that the split would minimize the number of rodeos, but it would not equalize the number of rodeos among the regions. Schoonover proposed that contestants should be restricted to entering six or seven rodeos with the five best being counted for points. He said that the trade-out rule was good, but "the interpretation of this rule seems to be the main stumbling block." He pointed out that limiting the number of rodeos for contestants would help in budget preparation each year. However, if limited, rodeos at some schools might not be as attractive as others, so the entries would suffer. Schoonover said, "I promised Hoss Inman that I would write to him giving him my recommendations on what should be done about splitting the region."[70] Schoonover sent these suggestions to Inman on June 17, 1959.

Letters fanned the flames of controversy by adding another smoldering issue. In November, 1959, Montana State adviser Charles Bowman wrote to NIRA secretary-manager Hoss Inman and Lamar College adviser James Heath reporting that at the NIRA board meeting on December 31, 1958, the advisers "agreed on a National Adviser elected by the advisers, but we allowed the Executive Committee to select Red Heath for the balance of the year. He stated he would be glad to serve for that period only and asked to be replaced at the national meeting at Klamath. This was not done and therefore is now vacant." Bowman, president of the Rocky Mountain Faculty Rodeo Conference, said, "The proposed constitution and bylaws that your office sent" have several points that school administrators will not agree to, such as no vote for administrators, a student executive committee with unlimited powers, no provision for advisers' electing the national adviser, and mandatory entry fees.[71]

The NIRA, being a student-led organization, had created problems with college and university administrators, so several cosmetic remedies had been instituted. The composition of the executive committee in the 1949 Constitution was the national officers, the three regional directors, and the faculty advisers of the three regional directors. However, the faculty advisers had no vote. The 1950 Constitution added the faculty advisers of the officers and regional directors, but they still had no vote. In a resolution at the 1950 convention, the delegates acknowledged the invaluable assistance to the NIRA given by advisers, such as Bob Denhardt, E. E. Turner, Dr. R. S. Jackson, and Hyde Merritt.[72] Even though the link to permanent status on college campuses involved college administrators, the students maintained complete control.

The expanding controversy forced the idea of a split in the NIRA. Montana State adviser Charles Bowman wrote that the Rocky Mountain and the Great Plains regions were weighing the idea of forming a separate conference if the NIRA refused to meet their requests. Bowman had made two changes to the 1955–56 NIRA Constitution and Bylaws and sent it to all clubs in the two regions, and a majority of the schools had approved it. The first was in Article III National Officers. The national board would be a 50-50 representation with the NIRA president being a faculty adviser. The second point was to leave the subject of entry fees out of the constitution.[73]

Letter writing resulted in meetings of the disgruntled members. Charles Bowman mentioned two meetings to Hoss Inman: "Recently I made a trip to Fort Collins, during which time I visited with Jim Scott of Fort Collins, [C. O.] Schoonover of Laramie, and [Dale] Stiles of Casper. There is a strong desire to hold a meeting at Casper December 18, 1959. Stiles will contact you in regards to this matter. While in Casper, Stiles received a call from you and Heath that brought up several questions I feel should be answered." Bowman said that he had asked the Montana State Club to arrange for a meeting of the clubs at Pocatello, Idaho, for organizational purposes.[74]

The NIRA attempted to meet some of the demands of the dissenters. NIRA secretary-manager Hoss Inman responded to Charles Bowman's requests in a letter on November 17, 1959, to Dale Stiles, secretary of the Rocky Mountain Faculty Rodeo Committee and Casper College adviser. Inman asked that his letter be read at the November 21 meeting at Idaho State, which Inman could not attend. Inman wrote that a majority of schools had approved the new constitution with only three schools from the Rocky Mountain Region casting dissenting votes. Inman said, "We are charged with the responsibility of directing the activities of the entire NIRA and will carry out these responsibilities to the fulfillment of the wishes of the majority and not the wishes of any two or three schools or one or two persons. We realize that there are cases where the constitution will work a hardship on some schools and clubs, and these problems will be taken up at the first directors' meeting which is planned for January in Denver." Inman suggested that all matters go through "the normal channels of progress that consists of the members conducting their business through the regional director and national office and the advisers through the national adviser."[75]

The meeting at Casper College on December 18, 1959, started as the Rocky Mountain Faculty Rodeo Conference and ended as a new organization, American Collegiate Rodeo Association (ACRA). The Rocky Mountain and Great Plains Regions sent eleven faculty representatives from ten schools: Montana State, Utah State, Western Montana College, University of Wyoming, Sheridan College, South Dakota College, Dickinson State Teachers College, Colorado State University, Chadron State Teachers College, and Casper College. Washington State, Montana State, and Northern Montana College voted by proxy using letters of authorization. The Great Plains Region director James Moore and sixteen other students attended. The schools "could not continue rodeo as a college sport under the present type of administration from the NIRA." Justification was that administrators of the American Association of Land-Grant Colleges and State Universities would not sanction college rodeo as such after their November meeting in Saint Louis, Missouri, without some type of faculty control. A letter from Dr. R. R. Renne, president of Montana State College, was read to this effect.[76]

The group developed bylaws for the ACRA. Dr. R. W. Roskelly of Utah State University made a motion that "the schools of these two regions disassociate themselves from the NIRA." Don Lee of Montana State College seconded the motion; the motion passed with no dissenting vote. The structure of the board was to be a faculty president, who would vote only in case of a tie and a faculty vice president, who would act only in the absence of the president. The executive board would have two faculty advisers and two regional student directors. The two regions would remain the same for one year. They recommended that the affairs of the secretary-manager's office be run through the business office of the school wherever the secretary is employed. They tabled this so that the executive officers could recommend ways to handle the funds.[77]

ACRA elected officers the same day they organized it. Officers were President Charles C. Bowman of Montana State College; Vice President Dr. Carroll Schoonover of University of Wyoming; and Executive Secretary-Manager Dale Stiles of Casper College with Dr. James Scott of Colorado State University as the Great Plains adviser. President Bowman was requested to call Lex Connelly of the Rodeo Cowboys Association to "inform him of our actions and our intention to cooperate fully with the RCA."[78]

Excitement and optimism started the 1950s for the new student-led college rodeo organization. Developing the organization, stabilizing the leadership and finances, publicity, and a newspaper or magazine to dispense collegiate rodeo news proved to be a continuing challenge. The membership of individuals and schools grew rapidly as the organization worked to standardize rules and establish balanced regions as well as find a location for the annual national championship finals. Cowgirls defined their events and carved a niche for themselves in the NIRA. Many initial problems had been solved; however, the NIRA faced critical times as the 1950s closed. With two regions abdicating to start a new college rodeo association, decisions by the NIRA board and the new ACRA board would either destroy or strengthen college rodeo. The nature and character of college cowboys and cowgirls would be tested by this challenge to their sport.

CHAPTER 4

1960s—NIRA Tested
and Nomadic Finals

The 1960s began with two college rodeo associations instead of one. In 1959 a group of disgruntled cowboys and faculty sponsors had split from the National Intercollegiate Rodeo Association (NIRA) and formed the American College Rodeo Association (ACRA). Compromise resolved the issues that separated the two organizations, resulting in one organization, a stronger, more stable NIRA. It also grew stronger with the hiring of a secretary-manager, who worked for a university and maintained a national office in one location. A bonus came with the new secretary-manager whose wife managed the office. But the rodeo finals continued seeking a permanent home during the 1960s. After resolving the divisive issues in the early 1960s, the NIRA grew in size, strength, and competitive quality, but it continued to have problems.

The 1960 NIRA board agenda focused on crisis resolution. The board met in Denver with two of the regional directors missing. The directors from the Rocky Mountain and the Great Plains Regions had joined ACRA, organized on December 18, 1959. National adviser Red Heath of Lamar College; Southwest Region director Ross Caton; Southern Region director Jerry Moore of Sam Houston State; Pete Lewis of Sul Ross State; Hoss Inman, secretary-manager; Sonny Sikes, Sam Houston State faculty adviser; and Dick Eddler, NIRA office secretary, attended the meeting. The board addressed the problem: "In all cases the Board tried conscientiously to act in the best interest of all of the regions.

Members of the Board expressed their regret that due to circumstances beyond their control, the rest of the Board could not attend."[1]

The grievances that had split the NIRA motivated the board to create an acceptable compromise at the January meeting. Since Colorado State and other schools in the Rocky Mountain Region had not joined ACRA, the Rocky Mountain Region had a board representative. National adviser James (Red) Heath requested that the NIRA give faculty members a vote in the organization. The board approved NIRA secretary-manager Hoss Inman's proposal to add two new people to the management structure, H. A. Pedersen of Oregon Technical Institute as the Finals Rodeo Director and J. Woodson Railey as the NIRA attorney. Inman proposed diversification of responsibilities so that the part-time secretary-manager could manage the full-time job. Through a newsletter, Inman attempted to create a better flow of information among the schools about rodeo dates and other information.[2]

The changes resulted in four amendments. The first stated that a school sponsoring a rodeo did not have to pay 5 percent of its net profit to the NIRA. The second stated that entry fees were at the discretion of the school sponsoring the rodeo. The third provided for the election of five faculty advisers in each region. The fourth change expanded the point-award events to include the girls' barrel race and the optional girls' event. A team would still consist of one to six members. A coeducational college could have two girls on the team, and an all girls' school, a full team of girls. The member-school rodeo clubs had to pass the amendments for them to become effective.[3]

ACRA continued with its plans to have a fully functioning organization as quickly as possible. Ten rodeos scheduled between April 30 and May 29, 1960, were approved. Plans were made for a regional finals to be held on June 4 and 5 at Casper College in Casper, Wyoming. Students had to have ACRA cards to enter. Dale Hewson, Dickinson State Teachers College rodeo adviser, of Dickinson, North Dakota, wrote Jim Moore, University of Wyoming regional director, requesting two changes. First-quarter freshmen should be eligible to compete, and a finals rodeo should be planned so that "the organization may have adequate time to work out the necessary details for each event."[4]

Second thoughts about joining the new organization started to surface among the schools. In a letter from ACRA executive-secretary Dale Stiles to ACRA president Charles Bowman at Montana State College, Stiles raised questions about ACRA and one school's decision to stay with the NIRA. He stressed four points. Dickinson State had mentioned holding the finals. A uniform entry blank for all ACRA schools was needed. An explanation of "the soundness of ACRA with schools who are not entirely familiar with the association" was needed and a review of the ACRA constitution and bylaws. Stiles indicated that all the schools might not join ACRA: "I talked to Dr. Schoonover yesterday, and he said that Colorado State University had definitely decided to stay with the NIRA." CSU's request to enter an ACRA-sponsored rodeo at South Dakota State College was approved, but with the understanding that it would be the only time unless CSU joined ACRA. They approved CSU's request due to the shortage of SDSC contestants caused by a conflict of dates."[5]

ACRA board members met with the RCA in Denver to formalize an agreement between the organizations. Bowman said, "I received a letter from Oral Zumwalt informing me that the RCA will allow the ACRA to use RCA producers for the production of their shows. They are also allowing the NIRA to do the same. There are indications that the RCA producers are quite aware of the problem that we are trying to correct."[6] Eventually, Lex Connelly of the RCA met with representatives of NIRA and ACRA to encourage reconciliation of the two organizations' differences.

At the last minute, several schools decided to remain with the NIRA. The April, 1960, ACRA Member Clubs newsletter stated, "Washington State College in Pullman, Washington, has indicated that they would like to join next year but have already paid dues to the NIRA." The University of Idaho did the same. Colorado State University had already chosen to remain with NIRA. Thirteen schools from eight states had joined ACRA: four from Montana, two from Utah and Wyoming, one each from Idaho, North Dakota, South Dakota, Nebraska, and Colorado. Eighty-four students from nine schools paid their dues to the new organization.[7]

After a year of controversy, the two organizations reunited after schools approved the NIRA constitutional amendments that settled the problems. During the fall of 1960, schools that had joined the ACRA returned to the NIRA. With the changes, faculty had equal representation on the national board, and women were accepted as team members. The schools from the Rocky Mountain and Great Plains Regions sent membership dues and their rodeo dates for approval. Once again, college rodeo had one national organization.

After resolving the crisis, the NIRA officers looked at issues, such as the agreement with the RCA and the financial report. When the NIRA and the RCA met,

The 1959–60 NIRA board met with the RCA board to try to resolve the problems that caused the split in the NIRA. RCA board members (seated, left to right) *Clark McEntire, Willard Coombs, Dale Smith, unidentified, Guy Weeks, 1960 RCA president Jack Buschbom,* (back, left to right) *Bill Fedderson, two unidentified, Sonny Sikes, Jerry Moore, NIRA president Ross Caton, Bill Ward, Harley May, Buddy Groff, NIRA secretary-manager Hoss Inman, Paul Bond, unidentified, Deb Copenhaver. Photo courtesy of Sonny Sikes, Huntsville, Texas, and NIRA Alumni archives.*

they made one change. They limited NIRA contestants to one summer rodeo. The other item, a review of the income and expense statement from the 1959 finals rodeo at Klamath, Oregon, revealed that the finals rodeo had a fifteen hundred dollar loss. Travel expenses of $1,800 caused the deficit. The board agreed to move the finals to a more central location, such as Albuquerque, New Mexico, or Pueblo, Colorado. However, due to lack of time, the board closed without planning the 1960 finals.[8]

The lack of leadership, once again, confronted the NIRA officers when the secretary-manager resigned on June 17, 1960. Hoss Inman had successfully led the NIRA through a major crisis and back to unity, so he wanted to return to his other businesses. The board hired Sonny Sikes, a knowledgeable, experienced Sam Houston State NIRA rodeo coach. He had competed for Sam Houston State for four years, won four national championships, earned a degree in animal science, and returned to teach at the university. Since Sikes was affiliated with a college, the NIRA voted to hire him. Sikes moved two file boxes and a typewriter into his office at SHSU and set up the NIRA office where it stayed until 1964 when he moved it to his home. Sikes succeeded at his two full-time jobs because his wife Joanne managed the office, kept the records, and published the newsletter. With the leadership of the Sikeses, the NIRA national office found stability and permanency for the next nineteen years.[9]

Once again, the NIRA board aggressively sought national publicity along with some changes. The 1964 agenda showed that the NIRA had some innovative ideas for expanding the organization. The board negotiated again with ABC television to televise the finals and a proposed East-West match rodeo. Ironically, the same year the RCA headed the opposite direction. "On April 1, 1964, citing the best interests of rodeo, the RCA Board of Directors agreed that no local television stations would be allowed to film rodeos." The NIRA board had contacted an advertising agency, Fidelity Advertising, for a proposal. The board also planned to discuss protective headgear for college cowboys and insurance for the members. Two agenda items addressed women's events and women's representation on the board.[10]

The original board recognized the need for a publicity director; however, the NIRA waited eighteen years to hire a marketing expert and add some incentives. In September 1967 the board hired Del Higham of Dixie College, St. George, Utah, to market the NIRA. His contract of $200 a month expired at the beginning of the 1968 finals rodeo. Higham found many ways to publicize the 1,163 NIRA members. The NIRA also gave a $100 scholarship to the champion and $50 to second place at the finals and first and second in the NIRA standings. The NIRA awarded Ray Davis, *Western Horseman* staff writer, an honorary membership for his articles.[11]

The NIRA had tried different ways to gain greater media exposure for the finals and the sponsors. In 1962 the American Broadcasting Company filmed the finals, narrated by Lex Connelly, former RCA executive manager, and broadcast on June 8, 1962, on *Wide World of Sports*, a regular Sunday program. Producer Dick Kirchmer said, "We've filmed rodeos before, but this was the fastest moving one we've ever produced."[12] The National Broadcasting Company videotaped the 1965 finals short-go on Saturday afternoon for release on August 1, 1965, on *Sports in Action.*[13] For publicity, the 1962 national champions received a week's paid vacation to a Colorado dude ranch.[14] The 1967 national all-around champion A. C. Ekker of the University of Utah rode in on a horse and drove away in a 1967 Ford Mustang convertible, donated by Ford Motor Company for six months.[15]

A different way to market the 1967 rodeo finals at St. George, Utah, proved to be a success. After being selected rodeo hostesses, three Dixie College co-eds, Helen Harmon, Jolene Gentry, and Sandra Sorenson, with the help of Bonanza Airlines, appeared at rodeos in the western states. They met with newspaper, radio, and television representatives at each place, and were invited to speak at the Southern California Sportscaster's Weekly Luncheon in Los Angeles. "Because of a tight schedule, the women were met at Los Angeles International Airport and whisked by helicopter to downtown LA. The helicopter was met by a special car and a police escort, which hurried the three, with a couple of split seconds to spare, to the site of the luncheon." Then, Harmon served as official hostess for the Miss College Rodeo contest.[16]

The new publicity director's constant flow of news exposed the NIRA to a national audience. Del Higham initiated a series of memos in January, 1969, informing the board about public relations activities, and he sent information to the NIRA members on effective ways to be interviewed. Higham requested that the finals qualifiers send information to him to use in news releases. He designed and produced business cards for the national board and an NIRA brochure, which he sent with a letter to college presidents. Higham had written the Joey Bishop Show, the Art Linkletter Show, the Donald O'Connor Show, and the Steve Allen Show trying to get a spot. He did not, but 1969 Miss College Rodeo Terry Jo Stephens of Montana State University rode in the Rose Parade and gave a "nice plug for the NIRA on the CBS Network."[17] Higham contacted many national magazines, such as *Time, Life, Newsweek, Holiday, Farm Journal, Family Circle,* and *Sunset Magazine.* Replies from the media to Higham expressed interest, but a six-month to a year lead was needed.[18] *Sports Illustrated* published an article on July 1, 1968, about the NIRA. In April Higham contacted *Wide World of Sports,* the ABC network, and Intermountain Radio Network (IRN), which included seventy-eight radio stations in five states. IRN agreed to do approximately three thousand spots two weeks prior to the finals and the last two days of the finals.[19]

The NIRA board continued to develop ideas to strengthen the organization. In 1965 student president Dick Claycomb, along with faculty president Dr. Joseph Feathers, presided over a nineteen-member board from six regions that worked diligently to create a more cohesive board and organization.

The board established new regional event directors to divide the regional student directors' workload. Student directors needed to focus on larger issues that occurred at each rodeo. With an elected person responsible for each event at a rodeo, the regions functioned more professionally. For example, in 1965 in the Southwest Region, Wanda Boatlee Driver of Texas Tech directed the goat tying; Skipper Driver of Texas Tech, the ribbon roping; J. M. Bradley of Eastern New Mexico University, the bareback riding; Kenneth Cunningham of ENMU, the saddle bronc riding; Sherrill Overturff of Sul Ross State, the calf roping; Lebert Saulsberry of New Mexico State, the steer wrestling; Eddie Puckett of South Plains College, the bull riding; and Paulette Taylor of Hardin-Simmons, the barrel racing.

The NIRA progressed toward using a business management plan. In 1965 defining the secretary-manager's job description helped: "He shall be a staff member of a member college or university and shall qualify by existing standards. He votes only in case of a tie." The secretary-manager would conduct the correspondence, make an annual report and financial report, and write brief quarterly financial reports. He would produce a monthly newsletter in April, May, and June and issue all official documents, receive all money due to the association, and pay all bills. He would handle the money for the finals rodeo, the scholarship money, and work to improve the association for a monthly salary of $250 with an expense allotment.

Student/faculty leadership problems, however, nagged. For example, in April 1965 Irving M. Munn, Great Plains Region faculty director of South Dakota State University, wrote to Sonny Sikes, secretary-manager, about a "little scene" at the Regional Governing Board Meeting in Manhattan, Kansas, where the "Great Plains Region Student Director was nailed to the wall by our students and faculty for preempting the prerogative of tampering with college rodeo dates." He stated that "the regional faculty advisers at a privately scheduled meeting at Manhattan, Kansas, resolved that the regional faculty adviser appoint a faculty-scheduling committee to work with student representatives of each club to schedule all rodeos by the end of the last semester of the previous school year."[20]

A constant search for a permanent location for the college finals rodeo continued to consume a sizable amount of time of the NIRA officers. The Montana State University Rodeo Club co-adviser Bud Purdy requested information about possibly producing the finals rodeo at Bozeman, Montana. After receiving the information, Purdy wrote W. A. Harris, national faculty vice president at the University of Wyoming, in 1965 that they would like to have the rodeo at their field house, but "we need a rich uncle to back such a venture."[21] Harris had sent Purdy some financial information and some suggestions. Harris said, "The Laramie Jubilee Committee had expenses of $15,000, which was about $2,000 more than their income which included $2,500 from the TV rights. The gate receipts were $7,300." Harris suggested that Pete Burns of Laramie, Wyoming, and Jim Roush of Douglas, Wyoming, be approved as rodeo coproducers for the 1966 finals at Vermillion, South Dakota.[22] Both men knew college rodeo from experience. In 1949 Burns had attended both the NIRA organizational meeting and the first NIRA convention. Roush had served as the University of Wyoming Rodeo Club president in 1950–51.

The NIRA board benefited from having dual membership of a faculty and students representing each region. Montana State's Dave Holt, 1966–67 national student president, led the board of directors through a series of issues that strengthened the growing organization. By 1967 the board had stabilized with a faculty and a student representative from each of the six regions and three women representatives. The board represented 961 members and 486 permit holders from eighty-one colleges and universities.[23]

The NIRA board created regional governing boards and made insurance available for the members. On the regional governing board, one boy, one girl, and a faculty adviser served from each of the member clubs with an elected student director and faculty director completing the board. At the national convention, each member club could have two voting delegates.[24] A new region was also initiated increasing the number of regions to seven. The state of Montana was dropped from the Rocky Mountain Region and combined with Washington, Oregon, and Northern Idaho to form the new Northwest Region. A letter to each member explained the NIRA insurance. A letter from D. Lee Johnston of the insurance company stated that "the biggest number of claims came from bull riders with the actual amount of money claims running around 75 percent of the total—from bulls. The average claim looks like it is going to be about $225."[25]

Solutions to unequal numbers of contestants in regions and rodeo production issues eluded the NIRA student president Warren Moon Jr. of Texas A&M in his search for answers in 1968. The number of contestants in each region varied considerably, making it difficult to qualify for the finals in the larger regions. The Southwest Region, one of the largest regions, proposed on May 11, 1968, that points be given by dollars won. However, since some regions did not have entry fees, the smaller regions would never have a chance to accumulate the points that a larger region could. The number of years of eligibility, even pens of rodeo stock, limited entries at the finals, penalties for being blacklisted, and selection of the 1969 finals site also caused heated debates.

Although nomadic during the 1960s, the NIRA finals produced memorable circumstances and champions who later won world titles in professional rodeo. The 1950s NIRA champions Harley May and Jack Roddy became world champion professional cowboys. The 1960s started a stream of college cowboys moving into professional rodeo competition. However, the finals needed a travel agent to keep up with its moves to six states and eight cities in ten years. The 1960 finals went to Clayton, New Mexico, a small ranching community in the northeast corner of the state. The Clayton Rabbit Ear Roundup Association had sponsored the 1959 Women's Professional Rodeo Association's national finals barrel race and 1960 PRCA steer roping finals.

A fiercely competitive school, which had a team at the first finals, finally won a team trophy in 1960. Even with Rocky Mountain and Great Plains Regions schools pulling out to join the new national association, the 1960 finals started on schedule. Cal Poly at San Luis Obispo won its first men's team championship, the first of five. Two Cal Poly cowboys won event titles in close contests. For the second year, Bill Nielson won the ribbon roping, only sixteen points ahead of Clyde Fort of Texas Tech, a second-generation roper, trained in the Lovington, New Mexico, area of his father, world champion calf roper Troy Fort. Cal Poly's Riley Freeman won the steer wrestling, only forty-seven points ahead of Jack Burkholder of Texas A&I. Marvin Smith, Jim Walker, Jack Sparrow, and Ray Bunnell rounded out Coach Bill Gibford's first champion Cal Poly team.

The first finals of the 1960s ended a stellar college rodeo career and started another one. A record-setting college career climaxed in 1960 as a roping brother duo from Texas A&I put sports writers' pens to the paper. Jack Burkholder finished his phenomenal college roping career in 1960 with six trophy saddles, four being consecutive calf roping championships, an un-equaled NIRA record. Kenneth Burkholder challenged Jack's fast calf roping loops. The brothers finished one and two with only five points separating them: 522 points and 517 points with two hundred points for third place. Jack captured the reserve championship in steer wrestling and third in the all-around. Kenneth took fourth in the ribbon roping and fourth in the all-around.

As Burkholder closed his college rodeo career, another cowboy moved into the spotlight. Occasionally, a true all-around champion comes along, and Edd Workman of Lubbock Christian College fit that category. Workman won two saddle bronc championships and dominated the all-around standings for three years while pressing contestants in almost every event. In 1960 through 1962, Workman was all over the place. He was the 1960 all-around and saddle bronc champ and finished third in bareback riding, calf roping, and steer wrestling. In 1961 he took the all-around again and placed second in the bareback riding and saddle bronc riding, third in the ribbon roping and steer wrestling. Again,

Texas A&I calf roping champion Jack Burkholder, shown roping at San Antonio, Texas, in 1964, set the record for most consecutive NIRA calf roping championships in 1960 by winning his fourth championship. Photo by Ferrell Butler, Mesquite, Texas, courtesy of Jack Burkholder, Edinburg, Texas, and NIRA Alumni archives.

in 1962 Workman was number one in the all-around and the saddle bronc riding. With his third consecutive all-around, Workman moved up into a class with Harley May that no one else has entered.

Record firsts piled up at the 1961 national finals. For the first time, Sam Houston State won the first national champion women's team title. For the first and only time, the University of Wyoming won the men's team championship. All the team members hailed from Wyoming and still called Wyoming home in 1999: Al Smith, Frank Shepperson, Leon Cook, Fred Wilson, Jerry Kaufman, and Jim Moore.

Winning both team championships with two married couples on the Sul Ross State teams brought another first. At the 1962 finals at Littleton, Colorado, unity and competition went hand and hand with Ruth Foster and Mereva James married to Melvin Foster and Bill James. Mereva James finished third nationally in the barrel race. Ruth Foster added points for fourth in the goat tying first go. All three members of the Sul Ross women's team qualified for the short round in barrel racing. The third member Donna Saul, on Yeller her palomino gelding, won the all-around and goat tying titles. Lorraine Taylor of Northern Montana College beat the three Sul Ross barrel racers with a five-point margin, winning NMC's only national championship. One husband, Melvin Foster's 11.6 in the calf roping, won the last go. The other husband, Bill James, won the ribbon roping and calf roping titles, but James had to share the calf roping title with Dub Cox of New Mexico A&M, the first NIRA tie for a championship. Sul Ross's George Eads won the bull riding after scoring 169 on his final bull. At that time, judges scored one hundred for the animal and one hundred for the rider.

The 1963 all-around and bareback champion watched his son win identical championships exactly thirty years later. Western Montana College's Shawn Davis, a cowboy associated with college and professional rodeo in a variety of ways for years, had won the 1961 saddle bronc title. Davis, later called "the professor," became coach at the College of Southern Idaho and NFR executive general manager. Shawn was Zane's rodeo coach at CSI when Zane won identical championships. While watching, Shawn, three-time world saddle bronc champion, said, "I was never this nervous when I was competing myself."[26]

Camaraderie that develops among contestants is invisible in the record books. Shawn Davis and Buz Cowdrey grew up together and marked a trail of success in rodeo and business while remaining lifelong friends. At the 1961

Shawn Davis, three-time NIRA champion, three-time world saddle bronc champion, and College of Southern Idaho coach, rides a bronc at a Burwell, Nebraska, PRCA rodeo in 1976. Photo by JJJ Photo, Ord, Nebraska.

Montana State College regional rodeo, Davis won the all-around and the saddle bronc riding, then took third in the bareback riding. Fellow Western Montana College teammate Buz Cowdrey won the bull riding championship and finished fourth in the nation in 1962.[27] Davis's rodeo career started when he sneaked out to practice in the Cowdrey's practice pen. Davis said, "On the way home through the pasture, I would stop at a pond and add some mud to cover the dirt to hide my rodeo experiences." Davis saw Cowdrey at least once a year when Cowdrey and his wife Judy hosted a dinner in their spacious home during the CNFR for the WMC rodeo team and alumni, along with the NIRA Alumni Board of Directors of which the two friends were both charter board members.[28]

Casper College started a winning streak in 1963 that set an unmatched record for two-year schools. They tied Sul Ross State University's record of four consecutive men's team championships set in 1949–52. Other two-year colleges have won a maximum of three team championships. CC's coach Dale Stiles, the 1949 NIRA national saddle bronc champion, knew how to recruit and how to run a program that kept them coming.

The powerhouse Casper cowboys in 1964 continued with one cowboy winning three titles. At the finals at Douglas, Wyoming, Dale Stiles's cowboys won three national championships and the team trophy. Casper's Pink Peterson rode his way to a bareback, an all-around, and a shared championship in the saddle bronc riding with Lamar College's Ned Londo, both with 539 points.

A University of Wyoming cowboy won a 1964 championship, added another in the professional ranks, and raised an NIRA champion. Frank Shepperson became UW's first steer wrestling champion and won the 1975 professional steer wrestling title. His daughter Amy won the 2000 NIRA breakaway gold buckle for the same school.

The 1965 finals rodeo, billed as "NIRA World's Championship Rodeo," moved to Laramie, Wyoming, to test the college contestants' skills on the rodeo stock of Hyde Merritt, Bill McKee, and Summit Rodeo. At the 1965 awards banquet on Saturday night following the finals, Coach Dale Stiles accepted for Casper College the five-foot traveling trophy permanently.[29] Casper's team members took trophy saddles in two events and the all-around. Pink Peterson added his second consecutive all-around and saddle bronc riding championships. Claude Wilson won the bareback riding title, and Ned Londo came in second in the saddle bronc riding. Londo qualified for the professional finals four times in saddle bronc riding. Adding team points were Tom Jarrard, Bill Peterson, and Wayne Not Afraid.

A 1965 NIRA champion took the responsibility of educating judges for professional and college rodeos. Utah State's Jack Hannum won the first and only calf roping championship for his school. Hannum, a five-time National Finals Rodeo qualifier, started working in 1972 for the PRCA as the supervisor of the Wrangler PRCA pro-officials judging program and continues today training judges. Wrangler's decision to sponsor the education of judges is a benchmark in rodeo. This program, attended by many college rodeo coaches, raised the quality of rodeo by helping to standardize judging and make it more consistent. When the PRCA started hiring full-time Wrangler judges, it added a consistency to judging and an expectation for quality in the events that elevated rodeo to a new level of competition.

The world-class talent at the 1966 finals rodeo spotlighted the growing importance of the college rodeo experience. Names of young, talented future world

Casper College, the 1966 NIRA national champion men's team, set a record of four consecutive championships, the most ever won by a two-year school. Team members are (left to right) Tom Jarrard, Ned Londo, Claude Wilson, Ralph Betz, Bill Peterson, Pink Peterson, and Coach Dale Stiles; boy, Roger Stiles. Photo by Bob Clore, BCR Awards, Manhattan, Kansas, and courtesy of NIRA Alumni archives.

champions or National Finals Rodeo qualifiers like Joe Alexander, Ivan Daines, Stan Harter, Bobby Berger, and Phil Lyne crowded the final 1966 NIRA standings. Coach Dale Stiles's Casper College cowboys finished with two event titles and their fourth team championship. Casper's champion bareback rider Joe Alexander of Cora, Wyoming, later won five consecutive world championships and two consecutive PRCA championships making Alexander's name legendary. Texas Tech's Garland Weeks, the 1995 Official Texas State Sculptor, claimed third place in bareback riding. Weeks's rodeo experiences inspired his creative spirit and talent, leading to his award-winning bronzes.

The challenge for championships at the 1966 college finals focused on talent that would prove itself over and over. At the end, only five and a half points separated the champion, Casper's Ivan Daines, many times NFR qualifier, and Cal Poly's Bobby Berger, the 1977 PRCA saddle bronc and 1979 world champion saddle bronc rider. Two other names that became famous in the rodeo world followed: Ned Londo of Cal Poly took third, and J. C. Bonine of Eastern

Joe Alexander, 1966 NIRA bareback champion, rides at a PRCA rodeo at Burwell, Nebraska. Alexander won five consecutive bareback world championships and two PRCA championships. Photo by JJJ Photo, Ord, Nebraska.

New Mexico University, fourth. The multi-talented Daines left his mark on rodeo production at the famous Canadian Innisfail Rodeo and by singing old favorites, such as "The Strawberry Roan" and new ones like "Rodeo Coach," dedicated to Coach Dale Stiles. Daines became known for the Ivan Daines Country Music Picknic [*sic*] & Campout held the first weekend in August each year in Innisfail, Alberta, Canada. Arizona State's Stan Harter, many times NFR qualifier in calf roping, won two 1966 NIRA championships: calf roping and ribbon roping. Harter served as the West Coast Region student director for two years.

Members of the 1967 champion men's team influenced rodeo in several ways. More than 180 contestants from seventeen schools headed to St. George, Utah, to compete at the Dixie College–sponsored finals. In 1967 Tarleton State University, which had joined the NIRA in the fall of 1965, won its first men's team championship with Billy Albin, Charles Bitters, Johnny Edmondson, Bobby Hungate, Randy Magers, and Terry Walls, a harbinger of their future rodeo success. Edmondson later married Diltzie Bland, and they raised third-generation NIRA contestants Carter and Lorissa Edmondson. Diltzie's mother,

Rosemary Bland, started the family tradition of competing in the NIRA at Texas Tech. Randy Magers, many times bull riding NFR qualifier, returned to Tarleton to coach its rodeo team in the early 1990s. Terry Walls had a wreck near Gainesville en route to Utah and was replaced by Lionel Lane.[30] However, Walls later started his own rodeo stock company, Terry Walls Rodeo Co., and produced professional and college rodeos starting in the 1980s. His daughter Schelli and son Trent both were regional champions, and Trent qualified for the 1998 NFR in calf roping.

The 1967 finals was a preview of professional rodeo champions. With the talent at the finals, all-around champion A. C. Ekker of the University of Utah worked to earn it. Ekker won the all-around by only ten and a half points. Ekker and Phil Lyne of Southwest Texas Junior College finished one and two in the ribbon roping, also. Lyne, five-time world champion who competed at both ends of the arena, was considered one of the best multi-talented cowboys ever. Cal Poly's Dan Freeman edged by bareback rider Joe Alexander of Casper College. Black Hills State saddle bronc rider Dave Dahl, who later specialized

Casper College cowboy Ivan Daines of Innisfail, Alberta, Canada, won the 1966 NIRA national saddle bronc riding championship and went on to leave his mark on international rodeo through competing, rodeo production, and rodeo music. Photo by Bob Clore, BC Rodeo Awards, Manhattan, Kansas, and courtesy of NIRA Alumni archives.

in custom-made bronc saddles, beat Casper College's J. C. Bonine and Ivan Daines. ABC's *Wide World of Sports,* in a special on the rodeo finals, interviewed the calf roping champion, Mesa Community College's Sherrick Grantham. The steer wrestling champion Butch Myers of Southern Colorado State and bull riding champion Bobby Berger of Cal Poly would cause sports writers to take note of the quality of cowboys coming out of the NIRA when they both won world championships.

For the second time, two teams from the same school won both titles. At the finals of July 2 to 7, 1968, in Sacramento, California, Coach Sonny Sikes's Sam Houston State teams won both team championships. Both of Eastern New Mexico University's teams stalled at second place. Sam Houston team member Becky Berggren from Scottsbluff, Nebraska, won top goat tying points in the first and short rounds and second in the average. Kay Steele Campbell and Willie Gregson Little placed in the barrel race. Steele Campbell split third and fourth in the average.[31] Earning the record for Sam Houston State were team members Carl Deaton, Ron Williams, Bob Smith, Bill Burton, Jim Daniel, and Billy Thomas. SHSU's Dan Harris and Buster Brown competed at the finals, also. SHSU steer wrestler Carl Deaton entered the finals in twelfth place with Butch Myers of Colorado State, the 1980 world champion, leading the steer wrestling. Deaton finished with a total of 17.9 seconds on three steers, beating Myers by twenty-two points. SHSU calf roper Ronnie Williams missed the gold but added team points with reserve titles in calf roping and ribbon roping with Buddy Draper of Southern Colorado State taking the ribbon roping honors. Phil Lyne of Southwest Texas State College won the all-around and calf roping titles; Eastern Montana's J. C. Bonine, the saddle bronc riding; Mesa College's J. C. Trujillo, the bareback riding; and South Dakota State's Don Reichert, the bull riding. Later, Reichert rode professionally and managed the Badlands Circuit.

The potential economic impact of the NIRA rodeo finals attracted the attention of two places in 1969. The finals at Sacramento had produced a profit of almost $11,000.[32] The board marked the third week in June as the best dates for the finals rodeo. Cal Expo representatives Lex Connelly, Kay Haley, and Larry Gately invited the NIRA to make the Cal Expo in Sacramento, California, its permanent home."[33] However, Dr. Charles Schad of Black Hills State College of Spearfish, South Dakota, invited the CNFR to Deadwood, South Dakota, which was chosen.

Phil Lyne led the growing list of NIRA champions who became professional

Sam Houston State won both the men's and women's team championships in 1968, only the second time in NIRA history. Members are (left to right) *Ron Williams, Coach Sonny Sikes, Bob Smith, Carl Deaton, Bill Burton, Jim Daniel, Dan Harris, and Buster Brown,* (front, left to right), *Becky Berggren, Willie Gregson Little, and Kay Steele Campbell. Photo courtesy NIRA Alumni archives.*

rodeo legends. Sam Houston State's Lyne repeated his 1968 all-around and calf roping titles in 1969. Lyne then won the same two world championships in 1971 and 1972. However, Lyne said, "My favorite event is bull riding." Lyne, taught to rope by his dad on their ranch at George West, Texas, learned to ride bulls from his friends. Lyne won the Linderman Award four times: 1970, 1971, 1972, and 1976, given to the professional cowboy considered by many to be rodeo's best true all-around cowboy.[34] To qualify for the award, a contestant must win at least $1,000 in each of three events, including a rough-stock event and a timed event. Lyne became the only professional cowboy to win the NFR average championships in three events. He added a fifth world championship in 1990 for steer roping although he had quit rodeoing full time after 1972 to help his wife Sarah raise their two daughters, Amanda and Samantha, on their ranch in Cotulla, Texas.

Another university moved into the championship circle, joining the ranks of top NIRA competitors. At the 1969 finals, Eastern New Mexico University won its first men's team title with its multi-event cowboys. The women had won their first in 1967. ENMU's Virgil Lawson won the region in all-around and steer wrestling, a second in bull riding and a fourth in ribbon roping. Ross Chesser came in fourth in steer wrestling. Ben Calhoun won the region in bull riding with a fourth in the all-around and a sixth in bareback riding. John Wilson was fifth in saddle bronc riding, and Lon Sultemeier was fifth in the bull riding. Calhoun finished fifth in bareback riding in the nation and second in bull riding.

At the twentieth anniversary finals rodeo in 1969, two other event winners became legends in the rodeo. Eastern Montana's J. C. Bonine won the 1969 NIRA saddle bronc championship, his second consecutive title. Only six other NIRA saddle bronc riders have won two consecutive championships. Bonine won the world saddle bronc championship in 1977. Sheridan College's Chris LeDoux beat the 1968 bareback riding champion J. C. Trujillo by seven and a half points. LeDoux and Trujillo used the NIRA for a springboard into world championships.

A legend in professional rodeo, Phil Lyne, who competed for Southwest Texas State and Sam Houston State and entered five events, duplicated the two championships that he won in 1968 by winning the 1969 all-around and calf roping championships in spite of ankle-deep mud at the finals in Deadwood, South Dakota. Photo by James Fain, Logan, Utah.

J. C. Trujillo, the 1968 NIRA bareback riding champ, finished his degree in elementary education at Arizona State University followed by twelve trips to the NFR and a bareback riding gold buckle in 1981. Trujillo branched out in business, but it included rodeo. He put on rodeo schools with champions Shawn Davis and Gary Leffew. While in charge of special events at Steamboat Ski and Resort, he helped found the now-famous "Cowboy Downhill" ski race. He and his wife Margo and their two daughters live on their ranch southwest of Steamboat Springs, Colorado, where they all help with the family business, J. C. Trujillo Guide & Outfitters.

Chris LeDoux, the 1969 NIRA bareback champion, capped his rodeo career with a world championship and a singing career. LeDoux celebrated the United States bicentennial year of 1976 by winning the world bareback riding title. He provided another avenue of insight for the public with his songs about rodeo. LeDoux, typical of a new type of college cowboy, was not ranch raised. After he was exposed to rodeo, he knew that he had found something that he loved.[35] LeDoux started riding in junior rodeos at age thirteen in Denison, Texas. Since LeDoux's father was in the Air Force, Chris had lived in France and several different states before he moved to Texas and learned "to love rodeo." During his sophomore year, his family moved to Cheyenne, Wyoming. After graduation, LeDoux attended Casper College on a scholarship followed by Sheridan College and Eastern New Mexico University. His love for "family, freedom, the West, and cowboy ways" was transformed into songs, leading to his career in music after rodeo. The songs LeDoux chose to sing reflected his love for rodeo, such as "I've Got to Be a Rodeo Man" and "She's in Love with a Rodeo Man."[36]

In the 1960s two landmark decisions changed women's events. The first was a change in the barrel racing rules. When a cowgirl hit a barrel, instead of being disqualified, she would receive a five-point penalty. In 1964 the NIRA board considered changing ribbon roping to a woman's event and eliminating goat tying. Another event for women, breakaway roping, was considered, but the board voted to try it on the regional level until details could be worked.[37] At the 1968 board meeting, faculty director Tommy Buckner moved to add breakaway roping as the third standard event for women, but the motion was tabled. The next day, on July 2, the board passed it with nine in favor and three opposed. Breakaway roping became the third standard event for women and would remain until the fourth, team roping, would be added more than a decade later. Another landmark decision for women occurred: the NIRA board

Country singer Chris LeDoux rides at the 1969 CNFR to win the NIRA bareback championship. He won the 1976 world championship. Photo by James Fain, Logan, Utah.

added a Girls National Director, serving as a representative for all girls events and regions.[38]

Preparing NIRA cowgirls for college rodeo queen competition started at regional rodeos that staged queen contests to train for the national competition. Success of the preparation showed in the titles of Rebecca Ramsey from Texas Tech, a member of the Southwest Region, who won the 1964 Miss College Rodeo and other major pageants, such as the Miss Rodeo Texas and Miss Rodeo International pageants.[39] Southwest Texas State College's Carolynn Seay Vietor won the 1965 NIRA goat tying reserve championship and the triple-crown championships: 1965 Miss College Rodeo, Miss Rodeo Texas, and Miss Rodeo America. She continued to leave her mark on rodeo by serving as president of the Women's Professional Rodeo Association (WPRA) and as a 1992 NIRA Alumni (NIRAA) charter board member.

NIRA cowgirls continued to prove that they could be beautiful and athletic by winning national championships and the Miss College Rodeo crown. Texas Tech's Marianne Munz Brunson, the 1967 and 1968 goat tying champ, finished with the Miss College Rodeo crown and a chance to compete for Miss Rodeo America. Munz, who earned a master's degree in food and nutrition, added Brunson to her name in 1968 when she married Ron Brunson, an Eastern New Mexico University civil engineering graduate. Marianne represented a new type of college rodeo student. A city girl who liked horses, she and her sister Nancy got the "horse bug" while they were in elementary school. Their father, an industrial arts instructor in Alvin, Texas, borrowed a horse to check the durability of his daughters' interest in horses. It lasted. In 1967 the goat tying national runner-up Nancy Munz trailed her sister Marianne by twenty-three points.[40]

One cowgirl moved into the triple-crown winner's circle for consecutive identical event championships, joining an elite group of three cowboys. She matched bull rider Ira Akers and all-around champions Harley May and Edd Workman. Only one cowboy exceeds their record: Jack Burkholder with four in calf roping. West Texas State cowgirl Mike Reid Settle, inducted into the National Cowgirl Hall of Fame in 1977, won three consecutive barrel racing championships in 1959–61. No other cowgirl has matched her record. In 1960 Reid Settle tied her goat for fourth place and took number two in the all-around in a photo finish with all-around and goat tying champion Sam Houston State's Karen Mangum. With over a thousand points for each won during the year, Mangum won the title with eight and one-quarter points more than Reid Settle.

Women's team championships, after twelve men's team championships, were awarded for the first time at the 1961 finals at Sacramento, California. Sam Houston State won the first women's team national championship. Coach Sonny Sikes watched as Flossy Brandes picked up a barrel racing reserve championship, and Karen Bland did the same in tie-down calf roping. The May 1961 NIRA newsletter for the Texas Western College rodeo results reported the first awarding of a women's college rodeo team trophy at a regional rodeo. New Mexico State University's cowgirls took first place at TWC with NMSU's Sara Cox winning pole bending, not a common college event. Cox won the all-around by splitting first place in the average in barrel racing with Sul Ross's Mareva James, whose son Billy James qualified for the NIRA finals in team roping in the 1980s.[41]

Another cowgirl event passed into history in 1961; for the second and last time, a woman won a calf tying championship. Occasionally, instead of goat tying, a rodeo producer used small calves because goats were unavailable. This happened in 1959 and again in 1961. Everyone watched Donna Saul of Sul Ross race to a calf tied to a stake, flank and tie it to win the calf tying saddle.

Texas dominated the women's team championships for two years; however, Colorado State University took over in 1963 and 1964, winning both women's team championships and two event titles. CSU's Leota Hielscher was the 1963 all-around, and CSU's Sally Spencer was the number one goat tier. In 1964 all-around went to another Colorado cowgirl, Marie Mass of the University of Southern Colorado, along with the reserve championship in goat tying. Mass became her college's only cowgirl NIRA champion. The barrel racing champion Carlee Obervy became South Dakota State's first NIRA champion. Karen Coleman Smith won Montana State University's first goat tying championship. In 1966 CSU's barrel racer Cleonne Skinner Steinmiller capped the winning streak for CSU, the last national champion for it.

In 1965 the records show that one university was becoming a perennial powerhouse. At the 1965 awards banquet, NIRA secretary-manager Sonny Sikes put on his Sam Houston State coaching hat to accept the second national women's team championship for SHSU and watch SHSU's talented Becky Berggren awarded the all-around and barrel racing trophy saddles.

The cowgirl events reflected their growing competitiveness as dual winners of championships in one year happened only once from 1966 to 1969. In 1966 the Arizona State women gathered enough points to be ASU's one and only champion women's team. The event championships went to three different schools. Marianne Munz Brunson wore the goat tying buckle home to Texas Tech and repeated it in 1967. The 1966 all-around champion Montana State's Carol O'Rourke Smith later watched her husband Bill Smith win the world in saddle bronc riding three times. Kansas State's Barbara Socolofsky won the 1967 all-around championship, the only one for Kansas State. Barbara Baer of Cal Poly beat Donna Kinkead of Eastern New Mexico University by five points to win the 1967 barrel racing saddle. Kinkead, Linda Blackburn Sultemeier, and Linda Griffin earned ENMU its first national rodeo team title.

A duo of event championships were once again won. ENMU's Donna Kinkead followed up with two 1968 championships. Kinkead followed the 1967 barrel racing champ Barbara Baer of Cal Poly by twenty points, but Kinkead made up the difference in the short-go and the average. Kinkead, also serving on the NIRA board, won the all-around with another Cal Poly cowgirl, Nancy Robinson Petersen, a close second. Southwest Texas State College goat tier Mary Fuller put the only woman's national championship in the SWTSC record books. Fuller beat the Munz sisters of Texas Tech. Fuller, who earned a master's degree in animal nutrition, went to work for Ralston Purina in St. Louis, Missouri, in 1973 as an animal nutritionist in pet foods. She was granted a patent in 1981 for flavor enhancement in dog foods.[42]

A new standard event and a cowgirl team that would dominate championships caught the attention of fans at the NIRA's twentieth anniversary rodeo finals. In 1969 at Deadwood, South Dakota, Tarleton State University's Sally Preston showed fans that cowgirls can rope by winning the first breakaway roping championship after it became a standard event. Teammate Angie Watts Averhoff won the goat tying, but not easily, with the Munz sisters in hot pursuit. That launched the TSU women's team winning cycle that lasted three years, then lay dormant for thirty years. From 1969 to 1971 TSU's women claimed three team championships and four event championships. The competition was tough as the Cal Poly cowgirls took two event championships back to California. Cal Poly's Barbara Baer, the 1967 barrel racing champion, added the 1969 championship with TSU's Karen Walls taking second. Cal Poly's Nancy Robinson Petersen won the 1969 all-around championship after coming close for several years.

Thirty years later, two all-around champions met again when their daughters competed on the same team. The 1969 all-around champion Cal Poly's

Nancy Robinson Petersen and Eastern New Mexico University's Linda Blackburn Sultemeier, the 1970 all-around champion, met at the college finals. Three decades later, they met again at the college finals. After college, Nancy moved to Montana, and Linda stayed in New Mexico. Their daughters met in Texas. Nancy's daughter, Jody, and Linda's two daughters Christi and Kelli accepted rodeo scholarships at Vernon Regional Junior College, Vernon, Texas, and qualified for the 1996 finals by winning the Southwest Region team championship with Jody winning the all-around and the breakaway roping titles. The Sultemeiers's father Lon of ENMU, finished fifth in bull riding in 1969 in the Southwest Region. These two families illustrate college rodeo networking continuing into the second generation.

Another unique experience was a repeat performance for Texas Tech cowgirls. In 1965 Texas Tech cowgirl Eileen Cochran won the goat tying championship, the first women's event title for her school. Twenty-two years later in 1987, Eileen's daughter Karen Cochran Smith won the first breakaway roping championship for Texas Tech.

Many college contestants consider their rodeo years at college as their best because of the team spirit and the competition with the same schools at the regional rodeos. Tarleton State Coach Randy Magers said that his college rodeo years were more fun than his professional years because of the team concept. He said, "We all traveled together, so we had a lot of fun." He told about their preparations for their first trip together. The father of one of the team members owned a funeral home. Magers said, "He gave us some casket boxes that we used to build a camper for the pickup. It worked well. Three slept on the top and three on the bottom in the camper."[43]

The NIRA celebrated its twentieth anniversary having weathered financial problems, rapidly changing leadership, and lack of acceptance as a new college sport. The NIRA's relationship with colleges and universities improved when it gave college faculty and administrators a vote on the board. A permanent office location brought better communication between the national office and the regions resulting in a growing consistency in regional rule enforcement. The more women's standard events resulted in more cowgirl contestants with a growing expertise. Rodeo scholarships raised the quality of competition in all of the events resulting in more college contestants winning professional titles. However, during the 1960s, the finals rodeo moved nine times in the ten-year period, so the NIRA still had major issues to resolve.

CHAPTER 5

1970s—Powerhouse

Universities, Champions,

and Change

The new rodeo training ground, college rodeo, produced subtle but positive changes in the 1970s in its own organization, which also affected professional rodeo. College administrators mellowed toward college rodeo programs as scholarships advanced them. Strong personalities along with a nationally known celebrity spread the well-kept secret of college rodeo; however, without a media person, college rodeo remained out of the mainstream of sports journalists. The second generation of college rodeo athletes built on their parents' NIRA experiences, honing a new standard of excellence in rodeo competition. University teams dominated the winning of championships while a hint of the importance of two-year schools was surfacing. College rodeo champions monopolized the collecting of professional gold. With a variety of degrees, cowboys and cowgirls filtered into many professions, spreading rodeo with some returning to coach college rodeo. The NIRA numbers grew as it refined its rules, and the production of the finals (named College National Finals Rodeo in 1971) rivaled the professional finals, but not without the dedicated efforts of many coaches and volunteers.

Colleges and universities started pursuing enrollment numbers, so adding a coed sport that did not have a cap on the number of competitors raised administrators' interest in funding college rodeo programs. Visionary administrators started to prepare for gender equalization in sports. For colleges and universities, rodeo could increase enrollment and add a federally mandated sport for women. College rodeo also benefited during this decade from the proliferation of two-year colleges. The two-year schools, in competition with the four-year schools, started awarding rodeo scholarships and hiring rodeo coaches instead of selecting a faculty adviser. Many two-year schools considered rodeo a sport, placed it in the athletics department, and funded it equally. Fueled by two-year schools, the quality of the competition and the number of contestants increased especially in the cowgirls' events.

Many school administrators recognized the advantages of hiring an experienced rodeo coach. With so many cowboys and cowgirls earning college degrees, some returned to coach rodeo programs, bringing recruiting and rodeo production experience. Having coaches with experience led to the proper care of the animals, satisfactory rodeo practice, and a network to contact recruits. With college administrators' support, coaches had adequate practice stock and support for the program. Satisfied graduates also recruited for the coaches, so rodeo programs grew.

College rodeo was changing, reflecting a positive direction for rodeo. The competition with its multiple events for men and women broadened the scope of rodeo. The regional rodeos and national finals provided opportunities for numerous cowboys and cowgirls and their families from the western states, many of the eastern ones, Canada, and Australia to meet. A network of rodeo families grew as the NIRA numbers grew, producing what some say is the best part, friends in almost every state. This college networking created strength, support, and a steady flow of new contestants for professional rodeo.

The NIRA itself matured with stability in the national office and with a permanent location for the national finals rodeo. The long-term part-time executive secretary (changed from secretary-manager) Sonny Sikes of Huntsville, Texas, with his wife Joanne Sikes, had brought stability, continuity, and credibility to the national office. With the finals crisscrossing the country during the first twenty years, it could not build an audience, provide constant volunteer help, or promote growth in its production. Articles about many of the finals rodeos, except for the first three years, mentioned mud and rain at many performances. So finding a permanent location with an indoor arena for the next twenty-six finals with only one hiatus gave college rodeo a margin of profit and an increase in production quality.

The NIRA directors accepted the 1970 bid of Bozeman, Montana, for the finals where it stayed until 1997 except for a 1979 trip to Lake Charles, Louisiana. The 1970 national student president Harlan Schott of the University of Nebraska said, "I was the 'Northern Kid' that kept our Board of Directors' meeting from adjourning until we had agreed to move the 'Finals' to a permanent indoor site (we were rained on at two or three 'Finals' I made, and I knew if the NIRA Finals were ever to be financially successful, we had to have a roof)."[1]

With the addition of three regions in the 1970s, the NIRA expanded. In 1970 under the direction of faculty president Melvin Griffeth from Ricks College, the board added Arkansas, Northern Mississippi, and Southern Missouri as the Ozark Region, the eighth region. In 1972 the NIRA added two more regions. The state of Montana, dropped from the Northwest Region, became the Big Sky Region. The new Central Plains Region included the states of Nebraska, Kansas, and the northern part of Oklahoma, including the panhandle of Oklahoma.

Some coaches added continuity and durability to the NIRA with their long tenure. Melvin Griffeth provided stability at Ricks College for twenty-nine years. He and his wife Rama maintained a policy of having the team travel together. By 1998 they traveled with two ten-horse trailers and a fifteen-passenger school van.

One coach had a significant effect on the NIRA. Walla Walla Community College in Washington added a rodeo program with Tim Corfield piloting the new varsity sport. WWCC became a top contender in the Northwest Region and nation, and Corfield became an integral part of the NIRA, ultimately becoming the NIRA commissioner. WWCC set the pace for a growing number of community colleges that established scholarship programs that attracted some of the top recruits in the nation.[2]

Lack of a salaried publicity director continued to inhibit publicity for the NIRA. Due to a heavy workload, Del Higham, part-time NIRA publicity director for several years, decided to resign his second job. The directors discussed the implications of losing Higham. The board wanted to continue the *Rodeo Collegian,* an annual magazine that Higham had initiated, designed, and published three times. The board commended Higham's excellent work and the quality of the *Rodeo Collegian.* The board decided to split Higham's job. D. K. Hewett, a former NIRA member, would publish the *Rodeo Collegian* and a monthly newspaper. The board voted to abolish the job of public relations director and hire a PR person for the finals.[3] The board also accepted Oklahoma City's Channel 9 proposal to televise the 1976 CNFR, but the sponsor later backed out.

The old media dilemma surfaced again in the fall of 1976. D. K. Hewett, editor and publisher of the *Rodeo Collegian,* lost his publication contract with the NIRA. Highlighting some problems with the NIRA, he said, "All it [NIRA] really gets done is sell membership cards, have a finals, crown champions, and get ready for the next year. Does it matter that in an organization with a gross income of nearly $150,000 per year, that there is no money budgeted for promotion and no specific plans for any?" He was concerned that no major sponsors were being recruited and that the NIRA was still an unknown college sport on the national scene. He continued, "Does it matter that most of the western equipment and apparel manufacturers know little or nothing about the NIRA, what it is or what it does?"[4]

A major advancement occurred when the College National Finals Rodeo joined the computer age in 1971. Student president Mack Abernathy from Sam Houston State and faculty president Bob Miller from Montana State University announced that a new rodeo results program was ready to be used at the finals. The idea for programming the computer to produce finals rodeo results came to Nick Shrauger, an MSU electrical engineer, as he watched the 1970 finals. The university had successfully used the computer to score cattle show judging, so Shrauger suggested that a rodeo results program could be created. Shrauger and MSU students Susan Temple and Dennis Smith talked with Bob Miller, MSU rodeo adviser, and Sandy Gagnon, MSU rodeo coach. They tried their new program at the 1971 MSU rodeo; then, with some revisions, they successfully used it at the 1971 finals. Instead of having to hand score three rounds and the average in nine events, the new program calculated the champions as soon as the results were entered. It also drew the stock and created publicity information.[5]

The electronic age came to barrel racing in 1971, and improvements were made in regional office personnel and procedures. At the 1971 winter board meeting, the directors voted to use electric-eye timers for barrel racing at the next finals. The Southwest Region had some accounting trouble with their regional rodeo secretary, so they hired an experienced rodeo secretary, Una Beutler of Elk City, Oklahoma, mother of stock contractor Bennie Beutler.[6] With faithfulness and expertise, Una served the Southwest Region for twenty years. When she retired, her daughter Dollie Riddle stepped in as regional secretary. Una's other daughter, Vickie Shireman, expanded the family tradition into the Great Plains Region. Having rodeo secretaries who were competent, knowledgeable, dependable, and honest strengthened the regions. With the stability brought by Una Beutler, her daughters, and other regional rodeo secretaries, rodeo reports became routine, and regional rules became more uniform.

The twenty-fifth year, a watershed year for the NIRA, saw the addition of a scholarship program. In December, 1974, the NIRA accepted the U.S. Tobacco Company's proposal to invest $74,000 in a scholarship program for the NIRA. Copenhagen/Skoal Scholarship Awards Program helped college rodeo grow like the GI Bill had helped increase the number of early-day cowboys who attended college. Jeff Stone and Red Springer of U.S. Tobacco presented the proposal that $60,000 be given to the regions with $500 to be awarded to each region's nine event winners, $1,000 to the men's team, and $500 to the women's team. At the finals, $1,000 would be awarded to each of the nine event winners and the women's team. The men's team would receive $2,000. Dr. H. L. Hutcheson, Great Plains faculty director, made the motion, and Gardner "Bud" Seaholm, Southern Region student director, seconded this historically significant motion, which passed unanimously. The proposal included providing Walt Garrison, former Dallas Cowboy football great and PRCA steer wrestler, to help advertise the college rodeos. This partnership gave the NIRA a financial shot-in-the-arm by helping struggling college rodeo programs provide scholarships to outstanding rodeo athletes. The first year forty-seven schools received scholarship money. Within twenty-five years and without opposition, U.S. Tobacco awarded $3 million in the name of NIRA champions to colleges and universities for rodeo athletes' tuition and books.

Walt Garrison, who joined U.S. Tobacco in 1974 after playing nine years as a running back for the Dallas Cowboys, was just the right man to promote the scholarship program and college rodeo. Garrison was "the company's first link with sports promotions, and it came about accidentally."[7] The year after the 1972 Super Bowl win by the Cowboys, an NFL film highlighted Garrison with two other football players who had unusual off-season activities. Garrison, who had started steer wrestling in high school, took a dip of snuff during the film clip. U.S. Tobacco called him to do a commercial, and Garrison eventually became a vice president of the company. Tom Pickett, from New Mexico and U.S. Tobacco's vice president for marketing, had been seeking a way to expand

NIRA Southwest Region rodeo secretary Una Beutler (right) *served twenty years, then her daughter Dollie Riddle* (standing) *took over. Her other daughter Vickie Shireman is the secretary for the Central Plains Region. Her son Bennie Beutler, a PRCA stock contractor, continues the family tradition with his company, Beutler and Son Rodeo Company. Photo by Sylvia G. Mahoney, Vernon, Texas.*

marketing into the sport of rodeo. Garrison was the perfect tie because of his dual involvement with the Cowboys and with rodeo. Garrison had belonged to the NIRA for two years while playing football at Oklahoma State University. The friendly, congenial Garrison became an immediate asset to college rodeo. Fans soon flocked to the CNFR to get Garrison's autograph. Garrison along with U.S. Tobacco's Red Springer logged thousands of miles promoting college rodeo by attending rodeos and giving interviews to newspapers and at radio and TV stations. Their efforts gave much needed exposure to the NIRA, still a relatively unknown college sport.[8]

NIRA alumni welcomed an announcement that an NIRA Hall of Fame, approved by the board, was to be established. In 1976 Sul Ross State University president Bob Richardson and Dr. Ernie Harman, SRSU Range Animal Science department head and rodeo coach, and David Moore, NIRA alumnus and president of Alpine's First National Bank, made a presentation to the NIRA board. The board gave official sanction to locate the NIRA Hall of Fame on the

Dallas Cowboy and PRCA steer wrestler Walt Garrison, with his wife Debbie, joined U.S. Tobacco and pioneered the NIRA scholarship program in 1974, which boosted college rodeo programs across the United States. Photo by Sylvia G. Mahoney, Vernon, Texas.

SRSU campus.[9] However, plans for the museum never materialized because Dr. Richardson and Dr. Harman both left the university, and the plans were left to gather dust. In the 1990s the NIRA Alumni (NIRAA) association with NIRA approval started an ongoing, unproductive nationwide search to find an established rodeo museum that wanted to add depth to its rodeo history by including the NIRA and college rodeo in its displays.

Unique NIRA awards reflected the influence of college rodeo on the professional direction that one of its cowboys took. When some of Bob Clore's friends received rodeo scholarships to Casper College, Clore, competing since age fourteen, said, "I was married and had two kids, and college was the last thing on my mind." However, Clore applied for and received a rodeo scholarship. The first year he took business administration classes and "an art class just to fulfill my humanities requirement. I found out I liked it." So Clore took a new career direction, graduating from the University of Northern Colorado with a master's degree in sculpture and painting and from the University of Kansas with a master of fine arts. After joining the art faculty at Kansas State, Clore agreed to be the rodeo adviser for the K-State Rodeo Club and was elected Central Plains Region faculty director, serving as the 1975–76 national faculty president. Clore found that over half of the clubs were going to rodeos sponsored by another organization, Central Plains Rodeo Association (CPRA). Clore and the K-State Club president set out to convert the CPRA to NIRA membership and form a new region. In 1972 the Central Plains Region was formed, and the renegade rodeo hands returned to the original herd.[10]

While serving on the national board, K-State art instructor and rodeo coach Bob Clore designed a new type of rodeo award, which led to his successful business, BCR Awards. He created a popular design for the NIRA that was cast in a plastic resin and covered with a bonded bronze finish.[11] After Clore's success with the NIRA, many other rodeo associations commissioned him. Clore became a charter member of the 1992 NIRA Alumni Board of Directors and a generous donor to its scholarship fund. As Alumni Director of Honors/Awards, Clore designed some new awards exclusively to honor former NIRA champions at the alumni reunions. Clore's humorous presentations at the reunions became annual crowd pleasers.

Personalities from CNFR productions became trademark names in the profession. Don Harrington, a former member of the University of Montana rodeo team who earned a degree in business administration, moved from the professional rodeo circuit to the mike at the CNFR at Bozeman. In fact, in 1972 Harrington announced the NFR and the National High School Finals Rodeo as well. After becoming president of Harrington's Pepsi Cola Bottling Company in Montana, Harrington remained close to rodeo, especially college rodeo, by becoming a sponsor.[12]

CNFR secretary Ellen Backstrom of Wickenburg, Arizona, who became as much a part of the finals as Bozeman, had the respect and admiration of all the contestants. Ellen's fan club of NIRA cowboys and cowgirls appreciated her rodeo expertise and her love for the rodeo family. She ably served until her health would no longer permit, then her daughter Sunni Deb Backstrom took over. Both earned the respect of the cowboys, judges, and stock contractors for their knowledge of the drawing of stock, the accuracy of keeping the finals records, and their ability to deal with the contestants fairly. Along with her rodeo expertise, Sunni Deb managed to find time to get the last laugh when the cowboys pulled a joke on her, a frequent occurrence.

Stock contractor Harry Vold with his years of experience brought a new level of professionalism to the CNFR. He became a familiar sight at the CNFR riding his trademark black horse, moving with the authority and dignity of one of his Brahma bulls. In the presence of a lady, Vold's hat comes off faster than a breakaway roper throws her loop. His manners and his knowledge of rodeo stock were as much a trademark as his matched black saddle horses and his world-class stock used during rodeo performances. Vold's rodeo stock expertise extended beyond the arena into a successful breeding program to raise them to buck. One bull Vold raised, Old Crooked Nose, garnered his own poster and fans. Canadian-born Vold started contracting stock to rodeos before the era of trucking, so he trailed them to and from Canadian rodeos. Later, he trucked them from his ranch near Fowler, Colorado, to all the major rodeos in the United States and Canada. Many of Vold's animals are champions as famous as the world-class cowboys they have helped to make. Cowboys roll their eyes when remembering their rides on Vold's bareback horses, such as Necklace and Smokey, and bull #33, and saddle bronc Rusty. Vold's stock brought the CNFR to the same level of competition as at the NFR.

The NIRA suffered the loss of a man in 1974 whose contributions continued to benefit contestants long after his name had passed into history. Robert N. Miller, who served in many capacities with college rodeo, had competed in the first collegiate rodeo at Montana State on May 24, 1947. After coaching rodeo at Cal Poly at San Luis Obispo, he returned to Montana State to teach and become the rodeo adviser. During Miller's many years on the NIRA board, he served as national faculty president and CNFR adviser. NIRA public relations director Del Higham said, "Although many people were involved in a national finals production, credit for the overall management must go to Bob Miller." In 1974 at age fifty-one, Miller died following complications resulting from a fall from a horse at his ranch. The NIRA dedicated the twenty-fifth anniversary issue of the official magazine the *Rodeo Collegian* to Miller and awarded two scholarships in his name, a two hundred dollar scholarship and a fifty dollar trophy, to the cowgirl and cowboy Rookies of the Year.[13]

Even with the growth and maturity of the NIRA, several controversial issues with team roping and the role of women continued unresolved. The 1975 board considered a proposal to let team ropers enter twice with different partners from the same school and to let women enter the team roping. Several objections were raised, such as the cost of changing the computer program to allow women to compete. In the past when one event was added another was dropped, so some suggested that allowing women to rope would take away some of the men's points. However, new federal regulations required gender equity between men's and women's sports. A committee reviewed the options. In 1975 the board approved a proposal by NIRA women's director Terri Reed to allow women to enter the team roping. Team ropers could enter twice in the region but only once at the CNFR. The board elected Dolly Hughes to be the Miss College Rodeo adviser, CNFR women's events supervisor, and CNFR goat contractor.[14]

Team roping had some other weak areas. Team ropers shared points, so they could win only half as many as the other events; however, some regions had only a few consistent ropers, so those ropers could accumulate an unbeatable lead. This became a much-debated issue for years without a satisfactory solution. Wayne Smith of Arkansas State University at Beebe crossed the Mississippi River headed east for the first time with a team roping championship, and he did it without competing at the 1976 CNFR. His lead, points earned at the regional rodeos, could not be beaten with finals points. The 1976 winter board members named second place Jack Pearce of Brigham Young University as co-champion and authorized a trophy saddle to be made for him. The board asked the Rules Committee to consider requiring anyone competing for a national title to compete at the CNFR unless physically unable to attend.[15]

Management, CNFR location, scholarships, and finances continued to be issues. In 1975, the board approved Sandy Gagnon, Montana State rodeo coach, as the CNFR adviser and gave Montana State a three-year option on the CNFR, which stretched into twenty-six years except for one hiatus in 1979. Gagnon had competed for MSU, earned his master of science degree in animal physiology from MSU, joined the faculty, and become the rodeo coach under Bob Miller. Bozeman had enthusiastically welcomed the college cowgirls and cowboys to the 1970 CNFR, establishing a long-term, strong relationship with the NIRA that benefited both groups. U.S. Tobacco Copenhagen/Skoal announced that they would raise their scholarship money to $100,000. However, when Miss College Rodeo 1975 Cathy Tvedt asked for increased support to include more travel to promote the NIRA, the minutes showed no response.[16]

The NIRA board struggled with financial shortfall problems and with shared CNFR responsibilities. In the review of the annual budget for the fiscal year that ended July 31, 1976, the total cash receipts were $163,797. Of this amount, $128,578 represented individual dues. The major expenses were $71,488 for insurance, $14,365 for the *Rodeo Collegian,* $11,982 for computer services, and $14,040 for salaries of the executive secretary, office manager, and office secretary. Although $2,600 in the red at year's end, the NIRA paid $4,000 to Montana State University to help defray their 1976 CNFR deficit.[17]

College and professional rodeos had common problems, such as having adequate, uniform stock, maintaining consistent judging standards, and encouraging well run, properly promoted rodeos. With 2,781 NIRA members from 152 member schools in 1975, the quality of the contestants demanded the best stock available for fair competition at the CNFR. Student president Gardner "Bud" Seaholm said this issue caused the board members to lock horns because they were not satisfied with the quality and uniformity of the stock. The board selected stock contractor Sonny Linger of Miles City, Montana, to put together stock from four rodeo stock contractors to even up the draw. He supplemented his pens with bucking stock from Brookman Rodeo Company, the Flying Five Rodeo Company, and the Bud Kramer Rodeo Company.[18]

After Wrangler started sponsoring professional rodeo judging seminars, the quality of college judging improved. However, judges trained for PRCA rodeo events often lacked experience in judging goat tying and breakaway roping. To correct the unequal judging experiences, the NIRA conducted a judging seminar at the 1975 finals conducted by Marvin Joyce and Larry Jordan, representatives of the Professional Rodeo Cowboys Association.[19]

Changes rattled the stability of the NIRA on its thirtieth anniversary in 1979. Longtime executive secretary Sonny Sikes shook the organization when he announced that he and Joanne had decided to retire from their NIRA positions. Sonny Sikes said, "We will stay in our present positions until the end of this fiscal year—July 31, 1979, which will give you six months, if necessary, to replace us and make the change." The board approved the Lake Charles Jaycees Rodeo Association's proposal to move the 1979 CNFR to Louisiana, another unsettling change. After nineteen years of leadership from the Sikeses and nine years of methodically returning to Bozeman, Montana, for the CNFR, all of that changed.[20]

Although the NIRA executive secretary's job was available, Walla Walla coach Tim Corfield had too many things on his mind to think about seeking the position. Being the 1979 NIRA faculty president included oversight of the CNFR's move to a new location. With his national board responsibilities, his coaching duties, his teaching assignments at Walla Walla Community College, and his family responsibilities with a wife and two daughters, Corfield had not stopped to consider the job until his path crossed the path of Coach Pat Hamilton of Sheridan College in an airport on the way to Lake Charles. Mrs. Hamilton, whose years on the board gave her insight into the politics of the organization, stopped Corfield and suggested to him that he had the personal qualities, rodeo knowledge, and management skills that were needed for the executive secretary's position. From that point on, the process was in motion, and Mrs. Hamilton was determined to see her plan succeed.[21]

Coach Pat Hamilton influenced the NIRA with her wisdom and her dry humor. Her touch was subtle, but recognizable. Coach Hamilton would stand on the sideline watching and analyzing before she would go to work quietly behind the scenes for the good of the NIRA. Although polite to strangers, she kept her distance until she gained insight. Once she dropped a wry bit of humor in a newcomer's presence, that person knew that Mrs. Hamilton had given her stamp of approval. Coach Hamilton, the only woman coach in the nation for several years, was accepted as an equal because she did an equal or better job. Due to her energy, enthusiasm, and rodeo knowledge, Mrs. Hamilton guided the Sheridan College rodeo program to a level of success that resulted in champions, such as the 1969 champion bareback rider and country singer Chris LeDoux and 1971 bull riding champion Wally Badgett, a 1974 NFR qualifier, a deputy sheriff, Montana rancher, and noted cowboy cartoonist. Badgett created *Ranchin' with Earl,* which has been exhibited at the National Cowboy Hall of Fame. Mrs. Hamilton, an instructor of anthropology, archaeology, geology, and Spanish, lived on the Triangle A Ranch with her husband and son. Ranch born and raised, she knew her business. As coach, Central Rocky Mountain Region faculty director, and national board member, Coach Hamilton left a legacy of cultivating quality in her students and giving wise direction to the NIRA.[22]

Returning to Walla Walla after the CNFR in Louisiana in June, 1979, the newly elected secretary-manager Tim Corfield had a major job of logistics. The NIRA records that had been in Huntsville, Texas, for nineteen years had to be moved to Walla Walla, Washington, and the office in operation before students returned for the fall semester. Before that, personnel had to be hired, a place for an office had to be found, and set up. Corfield said, "Just getting ready for the coming year would consume most of our time, but we've also got to get printing done with the new location and inform everyone and do everything else that goes with the change." While settling in, Corfield was mentally working on plans for the NIRA, especially plans to seek corporate sponsors. He knew the effect of U.S. Tobacco and Copenhagen/Skoal Scholarship Awards Program on the NIRA. He said, "They were our first and largest contributor of scholarships. Equally important has been the work they do—the staff they have hired and send out all over the United States—to help promote individual rodeos."[23]

With all the organizational efforts in the NIRA, the competition in the area was still the focus of the NIRA. The 1970s proliferated with NIRA champions who became ProRodeo legends. One legend, Tom Ferguson, exhibited his potential when his team, Cal Poly at San Luis Obispo, won the 1970 championship, and he won the ribbon roping title, the first of three NIRA titles. In 1973 Ferguson added calf roping and steer wrestling buckles. He set PRCA records by winning nine world titles and two PRCA championships. Ferguson's record six professional consecutive all-around championships between 1974 and 1979 stood until 1998 when another NIRA champion, Ty Murray, added his seventh all-around title. Ferguson also led the professionals across the one-million-dollar line in rodeo earnings. In 1999 at the ProRodeo Hall of Fame induction ceremony, Ferguson thanked four people for helping him succeed. Three were NIRA alumni: stock contractor Cotton Rosser, timed-event cowboy Jack Roddy, and calf roper Roy Cooper.

The competition for championships in the 1970s pushed the limits with almost equally matched athletes, who made professional rodeo history. The 1970 all-around and bull riding competitors went to the wire. Black Hills State College's Tom Miller won the all-around championship in a close race with Cal Poly's Tom Ferguson, and Melvin Dick, the reserve all-around, bareback, and saddle bronc champ. Miller, who returned in 1971 to win his second all-around championship, qualified for the NFR many times in saddle bronc riding, winning the 1975 and 1979 reserve world championships. University of Southern Colorado bull rider Doug Wilson finished first with 468 and a half points. Only fifty-six points separated the top four riders. Leander Frey of McNeese State had 457 and a half, and Jim Jacobsen of Montana State and Jack Ward of Sul Ross State both had 412 and a half.

The 1970s were an era of team championships for universities, multiple championships in fact. Three university teams won more titles in the 1970s than in any other decade. In 1970 Cal Poly won one team and four event titles.

Tom Ferguson won the 1973 NIRA steer wrestling and calf roping championships after winning the ribbon roping in 1970. He won nine world championships and two PRCA championships. Photo by James Fain, Logan, Utah.

In 1972 Montana State followed suit with an equal number. Sam Houston State University rounded out the powerhouse teams of the decade with five in 1974. Previously, SHSU had won a record six event titles in 1955, and Sul Ross State set an unmatched record of two team and four event titles in 1962.

As fast as the college champs put on their gold buckles, they were adding professional gold to their collection. The 1972 all-around winner Dave Brock, who had transferred to the University of Southern Colorado to compete for national faculty president, Coach Larry Thomas, placed second in ribbon roping, third in calf roping, and fourth in steer wrestling, leading his team to a second place finish in the nation. He repeated the all-around win in 1973 and took the ribbon roping for a second time after winning it in 1971 while at Casper College. He added a professional calf roping title in 1978.

With 2,286 NIRA members in 1973, qualifying for the finals became more challenging. To qualify, a cowboy or cowgirl or a team had to finish in the top two in one of the ten regions. For event championships, contestants brought points from their five best rodeos, but teams started with a clean slate. Two schools locked horns at the 1973 finals. Cal Poly was still chaffing over Montana State's win in 1972, which kept Cal Poly from adding its third consecutive championship. Longtime Cal Poly coach Bill Gibford, the 1970 national faculty president, and his team collected its third team championship in four years.

Ribbon roping had its swan song at the 1974 CNFR, and a new university challenged the perennial champions. University of Southern Colorado's Mike McLaughlin, son of five-time world champion calf roper Don McLaughlin, won the last NIRA ribbon roping championship. Eastern New Mexico University won its second team championship with Coach Mick Trujillo's team members later competing in the professional ranks: Gary Good, Tutt Garnett, Mike Retz, Alan Hennigh, Bobby Campbell, and James Ward, the number two bull rider.

Bull riding and bankers typically are not synonymous, but in 1974 they fit, showing the career expansion of college rodeo cowboys. Butch Bratsky of Montana State University proved his brawn with the bull riding championship and his brains by becoming a banker in Billings, Montana. A rodeo friend said about Bratsky: "We went on to ride bulls, and now we have to borrow money from Bratsky's bank. Who was the smartest?"[24]

Events still fluctuated. The NIRA sanctioned team roping again in 1975. Dawson College's Bill Parker and Phil Luman, whose brother Ken Luman was the 1966 world team roping champion, won the team roping title. Team roping had been a professional rodeo event at least since the record of world champions was started in 1929. However, at the first NIRA rodeos, team roping was an option. Often, wild cow milking or ribbon roping won out at the regional rodeos. In the 1950s five team roping titles were awarded with the last one in 1957.

The growing influence of college rodeo on the professional ranks was never more evident than at the 1975 CNFR. Four of the NIRA champions won world championships, and several others qualified for the NFR. The percentage of professional cowboys and cowgirls from the college ranks increased each year. After one year, some competed professional full-time competition, but many others earned college degrees. Montana State's Bud Munroe, the 1975 NIRA saddle bronc champion, won the 1986 world saddle bronc championship. Cisco Junior College's Roy Cooper, the 1975 NIRA calf roping champion, won eight professional world championships and crossed the two-million-dollar-career earning mark first.

The 1975 NFR showcased the quality of college competition as many qualified for the NFR while still in college or immediately after finishing. Twenty-two former NIRA members competed at the 1975 NFR. Jimmie Gibbs Munroe (1974 NIRA champion all-around and 1974–75 barrel racer), Colette Graves Baier (1973 NIRA barrel racing champ), and Kay Proctor competed in barrel racing. Seven of the fifteen NFR bull riders were former NIRA bull riders: Randy Magers, Jerome Robinson, Don Graham, Bobby Berger (1967 NIRA bull riding champ), Leander Frey, A. J. Swain, and Charlie Underwood. Tom Ferguson (1970 NIRA ribbon roping and 1973 calf roping and steer wrestling champ) and his brother Larry competed in the calf roping. Three former NIRA steer wrestlers qualified for the NFR: Bob Christopherson (1970 NIRA steer wrestling champ), Fred Larsen, and Frank Shepperson (1964 NIRA steer wrestling champ). The two NIRA team ropers at the NFR were Paul Hughes and Merrill Bond. NIRA saddle bronc cowboys competing were Tom Miller (1970–71 NIRA all-around champ) and Bobby Berger, his second NFR event. Bareback riding had four: Joe Alexander (1966 NIRA bareback riding champ), Jack Ward, J. C. Trujillo (1968 NIRA bareback champ), and Ben Calhoun.

The 1975 NIRA calf roping champion Roy Cooper, who won six calf roping world championships, joined an elite group of roping legends (left to right) Dean Oliver, eight world championships; Don McLaughlin, five world championships; and Toots Mansfield, seven world championships. Photo by Sylvia G. Mahoney, Vernon, Texas.

Second in the region qualifies a team for the finals, and sometimes it is all they need. Both team champions in 1975 were reserve regional champions. Since all teams started with zero points, they took advantage of the level playing field. Helping Montana State's team qualify for the CNFR and win the championship were Butch Bratsky, the defending bull riding champ, Grant Dunning, Kirk Webb, Kent Mosher, Jim Solberg, and Bud Munroe, the 1975 saddle bronc champ.[25]

Firsts crowded the NIRA records during the 1970s. Lamar College's Paul Hughes, the 1975 NIRA steer wrestling champ and many times NFR qualifier, made history when he was featured for a publicity exhibition in a matched steer wrestling with Walt Garrison at the CNFR. Garrison was injured in the match, so the matched publicity exhibitions were discontinued. Skip Emmett of the University of Tennessee at Martin won the 1975 all-around and the bareback riding championships, the first for a school east of the Mississippi.

College rodeo started in 1968 at the University of Tennessee at Martin. Dr. Niels W. Robinson, known as Doc Robby, agreed to sponsor the UTM rodeo team at the request of several students. With the "administration opposed to such dangerous activities due to liability in the event of an accident," Dr. Robinson and his group had an uphill struggle because "they had no money, no practice facilities, little support from the rest of the students, no real rodeo experience, and nowhere to hold a rodeo." Hard work brought solutions to these problems and success along with other all-around champions, such as Tony Coleman and George Mesimer. In January, 1994, Dr. Robinson died, and UTM honored him for his years of hard work promoting the rodeo program by naming the arena in the West Tennessee Agricultural Pavilion for him and inducting him into the UTM Rodeo Hall of Fame.[26]

The fourth year, Tony Coleman heard his name called for all-around champion. Coleman of the University of Tennessee at Martin won the 1977 all-around title only a few weeks after being awarded his bachelor's degree in animal science. He said, "Rodeo is the reason I've got a college education today." In 1978 Coleman returned to the university as rodeo coach. Coleman and his wife Mimi let the rodeo team use their farm and facilities for rodeo practice. Coleman became faculty director of Ozark Region and served on the NIRA board.

Names of members of the champion 1976 Southeastern Oklahoma State University team looked like a rodeo history book. In 1976 James D. Ward won SEOSU's first two titles—all-around and bareback riding. SEOSU's line-up included familiar names such as Roy Cooper, Billy Teague, Steve Bland, Jerry Beagley, and Tom "Buster" Record. Cooper's father, Tuffy, like Teague's father, Bill, earned places in NIRA history in the 1950s. Tuffy was a calf roping champion, and Bill Teague, 1954 national student president. Steve Bland's mother, Rosemary Beck Bland, started the tradition of college competition for her family at Texas Tech. So the SEOSU team was new, but the team members' rodeo bloodlines and experience ran deep. That same year, the son of a world champion calf roper, Mike McLaughlin of the University of Southern Colorado roped his way to a two-hundred-point lead in the calf roping.

The quality of the 1977 CNFR contestants showed the effects of the keen competition with three thosand members competing in the regions. SEOSU lost James Ward to a rodeo injury the week before the finals, but the five-man team won their second consecutive men's team championship. Jerry Beagley's eighty-two-point ride on Black Satin in the final round led to the bull riding buckle and helped his team win the championship. Beagley, the 1974 bareback riding champion from Medicine Lodge, Kansas, had earned his business degree and his private pilot license and was ready to make the professional circuit full-time. Four other SEOSU cowboys picked up points by placing second in the final go: Steve Bland in calf roping, Rick Bradley in steer wrestling, and Bill Teague and Buster Record in team roping. Defending calf roping champ Roy Cooper rounded out the team.[27]

The quality of college competition in 1977 resulted in only a few points separating first and second place even though some learned their event in college. Cal Poly's Chris Lybbert, the 1982 professional all-around and 1986 calf roping champ, won the calf roping just seconds ahead of second place Steve Bland and third place Roy Cooper, both from SEOSU. Steer wrestling champion Tarleton State's Steve Fryar learned his event while in college from a good teacher, Johnny Hampton of Stephenville. Fryar, also doing some cotton farming in his hometown of Big Spring, Texas, downed three steers in 21.65 seconds to win the championship his senior year.[28]

Sometimes it takes a wild card to make a champion. The 1977 team roping champion Thomas R. Maycumber of Washington State University got what he called a wild card. Maycumber had gone home empty-handed for three years, and the fourth year, he did not even qualify. He was not even in the top ten. But Jeff Knowles of Walla Walla Community College took him as his team roping partner to the finals. After the second round, they were leading by two seconds, but Bill Teague and Tommy Record of SEOSU stretched their steer in 12.41 seconds. Maycumber said, "We had to be 14 (seconds) or faster to win. We ended up with 12.5."[29]

Two-year-school contestants challenged the university contestants. Howard College's Jack Himes of Beulah, Colorado, the 1975 NIRA bull rider, Rookie of the Year, and HC's first national champion, added the 1977 bareback in spite of his thirteen broken bones with eleven of them in bareback riding.[30] Western Texas College's Joann Whitehead of Morton, Texas, had almost stayed at home. She said, "I was down about 16th in the standings, and it was so far up to Bozeman. But my daddy said, 'You earned it, and you're going.'" Whitehead had the fastest barrel run at the 1977 CNFR, won the three-run average, and the title.[31]

Many schools recognized the new rodeo program at SEOSU as a threat when it won its third consecutive men's team title in 1978. Even with the 1978 event champions on their teams, such as Joe Parsons, the 1978 calf roping champion from the University of Arizona, Samuel Edmondson, the 1978 steer wrestling champion from California State at Fresno, Hank Franzen, the 1978 all-around and bull riding champion from Casper College, David J. Griffith, the 1978 saddle bronc champion from Montana State University, and Jay Himes, the 1978 bareback champion from the University of Southern Colorado, the schools felt the effect of the rodeo experience and recruiting ability of SEOSU coach Betty Gayle Cooper Ratliff. One of her recruits, Olie Smith of the Del Rio, Texas, Smith and Altizer roping families, won the 1978 team roping title with teammate Tee Woolman, the 1980 and 1982 world champion team roper, taking second.

As the decade came to a close, the top-four list looked like a history book of rodeo legends. In 1979 cowboys finishing in the top four in various events— Brad Gjermundson, Jess Knight, Hank Franzen, John R. Davis, John W. Jones, Jade Robinson, and the 1979 steer wrestling champ Lance Robinson—would dominate events in the professional ranks. Blue Mountain's Mike Beers, the 1979 NIRA team roping champion, won the 1984 professional world championship. The calf roping champion Walla Walla's Dave P. Smith made it a good year for his coach Tim Corfield by winning WWCC's second championship. However, Smith's potential was not realized as his career ended on July 2, 1990, when he and three other cowboys headed to the Ponoka Stampede finals in Alberta, Canada, died in a plane crash on Mount Rainier in Washington state.

By the end of the decade, more champions were choosing rodeo rather than being born into it. That was true of the 1979 all-around champion Joe Peabody of State Fair Community College, Sedalia, Missouri. His parents did not rodeo, but they did farm near the University of Wisconsin where a few NIRA cowboys came to tie calves and dog steers. Peabody tried all the events at high school rodeos. He said, "In the steer wrestling, I had read an article in the *Western Horseman* magazine on how to get down on a steer. I did that beautifully, with no problems. However, the article was to be continued the following month so when it came to shaping and throwing the steer I had problems." Peabody's points were short the first three years of college. He said that "he attributes that to the quality of the competition." Peabody's fourth and last year proved that "champions are made, not born."[32]

Cowgirls reached a new level of expertise in the 1970s. A soon-to-be famous rodeo professional, a Cal Poly cowgirl, Sharon Meffan Camarillo, won the goat tying title, the fifth for Cal Poly in 1970. Rodeo also provided Sharon an outlet for her talents. She created a rodeo clothing line and became a nationally known rodeo television commentator.

Some 1970s champions later produced second-generation NIRA contestants. Eastern New Mexico University cowgirl Linda Blackburn Sultemeier won the reserve championship in breakaway roping and goat tying giving her the 1970 all-around saddle, one used later by her three girls, Christi, Kelli, and Ashley. Utah State's Saundra Curlock Sorensen beat Sultemeier by twenty-two points in the breakaway roping. In 1999 Sorensen watched her daughter Stacie Sorensen win the breakaway roping for the University of Nevada at Las Vegas.

Some 1970s cowgirls set records that still stand, such as consecutive team championships. Tarleton State's women's team won championships in 1969, 1970, and 1971. Although TSU had produced intercollegiate rodeos prior to the organization of the NIRA, it did not join the NIRA until 1965. The 1967 TSU men's team won its first and only men's team championship. Four TSU cowgirls won championships in three years along with the three team championships. In 1969 Angie Watts Averhoff won the goat tying, and Sally Preston, the breakaway roping. In 1970 Connie Wilkinson Wood won the barrel race. In 1971 Martha Tompkins added another barrel racing title, the last TSU woman's championship for twenty-eight years. In 1999 Watts Averhoff made the college circuit again, but this time as a spectator mother.

In the 1970s winning contestants came from states that had not produced champions in the past. A Missouri cowgirl won two championships, a first for her state. In 1971 Jan Wagner of Missouri State won the breakaway roping and all-around by placing second in the barrel race.

Women's team competition accelerated during the 1970s. Eastern New Mexico University broke TSU's three-year winning streak in 1972. ENMU coach Sally Pate, a staff accountant, had taken the coaching position when Bill Britton, the adviser, left in 1970. The power behind the ENMU championship was Kathy Richter, Martha Wright, and Betty Gayle Cooper Ratliff, who, using the famous Cooper loop, won the breakaway roping championship.

The Cooper-roping dynasty defined itself in the NIRA in the 1950s and 1970s. Betty Gayle Cooper Ratliff, one of three Cooper NIRA champions, was the first child of an NIRA champion to win a championship. She won the 1972 NIRA breakaway roping championship twenty-two years after her father Tuffy Cooper, a 1998 National Cowboy Hall of Fame honoree, won the 1950 NIRA calf roping championship. Her parents, Tuffy and Betty Rose Hadley Cooper, were one of the first couples of a growing number who met while competing at a college rodeo, got married, and raised kids who grew up and competed in college rodeo. Betty Rose's brother Tom Hadley won the first NIRA steer wrestling championship in 1949. Exactly twenty-five years after Tuffy won his title, his son Roy Cooper won the same title, 1975 NIRA calf roping champion.

The Coopers set the standard for adding professional gold to college gold. Betty Gayle won nine professional world championships before she lost her battle with cancer in 1999. Roy won eight professional world championships and two PRCA championships. In 1983 Roy, the Super Looper, won the triple crown in the professional ranks: all-around, calf roping, and steer roping. In 2000, Roy was the first professional cowboy to cross the two million dollar mark in career earnings. Betty Gayle is an honoree of the National Cowgirl Hall of Fame, and Roy, an honoree of the ProRodeo Hall of Fame. All three Coopers are honorees in the Lea County Cowboy Hall of Fame at Hobbs, New Mexico. Their brother Clay competed at the CNFR and the NFR.

Besides Betty Gayle Cooper Ratliff's gold buckles, she exemplifies the career college rodeo coach. B.G. started coaching at Southeastern Oklahoma State University at Durant, Oklahoma in 1976. Her teams won sixteen event and nine team championships for SEOSU, tying the team record of wins. However, SEOSU won all four women's and five men's team championships under B.G.'s tenure, a record of team championships for one coach.

The 1972 NIRA breakaway roping champion Betty Gayle Cooper Ratliff shows her roping style that helped the ENMU women take the 1972 team championship and enabled her to win eight world titles. Photo by James Fain, Logan, Utah.

In the mid-1970s, a school and a cowgirl made an indelible mark on the NIRA. In 1974 Jimmie Gibbs Munroe riding Billy won the barrel race and the all-around titles, and Cindy Galow, the breakaway roping and reserve all-around, helping Sam Houston State University win the women's team championship. Gibbs Munroe added her third NIRA title, 1975 barrel racing champion. Coach Sonny Sikes now could count four women's team championships.

While competing at the CNFR in the 1970s, a northern cowboy met a southern cowgirl and experienced one of the benefits of the NIRA. They married in 1980. Bud and Jimmie Gibbs Munroe ranch at Valley Mills, Texas, with their daughter Tassie Oline. They personify an often-repeated pattern of college cowboys and cowgirls. Bud was born into a Montana rodeo family. His father Dan, his mother Roberta, and his sister Butch Bonine all competed in rodeo. Bud won the 1975 saddle bronc championship for Montana State. Jimmie's rodeo roots ran deep, also. Jimmie, the granddaughter of Colonel Zack Miller of the famous 101 Ranch and Wild West Show, was raised on horseback competing in junior and high school rodeos. She went to Sam Houston State on a

Sam Houston State's Jimmie Gibbs Munroe won two 1974 NIRA championships, the all-around and barrel racing, and the 1975 barrel racing title, also. She won three world championships and two WPRA regular season championships. Photo by James Fain, Logan, Utah.

rodeo scholarship and served for two years as girls' director on the NIRA board. Bud also served on the national board as the Big Sky Region student director.

The Munroes became legends in professional rodeo. Jimmie, who qualified for the NFR eleven times, won three Women's Professional Rodeo Association (WPRA) world championships. In 1975 she won the barrel racing, tie-down calf roping, and all-around. In 1976 and 1977, Jimmie, a 1992 National Cowgirl Hall of Fame honoree, won the regular season barrel racing championships. Under Jimmie's able leadership as WPRA president from 1978 to 1993, the WPRA grew and improved its image. Bud wore the 1986 world saddle bronc buckle. Bud's sister Butch married J. C. Bonine, the 1968 and 1969 NIRA saddle bronc champion and 1977 world saddle bronc champion.[33]

When a life is cut short, and the talent was extreme, pondering the potential results after the fact. Jennifer Haynes, multi-talented Albuquerque, New Mexico, cowgirl, helped win the 1975 and 1976 team championships for NMSU with Kathy Summers and Debbie Phillips. NMSU claimed fifteen event championships, but no team titles. Haynes, the 1975 NIRA triple-crown winner (all-around, breakaway roping, and goat tying), won six professional world championships. By the year 2003, only two other women had exceeded Haynes's NIRA record of four national titles. Only one other cowgirl had won three events in one year and that happened twenty-five years later, in 1998. With Haynes's four NIRA championships and six professional world championships won in five years between 1975 and 1979, she ranks among the few to win so much in such a brief time. However, Haynes did not live long enough to see her potential fully realized.

By the bicentennial year, cowgirls' competition rivaled the cowboys. Not contented to stay in the background, the cowgirls now called themselves women, not girls. The men shared the spotlight with the cowgirls as their numbers and skills increased. No longer did people go to the concession stand during the women's events. As the women's events became more competitive, being called "nanny whammers" and "can chasers" subsided. They trained right along with the cowboys, perfecting their skills, while riding horses trained for their events. They had parents who trained them or sent them to rodeo event schools. They started team roping with the men in 1977. However, another ten years passed before a woman won the CNFR team roping average, and another twenty years before a woman won the reserve national champion team roper. A champion is yet to happen. It was not long, however, before cowboys started complimenting some cowgirls with the statement, "She ropes

The 1975 NIRA all-around, breakaway roping, and goat tying champion Jennifer Haynes of New Mexico State, won the goat tying again in 1976. She won six professional championships. Photo by James Fain, Logan, Utah.

like a man." College rodeo competition with five standard events for men, three standard events for women, and one coed event promoted gender equity.

Title IX of the Equal Opportunities Act played a role in fielding women's rodeo teams. When SEOSU won the 1976 men's team championship, everyone started asking, "Where did that school come from?" By 1996, it had won ten women's events and four women's team titles. In the fall of 1975, SEOSU president Dr. Leon Hibbs started the rodeo program to complement the nine-year-old horsemanship program and to meet the Title IX mandate. Hibbs, who saw the advantage of adding a coed sport, said, "Title IX of the Equal Opportunities Act pretty well outlines that we need to have females involved in competition." Dr. Hibbs also hired a woman rodeo coach.[34]

Cowgirl competition reached a new level. New Mexico cowgirls from two universities won all the 1976 championships. ENMU's Chris Helker won the barrel race, and NMSU cowgirls won the other three and the team title. Jennifer Haynes won the goat tying, and Janet Stover Crowson, the all-around and breakaway roping. Twenty-five years earlier in 1951, Janet's father, F. C. Stover, had won the NIRA calf roping championship for NMSU. Janet went on to win the world title after qualifying numerous times.

Endurance is a factor in the pursuit of championships. The 1977 all-around cowgirl took four years to achieve her goal. Shelly Haskins Mueller wondered as she left the University of Wisconsin at River Falls if her fourth and final trip to the CNFR would be any different from the other three when she had gone in leading the all-around and left empty-handed. Mrs. Mueller did not count on winning. However, she said, "Everything went my way for once." Mrs. Mueller had quite a workload as well as having many miles to travel. She was serving an internship in a canning factory laboratory so that she could finish her bachelor's degree in food science. She and her husband John had bought a farm near River Falls and were raising beef cattle and horses, so they kept some calves and steers to practice. Her 1977 all-around championship plaque hangs alone on the University of Wisconsin's wall of honor.[35]

Sometimes longevity and luck combine with ability, skills, and a positive attitude to make champions. The 1977 champion Utah State ladies packed the power and the experience with the 1972 all-around champion Linda Miller Munns along with Vicky Leavitt and Cindy Coombs Lulloft on the team. They won Utah State's only NIRA team championship. Coombs Lulloft tied three goats in 29.02 seconds to win the title. The breakaway champion Sherre J.

Stoddard of Brigham Young University, who won with 9.97 seconds on three, represented the new cowgirl athlete. She said that the keys to winning were controlling your mind and daily practice sessions.[36]

In spite of the universities, a two-year school caught the winning spirit. Central Arizona College led by a skilled, athletic cowgirl Barrie Beach Smith, won the 1978 team title and added another the next year. Only ten two-year schools have won the challenge with four-year schools for a national team championship, and only one, CAC, has two women's team championships. Beach Smith's goat tying skills perpetuated the belief, helped by University of Arizona's Wendy Bryan, the 1972 and 1973 champ, that Arizona goat tiers are hard to beat. Arizona State's Pam Simon Sproul advanced the belief in 1974 with her title. With the goat tying title, Beach Smith became the 1978 all-around champion and Rookie of the Year.

NIRA cowboys and cowgirls had to prepare in a different way to head south to Lake Charles, Louisiana, for the 1979 College National Finals Rodeo from previous years when the finals were held in Montana. Veterinarian Dr. Sam Monticello explained how to "help insure that your horse maintains a good state of health during the performances" because of the "great variation in temperature and humidity." Competitors who had competed at the finals in Montana had to rethink their plans for the warmer, humid climate.[37]

The CNFR traveled south for the first move in the 1970s. The 1979 CNFR opened in its new southern location with Tom Hadley, 1949 NIRA steer wrestling champion, at the mike. Although the move changed many things, it did not affect the defending champions, Southeastern Oklahoma State University and Central Arizona College. Mountains or marshes, snow or humidity, they could win. For the fourth consecutive year, SEOSU claimed the men's team championship. SEOSU's Jimmy Cleveland won the bareback riding championship and Sabrina Pike, the goat tying. For the second consecutive year, CAC claimed the women's team championship and Barrie Beach Smith, the all-around.

As the 1970s ended, the NIRA had refined its rules, improved the CNFR production, grown in numbers and quality of competition, and supplied the professional ranks with an abundance of champion cowboys and cowgirls. Corporate sponsors awarded scholarships to the regional and national champions. As cowboys and cowgirls left college with rings on their fingers, both college rings and wedding bands, they had strengthened their rodeo skills, married into other rodeo families, created a national network of rodeo friends, and often wore a professional rodeo gold buckle. However, problems abounded. The deal to produce the finals in Lake Charles, Louisiana, had soured, so the CNFR was homeless again. The NIRA office was in transition, under new leadership, and in a new location. Financial insolvency continued to plague the organization. Lacking the budget to hire adequate personnel, the NIRA continued to be dependent on other organizations that had their own agendas. In thirty years, the NIRA had weathered many problems, and its leaders and sponsors had guided it to a level that the founders had only dreamed of achieving, but the NIRA still faced unsolved issues.

CHAPTER 6

1980s—Sponsors

and Superstars

The strong economy, the increasing number of rodeo programs at community colleges, and the quality of competition expanded the national organization during the 1980s. Contestants started driving better rigs and practicing to push the competitive advantage. Instead of one shared horse, most hauled a horse for each event they entered. With scholarships provided by sponsors and colleges and with the federal gender equity mandates in sports, the demand increased for the coed college rodeo program. Two-year schools, not in thrall to traditional sports, took advantage of the new way to attract numbers. Many two-year schools recognized rodeo as a sport equal to its other sports, so rodeo took its rightful place in the athletic departments of many of these schools. Cowgirl competition equaled cowboy competition in all aspects. The NIRA promoted efforts to attract corporate sponsors and to fine-tune its management system and the CNFR production. The setting was right for the NIRA to grow in size, quality, and recognition.

However, the NIRA had to solve some immediate problems, such as a new home for the College National Finals Rodeo. Executive secretary–general manager Tim Corfield, student president Mack Altizer, and faculty president Dr. Ernie Harman met with representatives from the city of Bozeman, Montana, to negotiate a new CNFR contract after the abortive move to Lake Charles, Louisiana. The NIRA finally agreed to become equal partners with Montana State University and the Gallatin Empire Lions Club of Bozeman. The three groups would share any profits or losses after paying the expenses of the finals. The NIRA lacked the staff to manage all the details of producing the finals and had no cash reserves to cover any losses. With the cost of the CNFR estimated at $66,500, the NIRA could not be a risk-taker, so the partners created a safety net for the NIRA. The Lions had previously produced and sold the rodeo program as a fund-raiser that had annually netted about $12,000 to $13,000 for them, so they were eager to be involved.[1]

With the three partners agreeing to share financial responsibility for the CNFR, plans for the return of the 1980 finals rodeo to Bozeman, Montana, began with a review of the stock contracts. The major expense was the $28,000 for stock. Cost of the rough stock supplied by Harry Vold, Stephens Brothers, Joe Kelsey, and Jim Sutton was $21,000. A hundred head of steers was leased from Jack Kelly of Deer Lodge, Montana, for $3,000, and a hundred head of calves from Bud Bolinger of Bozeman for $4,000. President Altizer donated the twelve goats.

The NIRA assessed other CNFR expenses including advertising and personnel. The advertising budget was $9,000, augmented by $3,000 each from U.S. Tobacco Company (USTC) and Miller Brewing Company. USTC supplied posters, bumper stickers, and armbands. Personnel expenses included $2,000 for a public relations person, $2,000 to $2,500 for judges, $900 to $1,000 for timers, $1,000 for an announcer, $800 for the rodeo secretary, $1,000 for the clown, and $1,000 for the computer scoring, $500 for security, $750 for parking, and $1,500 for setting up and taking down the arena.

The contestants' awards and activities added even more expenses, so the NIRA chose to solicit corporate sponsors and to accept help from the Lions Club for those expenses. Corporate sponsors were needed for the $1,000 for team award plaques and the $6,550 for the trophy saddles. Miller Brewing Company would pay the $4,000 for the Sunday afternoon contestants' barbecue with the Gallatin Empire Lions Club preparing and serving it. The forty-seven-member Lions Club would sell and collect tickets for the performances, produce and sell the rodeo program, stable the two hundred horses for contestants, and operate the concession stands. The Lions would pay the $3,000 for the cost of the Miss College Rodeo Contest.

A report from two major corporate sponsors added optimism to the 1980 summer board meeting. Red Springer, director of marketing for U.S. Tobacco, announced that the Copenhagen/Skoal Scholarship Awards Program would donate $125,000 during 1980–81. They had donated nearly a half million dollars to collegiate cowboys and cowgirls.[2] A representative from Miller Brewing Company had been contacted in February, 1979, by someone from a Northwest Region college rodeo about sponsoring a rodeo, which was approved by the national office. Miller gave $39,250 in scholarships to teams in 1980, and Miller coordinator Bill Glossen announced that in 1981 the amount would be $42,750.[3]

New sponsors, new promotions, and upgraded facilities completed the plans for the 1981 CNFR. The CNFR producers hoped to cover the $105,000 budget and exceed the $4,000 profit made in 1980. New corporate sponsors added excitement. Wrangler Western Wear, Nocona Boot Company, Circle Y saddles, and Bailey Hat Company created various types of partnerships. U.S. Tobacco hired Mizlou Television Network to televise the 1981 CNFR. Miller Brewing Company and Nocona Boots supplemented the $150,000 package deal. The Lions Clubs' creative promotions included donated colts for fund-raisers, golf tournaments, CNFR souvenirs, museum-sponsored Western art shows, buffalo barbecue, special fishing trips, a bucking horse sale, and equestrian drill teams. The trademark jack fences around the arena in Brick Breeden Fieldhouse gave way to new pipe fences with center loading chutes.

The CNFR was finally making money, so the NIRA board optimistically prepared for the next year. The final balance sheet for the 1982 CNFR showed a net profit of $39,000 while gross receipts were $180,000, and expenses were $140,000. Although income was up by 12.56 percent from 1981, net profits were down 28 percent from 1981. Bids were opened for the 1983 CNFR. The board also approved the Nocona Boot Company–sponsored Crazy Olympics for the 1983 CNFR. The icebreaker, tension-reliever entertainment awarded money to the winning teams.

Corporate sponsors continued to financially underpin many college rodeo programs with the annual scholarship money they awarded to regional and national champions. The mutual rewards for U.S. Tobacco and the NIRA encouraged them to continue their association with each other. U.S. Tobacco awarded $135,000 annually with $102,300 of the money going to regional winners and $32,000 to national champions. Guided by Walt Garrison, vice president/director of sales, who had pioneered the Copenhagen/Skoal College Scholarship Award Program in 1974, U.S. Tobacco had topped the one million dollar figure in scholarships in a decade with the NIRA. In 1986 another man who fit the job promoting college rodeo joined U.S. Tobacco. Randy Barnes, the U.S. Tobacco event coordinator, joined Garrison and Darrell Barron at the CNFR in 1986. Barnes, raised on a ranch in Nuevo, California, had competed on the Hartnell College and Cal Poly rodeo teams in steer wrestling.

The dedication to the NIRA of corporate sponsor representatives was never more evident than when Bill Robinson died in 1984. While at a Southwest Texas State University rodeo February 27, 1984, an aneurysm fatally struck William H. "Bill" Robinson, and he died at an Austin, Texas, hospital. Robinson, sales promotion manager for U.S. Tobacco Company, worked with Walt Garrison at the Lewisville, Texas, office. They traveled to rodeos throughout the country promoting Copenhagen/Skoal products and promoting the NIRA personally and professionally. Reared in Irving, Texas, Robinson competed as a PRCA steer wrestler for a number of years before joining U.S. Tobacco. His family requested that memorials be given to the Bill Robinson Memorial Foundation Fund for a college rodeo scholarship, awarded annually to a steer wrestler.

However, one corporate sponsor pulled out in 1986 after seven years. NIRA executive secretary Tim Corfield said that, "Miller's constant corporate personnel changes caused them to lose sight of why they were in rodeo." The other reason was "due to the national push on drinking and not driving and the push to raise the drinking age."[4] Miller Brewing Company had contributed to the growing success of the NIRA and the CNFR. In the seven years that Miller was an NIRA sponsor, they contributed more than $1 million to sponsor and promote college rodeos. In 1985–86, Miller gave $100,00 to more than 120 individual college rodeos to help defray the cost of advertising and producing a rodeo. At the 1986 CNFR, Miller awarded $10,000 in team scholarships and provided original design Gist buckles for the CNFR and NIRA champions. They awarded regional team champions $26,000 in scholarships. Miller also awarded the men's all-around champion a new two-horse trailer and Miss College Rodeo a $500 scholarship.[5]

Along with the award money, Miller Brewing Company provided a famous-name cowboy to promote college rodeo. Each year at the CNFR, Henryetta, Oklahoma, cowboy Jim Shoulders, sixteen-time professional world champion, made promotional appearances with his pet Brahma bull, Bufford T. Lite. Shoulders, five-time all-around, seven-time bull riding, and four-time bareback riding champion, signed autographs, entertained with his homespun humor, and provided photo opportunities for fans at various locations in the Bozeman area during the CNFR.

Working together during the 1980s, the NIRA, Montana State, and the forty-seven-member Lions Club created activities that transformed tourists into rodeo fans. Lion Gene Surber said that he had donated an hour a day from September to December and two hours a day from January to June. Surber recognized that volunteers could not continue to carry the CNFR production load that grew each year. Surber said, "The CNFR is in its infancy as to where it's going to go. But in order to become a success, it will need a full-time director with a budget of a couple hundred thousand dollars."[6]

Some national exposure for the NIRA came from advertising and promotional efforts during the 1980s. Bruce Parker, CNFR publicity director, told the board that advertising had been expanded to regional advertising, not centered just in Montana. If the advertisements went out of state, the state of Montana matched expenses dollar for dollar. CNFR publicity was sent to each of the contestants' hometowns. The Colt Giveaway Program, the Miller barbecue, and the VIP program for presidents and vice presidents of rodeo colleges and universities were continued. The awards presentation was moved to Saturday night after the finals instead of Sunday. Five major corporate sponsors funded many of the promotion efforts: U.S. Tobacco, Nocona Boot Company, Miller Brewing Company, Circle Y Saddles, and Wrangler. The Wrangler Judging Program, *College Rodeo Magazine,* Texas Ad Agency's program insert for regional rodeos, and the Miss College Rodeo Pageant helped promote the NIRA.[7]

A method of publicizing the NIRA, a magazine, was dropped while another one, an insert, was considered a success. The *College Rodeo Magazine* was not meeting the needs of the NIRA, so the board voted in 1985 to close its account with the CRM and publish NIRA information in the *ProRodeo Sports News.* Nancy Gilmore's Texas Ad Agency college rodeo insert, which was used by ninety-six of a possible 120 NIRA rodeo hosts, was working. The insert carried generic information about the NIRA with photos to illustrate the various events and regions of the country.[8]

The need for an NIRA publication was debated again with no apparent solution. In 1987 a publications committee recommended that Nancy Gilmore of Madisonville, Texas, the editor of the NIRA rodeo insert, be approved to produce a publication that she compared to a yearbook. It would cover the CNFR, national champions, directors, and regional wrap-ups. The committee requested that Billy Huckaby of Joshua, Texas, publish a sample paper for the CNFR. The committee also recommended that having an NIRA section in the *ProRodeo Sports News,* the professional rodeo newspaper, should be investigated.[9]

The NIRA partially addressed the problem of adequate staffing by hiring a CNFR manager, another attempt to channel marketing and public relations into the main stream of the NIRA management system. In November, 1983, the board hired Larry Davis of Bozeman to manage the CNFR and promote it on a state and national basis. Davis's job description included managing block tickets and sales, overseeing the public relations campaign, coordinating the parade with the help of the Gallatin Saddle Club, organizing the awards ceremonies and banquets, and obtaining state matching funds through a Montana Department of Commerce program. He coordinated the three entities that shared equally in the promotion and production of the CNFR—Montana State University, the Gallatin Empire Lions Club, and the NIRA.[10]

With the CNFR in the black, it had become a marketable commodity, so by 1987 the NIRA started soliciting bids periodically for a site contract. The contract with Bozeman expired in 1989, so the issue of CNFR site selection garnered spirited discussion in 1987. Tim Corfield, NIRA executive secretary–general manager, said that since no specific guidelines existed for the process of selecting a CNFR site for 1991, he would create an outline.[11] The overall budget for the CNFR was approximately $300,000. CNFR manager Larry Davis reported that the 1987 CNFR showed a profit of $47,000 that would be split among the three partners: NIRA, MSU, and Gallatin Empire Lions Club. CNFR committee chair Howard Ross presented a proposal to extend the CNFR's contract with Bozeman after the 1989 deadline. After fielding many ideas, the board approved a two-year extension to give a committee time to set criteria for bids and to investigate possible future sites for the CNFR.[12]

The NIRA management system still contained major flaws. The executive secretary–general manager's responsibilities would have kept a full-time administrator with several secretaries busy, yet the position was still part-time. Tim Corfield not only had the responsibility of overseeing all aspects of the NIRA and the CNFR, but he also taught full-time and coached at a two-year school. The CNFR manager was not a member of the NIRA, so he legally could not contact and make agreements with sponsors, which flawed the management chain. NIRA faculty president Dr. Darwin Nielsen suggested that the requirement that the executive secretary be affiliated with a member school be dropped and that they hire a public relations firm, or an office manager to be available full time.[13] In spite of the obvious need for a full-time executive secretary, the lack of money kept the board from approving a full-time position for more than ten years.

The quality of the CNFR was never more evident than in 1989. Since long-time CNFR secretary Ellen Backstrom's health precluded her continuing, the board hired her daughter Sunni Deb Backstrom and Shirley Churchill and Geri Pursley, experienced timers requested by Sunni Deb. Four Wrangler PRCA judges, George Gibbs, Larry Davis, Billy "Red" Rogers, and Jade Robinson, stock contractor Harry Vold, and pickup men Kenny Claybaugh and Brad Churchill got the nod. Barrelman Jess Franks of Flora Vista, New Mexico, was approved with comments that he is the best in the business. John Marchello's Vacquero Livestock & Feed, Inc. of Tucson, Arizona, would furnish the calves. The board wanted quality calves so they accepted Marchello's bid of $5,400, even though it was not the low bid. The board unanimously selected member Dr. Darwin Nielsen as the CNFR adviser and Darrell Barron, Copenhagen/Skoal representative, as CNFR arena director. Photographer James Fain of Logan, Utah, would record the CNFR action and donate pictures of the NIRA board and CNFR event winners. CNFR announcer went to Jim Thompson of Sturgis, South Dakota. Hardee's joined U.S. Tobacco and Wrangler in the $100,000 sponsorship bracket. Circle Y of Yoakum and Resistol Hats came in at $20,000 each. Frontier Trophy Buckles added $12,000 in sponsorship dollars.

The funding of Miss College Rodeo (MCR) created a board debate. When the 1989 MCR, Kelly Freitag of Kansas State University, passed her crown in June, 1989, to Amy Crain, Southwest Texas Junior College, she ended an unequaled year of college rodeo promotion in spite of the fact that she had been accepted into the college of veterinarian medicine. She had traveled forty thousand miles to visit the eleven regions, several major apparel markets, continued to rodeo in her region, and maintained her grades as a full-time student. She requested financial assistance from the board for travel expenses. The $20,000 raised by previous Miss College Rodeo coordinator Mrs. Pam Garrison was nearly depleted. The board suggested finding a sponsor for MCR as the NIRA was operating close to the bottom line.[14]

With use during the 1980s, the NIRA rules proved to need refinement. The six-year rule for eligibility settled a problem that had been debated periodically since the NIRA was organized in 1949. Approved at the 1980 summer board meeting, the rule, which took effect in 1980–81, stated, "Each prospective NIRA member will have six consecutive NIRA years from the date of his/her high school class graduation to complete four years of NIRA eligibility." Board members also decided to reward students for serving on the national board or serving as regional student directors. These students would receive seven years to complete five years of NIRA eligibility.[15]

The NIRA changed the team and individual rules for qualifying for the CNFR after it was tested in 1982. In the 1983 rule book, the new rule stated, "If a contestant has not competed in at least one regularly scheduled regional rodeo, that contestant will not be eligible to compete as a team member at the CNFR."[16]

The team to test the qualifying rule for teams and individuals in 1982 was a freshman two-cowgirl team from New Mexico Junior College. Coaches have all kinds of strategies for winning. For NMJC coach Sylvia G. Benge Mahoney, it was recruiting the best since she did not have a background of rodeo competition. The names of Tami Noble of Yale, Oklahoma, and LaRae Higgins of Peoria, Arizona, showed up everywhere in the high school winner's columns. Convincing cowgirls of their quality to try a little school like NMJC when major rodeo schools dangled scholarships was not easy. They came, they won, and they qualified for the CNFR. Noble added $1,500 of Copenhagen/Skoal scholarship money to NMJC's fund by winning the Southwest Region all-around and barrel racing championships and second in the goat tying. Between the two of them, Nobel and Higgins qualified as a team for the CNFR. However, to compete as a team at the finals, an NIRA rule stated that a team must have three cowgirls. Now, generally that would have been easy, but NMJC had a shortage of cowgirls. In fact, not another pair of boots on feminine feet could be found that was a bona fide student and cowgirl at NMJC.

One responsibility of the NIRA executive secretary–general manager was to interpret the rules. NMJC coach Benge Mahoney called NIRA executive secretary Tim Corfield, who gave a glimmer of hope to the cowgirls. As the NIRA rule stood then, the team needed an NMJC student with a 2.0 GPA who would be willing to compete in one event at the CNFR. Noble and Higgins headed for their roommate Lori Wafer, who competed in tennis for the college. Assuring her that having ridden a horse as a child at her grandfather's place predisposed her to having a penchant for rodeo and convincing her that her grand-

The 1982 NIRA reserve champion women's team members from New Mexico Junior College are (left to right) *Lori Wafer, Tami Noble, 16-time world champion Jim Shoulders, who presented the award, Coach Sylvia G. Benge Mahoney, and LaRae Higgins Branham. Photo by James Fain, Logan, Utah.*

children would love to hear the story some day, Wafer entered. Higgins had an old, slow barrel horse for Wafer to ride. At the CNFR, with the bravery of a woman on a mission, Wafer made it around the barrels. As Coach Benge Mahoney watched by the fence, one other coach said, "That horse must be sick the way he's going around the barrels." He did not know that he had just watched the most outstanding run of the rodeo. Higgins's 3.3 won the breakaway roping in the short round and was second to Southeastern Oklahoma State University's Sabrina Pike in the average. Higgins sat firmly behind Pike in second spot for the CNFR all-around, sharing second with Cheryl Overfelt of the University of Southern Colorado. Noble won the 1982 Rookie of the Year award. With all the excitement, Coach Benge Mahoney said, "I had no idea that our team was in second place when the final CNFR gate slammed. My team finished second to Betty Gayle Cooper Ratliff's powerhouse SEOSU team. How exciting especially since we are friends, and we both grew up in Lea County, New Mexico." Five years later, Coach Benge merged her name with the coach of the 1982 champion men's team, John Mahoney.

Equalizing the earning of points in the eleven regions continued as an unresolved problem. Some regions, such as the Southwest Region, had fourteen or more schools that fielded teams, while other regions had so few contestants they had two rodeos on one weekend. As a remedy, the board approved a maximum of ten rodeos in each region with each having a minimum of one long go and one short go. One plan that failed was the requirement that all regions should hold a regional finals rodeo starting with the 1986–87 season.

As more educated college cowboys made a successful move from the college circuit to the PRCA tour, the idea of rodeo as a business became more prevalent. In the fall of 1986, the PRCA governing board was in a state of turmoil. A new format designed to create a more business-minded governing board included the contestants, rodeo committees, stock contractors, and contract personnel. Three of the four elements had always considered their part of producing a rodeo a business. Now the contestants were trying to define their part as a business and maintain a voice in what was originally the cowboys' organization.[17] The PRCA board had approved "an internal reorganization intended to be responsive to the expressed needs of various elements within the rodeo industry. The contestant members of the competition committee will appoint four representatives to serve on the restructured PRCA board of directors." Two business individuals, two stock contractors, two rodeo committee members, and a contract-acts representative completed the board.[18] On January 1, 1988, the PRCA hired Lewis Cryer as its first-ever full-time commissioner of the PRCA. The board hoped that Cryer would bring some much-needed athletic management skills gained while he was the commissioner of the Pacific Coast Athletic Association.

With a change in the national board politics and with the changing gender role in college rodeo, a benchmark year for cowgirls occurred in 1985. For the first time, a woman served as the NIRA national faculty president, and a woman won the team roping average at the college finals. Board members composed of regional faculty directors elected Merrill Adams Angermiller as the national faculty president. Angermiller, instructor of journalism and coach at Southwest Texas Junior College, brought NIRA experience to the board, as she had competed for Eastern New Mexico University. Angermiller was a harbinger of the rapidly changing role of women in the administration of college rodeo. In the arena, gender was losing its distinction. Sul Ross State's Tami Noble won the team roping average with her partner Jeff Medlin of ENMU. She knew how to rope and how to invite the right partner to rope with her.

Cowgirls closed the gap in competition and leadership between them and the cowboys in the 1980s. The NIRA board elected their first female student president in 1989 to preside over the national board. Having students run their national policy-making board was unique in college sports. The contestants themselves helped determine their own fate by having a voice in the NIRA decision making. Basic to the original charter of the organization, this aspect had fostered a rodeo-knowledgeable twenty-three-member national board of directors composed of one student and one rodeo coach from each of the eleven regions elected by the students and coaches. The board, open to male or female membership, also elected a board-member coach as national faculty president to serve with the student president.

The first female national student president was exceptional but typical of many rodeo students. Molly McAuliffe Hepper, whose family was in the ranching business, was raised in Fort Klamath, Oregon, a little town with a post office. As this area was seasonal cattle pasture country, the McAuliffe family moved to northern California for winter pasture. While doing the daily chores, McAuliffe Hepper's dad taught her to rope. She said, "My dad had always liked to rope, so he got my brother involved in roping. I was either going to be left out or I had to join the crowd, so that's how I started to rope. It has been really neat for us because it is the one thing that our family does together." McAuliffe graduated with a degree in history from Montana State University in 1990 and added Hepper to her name. While spending her first two years at Blue Mountain Community College, McAuliffe Hepper, as a freshman, won the 1986 NIRA all-around championship and the Northwest Region all-around and breakaway roping titles. In 1987 she was runner-up to the national all-around. She said, "You are not always going to win. It makes you become more of a person to learn how to deal with loss." McAuliffe Hepper now teaches school in Oregon and goes to team ropings with her husband, Gary.[19]

The 1989–90 NIRA faculty president, Bob Doty, Western Texas College coach, supported McAuliffe Hepper. Doty brought a wealth of rodeo knowledge to his new position. Doty, raised on a farm and ranch at Lueders, Texas, earned two degrees while competing in the Southwest and the Southern Regions. After graduation, Doty taught vocational agriculture at Big Spring, Texas. WTC coach Van Rigby told Doty that he (Rigby) was moving, so Doty became the WTC rodeo coach in 1979.[20]

The 1989–90 NIRA national student president Molly McAuliffe Hepper of Montana State
University was the first woman elected to the position. Shown with her are (left to right)
national faculty president Bob Doty of Western Texas College, McAuliffe Hepper, past
national student president Rocky Patterson of Panhandle State University (Oklahoma),
past national faculty president Bud Young of Northwest Mississippi Community College,
and executive secretary–general manager Tim Corfield of Walla Walla Community
College (Washington). Photo by Sylvia G. Mahoney, Vernon, Texas.

Leadership on the board often went hand in hand with leadership in the
arena. After his first year as WTC's coach, Doty had a team qualify every year
for the CNFR, not a small accomplishment in the Southwest Region. Doty's
men's team finished second in 1981. In 1986 his men's team won the title. Two
of his calf ropers won championships: James Zant in 1982 and Keith Hudson
in 1986. However, Doty could not pass by the four-year school challenge, so
he accepted the coaching job at Tarleton State University. In 1999 Doty's TSU
women's team missed winning the national championship by seven and a half
points. Team member Jennifer Smith did win the all-around and the barrel
racing. Doty's rodeo philosophy has worked. He said, "You have to be a tough
competitor to win. You don't have to be smarter; you just have to work harder."[21]

Many successful rodeo programs can be traced to one person whose love
for the sport enabled them to overcome odds to ensure its success. NIRA president Bob Doty received his gavel from Bud Young, Northwest Mississippi

Community College, who finished his second term as national faculty president. Young believed in college rodeo so much so that he single-handedly held the Ozark Region together for many years and helped to start other schools' rodeo programs. Young was awarded the key to Murray, Kentucky, for helping to start the Murray State University rodeo program. He started the NMCC program in September, 1973. Three years later, Young was elected Ozark Region faculty director and served every year except two until 1990. Young attended every rodeo in the Ozark Region, which extended from Mississippi to Michigan.

The NIRA always focused on the CNFR. The contestants celebrated when they heard that the finals were returning to Bozeman in 1980 for reasons vastly different from the financial concerns in the board members' minds. "I am so glad the contestants following us can experience going to The Molly Brown," said one cowboy, and others chimed their agreement. For the contestants, experiencing The Molly Brown was spending the hours after the rodeo in a crowded local entertainment place. The cowboys and cowgirls danced to a live band, played pool, and got to know cowboys and cowgirls from all over the United States. Other contestants approved the move back to Bozeman because of the trout fishing in the clear Montana streams, white water or float rafting, and snow skiing.

For most contestants, competition at the CNFR put blinders on them until the champions wore buckles. The 1980 CNFR qualifiers headed to Bozeman to compete for the national titles. Two attitudes showed among the contestants. Some thought that the Southeastern Oklahoma State cowboys surely could not make it five consecutive team championships, but others thought they could. Not only did the SEOSU cowboys win, the cowgirls did, too, only the third time for both titles to go to one school.

More and more colleges sent formidable cowgirl teams. The SEOSU's 1980 women's team championship came down to the final breakaway calf. Utah State's Lori McNeil won the barrel race, putting her team in first place. SEOSU trailed Utah State by 153 points. The outcome hinged on the last loop of SEOSU's Sabrina Pike, who was in second place in breakaway roping with a combined time on two of 7.9. Utah's Lori Miller had a combined time of 6.3. The event and team championships depended on the two ladies and their loops. Pike roped in 2.5 seconds, the fastest time of the rodeo, the championship loop. Miller's loop slipped off the top of her calf for a no-time. SEOSU won its first women's team title.[22]

145

Members of the 1980 NIRA champion SEOSU women's team, pictured with NIRA student president Dean Churchill, and coach Betty Gayle Cooper Ratliff, were (left to right) *Cindy Perrin, Lori Primrose, Sabrina Pike. Also pictured, Gene Surber, Gallatin Empire Lions Club. Photo by James Fain, Logan, Utah.*

College rodeo kept attracting cowgirl champions from atypical rodeo states. The 1980 all-around and goat tying championships went to Arkansas and Missouri schools. University of Central Arkansas's Lea Erwin placed in the breakaway roping and barrel race, giving her the all-around title. University of Missouri at Columbia's Phyllis Crouse, the goat tying champion, changed the opinion that goat tiers come from the Southwest.

With parades and painted Western themes on business windows, the cowgirls caught the excitement that pervaded the opening of the CNFR. In 1981 tiny Anna Crespin Gardner and her horse Quittin' John stole the hearts of the CNFR rodeo fans as the cowgirl and her horse raced around the barrels, to the goats, and after the roping calves. After the judge's last flag, Crespin Gardner's team, Eastern New Mexico University, took the team award. Her horse Quittin' John received the CNFR performance horse award given by *The World of Rodeo.* Crespin Gardner said that Quittin' John originally thought he wanted to be a bucking horse, but through a turn of events, he found he liked the timed events better, especially the ladies' events. Crespin Gardner was not a one-

Members of the 1980 NIRA champion SEOSU men's team (left to right) *Clay Cooper, Bob Sailors, Olie Smith, Ralph Williams, John Davis, and Jim Cleveland; also pictured, Coach Betty Gayle Cooper Ratliff, Sam Wagner, Gallatin Empire Lions Club, and NIRA student president Dean Churchill. Photo by James Fain, Logan, Utah.*

woman team. Kay Sewell and Becky Meek Lewis made the three a well-matched team, winning equally all year. When Coach Charles Chambers retired in 1998, Meek Lewis took his place as coach for a couple of years.

Cowgirl watching at the CNFRs helped to sell tickets and fill the stands. In 1981 Labette College in Kansas saw its one chance to win a national championship when Kendra Bennett came along with the fastest barrel horse. SEOSU's Sabrina Pike won the all-around championship, her third title on her way to becoming the winningest NIRA cowgirl. Pike's 906 points beat Rookie of the Year, Shari Simmons, who had 905. Pike said, "I wouldn't believe it until they handed me the saddle."[23] The breakaway roping title went to the University of Wyoming's Jean Fuchs Poythress, who won the same title in 1978 for Chadron State University, a Nebraska school.

The cowgirl teams in the 1980s matched the power of the cowboy teams. The fourth year of competition for Sabrina Pike, who competed on the 1982 SEOSU national champion women's team, put her in a class by herself. The Albuquerque cowgirl added all-around and breakaway roping to her 1979 goat tying, 1980 breakaway roping, and 1981 all-around championships. No other cowgirl had

147

won an NIRA title for four consecutive years. Her record five NIRA titles stood until another SEOSU cowgirl, Caryn Standifer Snyder, won five in the 1990s.

The 1983 finals ended the career of one cowgirl's horse that had become a favorite of CNFR fans. Eastern New Mexico's Anna Crespin Gardner made the victory lap around the arena twice on Quittin' John, once for the all-around and once for the goat tying. She along with Jinita Williams and Jody Palmer earned the team championship. After the finals, Crespin Gardner retired her horse Quittin' John, who had his own CNFR fans.

One champion women's team used the advantage of longevity and CNFR experience to win. Montana State coach John Larick's 1986 champion women's team is an example. Stacey Waldhauser, a junior, won the 1985 CNFR goat tying average. Mary Melaney, a senior, carried three regional all-around titles and three years of CNFR experience into the 1986 finals. She finished second nationally in the breakaway roping. Melaney made her mark in 1987 by becoming one of the first two PRCA female team roping contestants. The third MSU team member, Carrie Munson, a senior, was CNFR reserve all-around champion and third in the goat tying.

Sabrina Pike runs barrels at the 1980 CNFR, where she won the breakaway championship. She won championships four consecutive years with a record-setting total of five college championships. Photo by James Fain, Logan, Utah.

By the late 1980s, cowgirls from two-year schools consistently won event championships. In 1986 two-year school contestants won the women's national all-around, goat tying, and breakaway roping titles. Blue Mountain Community College in Pendleton, Oregon, had an outstanding freshman cowgirl Molly McAuliffe Hepper, the 1986 Northwest Region all-around, breakaway, and reserve barrel racing champion. She edged Nancy Rea of Southern Arkansas University by five points for the national all-around championship. Eastern Wyoming College's Shelley Meter tied three goats in twenty-three seconds to win the title. Sophomore Deborah Rogers of Scottsdale Community College won the breakaway roping title with a 3.2 in the short round.

A two-year school won the cowgirl team championship in 1987. In fact, the men's team title and six of the eleven event championships went to two-year schools. Scottsdale Community College took the women's. SCC's Kelly Harsh, whose mother Pat had also competed in the NIRA, won the goat tying title while Deborah Rogers added team roping points for the team championship.

Cowgirls from universities still won their share. Sherry Lynn Rosser, head majorette at Southern Arkansas University, added the second all-around championship to SAU's list of champions. The barrel racing champion Holly Foster from McNeese State University and her horse Angel made three smooth runs to win the sixth title for McNeese. Pam Benoit of McNeese added the Miss College Rodeo crown. The breakaway roping champion Karen Cochran Smith from Texas Tech won the seventh event championship for Texas Tech and made NIRA history by winning a championship at the same university twenty-two years after her mother Eileen Cochran won the national goat tying title, the third event title for the same university.

During the 1980s, rodeo fans came to watch the cowgirl events, especially the fast-action breakaway roping. In the 1988 breakaway roping, SWOSU's Donelle Kay Kvenild averaged less than three seconds a loop for a total time on three of 8.9. Teammate Shannon Lord tied for second place with a 9.4, and teammate Patricia Lynn Burrough made the top four with a 9.9. At the CNFR, Lord placed second in the all-around to West Hills College's Cathy Cagliari. WHC coach Bruce Hunt's cowgirls held the banner high for two-year schools. Cagliari added a double championship, the all-around and the barrel racing. Cagliari's mother Wanda, an NFR barrel racer in 1980 and 1981, started Cathy riding at age four, and she never slowed down.[24]

The 1989 CNFR opened with the number one all-around spot belonging to

Cathy Dennis of Southern Arkansas University, and it closed the same way. Dennis repeated her coach Sherry Lynn Rosser's 1987 national all-around title and added Rookie of the Year. Dennis, the youngest of Brent and Mary Dennis's five children, said, "My dad and I have raised and trained all my horses." Dennis, the 1989 Ozark Region barrel racing champion, rode Juggy, a full brother to Cindy, a mare owned by Rosser, the 1986 and 1987 CNFR short round winner. Dennis, who attended college on an academic scholarship, started her rodeo career when her "dad bought a real nice horse, and some friends encouraged me to go to some junior rodeos. My coach Sherry Lynn is the one who got me into high school rodeos."[25]

An unusual situation occurred in 1989 when one cowgirl won triple-crown reserve championships and helped her school win its first women's team championship. Cal Poly at San Luis Obispo won its first women's team title, and Julie Adair collected three national runner-up titles: all-around, goat tying, and breakaway roping (a tie with Cathy Dennis). However, this was not a one-woman show; Lynn Burns and Holly Foster pushed Cal Poly's points to 834, which was 334 points more than second place SWOSU, whose Shannon Lord won the breakaway roping title. Patti O'Maley, Idaho State University, won the goat tying title by twenty-five points. After accepting the national women's team award, Cal Poly–SLO coach Clay Robinson said, "It's great to win it and to win it for the first time, and they are all going to be back next year."[26]

That was not all that Cal Poly-SLO's women won in 1989. Team member Holly Foster, Wrangler poster personality, won the national barrel racing title, but she was upstaged by Angel, her horse, a three-year CNFR veteran. Holly said that she took better care of Angel than she did herself. Angel and Holly won the 1987 national barrel title; Holly's sister Kelly borrowed Angel in 1988 and won the CNFR average and reserve championship.

A two-year school, College of Southern Idaho had another national cowgirl winner in 1986. CSI sophomore Joni James was crowned the 1986–87 Miss College Rodeo at the final CNFR performance. The talented, beautiful Miss James, the daughter of Jerry and Karen James of Jerome, Idaho, did not slow down until she added the 1990 Miss Rodeo America crown on November 29, 1989, making her the first daughter of a former Miss Rodeo America to claim the crown. Joni's mother had won the 1962 Miss Rodeo America title. In the Miss Rodeo America pageant, Joni won all of the categories: personality, horsemanship, appearance, and speech.

Members of the Cal Poly at San Luis Obispo 1989 NIRA champion women's team are
(left to right) *Holly Foster, Julie Adair, Coach Clay Robinson, and Lynn Burns.*
Photo by Sylvia G. Mahoney, Vernon, Texas.

By end of the 1980s, more schools sent well-balanced men's teams to the CNFR, so no school dominated the finals. For SEOSU the lead changed several times before they made history in 1980. For the SEOSU men's team going into the short go, they had a forty-five-point differential with three heavy hitters close behind—Sam Houston State, Montana State, and McNeese State. SEOSU's Jimmy Cleveland made points in the bareback riding, but Southwestern Oklahoma State's Joe Eckert won the championship. McNeese added points won by bareback rider Phil Smith and bull rider Phillip Fournier, whose earlier eighty-point bull ride, the highest of the rodeo, brought a standing ovation from the crowd. Cleveland's ride on Harry Vold's bull C85 ended with Cleveland across the horns needing medical help, but Vic Carmen announced a seventy-six score, the second highest of the rodeo. Dawson Community College's Chuck Simonson, the 1979 bull riding champ and Rookie of the Year, rode three bulls to win the title. Clay Cooper, brother of Roy and Betty Gayle, Bobby Sailor, and John Davis gave depth to the team and gave SEOSU an unprecedented five consecutive team titles.

At the CNFRs, some contestants become favorites of the rodeo fans. Two 1980 event champions did. Dickinson State's Brad Gjermundson, the 1980 PRCA Rookie of the Year, won the saddle bronc riding title. The Marshall, North Dakota, cowboy's name became synonymous with saddle bronc riding by the time he won four world titles: 1981, 1983, 1984, and 1985. A cowboy from the famous roping Yates family, J. D. Yates and his partner Bret Tenary, both University of Southern Colorado ropers, made the short list with two 7.0-second runs and won the average. Yates and Tenary finished first and second in the nation. Yates had qualified for the professional team roping finals at age fifteen, only the second cowboy to accomplish this feat. He picked his dad Dick Yates to head for him. Dick had competed for Colorado State University in the 1950s and qualified for the CNFR three times, where he competed in five events. During the ninth round of the 1975 NFR performance, ABC Wide World of Sports captured J. D. and Dick's 6.2 run, the fastest time of the NFR. J. D. became an instant celebrity at age fifteen.

For only the fourth time in NIRA history, a cowboy won the triple crown. Lance Robinson had won Weber State University's first championship in 1979. In 1980 he won the steer wrestling, calf roping, and all-around. Robinson, who, cowboy style, gave credit to another cowboy for one of his titles, said, "I followed John W. Jones on both of my steers. He's probably the best bulldogger here. To follow a man like that after he's handled your cattle for you. It kind of makes my job easier." Robinson used his three steers consistently with times of 5.3, 4.3, and 4.8, which gave him the average and the first crown. In the calf roping, he felt the pressure of the first round win by SEOSU's Clay Cooper. In the final round, Robinson said, "My plan after the draw was to get him [calf] down because I didn't draw a real good calf." His plan worked for third in the average, giving him enough points to win the calf roping and the all-around.[27]

Cowboy watching equaled cowgirl watching. In 1981 the Montana cowboys from Dawson Community College broke SEOSU's five-year winning streak. Dawson's Chuck Simonson, the 1980 bull riding champion and the lone cowboy to cover three at that particular finals, faced the same challenge again. The bulls had won nine times, and Simonson, the last cowboy, faced Harry Vold's $10,000 Brahma-cross, F1, that had been ridden only once in 354 trips out of the gate. Simonson wanted eight seconds with F1, although the bull riding championship already had his name on it, and Dawson had its name on the national team title. "F1 ducked his head, pulling Simonson forward and forc-

Dickinson State saddle bronc rider Brad Gjermundson won the championship at the 1980 CNFR and was PRCA Rookie of the Year. He went on to win four world championships. Photo by James Fain, Logan, Utah.

ing him to blow his feet. Then, the bull threw his head back, cracking Simonson on the chin drawing blood," and stopping him short of eight seconds. Simonson finished second in the all-around behind University of Tennessee at Martin's George Mesimer. Dawson's Larry Peabody added 342 points and the bareback riding championship. Kevin Jeffries collected 231 more bareback points for the Dawson team.[28]

Dawson's national championship had a bittersweet ending. Dawson Community College, Glendive, Montana, was barred from regional and finals competition for a year following a ruling by the NIRA executive board. The suspension resulted "from irregularities in Dawson's course-requirement and attendance policies."[29]

College rodeo proliferated with names that were soon-to-be famous professionally. One name, John W. Jones Jr., later synonymous with steer wrestling, won the 1981 NIRA championship. This Cal Poly cowboy's three-head time of fifteen seconds tied with Jade Robinson of Boise State, but Jones's season points made him the champion. He also won the world steer wrestling titles in 1988 and 1989. Jones earned his spot on the list of Cal Poly NIRA steer wrestling

University of Southern Colorado's J. D. Yates won the 1980 team roping with his partner Bret Tenary, the reserve champion. Yates qualified for the NFR when he was fifteen years old where he roped with his father Dick Yates, a former NIRA roper. Photo by James Fain, Logan, Utah.

Cal Poly–SLO steer wrestler John W. Jones Jr. won the NIRA championship in 1981 and won the 1988 and 1989 world titles, also. Photo by James Fain, Logan, Utah.

champions, a list with a record eight champion steer wrestlers that sported famous names, such as Monty Roberts, Jack Roddy, and Tom Ferguson.

By the 1980s, experienced coaches produced powerhouse rodeo teams. In 1982 the Sul Ross State team revitalized by a new coach went to Bozeman with a cache of big names and claimed the men's team championship. Sul Ross coach John Mahoney recruited future world-class cowboys, such as Tuff Hedeman, Cody Lambert, Chuck Lambert, Chuck Kinney, Wes Smith, and Gip Allen. Five of the Sul Ross cowboys competed in three events each with Chuck Lambert competing in four for a total of nineteen chances for the six cowboys to make it to the short round. Cody Lambert and his brother Chuck finished first and second in the CNFR all-around average, banking 651 points.

Even with the Sul Ross six-man team, the ride that determined the team championship depended on the last cowboy, Tuff Hedeman. In his character-istic style of riding the front of the bull with his knees bent and his toes straight like a jockey, Tuff turned on his famous mentally inspired staying power to win the final round in bull riding. Coach John Mahoney chose Tuff, the youngest cowboy on the team, because he believed in Tuff and his ability. Was he ever right! In the final round, the score was bulls, seven; cowboys, three. Tuff exhibited the talent that made him a three-time world bull riding champion, a PBR champion, and a name recognized nationally. Tuff's ability, riding style, personality, and championships put his face on corporate sponsors' posters and ads, in books, in a TV documentary, a movie, and his name in the ProRodeo Hall of Fame in 1997. His and Cody Lambert's friendship with bull rider Lane Frost put Tuff's and Cody's names on the movie marquees advertising *Eight Seconds,* the life of Lane Frost.

In the 1990s lifetime friends Tuff and Cody took advantage of rodeo fans' fascination with bull riding by spearheading the organizing of the Professional Bull Riders (PBR). Through Tuff Hedeman and Cody Lambert's efforts, college bull riders saw their chances for professional rodeo profits skyrocket in 1993 with the incorporation of the new professional organization, which spread across the country like e-mail. The PBR, an organization governed by a board

Members of the 1982 NIRA champion men's team from Sul Ross State University are (back, left to right) *Coach John Mahoney, Cody Lambert, Chuck Lambert, Wes Smith, Tuff Hedeman,* (front, left to right) *Sam Koenig (qualified in steer wrestling, not on team), Chuck Kinney. Team member Gip Allen, not pictured. Photo by James Fain, Logan, Utah.*

of bull riders, was by invitation only. The stakes were high, the bulls were rank, and the riders were the best. The governing board included nationally known bull riders such as Hedeman, Lambert, Ty Murray, Clint Branger, Cody Custer, Ted Nuce, and Michael Gaffney. The PBR Bud Light Cup Series, televised by the Nashville Network, reached seventy million people in 1995.[30] The PBR expanded the field of fans and solved some inherent problems for bull riders, such as the chances of a champion cowboy drawing a dink bull while a novice rider drew the best bull. Cowboys could win more and be away from home less. "Bull riders in the PBR are riding for $5.5 million in 1999, and the Finals are worth $1.5 million," said Hedeman.[31]

By the 1980s, the CNFR was a preview of world-class cowboys. At the 1982 finals, the Sul Ross cowboys beat a roster of future NFR qualifiers. Just to name a few, there were Dave Appleton of Western Texas College, Marty Melvin of South Dakota State University, Rocky Steagall of Blue Mountain Community College, Clay Parsons of Central Arizona College, Philip Fournier of Southeastern Oklahoma State and his brother David Fournier of McNeese State, Robert Etbauer of Panhandle State, Skeeter Thurston of Casper College, David

Three-time world champion bull rider Tuff Hedeman's last ride at the 1982 CNFR determined the men's team championship for Sul Ross State University. Tuff helped organize the Professional Bull Riders (PBR) association, won a PBR championship, and appeared on the sponsor's poster. Photo by James Fain, Logan, Utah.

157

Peters of Sam Houston State, Jerry Alley of Southwest Texas Junior College, Jade Robinson of Boise State, and Clay Robinson of Weber State. Scott Breding of Miles Community College won the 1982 bull riding title, and James Zant of Western Texas College did the same in calf roping.

Once a rodeo coach established a reputation for excellence, former students recruited for the program. Quality recruits poured into Coach John Mahoney's program at Sul Ross. In 1983, Mahoney had two regional champion teams with four event champions and the top four all-around cowboys. However, no longer did a few schools dominate the finals; luck played a role in winning. The Sul Ross cowboys' ace in the hole though may have been their camaraderie. Fun and friendship melded the group into a unit that seemed to emit energy. Coach Mahoney's thirteen men who qualified for the 1983 CNFR presented a selection problem for him. He had to choose six cowboys for the team. His selection of Tuff Hedeman, Cody Lambert, Cody Carruthers, Lynn Williams, Ty Springer, and Mark McKinley proved itself as they won the 1983 team title. Chuck Lambert's nine-year-old sorrel mare called Ginger out of Jet Smooth and a Double Bid Mare won the first NIRA Steer Wrestling Horse of the Year Award. Sam Houston State alumnus Rusty Davis originated the award because he "wanted to give back to College Rodeo part of what he took out of it."[32]

The 5,228 rodeo fans at the 1983 CNFR watched the timed-event cowboys wrestle with a different breed of roping calves. University of Arizona calf roper Clay Parsons's time of 36.7 on three head was outstanding for the calves. Clay duplicated his brother Joe's 1978 calf roping title, only the second brother duo to do so. The Pinzgauer calves, large-boned red-haired calves with a distinctive white topline that extended in a jagged pattern down their backs, proved to be wrestling rather than roping matches for many cowboys. The Pinzgauer calves disrupted the competitive edge again in 1984. Weber cowboy Kyle Kosoff roped all three of his Pinzgauer calves, happy to make it after watching other world-class cowboys, such as New Mexico Junior College's D. R. Daniel, the Southwest Region calf roping and steer wrestling champion, put out of competition in a wrestling match with the kicking calves.

Celebrating the CNFR's thirty-fifth anniversary, the fans saw more world-class champions. Texas Tech's Derek Clark's saddle bronc riding style won him the 1984 national championship and later qualified him fourteen times for the professional finals. Clark announced his retirement from full-time professional competition in 2000. In the final round in 1984, Clark rode Harry Vold's

Pinto Pete, the same horse that the 1983 champion drew. Blue Mountain's Mike Currin won the steer wrestling buckle. Currin's rodeo career ended July 2, 1990. Currin and three other nationally ranked professional rodeo cowboys Randy Dierlam, David Bowen, and Dave P. Smith, the 1979 NIRA calf roping champion, died when their private chartered plane crashed into Mount Rainier in Washington headed to the finals at the Ponoka Stampede in Alberta, Canada. Dierlam of Southwest Texas State University finished fourth in the nation in calf roping at the 1984 finals, helping his team win their first national championship.[33]

Seldom will a school produce two dominating teams, especially in regions with a dozen or more good teams, but in 1985 the Sul Ross teams did in the Southwest Region and the Southwestern Oklahoma State University teams did in the Central Plains Region. Sul Ross took the women's team championship, and SWOSU, the men's.

Both 1985 Sul Ross State University teams, coached by John Mahoney, headed to Bozeman with Southwest Region champions in five events. In fact, Sul Ross's Tuff Hedeman and Todd Watkins held the top two spots in the Southwest Region in the all-around, the bull riding, and the saddle bronc riding with Les Hale and Brad Wilson first and second in the team roping and Ken Browder first in steer wrestling.

Both 1985 SWOSU teams, coached by Don Mitchell, went to the CNFR with both Central Plains Region team championships, the all-around titles, three women's event titles, the saddle bronc title, and the steer wrestling title. SWOSU's regional all-around and saddle bronc champion Sam Houston Willis settled for reserve national all-around to Kent Jude Richard of McNeese State University though Willis won the CNFR all-around. Mike Merchant of the University of Tennessee at Martin brought in enough regional points to win the saddle bronc even though Sul Ross's Tuff Hedeman won the short round on Miss Descent. Merchant's championship was a fitting finale for the four-time bronc riding regional champion who earned a bachelor's degree in agricultural science.

Even with the two universities winning the 1985 team championships, the calf roping, team roping, and the bull riding championships went to other schools. The champs later proved their skills in the professional ranks. Southwest Texas State University's Lanham Mangold won the calf roping with a combined time of thirty-two seconds. Cal Poly's Nolan Twisselman won the team roping championship with his partner Clay Hurst of West Hills College. One of two cowboys to ride three bulls, Clint Branger of Northwest Community College, scored seventy-eight on Vold's bull #140 to win the short round and the title.

In spite of the universities' advantages, the decade of men's championships for two-year schools started in 1986. Western Texas College coach Bob Doty lived the dream of college rodeo coaches when both of his teams qualified to compete at the CNFR. This was the sixth year for Doty to take a WTC team to the CNFR, and it paid off. WTC went into the NIRA records as the fourth two-year school to win a coveted national team title in the thirty-seven-year history of the NIRA. During the next decade, six more two-year schools would win national team titles.

Bob Doty's 1986 WTC national champion men's team with talented freshmen placed second to Tarleton State in the Southwest Region. Paul Yorks, a twenty-four-year-old freshman from New York State, placed second in the steer wrestling average, and Tobin Tate added points in the bull riding. Keith Hudson, the only WTC freshman to make the short round, had won the Southwest Region calf roping title, and he won the national title.

Sometimes the drama outside the arena is the story maker. Sul Ross's Glyn Hutto and WTC's Keith Hudson were standing by the fence watching the final calf ropers after they both had roped theirs in 10.8 seconds. They went into the short round seventh and eighth in the average, a seldom-reversible place in the CNFR short round. Hutto was entertaining Hudson and others with his cowboy comments when two ropers missed. After two more roped with their times being 13.2 and 18.4, Hutto and Hudson looked at each other surprised. Winning the average had become a possibility for them. They had third and fourth cinched. Only two ropers left—the excitement became electric. A 15.3, then West Hills College's Clay Hurst, the West Coast Region all-around, team roping, and reserve calf roping champ, had the last calf. West Hills entered the short round leading the men's teams with WTC in third with only fifty-five points separating them. Hurst's 14.8 placed fourth in the round. Hutto won the CNFR average, and Hudson took second. Hudson stood there shocked when Zeb Bell announced that Hudson was the 1986 national calf roping champion.

By the mid-1980s, a coach at a two-year school on the west coast was recruiting the best cowboys in the country. At West Hills College in Coalinga, California, Coach Bruce Hunt recruited Clay Hurst, a sophomore from Buncombe, Illinois. Although not from roping country, he did know how to handle a rope. In 1986 Hurst with partner Cal Poly's Nolan Twisselman, the 1985 NIRA team roping champion, watched eight of the team ropers have problems, but the ninth team Johnny Emmons of Vernon Regional Junior College and Shane Hudman of Odessa College had a 7.2, giving them 22.1 on three. Hurst and Twisselman needed an 8.1 to win. Their 6.2 seconds won the CNFR average and the national team roping and all-around championships for Hurst.

With experienced coaches, two-year schools started to have more success. The 1986 bull riding and the saddle bronc champions both came from two-year schools coached by men who once competed in the NIRA themselves. Odessa College coach Jim Watkins had ridden bulls while attending Sul Ross State. College of Southern Idaho coach Shawn Davis had won three NIRA championships and three professional ones. Watkins understood bull riders and how to recruit them. His recruits looked like the who's who of professional bull riders. In 1986 Odessa College sophomore Jim Sharp, the Southwest Region all-around, saddle bronc, and bull riding champion, was noted for making bull riding look so easy that the judges often hoarded the points. At the CNFR, Sharp went into the final round leading the average. Four cowboys rode

Odessa College bull rider Jim Sharp won the 1986 and 1987 NIRA championships and two world championships. Photo by JJJ Photo, Ord, Nebraska.

all three. Sharp finished three points behind Paul Latham of Panhandle State in the average, but Sharp had a runaway in the national standings. Coach Davis watched freshman Frank Patrick Norcutt ride Chief Joseph to win the short round, the average, and the national saddle bronc championship.

The name Sharp became a household word in bull riding circles. Odessa College's Jim Sharp, the 1986 bull riding champion, added the 1987 title. Bull riding fans knew by watching Sharp ride that they were watching a future professional bull riding champion, and he was in 1988 and 1990. Sharp won the $50,000 bonus round at the 1987 Calgary Stampede. In 1988 he rode all ten NFR bulls, the first ever. Sharp along with his traveling buddy world champion Tuff Hedeman rode the bulls featured in the movie *My Heroes Have All Been Cowboys*. Hedeman rode the bulls for the leading man Scott Glenn. Sharp and Richard Rule rode all the other bulls.

Sometimes a year marks a decade with evidence of significant change. It did in 1987, the year Lane Frost won his world bull riding championship, and John Growney's Red Rock, the 1987 Bull of the Year, was scheduled to be retired. Before this would happen, Frost and Red Rock met in a phenomenal seven-time challenge of abilities. Frost won four; Red Rock, three. In 1989 Frost lost his life in an encounter with a bull at the Cheyenne Frontier Days Rodeo and was buried in Oklahoma by Freckles Brown, the bull rider who rode Tornado, the unrideable bull. Team roper Secretary of Commerce Malcolm Baldrige died in 1987, and bareback rider Bruce Ford tied the legendary Joe Alexander's record of five professional championships. The Dodge National Circuit Finals, the first finals for the PRCA's twelve circuits, was held in Pocatello, Idaho. Barrel racer Charmayne James entered the 1987 NFR with more money won than the all-around standings leader. The PRCA changed the governing board format and hired its first commissioner. The CNFR made the *Wall Street Journal* in Ruth Rudner's "Rodeo Days at the Old College Corral." She said, "There is no way not to fall in love with them all, all these cowgirls and cowboys competing in college rodeo. Young and earnest and gutsy, many have been rodeoing since they were small children."[34]

Universities once again started winning men's team and event championships. In 1988 Montana State succeeded in winning a team championship again. John Larick's MSU cowboys won three of the event titles along with the men's team championship. MSU cowboy Ken Lensegrav, who attended his first college rodeo club meeting with his parents when he was two weeks old, proved to be the all-around man and champion of his favorite event, bareback riding. Lensegrav wore the 1987 PRCA Rookie Bareback Riding Champion buckle.[35] Teammate Rex Phillips wore the NIRA bull riding buckle. National College's Cory Ferguson won the steer wrestling title. Ferguson, who later worked as a Copenhagen/Skoal sales analyst and coordinator of rodeos, was inducted into his college's Rodeo Hall of Fame in 1997. Tarleton State University's David Key roped with New Mexico Junior College's Joe McKown, to win TSU's first team roping championship.

Two cowboys from two-year schools won two championships to keep the four-year schools from making a sweep. Western Dakota Vocational Tech Institute's Eudell Larsen, the regional saddle bronc, bareback, and all-around champ, won the bronc title. Blue Mountain calf roper Bradley Goodrich's 17.5 on two and his 10.9, the best in the short round, gave him the title.

By the end of the 1980s, professional rodeo was predominately college-produced contestants. For example, in 1988, Australian Dave Appleton, a Western Texas College alumnus, won the world all-around championship. Jim Sharp, 1986 and 1987 NIRA champion bull rider from Odessa College, won the world bull riding title. Shaun Burchett, New Mexico Junior College alumnus, added his second gold buckle in steer roping. John W. Jones Jr., a Cal Poly alumnus and 1981 NIRA steer wrestling champ, won the world title. Clint Johnson, South Dakota State University alumnus, won the saddle bronc title with two other former NIRA cowboys in second and third, Brad Gjermundson and Bud Munroe.

The fortieth anniversary of the NIRA added some first-ever records at the 1989 CNFR. Seventy-one colleges and universities from the eleven regions qualified 356 cowboys and cowgirls. Ty Murray of Odessa College won a triple crown, helping his team win the title. Murray won the all-around, saddle bronc riding, and bull riding, only the fourth NIRA cowboy to achieve triple-crown status. Murray, who had won seven professional all-around gold buckles by 1998, first competed at the 1988 CNFR, but he did not win a title. However, Murray said, "Wanting to win the all-around title kept me in college for another year." Murray settled an old debt in 1989 with Rusty, Harry Vold's former bucking horse of the year. Murray said, "The first time Rusty and I met, I rode him, but the second time, he threw me off. He is hard to get out on, so I tried a new strategy on him, and it worked." On their third encounter, Murray settled the tie with Rusty by marking a seventy-nine and winning the saddle bronc championship.[36]

The Texas two-year college at Odessa moved into the college rodeo records and into the ranks of schools to beat. No team had ever won the team title and four of the seven individual titles. Teammate Shawn McMullan's national calf roping champion completed the record-setting finish. On the way to the 1989 CNFR, McMullan had twisted his knee while roping a calf at Elizabeth, Colorado. He had called his parents to tell them not to come to the finals, but "OC trainer Jim Carlson used a lot of ice and heat; my parents came, and I won."[37] Coach Jim Watkins said, "We're also pleased to have won Odessa College's first national team title." Coach Watkins, who competed at the CNFR for four years, raised three talented children with his wife K. C. Watkins. Todd, Jamie, and Ty won numerous American Junior Rodeo Association championships while growing up, and they continued their winning ways in college. Coach Watkins competed in bull riding for ten years in the PRCA until an injury sidelined him; then he took a teaching job at Crockett Junior High School in Odessa until his retirement in 1997. He continued to coach rodeo at Odessa College after he retired from the public school system.[38]

A tragic wreck ended the roping-talented Shawn McMullan's life before

Members of the Odessa College 1989 NIRA champion men's team are (left to right) *athletic director Jim Segrest, 1989 calf roping champion Shawn McMullan, Chad Ramirez, Bubba Flores, triple-crown champion Ty Murray, Linn Churchill, Kevin Bennett, Coach Jim Watkins,* (kneeling) *athletic trainer Jim Carlson. Photo by Sylvia G. Mahoney, Vernon, Texas.*

the depth to his talent could be established. McMullan was killed on August 17, 1996, in a head-on collision forty miles east of Portland, Oregon. Jarrod Grieve of Australia and Stran Smith of Tell, Texas, escaped without serious injury. McMullan, son of Glenda and Kenny McMullan, was a four-time NFR qualifier, who was ranked eighth in the world at the time of his death. McMullan grew up on a ranch ten miles from Iraan, Texas, where his dad "took from several ropers' styles and taught me. We roped about twenty calves a day every day after school."[39]

Another collegiate phenomenon toppled professional records. Ty Murray's records attested to his innate talent, early training, and champion's attitude. At age two and a half, Murray's bull riding career started. His dad Butch Murray, a former bull rider, put little Ty on calves, put his finger in Ty's belt loop, and ran along beside him. At age eight, Ty progressed to steers, then to bulls at age nine. Ty said, "At my first Little Britches bull ride, I expected a steer and found an 1,800-pound bull. That bull was so big that he had horns longer than my arms, but I rode him." Ty said that his second bull ride was not so successful.

Odessa College cowboy Ty Murray won three NIRA championships, all-around, saddle bronc riding, and bull riding, helping his team win the 1989 national championship. Ty broke the record for world all-around championships when he won his seventh in 1998. He was the world champion bull rider twice. Photo by James Fain, Logan, Utah.

165

"The bull was a muley, so after that first one, I didn't think that one could buck me off. I didn't know much. He spun to the left, and right at the whistle, he bucked me off and stepped on my face and broke my jaw. Up to that point, I had always had trouble keeping my toes turned out and keeping my spurs in the steers and the bulls. Since I had my jaw wired shut, I have never had trouble keeping my toes turned out and sticking the iron to them." Murray had a champion's attitude. He said, "Every time I ride, I win something or learn something." He would rather be ninety or bust every time he rides. He does better if he gasses it every time rather than trying to safety-up and do just what it takes. In December, 1989, Murray's NIRA triple-crown year, at age twenty, he won his first world all-around championship, the youngest ever. Rodeo ran deep in Murray's family. One year Ty was in a dead heat with his uncle Butch Myers, brother to Ty's mother, Joy, for the professional all-around championship.[40]

With 25,000 spectators at the CNFR in 1989, it had come of age. The NIRA had 2,300 members (1,594 men and 706 women) on two hundred college and university campuses. "The CNFR is," said Gordon Clark, CNFR manager, "the best rodeo in the nation, second to none." Clark, who once competed in the NIRA and served on the national board, added, "We have the best of both worlds: individual champions and team championships. It is a real crowd pleaser."[41] Noted stock contractor Harry Vold said, "The CNFR is equal to the NFR in the quality of competition between the contestant and the stock and in the production of the rodeo."[42] However, Tim Corfield, NIRA executive secretary–general manager, said that the NIRA was still a well-kept secret.[43] Except for a few, the CNFRs had been held in sparsely populated parts of the country. It had achieved maximum potential for the area.

Forty years young or forty years old? The NIRA was both. It continued to set new records and gain new fans while maintaining its original goal of pairing rodeo competition with earning a college education. The CNFR was making a profit, and the NIRA had a stable management system and administration even with the part-time secretary-manager's position. In the 1990s, the NIRA hoped to be totally independent by becoming financially solvent. The NIRA leadership was determined to accomplish this in the next decade.

CHAPTER 7

1990 to 1996—Independence
and Photo-Finish Finals

As the National Intercollegiate Rodeo Association (NIRA) approached the final decade before its golden anniversary, it continued a stable growth pattern. However, change brought by deaths and retirements took its toll on the organization. The level of competition accelerated providing a growth in the number of College National Finals Rodeo (CNFR) fans, improving its marketability and making it a candidate for organizational independence. Bids for the CNFR resulted in the finals remaining in one place for the first seven CNFRs in the 1990s. The contestants built on previous contestants' experiences and, with the expanding economy, invested in quality horses and equipment to push the competitive edge. The NIRA refined the CNFR qualifying rules and added more rounds, resulting in exciting photo finishes. The NIRA was determined, with the help of corporate sponsors and a new level of competition, to achieve the independence and national recognition that other college sports enjoyed, but that required moving the CNFR, which created new problems.

Deaths altered the face of the NIRA but brought members and alumni together as they memorialized their friends. Twenty-eight-year-old Shaun Burchett, a New Mexico Junior College CNFR calf roping qualifier, died on January 26, 1992, in a Sherman, Texas, hospital after a vehicle accident near there. In his brief life, the former NIRA cowboy won two world steer roping titles, three reserve, the 1982 PRCA Rookie of the Year, and set a new world record for the fastest steer roped, an 8.5 seconds. The sudden death on September 3, 1993, of the first NIRA all-around cowgirl Jo Gregory Knox, wife of Tee Knox, of Midland, Texas, created a vacancy on the NIRA Alumni board. University of Wyoming bull rider Sean Murphy died on October 8, 1993, when a bull threw him against the bucking chutes, spun around, and stepped on him, causing his fatal injury. PRCA and former NIRA cowboy Marty Yates died in a vehicle wreck on November 18, 1993, near Huckaby, Texas. Twenty-five-year Panhandle State coaching veteran Dr. Lynn "Doc" Gardner died on April 3, 1996, leaving a legacy of world-class cowboys recruited such as Robert Etbauer, Dan Etbauer, Craig Latham, and Tom Reeves.

Retirements in the NIRA left major vacancies. Utah State University rodeo coach and professor of ag-economics Dr. Darwin Nielson ended his twenty-five-year coaching career at the 1994 CNFR. Nielson's CNFR job was indispensable, but not glamorous. He had done the groundwork at the CNFR arena for seven years. Each morning by 3:30 A.M. Nielson was working the arena, preparing it for the 6 A.M. slack. Nielsen locked up about 11 P.M. after dragging the arena again. Another regional director Frank Adams, Cochise College professor of agriculture and rodeo coach, who retired from his longtime board service, was honored by his region with a handmade saddle.

Another coach whose name traversed the history of the NIRA retired in 1996 after coaching for fifteen years at the University of Wyoming. Pete Burns's years at UW started in 1946 as a track and basketball athlete. By 1947 his college roommates had converted him to being a steer wrestler, bareback, and bull rider. By 1951 Burns was competing full-time professionally. In college rodeo, Burns attended the NIRA organizational meeting in Dallas in 1949. In 1958 Burns started a rodeo stock contracting company, Summit Rodeo Company, and contracted his stock for national finals rodeo at every level from high school and college to professional.

Retirement by a sponsor highlighted the influence of an individual working within a corporation. At the 1996 CNFR, Walt Garrison, vice president of U.S. Tobacco Sales and Marketing Company, Inc., announced his retirement. The NIRA honored him by hanging his Dallas Cowboy Number 32 on a banner in the arena, where it was to be displayed at every CNFR. Garrison pioneered the idea of scholarships for college cowboys and cowgirls, helping thousands earn degrees. The year that Garrison retired, U.S. Tobacco's total donation to college rodeo scholarships exceeded $3 million. Randy Barnes took Garrison's position.

In spite of the losses, the NIRA continued to expand in all areas. The first female NIRA national student president finished her year at the 1990 CNFR. Montana State's Molly McAuliffe Hepper said, "I'm glad that I served on the board. It has been a great learning experience. I've learned to be more concerned about people other than myself. I've met a lot of people, and it has been a successful year financially."[1] McAuliffe Hepper, a role model for both male and female presidents, exemplified the quality of students that the NIRA attracted. Along with competing at the CNFR and serving as student president, in May, 1990, McAuliffe Hepper wore a Montana State University mortar board, having achieved a perfect 4.0 grade point average.

Molly McAuliffe Hepper highlighted some important issues that came before the board during her tenure. "One," she said, "was inviting the Canadian event champions to compete in the 1990 CNFR. The forming of a twelfth region is a possibility. It could be a big step in the growth of the NIRA." One Canadian Intercollegiate Rodeo Association contestant, Patty Jo Gulick of Lakeland College in Vermilion, Alberta, finished fifth in the breakaway roping average. A Canadian alliance with the NIRA, however, was not established. McAuliffe Hepper said, "Another important progressive step was the addition of $64,500 to the Copenhagen/Skoal Scholarship Awards so that the annual award starting in 1991 will be $200,000." Another issue was the awarding of a three-year contract for the CNFR to Bozeman, Montana, starting with the 1991 CNFR. McAuliffe Hepper said, "Bozeman has done an outstanding job. However, there have been some excellent presentations, very professional. I think that it will give everyone a broader perspective of the CNFR and its possible growth."[2]

Several cities had submitted bids in 1991 for the three-year contract to host the CNFR. Rapid City, South Dakota, Ogden, Utah, and Lubbock, Texas, were sites visited by the five-person selection committee: West Coast Region student director Holly Foster, Southwest Region faculty director John Mahoney, Rocky Mountain Region faculty director Dr. Darwin Nielson, Central Rocky Mountain Region faculty director Jeff Dorencamp, and NIRA executive secretary–general manager Tim Corfield. All the bids were well done and lucrative, but Bozeman had enough support to convince the committee that the CNFR should stay in Bozeman.

Bozeman had grown accustomed to the economic surge produced by the multimillion dollars brought to town by the college rodeo teams, their families, and their fans. Due to this, in 1994 they outbid Albuquerque, New Mexico, and Oklahoma City for the right to host the 1995 CNFR and two more. Since college rodeo was not a household word, few cities bid on the CNFR. Most knew rodeo as an individual sport with cowboys and cowgirls coming to town competing then going on down the road. Having college rodeo teams come to town and stay ten days was a secret known only by Bozeman. In the twenty-five years that the CNFR had called Bozeman home, sports and entertainment in the United States had become primary goals of many Americans with money and time to pursue their favorites. Bozeman and the CNFR benefited from this trend.

Change rattles minds, creates a flood of opinions, and brings upheaval, but change and progress are partners. CNFR site selection time in 1996 ignited all of these attitudes. Rumors about moving the CNFR to a new location created speculation at the 1996 CNFR. NIRA general manager Tim Corfield corroborated the rumor that the finals would be in a new location in 1997, but the decision had not been a simple decision. Reasons that he gave for moving were partly economic due to ticket sales being "maxed out long ago" in the small community of Bozeman and local sponsorship opportunities being limited. A second reason was facilities. "Conditions for contestants have always been mediocre at best. Horse stalling was cramped and inconvenient. Traffic to and from the field house can be a nightmare."[3]

In November, 1996, Rapid City, South Dakota, got the nod to host the 1997 CNFR, ending the twenty-five-year stay in Bozeman. Two South Dakota rodeo promoters, Jim Sutton, a second-generation rodeo producer from Onita, South Dakota, and David Allen, the 1992–96 CNFR executive director, formed a partnership to move the CNFR to Rapid City. Sutton's rodeo credentials were impeccable. His family began producing rodeos at their home ranch in 1926. Allen, former Deadwood, South Dakota resident, owned a sports marketing firm in North Carolina that represented NASCAR race teams and produced rodeo events.

Production of the CNFR required more than setting a date. Time had to be allowed to set up the arena. As had been the practice for many years, Brick Breeden Fieldhouse on the Montana State University campus was not available to the 1991 CNFR to start preparations until twenty-four hours before the CNFR stock was scheduled to be worked in the arena. MSU was on the quarter system; Saturday morning June 15, 1991, the MSU graduation ceremony was held. A crew of about twenty people could not start the breakdown until 1 P.M. Saturday. The crew moved two thousand chairs and a stage; then, a dirt floor was laid; and fences, pens, and chutes were set up. The arena dirt was stored during the year on the parking lot under a tarp. This dirt, along with two hundred yards of sand, was hauled in with a paddle-wheel scraper, leveled with a road grader, then worked with a tractor. CNFR adviser Darwin "Doc" Nielsen was on hand working and overseeing the project. In 1992 MSU changed from quarters to semesters, making it possible to have commencement earlier.

After a few years, management of the CNFR had become enmeshed in politics with three entities having equal shares of the profits and losses of the CNFR: Gallatin Empire Lions Club of Bozeman, Montana State University, and the NIRA. To make the changes in favor of the NIRA, it had to weather a major amount of hostility. After several heated meetings, the NIRA Board totally restructured the CNFR governing body enabling the NIRA to regain control of its destiny. No longer would it share profits, losses, and power with the Lions Club and Montana State.

The new CNFR agreement defined areas of responsibility for the volunteers and for the NIRA. A CNFR committee included many of the longtime faithful Lions Club volunteers. The committee was responsible for ticket sales, advertising, and volunteers to run the gates and other positions during the CNFR. Gordon Clark, CNFR manager, was responsible for the production of everything for the rodeo outside the arena, which included seeking sponsors. The NIRA board was responsible for the rodeo production in the arena.

Along with the new three-year contract with Bozeman and Montana State University, the NIRA made some management changes. They decided to hire a full-time, experienced marketing person, who would seek corporate sponsors, boost media exposure, and promote attendance at the finals. The NIRA board hired David Allen, a sports-marketing-firm owner with offices in Atlanta and Chicago, but it was a part-time position. Allen's credentials qualified him for the position as he had worked for the Professional Rodeo Cowboys Association media department, Wrangler Jeans special events, and sports marketing with Frankel and Co., of Chicago.

The CNFR improved in quality when the board instituted a new solution to an old problem. At the 1993 CNFR, for the first time, a "sudden death" format reigned; all contestants started with zero points at the finals. Another 1993 change specified that points earned at ten rodeos, instead of seven, would determine the regional championships.

Qualifying for the CNFR was a never-ending issue. A new idea, proposed in 1993, was to pair regions for competition with the top five teams and contestants progressing to a chute out. After the chute out, the top fifteen in each event would then qualify for the CNFR making more rounds possible. This idea imitated the NFR, which had fifteen contestants in each event. This idea hit the proverbial fan and spun out of control after the 1994 CNFR. The new NIRA student president Tyler Keith of Cal Poly at San Luis Obispo and faculty president Russell Walter of Laramie County Community College in Wyoming faced this issue while they were becoming accustomed to the title of president. The board had debated numerous plans to reduce the number of CNFR contestants and raise the number of go-rounds so the quality of the contest could be enhanced. Fewer contestants would also help to resolve complaints of uneven pens of stock. Keith called a special board meeting at the CNFR. After much discussion, the board decided to have a special meeting on September 14, 1994, in Denver, Colorado, to continue looking for a solution. The Top Five Rule was designed. Individuals, when counting all ten rodeos, must place first or second in their region in an event or the all-around. Team members could enter only the events in which they placed fifth or higher in the final year-end regional standings. Student directors on the NIRA executive board could enter any event in which they finished fifth or better.[4]

Opposition immediately surfaced. The Central Rocky Mountain Region requested a ballot be mailed to NIRA members on January 19, 1995. Pete Burns and Bill Laycock of the University of Wyoming prepared a position statement for opposition to the Top Five Rule. The following points were made: Fewer full teams would qualify, and most team members would be eligible for one event only. Most second place teams would not be complete. Team competition would diminish when members competed in only one event. Regions with fewer contestants would have an advantage. "College rodeo is attractive to University administrators solely because of the team concept and team, not individual, performance." Scholarship money would be concentrated in fewer students to stay competitive.[5]

The NIRA board produced a rebuttal statement to the controversy about qualifying for the finals. More go-rounds at a finals and an even pen of stock would reduce the impact of luck of the draw. Contestant skills had improved at the college level, but the conditions at the CNFR had not changed to reflect that improvement. No team member would be allowed to compete at the finals based on team membership. The records of CNFR team championships showed that winning the national championship often depended on the points of one or two women or two or three men. These team members were the same people who won the region and qualified for the CNFR. The Top Five Rule was voted down eighty-eight to sixty-six. Also, CNFR manager David Allen could not find financing for each level of the competition. The 1995 CNFR format remained the same.[6]

A major longtime sponsor continued to foster growth in the NIRA with its scholarship program. In 1990 the U.S. Tobacco Company (USTC) celebrated its sixteenth year of affiliation with the NIRA and its two million dollar mark in scholarship awards. In appreciation, the CNFR contestants presented Louis F. Bantle, USTC chief executive officer and president, with a watch for providing the leadership that resulted in the two million dollars for scholarships. The Copenhagen/Skoal Scholarship Awards Program gave $200,000 to teams and event winners during 1993, its eighteenth year sponsoring the NIRA.

To showcase academics along with athletics, USTC initiated academic scholarships in 1991. Three CNFR contestants with perfect 4.0 grade point averages collected the first Copenhagen/Skoal Scholarship Awards Program academic awards. The 1991 calf roping champion Southwest Missouri State sophomore Randy Orr, Western Texas College sophomore Troy Cattoor, and Southeastern Oklahoma State sophomore Jeana Bowman took the first academic honors.

Sponsorships grew, helping to expand the NIRA services. USTC announced that the Copenhagen/Skoal Pro Rodeo traveling scoreboard would make its debut at the 1993 CNFR. Three new corporate sponsors joined the NIRA: Tony Lama, Award Design Medals, and the Professional Rodeo Cowboys Association. Other sponsors gave their approval for another year: Wrangler, Resistol, Corral West Ranchwear, Justin, Universal Athletics, Billion Dodge, State of Wyoming-Tourism, and Harrington Pepsi.

The NIRA finally published its own newspaper after trying various newspapers. Paulette and James Moss of Moss Publishing published The *NIRA News* in Riverton, Wyoming, for several years. The NIRA next awarded the bid to the *College Cowboy* owned by Jeanne Carpenter of Kalispell, Montana. Following these two, *The Collegiate Arena* made its debut at the 1996 CNFR. The NIRA decided to publish its own paper in Walla Walla, Washington, using Kay Lynn Beard as publication manager. Tim Corfield, NIRA general manager, was editor of the newspaper, published monthly from October through June. The full-color cover emulated the quality of the professional rodeo publication.

More women team members, new qualifying rules, and another go-round strengthened the CNFR competition, For the first time in 1996, women's teams had four members instead of three because of the increase in female contestants and the adding of a fourth woman's event, coed team roping.[7] Women made almost one-third of the NIRA contestants in 1995–96 with 2,189 (67.6 percent) being men and 875 (32.4 percent) women. Twenty-one NIRA coaches were female.[8] Another change was a new rule that limited event entries to the top five or 30 percent of the regions point earners, whichever was greater. Previously, team members at the finals could enter any event in which he or she had placed during the year. Other major changes included the adding of a third round with the top twelve instead of ten advancing to the short round.

The new qualifying rules for the 1996 CNFR improved the quality of competition without reducing the number of contestants. Three hundred fifty-four contestants from eighty-six of the 142 member schools qualified to compete at the 1996 CNFR. The previous year, 356 contestants had competed at the CNFR.

Ingenuity directed many college rodeo program fund-raisers, which were necessary to fund programs not included in college budgets. Coach Bud Young's cowhands at Northwest Mississippi Community College produced their fourth Bull-A-Rama at the college farm arena on September 18, 1993, a harbinger of the success that the Professional Bull Riders (PBR) would later have.[9] Coach Shawn Davis's cowboys at the College of Southern Idaho hosted their annual CSI Rocky Mountain Cowboy Championship Boxing Smoker in Twin Falls, Idaho. Davis said that the competition resulted accidentally from a fistfight after a game of touch football. The following day when the fighters were in Davis's office explaining their side, the host of an annual boxing match called looking for fighters so that he would not have to cancel the match due to bad weather. Davis's eighteen volunteers won 80 percent of their first rounds. By 1993 more than two thusand seats were sold for the annual fund-raiser.[10]

One major rodeo program worked to survive university budget cuts. The teams of Montana State coach John Larick had four national champion team trophies, but in the middle of the 1993 season the university informed Larick that the athletic budget would no longer fund his program. Larick needed to raise more than $100,000 to run his program. The National Collegiate Athletic Association (NCAA) dictated that all schools must have fourteen athletic teams to remain in Division I. MSU had twelve, and one was a non-NCAA sport, rodeo, so MSU removed rodeo to make a place for two more NCAA sports.[11]

Instead of quitting, Larick showed the character that had earned him respect when he started coaching in 1971 at Hartnell College in Salinas, California. After eleven years at Hartnell, Larick moved to MSU. With the success of his program, MSU produced many supportive rodeo alumni, who helped Coach Larick raise $100,000 in sixty days to save his rodeo program. However, Larick said that repeating this would be asking too much of his alumni. He pointed to the CNFR held on MSU's campus and applied some leverage to the MSU administration. Larick said that with the MSU rodeo program out of the picture, attendance at the CNFR would suffer, and the school's finances would decline. The administration recognized the ramifications of its decision, so the MSU rodeo program was placed back on college funding.[12]

The idea of an NIRA alumni association, after years of being bantered about, took root at the 1991 CNFR. While Sylvia Gann Mahoney was doing research on the history of college rodeo, people often asked her about an alumni association. After Mahoney interviewed NIRA champion Betty Sims Solt, they decided to start an organization. With approval of the NIRA board, they set a fact-finding meeting for June 22, 1991, at the CNFR. Barry Davis, Western Oklahoma State College coach, and Julie and George Howard, coaches of Southwestern Oklahoma State University joined them. They set June 19 and 20, 1992, as the dates for the first reunion of the NIRA Alumni (NIRAA) at the CNFR. Mahoney wrote bylaws and a handbook. Using her contacts from her research, she selected a board of directors with one director from each of the eleven regions along with ten other directors.

The first NIRAA reunion in 1992 was a major success. President Sylvia Gann Mahoney of Vernon, Texas, and the other twenty board members had worked all year spreading the word about the new organization. Betty Sims Solt took on the secretary-treasurer's job, Paulette Moss, media director; Evelyn Kingsbery, historical collection director; and Bob Clore, awards director who designed the official logo and former NIRA champions' awards. The reunion included introduction of all alumni, awards, cowboy poetry, music, the collection of oral history and memorabilia, and honoring the champions from each decade by being on panels and giving them awards along with introducing them at a CNFR performance.

The NIRA Alumni announced that they would award a $500 scholarship annually to each of the Rookies of the Year. Winning the first one for the cowboys was the 1996 saddle bronc champ Jeremy Crane, a freshman business

*Some of the fifty NIRA alumni who attended the First Annual NIRA Alumni Reunion in 1992
are* (front, left to right) *Bob Clore, Kansas; Charlie Rankin, Texas; Betty Gayle Cooper Ratliff,
Oklahoma; Betty Sims Solt, New Mexico; Pat Dunigan Marr, Texas; Sally Jane Mosby,
Montana; Molly McAuliffe Hepper, Oregon; Sonny Sikes, Texas; Charlie Martin, Texas;*
(back, left to right) *Randy Witte, Colorado; Butch Morgan, Colorado; Tom and Linda Parker,
Wyoming; Bill Laycock, Wyoming; Darla Doty, Texas; Buddy Cockrell, Texas;
Jack and Evelyn Kingsbery, Texas; Jim Sims, Montana, and Sue and
Randy Magers, Texas. Photo by Sylvia G. Mahoney, Vernon, Texas.*

administration major from Dickinson State University. Western Texas College
freshman breakaway roper and barrel racer Tona Wright, who took second in
two events at the finals, won the cowgirls.

The NIRA established a foundation to broaden the scope of its services. On
September 10, 1994, a group met in Denver, Colorado, to organize the National Intercollegiate Rodeo Foundation, Inc., a nonprofit organization. The
purpose was "to create and support educational and charitable activities that
better the sport of collegiate rodeo and benefit disadvantaged persons who
have some relationship to the sport of rodeo."[13] The charter board consisted
of five members. The NIRA national student president and national faculty
president were ex-officio members of the board. Elected as the first president

was Tim Corfield, NIRA executive secretary–general manager. Other officers were vice president, John Mahoney, Vernon Regional Junior College rodeo coach; secretary, Varr Myers, Central Arizona College rodeo coach; treasurer, Russell Walter, faculty president; and Tyler Keith, student president.

Another first for the NIRA was the arrival of a Japanese television crew that filmed portions of the 1991 CNFR for a TV series of fourteen five-minute documentaries aired on TV in Japan every Saturday from June 29 through September 28. Although only five minutes were shown, it had an audience of six million people. The TV series, sponsored by a U.S. company, promoted the United States as a primary destination for Japanese travelers.[14]

Another event showcased college rodeo to its neighbors south of the border. During the Thanksgiving 1992 holidays, NIRA cowboys and cowgirls from Tarleton State University traveled to Saltillo, Coahuila, Mexico, to match competitors at La Universidad Autónoma Agraria Antonio Narro, to learn each other's cultural ways and rodeo techniques. They participated in the exhibition-type rodeo before a packed crowd of 1,500 people. The following week the Mexican team visited Stephenville, Texas, and experienced an exhibition rodeo with TSU demonstrating the NIRA sanctioned events, a barbecue and dance, and gifts of purple TSU rodeo jackets.[15]

A new NIRA program, RAWHIDE, started in 1993, earned praise. The program proposed to educate students about the risks of drug and alcohol use and abuse. The student-based program, field tested in the Northwest and Big Sky regions and coordinated by Pat Beard, a former NIRA member, set up alternative post-rodeo entertainment for athletes. Rodeo role models, who introduced the program, were world champions Clint Corey and Mike Beers, world champion Wrangler bullfighter Loyd Ketchum, and NFR bareback rider Bob Logue.

Fans showed approval for two major CNFR events although both were short lived. One event was the crowning of Miss College Rodeo. The 1990 Miss College Rodeo Nancy Reese of the University of Colorado crowned Scottsdale Community College's Angel Antan with the 1991 tiara. Miss Antan reigned as the last Miss College Rodeo because the NIRA office issued a notice on February 28, 1992, that due to a lack of funding, the contest would be dropped.[16] Another favorite was Crooked Nose, Harry Vold's famous poster-personality bull with the solo horn, who seemed to hunt barrel man Jess Franks for a crowd pleasing encounter as announcer Zeb Bell detailed the danger. Vold retired Crooked Horn to his ranch in Colorado to raise sons.

Some other events were added to draw crowds to the CNFR. The First Annual CNFR Bucking Horse Sale was scheduled at the 1995 CNFR. The CNFR Open Barrel Racing and Team Roping Jackpots were three-day events. Featherlite trailers joined the CNFR as a sponsor. As a fund-raiser, the cowboy calcutta auctioned all three CNFR rounds and the short go.

At the 1990 CNFR, the winning contestants required some luck to win gold buckles. The 274 men and 101 women contestants added their CNFR points to their regional points won during the ten-rodeo season. The twenty-two teams started with blank sheets as six professional rodeo judges put their pencils to the books: Butch Kirby, David Glover, George Gibbs, Tommy Keith, Billy "Red" Rodgers, and Jade Robinson.

Typically, the national leaders at the beginning of the CNFR do not win the gold. Points in two events eluded College of Southern Idaho's Zane Davis, incoming all-around leader, but Davis claimed the all-around and 1990 Rookie of the Year award. Davis said, "I didn't draw very well, so I'm happy that it turned out well, especially since I've chosen to be out for the next two years on an LDS church mission to Brazil."[17]

After returning from his two-year mission trip, Zane Davis proved that history does repeat itself. At the 1993 CNFR, Zane Davis, College of Southern Idaho, said, "Two days before I came up here, I went out to the barn. Six dusty old saddles were hanging on the wall. I walked over to one, and I dusted it off. It read, 'College Champion Bareback Rider 1963,' another read, 'College All-Around Champion 1963.' I thought, I'm going to win the nation in bareback riding. Dad did it thirty years ago, and I'm going to do it this year."[18] Davis's first seventy-three in bareback riding placed fourth. Five points separated first from tenth. Next round, Davis repeated a fourth place. After two rounds, Davis led with a total of 147 points, all points won at the finals. With a ten-point spread from first to tenth, Davis used Breezy Thistle for a seventy-five-point score to win the 1993 bareback riding and all-around championships, identical to his father Shawn Davis's championships thirty years earlier. Davis said, "Happy Father's Day" to Shawn, his CSI coach, and three-time professional world saddle bronc champion.[19]

Injuries eventually sidelined both Davis cowboys. In 1968 Shawn's bronc fell on him during a rodeo at Thompson Falls, Montana, damaging both of his shoulders, his spine, and his back. But the accidents did not stop there. After Davis lay in the sun for two hours waiting for the ambulance, his hand was

The 1990 NIRA all-around champion Zane Davis of College of Southern Idaho shows his awards to his college coach and father Shawn Davis, who won the same title in 1963 then went on to win three world saddle bronc championships. In 1993 young Davis duplicated the two NIRA national championships that his father had won thirty years before, all-around and bareback riding. Photo by Sylvia G. Mahoney, Vernon, Texas.

slammed in the ambulance door as they loaded him. Davis then had to wait while they loaded an injured bull rider. Davis said, "There was no doctor, just a veterinarian. On the way to the Missoula hospital 100 miles away, the ambulance ran out of gas and had to coast down the Rocky Mountain highway." The Bishop, as his friends called him because of his strong affiliation with his church, was in a body cast for six months and had a thirteen-month recovery period. Shawn's son Zane suffered injuries on his last horse at the 1993 finals. Zane's boot hung up in the cantle on a saddle bronc, and he broke his neck when he landed. After a nine-month recovery period, he broke his arm. Then, at a professional rodeo, a horse kicked Zane in the head causing a brain hemorrhage, so Zane hung up his spurs.[20]

Most coaches stressed athletic and academic excellence. Coach John Larick and his 1990 champion Montana State men's team, the fourth for MSU, exhibited both. Larick said, "I'm especially proud of this team because they are all on the honor roll and are going to graduate. Jeff Kvamme graduated last Saturday night along with fourteen other NIRA members."[21]

The MSU 1990 blue-ribbon team could attest to athletic bloodlines and skills. MSU's 1990 national champion team fielded two second-generation NIRA cowboys. Jeff Miller's father Tom Miller won the 1970 and 1971 NIRA all-around buckles competing for Black Hills State College. Bill Melaney's mother, Sue Burgraff Melaney, while at MSU, had won the 1961 NIRA all-around buckle, the first woman's championship for MSU. Bill's sister Mary Melaney was a member of the MSU 1986 NIRA champion women's team, the first women's team championship. Team roper and calf roper Chris Witcher won the rodeo all-around. Two other MSU team members Shawn Vant and Dan Mortensen excelled in the PRCA. Mortensen, ranked in the 1990 PRCA top ten in saddle bronc riding at CNFR time, went on to win five world saddle bronc titles and one all-around title by 1998.

MSU's Vant, a junior, won the national all-around, the CNFR all-around, and national bareback championships in 1990. His seventy-seven on Snappy Jack was the highest score of the rodeo. The Canadian cowboy credited his stepfa-

Members of 1990 NIRA champion Montana State men's team are (left to right) *Bill Melaney, Jeff Miller, Jeff Kvamme, Coach John Larick, Chris Witcher, Shawn Vant, and Dan Mortensen. Photo by Sylvia G. Mahoney, Vernon, Texas.*

ther Bill Robinson, the 1963 bull riding average winner, for starting him in rodeo. Raised on "a little ranch just outside town," Vant said, "We had an indoor arena at home. I just got on there all the time."[22] Mortensen won the 1991 saddle bronc championship, but after the first round, he thought that was impossible. Mortensen said, "I fell off my first horse in the first round." He then rode Border Patrol for a seventy-six score, the best of the rodeo. Mortensen, whose childhood was spent on a "little place, three and a half acres outside Billings," said, "I was taught to ride broncs by my dad and polished by my coach Ike Sankey at Powell, Wyoming."[23]

Prospects of championships rose and fell creating photo-finish excitement at the CNFR. The 1990 NIRA bull riding champ Casey Gates of Fort Scott Community College spent a nerve-wracking final round before the results were in. Of the six bull riders with scores on two bulls, Gates's 158 points ranked first. In the final round, the bull AZ Copenhagen stopped Gates's hopes, for a while, when the bull tossed him before the buzzer sounded. However, only two riders heard the eight-second short round buzzer, Randall Thornton of Howard College, the CNFR bull riding champ, and Darrin Cook of Western Texas College. With only two having scores, Gates placed third in the average giving him the title by four points.

Champions came from every classification, freshmen through seniors, and every background, not just ranch or rodeo families. The 374 contestants started the 1991 CNFR with high expectations. For six days tension built as 266 cowboys and 108 cowgirls from eighty-seven colleges and universities vied for two national team championships, two all-arounds, and nine event championships. These contestants were from a pool of 2,263 NIRA members at 117 schools.

Some university coaches knew how to recruit six skilled, talented team members. Southwestern Oklahoma State University coaches Don "Doc" Mitchell and George Howard won the 1992 title with team members J. D. Crouse, Mark Gomes, Bob Griswold, Scott Mullen, Brian Rice, and Jack Sims. However, the event winners were from other schools, not SWOSU.

As cowboys gained in competitive skills, they started to specialize so that a cowboy like Casey Minton of West Hills College, who competed in four events, calf roping, team roping, bull dogging, and bull riding, was rare. In fact, Minton's prowess at both ends of the arena later earned him the 1993 Linderman Award for winning at least $1,000 in three professional events, with one being a timed event and one a rough-stock event. Minton's success, as every cowboy knows, rests in the quality of the horse he rides. Minton's nine-year-old dun gelding won the 1992 CNFR American Quarter Horse of the Year. "Willy," trained by Minton, proved to be as versatile as his rider; Minton rode him in all three timed events.

Sometimes in spite of CNFR points, regional points made championships unattainable, such as the 1992 team roping championship. Two Texas team ropers, Turtle Powell and Twister Cain from Vernon Regional Junior College, challenged Seth Weishaar of South Dakota State University. Although Weishaar did not win a point at the finals, he beat Turtle by six points and Twister by fourteen points, making them number two and number three in the nation.

Some colleges specialize in one event, especially a coach's event. Odessa College, known as the bull riding school of the Southwest, fielded a fourth bull riding champion in 1992, Jerome Davis. The new champion from North Carolina was the first college bull rider from east of the Mississippi to win an NIRA bull riding championship. Davis won the 1995 world bull riding championship. However, on March 14, 1998, a bull threw Davis on his head, shattering his spine and paralyzing him. Davis, who returned to a standing ovation at the 1999 CNFR, said that he believed he could beat the one percent chance his doctors gave him to walk again. With the help of a special saddle equipped with a back brace and cowboy grit, the twenty-six-year-old cowboy can ride across his hundred-acre farm, where he and his wife Tiffany manage two hundred head of bucking bulls.[24]

CNFR event competition started with zero points in 1993, so some of the 256 cowboys and 104 cowgirls won events by one point. The 1993 saddle bronc champion Cliff Norris, Panhandle State University, said, "I came into the final round with a one-point lead on Zane Davis, so I said to myself, 'whatever happens, happens.'"[25] Norris rode Class Act for a seventy-five-point ride; Davis rode Bad River to match Norris's score. The one-point difference gave Norris the saddle bronc title.

One point made the difference for the 1993 champion bull rider. Philip Elkins of Hill College, a freshman at the Texas school, said, "I had watched the CNFR on TV several times, so I had some idea what to expect. I started riding goats when I was five or six then calves, steers, junior bulls, and bulls, so I felt prepared."[26] Elkins, with one round left, stood fourth of ten, but only eight riders had succeeded on two bulls. Elkins had to make up a ten-point deficit to win.

He watched as the bulls scored six times. Elkins's eight seconds produced eighty-four points, the highest of the rodeo, good enough for a one-point lead and the championship.

The photo finishes at the 1993 CNFR continued. Two world-class calf ropers wrapped two in 20.7 seconds each. The two freshmen, Vernon Regional Junior College cowboy Shane Hatch and Southeastern Oklahoma State cowboy Blair Burk, the 1993 PRCA Rookie of the Year, took three rounds to decide the champion. Hatch's second round 8.5 was the fastest of the rodeo. Burk's third round came up dry and moved him to a seventh place finish. Hatch's final 9.5 won the final round, the 1993 national championship, and Rookie of the Year for him.

The team roping duo leading the national standings did not move at the 1993 finals even though they could not use regional points. University of Tennessee at Martin ropers Frank Graves and Brett Gould wanted to be the first college champion team roping cowboys east of the Mississippi. Graves and Gould's first 8.4 did not make the top ten, the next, a 5.4, was the fastest of the rodeo. SEOSU's Britt Bockius and Blair Burk won the final round with a 6.4, but the Tennessee cowboys' 6.6 run won the championship.

SWOSU coached by Don Mitchell, George Howard, and Shawn Wright won the $14,000 first-place men's team 1993 scholarship award. SWOSU also won the title in 1985 and 1992.

For only the ninth time, a two-year school won a team championship. Six cowboys from a Texas two-year school, Vernon Regional Junior College, won the 1994 championship with five university teams completing the top six. The school was relatively new to college rodeo, but the coach and cowboys were not. Three times, Coach John Mahoney had been to the winner's circle while coaching at a four-year school. The six sophomore VRJC cowboys rode in with two years' of college rodeo experience along with an impressive list of credentials. Along with the 1994 team championship, two VRJC cowboys finished in second place: Pete Hawkins, reserve bareback champion, and the 1993 calf roping champ Shane Hatch, reserve calf roping champion. Hawkins later became the 1999 reserve world champion bareback rider. This was Hawkins, Hatch, and Travis Griffin's second team try at the championship. Doug Fennell, Kirby Berry, and Mark Eakin, new to the team, brought years of rodeo experience. Griffin finished fifth in saddle bronc riding, and Eakin, sixth in calf roping. Eakin later coached rodeo at West Texas A&M.

Members of the 1994 NIRA national champion men's team from Vernon Regional Junior College, who collected the $14,000 scholarship from Annice Burkhalter, representative for Copenhagen/Skoal Scholarship Awards Program, are (left to right) *Doug Fennell, Pete Hawkins, reserve bareback champion; Travis Griffin, Coach John Mahoney, Burkhalter, Kirby Berry, Mark Eakin, and Shane Hatch, reserve calf roping champ. Photo by Sylvia G. Mahoney, Vernon, Texas.*

Sometimes championships happen in strange ways. The 1994 bull riding champ, University of Nevada at Las Vegas team member Beau Gillespie, scored an eighty-two, but Montana State sophomore Jason Jackson scored an eighty-four, the highest score of the rodeo. Gillespie was leading the average until Harry Vold's bull bucked him off. Vold's bulls finished the round with bulls, ten; cowboys, zero. Gillespie said, "I hate to win it on two, but I am happy to take it."[27]

Sometimes the champions are surprised with their titles. Panhandle State sophomore Marty McCloy said, "I was as surprised as anyone at what happened in the final round."[28] In the first round, the defending champion VRJC's Shane Hatch, roping on Jotta Jett, his 1994 American Quarter Horse of the Year, roped one in 9.8. Western Texas College sophomore Leddy Lewis matched Hatch's 9.8. So Hatch roped in 9.4, but McNeese State junior Jason Senior roped one in an 8.8, the fastest of the rodeo. With one round left, Hatch led the average with 19.2, with Senior at 21.1. Along came Marty McCloy with a 12.3 and a 10.8 for sixth in the average at 23.1. In the final round, Hatch's time stopped at 14.7, Senior's at 13.0, and McCloy's at 9.9. McCloy won the 1994 NIRA calf roping championship with Hatch second, and Senior third.

A surprise happened in the steer wrestling, also. The 1994 national champion steer wrestler Cal Poly-SLO junior Tyler Keith won the West Coast Region calf roping championship, fourth in the team roping, but he was not in the top twenty-five steer wrestlers. After three rounds, Keith, the new NIRA national student president, won with a total of 14.6, the eighth steer wrestling championship for Cal Poly.

Surprises in the team roping resulted from identical cowboys. Texas Tech sophomore Tye Maben and Howard College sophomore John Folmer roped one in a 5.8. However, the heeler for the team with the fastest time of the rodeo, a 5.4, appeared to be John Folmer, but it was his identical twin Wayne Folmer who roped with Tarleton State junior Turtle Powell. Maben and John Folmer finished with a 21.1 total, winning the 1994 NIRA championship.

Generally, the combination of tradition, longevity, and experienced coaches helps the winning teams. At the 1995 CNFR, two universities—Montana State University and Southeastern Oklahoma State University—added another NIRA team title.

Individuals' names often make the headlines with outstanding performances. MSU's Jason Jackson, the 1995 all-around and bull riding champion, was one of only two bull riders who made it to the whistle on three head. Jackson's eighty-seven-point bull ride on Jersey Joe Skoal in the final round earned his first bull riding title, his second consecutive all-around title, and led MSU to a men's team championship. Jackson became the first cowboy to claim back-to-back all-around titles since 1972–73.

In the 1990s, typically, champions won with consistent runs or rides. Two Louisiana consistent cowboys claimed two national championships. Chad Hagan, steer wrestler from the Louisiana school Northwestern State University, was eighth in the first round and third in the second round. The consistency showed when his total time on three head was 15.8, making Hagan the 1995 steer wrestling champ and giving NSU its first national championship. Louisiana bareback rider James Boudreaux of McNeese State University modeled consistency with scores of 78, 75, and 76 to take the 1995 bareback riding championship, the seventh event championship for McNeese.

Sometimes championships are won in spite of disadvantages. The 1995 team roping champions, Central Arizona College's Whip Lewis and Eastern Wyoming College's Paul Griemsman, had no chance to practice together before the CNFR. "Whip called and asked me to head for him," said Griemsman.[29] With a 6.9 in the first round and a 7.5, their combined times made them the leaders going into the final round. Their 8.7 was third, but good enough to be champions.

Trying to win a college rodeo national championship is like trying to win the Super Bowl. Many have the experience and talent, but few finish number one. The CNFR records show that successfully defending a championship is even more difficult. All but one of the 1995 NIRA event champions returned to defend their titles in 1996, but only one defending team and one defending event champion won again. Schools from six states claimed 1996 national champions: Oklahoma, Idaho, Wyoming, New Mexico, Texas, and North Dakota.

To sharpen the CNFR competition, in 1996 a third long round was added. The national champion men's team, College of Southern Idaho, benefited from the added round. Coach Shawn Davis said, "The third round made it possible for us to win the national championship."[30] Although Coach Davis had seen his team members win six national event titles during his twenty years of coaching, a national team championship had eluded his teams. All six members of Coach Davis's team won points in the first three rounds: J. C. Call, T. W. Parker, Jeffrey Rupert, Ryan Carey, Shawn Morehead, and John Roderick. Three of his men placed in two events, and five made it to the short round, and Call won the national all-around title.

The addition of another round in 1996 affected the outcome of the calf roping. Calf roper Jerome Schneeberger of Murray State College in Oklahoma followed Chance Henderson of the U.S. Air Force Academy by one second going into the final round. With the quality of the ropers, Schneeberger had to draw well to win. He did; he won the short round with a 9.5 to Henderson's 12.7 run. As a cadet, Henderson represented the diversity in college rodeo. The Air Force Academy had about sixty rodeo contestants.

Sometimes four rounds were not enough to provide a leader. In 1996 after the final round in team roping, two teams had identical times on four head: 37.7 seconds, so they shared the national championship title. Andy Bolton and Ben Blue of Panhandle State University in Oklahoma had a six-second lead going into the final round. In the final round, third place Buck Garcia and Joe Verastegui of Southwest Texas Junior College roped one in 6.2. Their shared title rests on some quick thinking and skill by the team of Bolton and Blue. When Bolton's head catch did not work, Blue changed ends and roped the horns while Bolton roped the heels in 15.7 for a total time of 37.7, a repeat of Garcia and Verastegui's time.

As the CNFR competition tightened, one point won many a championship. The 1996 CNFR Rookie of the Year, Jeremy Crane of Dickinson State in North Dakota, led the saddle bronc average by one point after three rounds. In the final round, his seventy-eight-point ride aboard Slick Quick earned second place points and the title. "I rode good, and I got good horses all week," said Crane.[31] The 1996 bull riding champ Aaron Williams of Hill College, Hillsboro, Texas, the only cowboy who had ridden three bulls, watched half of the bull riders buck off in the fourth round. As the eight-second whistle blew, Williams went flying through the air. "I didn't know if I made it or not," said Williams.[32] But the judges' watches showed eight seconds. Williams, the only cowboy to cover four bulls, won the national bull riding championship by a split second.

In spite of unusual circumstances and more rounds, typically, the winners were consistent and rode horses that fit them well. In the steer wrestling, Todd Suhn of the University of Wyoming led the average with a 6.4 or less on each of his first three steers. In the final round, he watched second place take a no-time and third place take a barrier penalty, so his consistency with a 6.3 in the final round earned the gold buckle. The American Quarter Horse Association (AQHA) named Suhn's 13-year-old sorrel gelding Super San Wood Horse of the Year in the CNFR men's division for the second time. At the time Suhn won his college title, he was fifth in the professional ranks in steer wrestling.

The fine line in barrel racing competition showed when two cowgirls had a photo finish. At the start of the 1990 CNFR, Elisa Nielsen of Utah Valley Community College trailed Holly Foster from Cal Poly by ten points in the national standings, but finished four–one-hundredths of a second ahead of her. Sophomore Nielson said, "My title is especially exciting because my horse and I have been together since the minute he was foaled twelve years ago. My mom trained him."[33]

Winning the all-around became more difficult as more cowgirls came to the finals entered in three events. The 1990 NIRA all-around champion Jimmi Jo Martin of the University of Wyoming came to the 1991 CNFR with three Central

Rocky Mountain Region buckles: goat tying, breakaway roping, and all-around. However, Martin said, "I did have a couple of lucky breaks here. My second goat got up right at six seconds (the qualifying time). I roped my first breakaway calf, and the rope broke off on his two hind feet."[34] Martin's goat tying started with a 7.1 run. She added a 7.2-second run, followed by an 8.8, which won the average, the goat tying title, and the all-around title. Martin's points gave University of Wyoming coaches Danny Dunlavy and Pete Burns their first women's team trophy.

In spite of the close competition, some contestants became crowd favorites. Leading the 1991 national all-around standings was a petite, talented, experienced cowgirl, Cal Poly-San Luis Obispo senior Julie Adair. Adair had been 1989 reserve national champion in three events: goat tying, breakaway roping, and all-around. Adair said, "With this being my last rodeo, I knew that it was going to be hard and that I needed luck. However, my first run in breakaway, I missed. I was pleased with my second run."[35] With a 3.0, she split third and fourth place breakaway points. She won the goat tying title, fifth place in the breakaway roping, and sixth in the barrel race to become the 1991 national all-around champion.

Another standout was the 1991 champion women's roper. Vernon Regional Junior College sophomore Lari Dee Guy came in second and left first. The Abilene, Texas, cowgirl, who some say ropes like a man, said that roping did not come easy for her: "I was left-handed, and Dad wouldn't let me rope left handed. I had to do everything right, or I couldn't catch one. Dad taught me the mechanics of roping. I had to know exactly what I was doing. I think it helped me."[36] At the CNFR Guy started with a 3.9, eleventh place. Then, she and VRJC sophomore Mitzi Mayes shared tenth place with a 3.5. Guy and junior Sonja Cosse of University of Nevada at Las Vegas shared first in the final round with a 3.4. Cosse took the average, and Guy took the nation.

Winning teams need a full complement of team members, and Coach Danny Dunlavy's 1991 University of Wyoming cowgirls fit the requirements. They did something unusual as they made it two years in a row, but with a completely different team. Dunlavy had two seasoned seniors from the 1988 CNFR, Shanna Newland and Toni Christinck and junior Lori Rhodes, all from Wyoming ranches. Newland roped a 2.4, the fastest of the rodeo. Christinck did the same on her first goat with a 7.7. Rhodes won the final goat tying round, and they won the team title.

An infrequent circumstance happened at the 1992 CNFR. A two-year school beat the universities to the finish line. Walla Walla Community College joined an elite group of winning two-year schools. Only ten two-year schools have won team championships. Coach Tim Corfield's Walla Walla cowgirls Penny Conforth Gardner won the all-around and Brenda Mays the breakaway roping.

The cowgirls continued to excel. In 1992 Texas A&M University barrel racer Mindy Morris of Seymour, Texas, paired with Doc's Three Bits, to break the forty-year championship hiatus for Texas A&M and set a record as the first champion cowgirl Aggie. The goat tying champion Lana Tibbetts of Montana State University, a cowgirl from a ranch thirty miles south of Terry, Montana, had won the goat tying Big Sky Region title four times, the all-around three times, and the 1991 national reserve championship. She beat Paulette Simonson of South Dakota State University by eighteen points. The South Dakota Sports Writers voted Simonson as the 1992 South Dakota Independent Female Athlete of the Year.

The cowgirls experienced photo finishes using the first sudden death format in 1993. Four cowgirls staked a claim to 17.1 on two goats. Vernon Regional Junior College's Tessa McCurley Cain tied hers in eight seconds to win the round. University of Utah cowgirl Andrea Allen set the fastest run of the rodeo, a 7.1 in the second round. At the end, SWOSU's Shelley Johnston's 1993 goat tying championship hung on one-tenth of a second. Johnston had 25.8, and Montana State cowgirl Kelly Stevens had 25.9. Johnston, who won the all-around, said, "I had mixed feelings about the sudden-death format. Everybody doesn't compete against each other through the whole year, so it seems to be more fair for everyone. It certainly worked for me."[37]

The one point difference in the championship races continued. Texas Tech cowgirl Lari Dee Guy, the 1993 breakaway roping champ, repeated the one-tenth of a second thriller. Stress seemed to produce consistency in Guy, the 1991 champ and 1992 reserve champ, as her first was a three flat, her second a three flat, and her third a 3.1. New Mexico State's Rachel Lacy's 2.6 took the first, and SWOSU's Shelley Johnston's 2.6, the second round. However, Guy's total of 9.1 beat Lacy's 9.2 for the championship.

The horse race thriller finished with four runs separated by only one–one-hundredth of a second. The 1993 champion Merilee McGraw of Garden City Community College in Kansas, riding Captain Seville, ran the barrels for a total of 42.05. One-tenth of a second behind her was a cowgirl from Oahu,

Hawaii, Heidi Ho, University of Southern Colorado, with a 42.15. The 1992 champion Mindy Morris of Texas A&M followed with 42.18 and 1992 runner-up Jamie Bean of the Texas school Tarleton State University was a 42.21. McGraw won the first round, and Morris the second with a 13.8, the fastest time of the rodeo. The final round joined the records of amazing finishes. Only one–one-hundredth separated the top four: McGraw, 13.90; Ho, 13.91; Morris 13.92; Bean, 13.93.

Coaches who recruited well from two-year schools were difficult to beat. SEOSU had four team championships by 1994. The three SWOSU cowgirls, coached by Don Mitchell and George Howard, were the number one team by the end of the first round, and they stayed, a rarity at the CNFR. SWOSU senior Shelley Johnston, the defending all-around and goat tying champion, won the first round in goat tying followed by a 2.7 in breakaway roping, the fastest of the rodeo. SWOSU junior Tori Woodard, a three-event cowgirl, won the second round in goat tying and barrel racing and finished as the reserve champion barrel racer and the all-around champion. Shelley's sister Kelley, a freshman, took fourth in the breakaway roping average. With 780 points, SWOSU had no serious challengers for the championship. Woodard, Kelley Johnston, and Shelley Johnston, the all-around runner-up with 295 points, demonstrated how a real team should work.

SEOSU returned in 1995 after being absent from NIRA competition for several years. The school had rebuilt its rodeo program after dealing with some NIRA infractions, which had forced the university to change directions for several years. SEOSU won their eighth national team championship. In 1996 Caryn Standifer Snyder along with teammates Tachana McCurley and Brenna Winship added the ninth team championship for Coach Betty Gayle Cooper Ratliff, making her the "winningest" coach in NIRA history.

Some cowgirls managed to get to the winner's circle every time, breaking records along the way. In 1995 SEOSU's Caryn Standifer Snyder proved her all-around cowgirl credentials by placing in all three women's events, setting a domino effect in motion. Next came the 1995 national goat tying title, followed by the all-around title, and the number one spot for her team. At the 1996 CNFR, Standifer Snyder joined a select five in NIRA history to win consecutive all-around titles. With her 1996 barrel racing gold buckle and her 1997 breakaway roping title, she became the only cowgirl to win four different events: three-events and the all-around twice. With five championships, Standifer

Southeastern Oklahoma State University's Caryn Standifer Snyder won the goat tying national championship in 1995 and the all-around on her way to tying the record of five NIRA championships. She won a championship in each of the three women's events and all-around, a first. Photo by JJJ Photo, Ord, Nebraska.

Snyder matched the record of another SEOSU cowgirl, Sabrina Pike, the only two in NIRA history. Standifer added Snyder to her name when she married the 1995 calf roping champ, T. W. Snyder.

A Cinderella story always captures the public's imagination. The 1995 barrel racing champion, Vernon Regional Junior College cowgirl Molly Swanson Powell, riding her black mare named Pecan, dominated the barrel race with her fast, snappy runs. The petite Montana cowgirl, who went to a Texas college, made headlines with her little mare that was a family-bred and family-trained cross between a Quarter Horse/Welsh mare and a Thoroughbred stud. Swanson Powell had run barrels on Pecan's mother before turning her out to be a brood mare. When Swanson Powell's name was announced for her second run at the 1995 CNFR, everyone stopped to watch as the first round winner did it again. Swanson Powell's second place final run took the gold buckle, the 1995 Rookie of the Year award, and her team's second-place finish in the nation with the help of team members Christi Sultemeier and Angie Meadors.

As cowgirl competition grew, it became more common to see CNFR contestants qualify for the professional finals simultaneously. Molly Swanson Powell

Vernon Regional Junior College barrel racer Molly Swanson Powell, riding her mare Pecan, won the 1995 NIRA national title and became a many-times NFR qualifier. Photo by JJJ Photo, Ord, Nebraska.

and Angie Meadors both qualified for the 1995 NFR barrel race, and both appeared on a popular cowgirl calendar. It was Swanson Powell and Pecan's first time to make the professional top fifteen barrel racers, but Meadors returned for her fourth NFR appearance. Swanson Powell continued to qualify for the NFR through 2002. Meadors, a Wrangler poster personality, continued competing also, adding to her barrel racing winnings revenue by modeling professionally.

During the first six years of the 1990s, the new qualifying rules for the CNFR had elevated the competition to a new level making it easier to market. Both Bozeman and the CNFR had benefited financially during their partnership. However, the CNFR had grown beyond the size of the facilities and sponsorships that Bozeman could provide. The rationale for leaving Bozeman was logical and realistic, but the emotional impact of changing from a familiar annual routine left both sides dreading the move. Change brought contradictions: fear of the unknown and excitement for the possibilities for improvement. The change impacted decision making for the NIRA leaders and added to the daily press of activities. Three years before its golden anniversary, the CNFR moved with the NIRA leaders believing that the move was necessary for growth and independence.

CHAPTER 8

1997 to 2003—A College Sport

and Big Business

The twentieth century ended with college rodeo contestants pushing the competitive edge and the NIRA becoming a big business. The accomplishments continued in spite of the earlier contestants' records that seemed unbeatable. The NIRA was knowledgeable, experienced, and independent, although not independently wealthy. It was branching into areas of service to its members, such as endowed scholarships, funding for injured athletes, recognition of academic excellence, collecting its history, and honoring its alumni. Following the lead of other collegiate sports, colleges and universities were hiring experienced rodeo coaches with the drive to win. The cowgirls, as had women in other sports, had entered the twentieth-first century equal to the cowboys as talented, skilled contestants. College rodeo kept true to its western heritage while joining the world of technology. Web pages touted college rodeo programs, and coaches responded to e-mailed questions with instant answers. Generally, college rodeo had become recognized as a college sport, not a show, and the NIRA was moving to a new level of self-determination. However, one era ended in 2001 with the changing of its longtime leader, and a new era began with a new leader and many unknowns for the future of the NIRA.

Internal changes occurred first for the NIRA with the announcement of leadership adjustments. After the 1996 CNFR, publication manager Kay Lynn Beard turned the NIRA newspaper over to Sarah Neely, who brought valuable experience from her years working for the ProRodeo Hall of Fame in Colorado

Springs, Colorado. Beard's reasons for leaving cited the demands of her full-time job as counselor and instructor at Walla Walla Community College and her family's rodeo production company. The *Tri-State Livestock News* in Sturgis, South Dakota, contracted the advertisement sales, the printing, and mailing responsibilities. The *Tri-State Livestock News* hired Colette "Koko" Knutson Gjermundson of Marshall, North Dakota, to expand the CNFR coverage by writing daily articles for the *Daily CNFR Editions.* Gjermundson's credentials included writing talent, a communications degree, and family rodeo roots.[1]

Promoting college rodeo as a sport, the NIRA made position titles comparable to other college sports and the PRCA. The NIRA general manager became the NIRA commissioner, combining the duties of CNFR director with NIRA executive secretary and general manager. NIRA commissioner Tim Corfield had given up his coaching job after twenty-three years, so he agreed to the new combination of responsibilities. Corfield, who joined the 1974 NIRA board as Northwest Region faculty director, had become the NIRA executive secretary–general manager in 1979. Along with this job and coaching, Corfield taught history and economics at Walla Walla Community College as well as directed his two daughters through the ranks of rodeo competition. As rodeo coach, Tim Corfield's Walla Walla Community College teams had won one team and five event championships. Corfield joined the ranks of an elite group of coaches from ten two-year schools who had won national team championships.

When the NIRA was finally economically able to expand its staff, it still lacked enough administrative personnel to adequately manage all aspects of the NIRA and the CNFR. Five people comprised the office personnel in 1998. NIRA commissioner Tim Corfield, whose four-year contract ended June 30, 2001, was the chief executive officer and manager of the business office, subject to the supervision and direction of the NIRA Board of Directors. Sarah Neely managed the *Collegiate Arena* and coordinated the NIRA Foundation and RAWHIDE. The NIRA newspaper had a circulation of about 3,600. RAWHIDE, defined as Rodeo Athletes on Wellness, was a program designed to strengthen rodeo participants' wellness scope and to educate them regarding alcohol and drug abuse. The office-business manager Donna Maiden was responsible for the personnel issues, encompassing salaries, office procedures, clerical services, job interviewing, and job evaluations. Her job included maintaining the financial records for the NIRA, CNFR, NIRF, and RAWHIDE. The rodeo secretary Lori

Brown maintained the addresses for all stock contractors, judges, and regional secretaries, assisted in assigning judges, and scheduled rodeos and judging seminars as well as compiled and maintained rodeo statistics. The membership secretary Claudia Kelly determined the eligibility status of college students, maintained membership lists, and processed CNFR applications.

The NIRA connected to the Internet and created a Web page with information about membership, scholarships, alumni, the foundation, and the CNFR. They eventually had weekly updates on the regional standings and daily updates during the CNFR.

With the growing number of contestants, finding adequate, quality stock became a constant problem for some of the regions. In 1998 the five male and six female student board members and eleven coaches reviewed the rule for the number of stock required at a rodeo. The burgeoning numbers of contestants in some regions made it impossible to find stock contractors who could supply uniform pens of timed-event cattle and bucking stock. The Central Rocky Mountain Region with 450 contestants requested that the minimum number of cattle be one-third of the number of entries instead of one-half the number. The board planned to rework the rule for drawing stock to compensate for judges who arrived an hour before the first performance.[2]

Eligibility and timers' qualifications caused debate. One issue was the suggestion that regional work-in-progress forms should verify that students were enrolled in twelve hours during the entire semester. Another issue was timekeepers' qualifications. At many rodeos, the timekeepers had never timed a rodeo, possibly never even seen a rodeo, so they lacked accuracy and consistency.[3]

To celebrate the twenty-fifth anniversary of U.S. Tobacco's (USTC) association with the NIRA, USTC awarded a new scholarship in 1999. Aaron Marts of Treasure Valley Community College in Ontario, Oregon, received the new, prestigious award, the Walt Garrison Top Hand Award. Each of the eleven regions had selected a nominee based on qualities modeled by Garrison: initiative, loyalty, tenacity, commitment, honesty, perseverance, integrity, and leadership. Marts received a $2,500 cash award, a custom trophy buckle, and a $2,500 scholarship for his school.[4]

Hearing one's name called at the CNFR scholarships awards ceremony highlighted a contestant's well-managed year. The Copenhagen/Skoal Scholarship Awards Program provided academic scholarships to eight 4.0 GPA students who qualified for the 1999 CNFR, the first year that all recipients had 4.0 GPAs.

In 2001 U.S. Smokeless Tobacco Company Scholarship Awards Program awarded $207,700 in scholarships to winning students' colleges.[5]

The NIRA signed two new national sponsors in 1998 and maintained other sponsors of long tenure. The newest national sponsor, Powder River Livestock Handling Equipment, agreed to sponsor the CNFR and provide a Powder River arena for CNFR competition. Another new sponsor, the National Institute for Automotive Service Excellence (ASE), donated twelve trophy saddles for the champions and $1,000 for the Long Haul Award, the first going to the University of West Alabama for traveling the farthest distance to compete at the 1998 CNFR. Longtime sponsor Copenhagen/Skoal Scholarship Awards Program announced that since 1974 they had donated $3.4 million for rodeo scholarships, and they would continue with their sponsorship program. Ariat International, Inc., had signed on in the fall of 1997 to provide over five hundred pairs of boots to contestants and a team scholarship to the RAWHIDE Team of the Year.

Another major sponsor for many years, Wrangler Jeans & Shirts had helped to correct a major early-day problem by training qualified NIRA judges. They agreed to continue sponsoring the Wrangler Official's Program, which funded judging seminars in all eleven NIRA regions. They also agreed to subsidize judging fees at all NIRA-sanctioned rodeos and provide support for judges fees and expenses at the CNFR.

As a safeguard for funding expanding services, the NIRA established the NIRA Foundation. By 1998 the Foundation had five categories for projects: scholarships, historical preservation, NIRA traveling exhibit, injured athlete relief fund, and general fund. They started with four $1,000 scholarships and increased it to eight with the criteria being a 3.0 GPA and financial need. Next, they promoted historical preservation in *The Collegiate Arena* ads. The Foundation produced a three-fold traveling NIRA exhibit, an injured athlete relief fund, and funds for the RAWHIDE program, which produced a kid's rodeo, an annual breakfast for coaches, and a *RAWHIDE Coaches' Handbook* on wellness, distributed for the first time in 1998.

As with all aging organizations, retirements, changes in coaching positions, and deaths created hard-to-fill vacancies. After the 1997 CNFR, Coach Ed Mayberry of Miles Community College announced his retirement after twenty-two years. "I was shotgunned into taking it because the person that had it didn't want it, and I knew which end of the horse to get on," said Mayberry. Mayberry had students qualify for the CNFR every year except one with Scott Breding winning the 1982 bull riding championship, earning an associate degree, and becoming the 1985 PRCA Rookie of the Year bull rider. Nacona Pauley won the 1995 breakaway roping buckle. The 1991 world champion bullfighter Loyd Ketchum rode bulls and earned an associate degree in auto mechanics at MCC. "Once I retire, I don't know the future of college rodeo here at Miles," Mayberry said, "It will depend on the legislature and the source of income for the program."[6]

Another legend in college rodeo, William O. "Doc" Beazley announced in 1997 that it was time to retire since he was eighty-one years old. As long as anyone in the Southwest Region could remember, on Thursday afternoon, the last weekend of April, as the pickups and trailers rolled in at the Hardin-Simmons arena on Grape Street in Abilene, Texas, Doc Beazley, a silver-haired dynamo, could be seen rushing around, usually on a white horse, making sure that everything was in order for the first performance. He had carried the NIRA banner high at Hardin-Simmons University for thirty-five years, long after the university, a charter member of the NIRA, quit fielding a rodeo team. His title at the university was vice president, but his legacy came from his commitment to maintaining a direct connection with horses and rodeo for the school that called itself "The Cowboys." Doc said, "The University has to keep its Western image. The Six White Horses, the Cowboy Band, and the NIRA rodeo all help to keep this image alive."[7]

A death activates the national rodeo network of phone calls and contacts. This was true on April 25, 1999, when Pat Larick, forty-nine-year-old Big Sky Region rodeo secretary and wife of Montana State University rodeo coach John Larick, had a heart attack and died while she and John were enjoying a Saturday evening at home. Pat left a large heart print on the NIRA. When the CNFR was in Bozeman, Montana, each year Pat and John opened the doors of their home, located in a Montana picture-postcard setting, to students, NIRA board members, their families, and friends who enjoyed catching up on the previous year's happenings while indulging in a feast that included grilled wild game and fresh rhubarb cobbler. As well as serving as the perfect hostess, Pat gave facts and statistics to the CNFR announcer each evening along with taking a cake to the rodeo office for the judges, rodeo secretary, and others who followed the aroma.

The century ended along with the life of one of rodeo's legends, Betty Gayle Cooper Ratliff, whose athletic ability and attitude helped set the standard in college rodeo and mold the future of women in rodeo. On November 12, 1999, in Durant, Oklahoma, nine-time world champion, B. G., so well known in the rodeo world that only her initials had to be used, died. In her eulogy given by Steve Massey in Durant to a church overflowing with her family, friends, and fans, he said that B. G. lived by the Code of the West, and he did not have to explain that to her friends. He said she "cowboyed-up" during her long, courageous fight with cancer so much so that it was difficult to tell how serious her condition was as she talked about it so positively.

The CNFR had exceeded the facilities and economic potential in its twenty-five-year stay in Montana, so the NIRA board moved the CNFR to a new location in 1997 to advance its promise as a commodity desired by sponsors and fans, while offering an economic advantage to a community. The NIRA board recognized the hazards of change, but it also recognized the economic rewards of a successful venture for the CNFR. When the NIRA advertised for CNFR bids, it discovered that many cities were seeking events like the CNFR to swell their economic base through fans who would flock to see collegiate contestants win record-breaking championships. The NIRA continued negotiations for sponsorships that would be lucrative for the NIRA, would help promote the CNFR on a national scale, and would help fund scholarships for the student contestants. The NIRA was expanding its efforts to achieve the national recognition and economic success that the professional finals had achieved.

Independence for the NIRA obligated it to take control of all aspects of the CNFR, moving toward professionalism in every detail. To eliminate a drawing contest for the contestants, the NIRA leased stock from six contractors, becoming its own stock contractor for the 1997 CNFR. They hired Bob Tallman, a ten-time PRCA National Finals Rodeo announcer whose familiar, rapid-fire voice mesmerized audiences while focusing on the arena action. The NIRA hired the world championship talent of Loyd Ketchum, veteran bullfighter and NIRA alumnus, to run interference for CNFR bull riders and barrel man Flint Rasmussen, a favorite of fans for his wry humor. The NIRA hired the best rodeo secretary, Sunni Deb Backstrom, timers, Shirley Churchill and Tami Vold Larsen, and pickup men, Brad Churchill and Kenny Carpenter.

The NIRA constantly promoted humane treatment of animals at the CNFR and in the regions. They held training seminars, such as the one at the 1997 CNFR presented by Terri Greer, director of PRCA animal welfare issues. She highlighted animal activists' activities, legislative issues, education on confrontation, materials available for research, and new ways to handle confrontation.

"Ms. Greer is offering tools for educating the non-horse public. It is a battle that we all need to consider our own," said Tim Corfield, NIRA general manager.[8]

The NIRA had been moving forward, expanding in all areas; however, a major crisis halted everything when the CNFR became homeless prior to the 1999 finals. After the 1998 CNFR, the promotional partnership of the NIRA with Sutton Rodeos and Champion Sports Group, which had contracted to produce the CNFR at Rapid City, South Dakota, dissolved. On August 14, 1998, "the NIRA Executive Committee, exercising directions provided by the NIRA Board, met in Denver and entertained proposals from Oklahoma City and Bozeman, Montana." A proposal by Las Vegas, Nevada, did not materialize because of "unpredictable construction progress on a new facility." Bozeman was selected "primarily due to the inability of Oklahoma City to deliver the dates of the week of June 14, 1999, the dates of first choice for the CNFR."[9]

Again, plans for a home for the 1999 CNFR failed for an unexpected reason. Prior to the meeting set for September 3, 1998, an antitobacco group appeared in Bozeman and welcomed the return of the CNFR but opposed the involvement by the Copenhagen/Skoal Scholarship Awards Program. The Montana State University fieldhouse, where the CNFR would be held, had banned tobacco products including samples for adults from U.S. Tobacco. The NIRA board "when faced with the choice of abandoning a 24-year sponsor that had provided $3.8 million for the education of college rodeo athletes," chose to "stand by a valued friend of college rodeo and a long-time sponsor commitment."[10]

The homeless 1999 CNFR still wielded bargaining power with its economic impact. Several places immediately indicated an interest: Casper, Wyoming; Fort Worth, Texas; and Redmond, Oregon. The bid deadline was December 12, 1998, the last day of the NIRA winter board meeting. Casper, in a close vote, got the nod. "Casper offered optimal dates for the event and statewide support," said Corfield.[11] Casper sweetened the deal with a television package, discounted rates for accommodations, an experienced media coordinator, and a welcome barbecue. Casper College rodeo coach Tom Parker said that "the tradition of rodeo at Casper College and Wyoming's love for the sport were big factors in Casper's landing the CNFR."[12]

When the CNFR had moved in 1997, to attract fans, the NIRA had refined the CNFR level of competition. The sudden death format with three complete and a short round raised the quality of the 1997 CNFR competition and lowered the chances of a fluke championship since all contestants started with a clean slate. Veteran rodeo fans recognized this when the 338 contestants competed at Rapid City, South Dakota, for a week.

Along with access to good horses, more cowgirls roped and rode better. Fans saw a cowgirl rope with the men and win at the 1997 CNFR. Vernon Regional Junior College cowgirl Jody Petersen, a 4.0 GPA student, qualified for the CNFR team roping, so she invited Josh Crow from West Texas A&M University to rope with her at the finals. Not all the cowboy ropers were convinced that roping with a woman would get them anywhere. Petersen and Crow roped their way to the team roping reserve national championship with a total time of 32.6 seconds on four head, the best ever for a cowgirl. Tami Noble of Sul Ross State University had won the CNFR average in team roping before the sudden death format was started. Ironically, both cowgirls had the same coach, John Mahoney, and invited partners who hailed from the same county in New

Vernon Regional Junior College cowgirl Jody Petersen Sarchett, (front, fourth from left) the only cowgirl to qualify to compete in the team roping at the 1997 national finals, won NIRA reserve national champion team roper with her partner Josh Crow from New Mexico Junior College, a first for a female. Petersen's 4.0 GPA won her an academic scholarship at the CNFR. Photo by Sylvia G. Mahoney, Vernon, Texas.

Mexico, Lea County. Cody Mathew Willson of Scottsdale Community College and Preston Williams of the University of Nevada at Las Vegas won the team roping with 27.1 seconds on four head, giving Williams the all-around championship, too.

Cowgirls continued to set new records. At the 1997 CNFR, SEOSU's Caryn Standifer Snyder became a five-championship cowgirl, shared with one other cowgirl. She tied for the breakaway championship, making her the only NIRA cowgirl to win championships in all three women's events and the all-around (not in the same year).

As the quality of CNFR competition tightened, fans saw numerous crossovers between the college and professional contestants. Cowgirls, like the cowboys, had started making the professional finals and the college finals the same year. The fans watched a University of Montana three-time NFR qualifier and second-generation barrel racer, Rachel Myllymaki Sproul, win the 1997 NIRA championship.

A new generation of CNFR women's team champions became apparent with the Weber State University four. The WSU cowgirls proved that to win, depth on a team was necessary. In 1997 each of the four team members of Coach Roger Johnson's WSU team won championship points. Kelli Fowers Tolbert won the goat tying and all-around titles, and Mistilyn Smith placed in the barrels. Fawn Kennedy Allen and Mindi Lee Smith won points in the goat tying. Together they earned 747.5 points, with second place University of Montana having 490 points.

The Lewis-Clark State College cowgirls followed the pattern in 1998 with four premier cowgirls. The cowgirls from the Lewiston, Idaho, school combined their points to win first. Jamie Richards placed in the barrel race, Katy Richards in the goat tying and breakaway roping, Angie Champneys and Tanya Lewis in the roping. The coaching team of Mike Fuller and Karen Fuller brought years of rodeo experience with them. Karen, a California native, competed at the 1979, 1981, and 1982 CNFR for Cal Poly at San Luis Obispo. Mike, a Blue Mountain Community College alumnus, was the 1982 PRCA Team Roping Rookie of the Year.

College rodeo event records continued to be broken at the CNFR, especially in the women's events. When the 347 contestants from eighty-one schools arrived in Rapid City, South Dakota, in 1998, Lynn Wiebe of Central Wyoming College won three championships, the all-around, goat tying, and the breakaway roping, a first. In the goat tying, Wiebe had almost identical runs of 6.9, 6.5, 7.0, and 7.3 seconds; however, three other goat tiers almost equaled her runs with no one having one more than 7.6 seconds. In the breakaway roping, Wiebe had a 5.9, 3.9, 3.2, and a 3.1 final run. The Ottertail, Minnesota, native who grew up on a dairy farm, said that she "wanted to go out West to be a cowgirl, so she left as soon as she graduated from high school." Wiebe said that she chose CWC because "it was a small school with a rodeo program, and Coach Rick Smith knows how to coach about winning."[13]

Two women's teams showed the quality of competition in 1999. The champions, the University of Nevada at Las Vegas, beat Tarleton State University by seven and a half points. The young UNLV rodeo program had a street-wise coach in Fredrick Preston as did TSU with its coach the old pro Bob Doty. Both coaches recruited cowgirls from two-year schools who could win in every event. Three of the four UNLV cowgirls—Stacie Sorensen, Katie Marvel, Nora Hunt—filled three of the twelve spots in the breakaway roping short round. Sorensen's 2.7 won the title, and Hunt's 2.8 tied for second in the round. Hunt's father Bruce Hunt, longtime coach at West Hills College, instilled a champion's mind and skills into Nora. Marvel's 2.6 collected a barrier penalty. Next event—goat tying. Hunt's 6.9 stood until Western Texas College's Jill Childers had an even faster 6.7—the championship time. Sorensen's 14.18 led the barrel race short go until TSU's Jennifer Smith clocked 14.06, winning the championship on her gray gelding Topper, the AQHA Horse of the Year in the women's college division.

The deep collegiate rodeo roots continued with the 2000 team champions. Western Texas College won the women's team title, a men's event title, and two rookie awards. Coach Greg Rhodes and his wife Canita Cass Rhodes both had years of college rodeo experience, so Coach Rhodes knew how to pick a premier quartet of team players. Jamie Standifer, riding her sister's eleven-year-old horse named Fancy, pushed Amanda Barrett of Texas A&M for the barrel racing championship, but Standifer had to accept second. However, Standifer's three hundred points gave her the Rookie of the Year and all-around buckle, making three for the family with her sister Caryn Standifer Snyder's two all-around buckles. Jill Childers, the 1999 goat tying champ, placed in the goat tying, and Tibba Smith, a third-generation NIRA cowgirl, placed in the breakaway roping. Tibba's grandmother Tibba McMullan competed for Texas Tech, her grandfather Kenny Smith roped for Sul Ross, and her parents Ken and Margo Smith competed for Howard College. Dave Brock, the father of the fourth team member, Brandee Brock, had won four NIRA event titles and a world calf roping title. WTC's Houston Hutto won the calf roping crown and the $500 NIRA Alumni Rookie of the Year Scholarship.

About the time a standard was set for winning rodeo teams, along came an exception to the rule. In 2001 Oklahoma State University's team had four barrel racers, their only event. Winning the lottery and winning the championship with all team members in one event are equal in probability. However, Janae Ward won the championship, and Julia Warner, second, points enough for OSU's first team championship. OSU had five event champions in the 1950s. Janae's dad James Ward competed for the 1976 SEOSU champion team and won the all-around and bareback riding, and her grandmother Florence Youree was an all-around Professional Women's Rodeo Association (PWRA) champion.

Some rodeo traditions never seemed to change, such as the acceptance of pain without complaint. In 1997 two points separated first and second for two WTC saddle bronc riders, Jeff Decker and Patrick Ellis. Decker's fifth place

The Oklahoma State University 2001 NIRA champion women's team proved to be the exception to the rule as the four team members were all barrel racers (left to right) Shannon Herrmann, Janae Ward (2001 NIRA barrel racing champion), Julie Warner, and Gretchen Benbenek. Photo by Sylvia G. Mahoney, Vernon, Texas.

going into the last round looked better as coleaders Rance Bray and Ryan Rodewald, both from Panhandle State, bucked off. Decker's ride won the championship, but his right arm snapped when he slammed into the arena floor. Using a quick-fix sling by medics, Decker collected his buckle and trophy saddle before his trip to the hospital.

The numbers of outstanding CNFR contestants continued to grow, and photo-finish titles continued. In 1997 steer wrestler Bernard Getten of Western Montana had a total time of 17.9 on four, Gus Ledoux of McNeese State University, a total time of 17.8. That tenth of a second also made freshman Ledoux the Rookie of the Year worth a $500 NIRA Alumni scholarship.

The new generation of champions had definitely arrived, especially in the 1997 CNFR calf roping. Champion Jerome Schneeberger of Murray State College in Oklahoma had 36.3 on four, and Trevor Brazile of Vernon Regional Junior College in Texas, 37.6. Both cowboys were professional ropers with Brazile wearing the 1996 Steer Roping Rookie of Year buckle. Brazile also won the 1998 Timed Event Championship, an invitational competition in five events for the twenty best timed-event professional cowboys, and the 2003 world all-around title.

Two university teams in one region consistently had competitive teams. Panhandle State University had battled all year with Southwestern Oklahoma State University in the Central Plains Region. PSU stopped SWOSU's chance for a fourth men's team championship. Coach Phil Martin's team claimed the 1997 team championship, PSU's first team championship, in honor of their late coach Doc Lynn Gardner. Back-to-back championships are scarce, but the six Panhandle State University cowboys won the 1998 team championship and two event titles. Josh McIntyre won the steer wrestling with consistent times of 4.4, 6.3, 5.5, and 6.3, and Travis Goad and Brian Dunning won the team roping title with consistent times of 5.8, 6.8, 6.4, and 5.9.

The talent and skill to win an NIRA championship is enough to make the NFR. The 1998 NIRA bareback champion Davey Shields of SWOSU and four other SWOSU cowboys, coached by Dr. Don Mitchell, competed at the 1998 NFR: Mark Gomes, Lee Akin, Lee Graves, and Eric Mouton, the 1997 world champion bareback rider. In 1997 Erick Blanton of National College had shut Shields out of the NIRA championship by seven points. In 1998 Shields shut Ross Coleman of the University of Nevada at Las Vegas out by nine points, but Coleman won the all-around and reserve in saddle bronc and bull riding. Shields had

*Sharing in the awards to the 1999 NIRA champion men's team from Southwestern Oklahoma
State University are* (left to right) *U.S. Tobacco representative Darrell Barron,
BCR Awards' Bob Clore, Coach Don Mitchell, six team members: Daniel Adams,
Jeremy Hennigh, Clark Dees, Shane Drury, Davey Shields, and Cody Navarre.
Photo by Sylvia G. Mahoney, Vernon, Texas.*

been trained under the watchful eye of his father, a twelve-time Canadian finals
bareback qualifier. Rodeo fans knew Davey Shields as a Canadian champion
and winner of the $50,000 Calgary Stampede bonus round. Shields married
Central Plains Region all-around cowgirl Sonya Coy before they left for the
1998 CNFR.

The NIRA's fiftieth anniversary and the final CNFR of the twentieth century
were a celebration of success for the NIRA and the CNFR. However, being a
1999 champion was on the contestants' minds. Perhaps someday, being the
last champions of the century would filter into their CNFR reride stories, but
for the moment, all-around champion Bryant Mikkelson of the University of
Montana had to be exact in his final steer wrestling run. Announcer Randy
Schmutz said, "Bryant has to have a 4.0 to be the champion." Mikkelson's
time was 4.0 giving him enough points to win the all-around, also. Winning
the $1,000 Bill Robinson Memorial Scholarship finalized the time in

Mikkelson's life that he "wished he could savor with his coach," the late Joe Druso, who had died of a heart attack the previous year at age fifty-two.[14]

Many novice fans were surprised when a team that was not even in the top five in the first two rounds won the championship. Coach Don Mitchell's SWOSU 1999 champion men's team did not win a round until their third chance. In fact, they were in nineteenth hole after two rounds. The SWOSU cowboys, with two NIRA champions and two NFR qualifiers, did not appear until the 1998 NIRA bareback and NFR qualifier Davey Shields won first in the third round. SWOSU had five of their six in the short round, but so did first place Panhandle State and second place Blue Mountain Community College. Third place Western Montana College had two. In the bareback riding, Clark Dees's dream of riding Hank Franzen's Khadafy Skoal came true, and he scored a short-round score of eighty-one. Davey Shields, on Jack Hammer, scored one point more, giving first and second place to SWOSU in the round. SWOSU's team championship made a total of six for Coach Doc Mitchell.

As the NIRA aged, it became its own resource for contestants. The 2000 NIRA champions had credentials that could be the envy of a blue-blood registry. Bunny Burghduff Pauley, mother of the all-around champion Jesse Bail of Panhandle State University, had competed at the CNFR for Dawson Community College in the early 1980s, and his dad Wade Bail rode broncs, one of Jesse's three events he competed in at the CNFR. Jesse's stepdad Bud Pauley competed in saddle bronc riding at the NFR from 1980 to 1985 and helped Jesse along the way, too. The Camp Crook, South Dakota, cowboy won 420 points of the 607.50 points that PSU earned on its way to its third national team championship. Bail won the Houston Livestock Show Rodeo in March 2000, qualified for the NFR three times, and won the PRCA Linderman award.

Numerous examples of second-generation NIRA contestants highlighted CNFR 2000. Before he could walk, champion team roper Levi Garcia of Tarleton State University started going to college rodeos with his father Jimmy Garcia, who roped for Eastern New Mexico University. The other duo roping champion Kurt Kiehne found his fourth year at the finals to have the right combination of a talented partner, a lucky draw, and a good horse (his brother Ned's paint horse). Two NIRA trophy saddles hang at the Shepperson's, the 2000 breakaway roping saddle for Amy Shepperson of University of Wyoming and 1964 NIRA steer wrestling saddle for her father Frank Shepperson of UW, also.

To qualify for the 2001 CNFR, the NIRA fielded for the first time a College Rodeo Championship Series (CRCS), providing more levels of competition to reach the national finals. NIRA commissioner Tim Corfield said, "The NIRA board was planning to add another level of competition to the system, which would attack the age-old argument about strong region–weak region and qualification to the CNFR."[15] The top ten contestants in each event from each of the eleven regions competed in one of four regional tournaments with the top seven CRCS winners qualifying for the CNFR. The top two regional champs got a bye to the CNFR. To be one of the CRSC hosts, a location had to seat a minimum of three thousand people and commit to a two-year contract. Two or three regions competed in each regional finals. Hobbs, New Mexico, Enid, Oklahoma, Bozeman, Montana, and Ogden, Utah, had the winning bids to be a host site for a regional rodeo competition.[16] "It has the "potential of creating more exposure for college rodeo and attracting additional corporate sponsorship, due principally to the added value generated by four CNFR type productions in markets where support is wide spread," said Corfield.[17]

After the turn of the century, at least one team championship was won by a two-year school each year. College of Southern Idaho won the 2001 men's team title and repeated it in 2002. Cody Demers won the all-around and reserve bareback riding titles both years to help Coach Shawn Davis's teams win the championship. In 2001 Demers won the saddle bronc riding title, and Cody Wright added points for reserve bareback riding champion.

CNFR 2002 and CNFR 2003 added to the historical records. Texas A&M, the first to field a college rodeo in 1920, won its first national team title, the 2002 women's team championship. Coach Al Wagner watched Johna Reeves and Kelsey Cox earn their winning team points in goat tying. In 2003 Vernon College won both team titles, the fourth time for a school to win both, but the first for a two-year school. Jackie Hobbs added the breakaway roping title to points won by other team members, Tessie McMullan, Shy-Anne Bowden, and Laura Hyde, to win the title. For the cowboys, Cade Swor won the reserve calf roping title and Sterling Smith, the rookie award. Coach Bobby Scott experienced a disadvantage of NIRA contestants competing professionally. Will Lowe, who was leading the bareback riding average going into the short round, turned out to compete at the ProRodeo Winter Tour Finale, which he won. However, with a big lead going into the short round and with the help of other team members, Swor, Smith, E. P. Luchsinger, Marty Eakin, and Cal White, the team won anyway.

Along with Texas A&M's first championship, the university received possibly the largest endowment for a college rodeo program ever. A calf roper from Denton, Texas, James E. "Punk" Sauls, a member of the 1949 Aggie rodeo team, left Sauls Exotic Farm at Cisco, Texas, and his Capri Restaurant in Addison to A&M, estimated at a million and a half dollars, with preference for rodeo team members.

The NIRA had honored its alumni at the NIRA Golden Anniversary Celebration at the 1999 CNFR. During the CNFR opening ceremonies, some of the champions from the previous fifty years returned to meet the new champions in the arena. Between rows of members of the Casper Troopers Drum and Bugle Corps, the CNFR average leaders ran to the center of the arena to meet their champion counterparts from years gone by. Former student and stock contractor Hank Franzen led a riderless horse and rode in the spotlight as a tribute to the late Casper College rodeo coach Dale Stiles, the first NIRA saddle bronc champion. The opening pageantry of the last performance was a tribute to the level of rodeo production that the NIRA board had achieved.

The Texas Senate honored the NIRA on its fiftieth anniversary with a resolution. The Senate Concurrent Resolution No. 67 was adopted by both the Texas Senate and House on April 26, 1999, and signed by Governor George W. Bush, President of the Senate Rick Perry, and Speaker of the House Pete Laney. The Resolution acknowledged the NIRA on its fiftieth anniversary and the "ties and traditions rooted deep in the heart of Texas." It highlighted the group that met in November, 1948, at Sul Ross State University to give life to the idea of a college rodeo organization, to the thirty-three cowboys and cowgirls from thirteen colleges and universities in six states that formed the NIRA at Dallas, to the first NIRA champions from Sul Ross, and to the first student president Charlie Rankin from Texas A&M, and to the fact that the NIRA was chartered on August 5, 1949, "in the Lone Star State," which adopted rodeo as its official state sport. " The Resolution stated that "the efforts of the NIRA have proven indispensable in gaining well-deserved recognition and acclaim for this beloved sport."[18]

Through the years, many coaches had experimented with ways to fully utilize the team concept to encourage motivation and camaraderie. Often, team members encouraged confidence and helped hone the skills of other members of the team. Coaches experimented with the concept that if individuals could have winning attitudes, attitudes of teams could encourage individuals to win. Members of the 1995 Southwest Region champion men's team from VRJC at Vernon, Texas, said that all the members started as individuals with common traits, then they melded into a unit that exceeded the limits of individual attitudes.

The common traits among the team members could be traced to their earlier years when a professional rodeo person opened the door to rodeo and the gate to practice. Fathers, uncles, friends, and stock contractors initiated the team members' entrance into the sport of rodeo. Each VRJC team member discovered that, as Kolt Dowdy of Burleson, Texas, said, "I liked it the first time I got on."[19] Travis Griffin of Alamogordo, New Mexico, said, "My dad and my uncle both rode bareback horses and bulls. When I was riding, something just clicked in my head. I thought, 'I can do that.' It felt really good."[20]

Trying an event and calling it fun led to the next level, which was learning the fundamentals of an event and keeping a positive attitude while "paying your dues" to gain experience. Kirby Berry of Cypress, Texas, said, "You always want to remember the fundamentals of riding bucking horses, which is tuck, lift, mash, drag, and set your feet."[21] Colin "Roudy" Bauer of Queensland, Australia, learned "from an old bronc rider who came to America back in the late 1960s. When I came to America, the horses were a bit more bucky here. They have sorted me out a bit more. It is good fun."[22]

The team members agreed that a positive attitude was easy to believe in, but difficult to maintain. Kolt Dowdy said, "When I broke my leg last year riding a bronc, I recovered because I just craved it. I wanted to get on all the time I was crippled, but I didn't until the doctor told me I could get on."[23] The team members agreed that keeping a positive attitude over "a long dry spell" was one of the hardest parts. Shane Hatch of Farmington, New Mexico, said, "A good attitude is when you ride out the back of the arena, no one should know if you just won the world or lost the world."[24]

When the cowboys headed to college with their common traits, the next factor in creating a winning team was the attitude of their college rodeo coach. Shane Hatch said, "To be a team, the coach needs to be a role model like John Mahoney. Nothing bothers him. Leadership, I would like to be able to do like Mahoney."[25] Travis Griffin explained, "John is an excellent coach. He thinks we are the best, and he lets us know it, too. That gets our spirits up. I think that has a lot to do with winning."[26] A coach's reputation helps to recruit a winning team. Colin "Roudy" Bauer said, "I have a friend in Australia who rodeoed in college in America in the early 1990s. He told me about John. That's why I am at VRJC."[27] The team members agreed that coaching a team requires more than having been a former rodeo contestant. As Dowdy said, "John is my role model because he keeps me in line to keep me from getting into too much trouble."[28]

Even the team members helped with keeping each other in line, and team spirit pushed the individuals beyond their limits. Kirby Berry said, "I'm a little bit older, so I always tell Doug and Kolt what they are doing wrong. I never lie to them."[29] Doug Fennell from Idabel, Oklahoma, said, "You ride like your competition. There are some guys here that sure ride good and have good attitudes. If you are around winners, you are a winner yourself." The camaraderie among the team members contributed to a winning attitude. Fennel said, "My pards, I kinda like to give them hell when they get on. I tell them, 'Don't embarrass me.' We are leaving here good friends."[30]

All agreed that college rodeo was the best direction to take in rodeo after high school. Shane Hatch, the 1993 NIRA calf roping champ, said, "After I won the college championship, it gave me a lot of confidence. I might have roped just the same before and after, but I had the confidence knowing I had the title under my belt."[31] Kolt Dowdy said, "At VRJC I learned how to weld and learned about growing up. I'm not going to be able to ride broncs all my life. I had a rodeo scholarship, so I decided to learn something else. I learned that I like to build stuff out of metal. I like the artistic part of building out of metal."[32]

This team scenario could be duplicated with almost every team that qualified for the CNFR. The team concept gathered traits that enhanced college rodeo programs as college rodeo evolved from its origins in the 1920s. Colleges and universities started to hire experienced coaches who used full scholarships to recruit experienced cowboys and cowgirls. A coach's goal was to have a balanced team with strength in each event. Coaches started using the point system to select the members of their teams for each rodeo. Since many coaches had forty or fifty students competing, selecting the six cowboys to represent the men's team and four cowgirls to represent the women's team was often like playing the lottery.

Coaching college rodeo added a new type of rodeo career, a professional position at colleges and universities, which required a college degree generally and experienced coaches. Schools were feeling the impact of Title IX, which mandated equal sports funding between genders. Since rodeo was coed and could have unlimited numbers, school administrators looked more favorably on funding college rodeo and including it in their sports departments so that their schools could be in compliance. Another major dividend was the national publicity that winning a championship brought, often to a small college.

By the late 1990s, universities seeking success for their rodeo programs raided other schools for experienced, successful coaches. In 1997 two nationally recognized coaches changed jobs. John Luthi moved from a two-year school to a university. He had been coaching at Fort Scott Community College in Fort Scott, Kansas, for sixteen years, when he accepted the job at the University of Tennessee at Martin. The Central Plains faculty director and coach at Southwestern Oklahoma State University at Weatherford, George Howard, who assisted Coach Don Mitchell, moved to the University of Wyoming. SWOSU teams had won five team championships while Howard coached there.

All college rodeo programs were not alive and well; some were struggling to survive. Los Angeles' Pierce College in California's San Fernando Valley was faced with a shrinking budget and problems from "a multitude of reasons that have to do with things that are unique to California," said Tim Corfield, NIRA general manager. Pierce's rodeo coach Ron Wechsler said that "three straight years of bad weather contributed to the event's final end." Since Wechsler's request for college funding had not gotten out of committee, the administrators "did not know of the rodeo's impending doom."[33] However, the alumni of Pierce College, an NIRA charter member, along with other supporters continued to add life and breath to the rodeo program so that its end had not occurred by 2001. As humorist Baxter Black said, "You reckon any Big Ten, Big 12, Small 16, Ivy League, Industrial league, WAC, SWAC Thwack or Humpback athletic conference has to send its players out selling cookies or magazine subscriptions to fund NCAA team expenses? Not likely. Unless, of course, it was the rodeo team."[34]

The twelve coaches in the Southwest Region in the fall of 1997 typified the talents and accomplishments as well as the changes that had occurred in college rodeo coaching. Originally, college rodeo students had a college administrator or instructor, usually from the ag department and called an adviser, to sign their official forms to comply with the NIRA's bylaws and the college rules. Later, college and university administrators saw the merit in hiring rodeo coaches to direct their programs, which included recruiting, rodeo practice, travel with the teams, and producing their college's annual rodeo.

The combined qualifications of the twelve Southwest Region coaches in 1997 showed that they had one hundred years of college rodeo coaching experience among them and a variety of other qualifications. Eight were members of the PRCA, and seven were former NIRA contestants. Two held Ph.D.s, five had master's degrees, and five had bachelor's degrees. Seven had degrees in agriculture. Three had teams that had won one national NIRA team championship, and one had four national team championships.

The four with the longest tenure had a combined total of seventy-two years coaching experience with each having at least one national champion team. The quartet of coaches were Charles Chambers of Eastern New Mexico University, John Mahoney of Vernon Regional Junior College, Bob Doty of Tarleton State University, and Jim Watkins of Odessa College. When Chambers retired in May, 1998, after twenty-three years coaching, he had claimed for ENMU the national 1983 women's team, all-around, and goat tying championships. The 1991 PRCA calf roping Rookie of the Year Brent Lewis was a Chambers' recruit.

Coach John Mahoney of VRJC, an eighteen-year veteran, had known the winner's circle at two schools. During the eight years that he coached at Sul Ross State University, Mahoney's teams claimed three national championships. The 1994 VRJC men's team championship made Mahoney the only rodeo coach to win a national team championship at a two-year school after winning one (several) at a university. At the end of Mahoney's coaching career in 1997 after serving as national faculty president, CNFR arena director, and NIRA Foundation director, his teams had won four national team championships, five event championships, and two Rookies of the Year. While coaching, 149 of Mahoney's students qualified to compete at the CNFR, seventy-eight from Sul Ross and seventy-one from VRJC. He took twenty teams to the CNFR, ten from each school. Twenty-five of his recruits went on to compete at the NFR: ten from Sul Ross, fifteen from VRJC. The world champions were Tuff Hedeman and Guy Allen from Sul Ross and Cody Ohl, Rich Skelton, and Trevor Brazile from VRJC. Mahoney, a 1998 Sul Ross Range Animal Science Hall of Fame honoree, became the only rodeo coach to marry a rodeo coach from another school.

Another coach, Bob Doty, went from a successful program at a two-year school to a university. After fourteen years at Western Texas College and four NIRA titles, Doty was recruited in 1994 by Tarleton State University. Doty's 1986 WTC men's team won the national championship. In 1999 Doty's TSU cowgirl Jennifer Smith took a duo of titles: all-around and barrel racing. On

In 1997 the twelve coaches in the Southwest Region typified the changes that had occurred in college rodeo: (front, left to right) New Mexico Junior College, Wayne Smith; West Texas A&M University, Kelvin Sharp; Texas Tech, Chris Guay; Weatherford College, Todd White; Western Texas College, Greg Rhodes; (back, left to right) Odessa College, Jim Watkins; Eastern New Mexico University, Charles Chambers; Sul Ross State University, Harley May; Frank Phillips College, Rodney Purswell; Southwest Region secretary, Dollie Riddle; Tarleton State University, Bob Doty; Vernon Regional Junior College, John Mahoney; and Howard College, Mike Yeater. Photo by Sylvia G. Mahoney, Vernon, Texas.

Doty's list of champions who became top PRCA cowboys were 1982 NIRA calf roping champ James Zant and 1986 NIRA calf roping champ Keith Hudson. Others were the 1988 PRCA all-around champion Dave Appleton, 1997 PRCA bareback champion Eric Mouton, 1988 PBR bull riding champ Michael Gaffney, and PRCA bareback riders Danny McLanahan and Cleve Schmidt.

Sixteen-year veteran Odessa College coach Jim Watkins, who had competed for Sul Ross, had an impressive list of championships. By 2003, his cowboys chalked up ten NIRA national event titles and one team championship. His list of cowboys looked like a Who's Who of bull riding: seven-time world all-around champion Ty Murray, world champions Jim Sharp and Jerome Davis, and NIRA bull riding champ Ben Duggar, two-time NIRA champion calf roper, the late Shawn McMullan, and NIRA bareback champ Cimarron Gerke.

Three of the coaches had four to eight years of experience. The 1985 and 1988 Southwest Region bareback riding champion Chris Guay, who had coached at Wharton College for four years, was hired in 1997 by Texas Tech University to be their first full-time coach even though Texas Tech was a charter member of the NIRA. Howard College coach Mike Yeater, eight-year veteran, was hired from Frank Phillips College, both Texas two-year schools. Coach Yeater, a former NIRA contestant, had served on the NIRA board and one of his team ropers John Folmer had won the 1995 NIRA championship. Frank Phillips College coach Rodney Purswell, one of two coaches who had a Ph.D., had coached for eight years. One of his students Joshua Peek won the 2000 steer wrestling NIRA national championship, Frank Phillips' first championship.

The other five coaches had three years or less of experience, but they were not new to rodeo. In 1998 Sul Ross State University coach Harley May quit after coaching four years for the school where he had won three championships in both 1949 and 1950 and two in 1951, followed by three PRCA steer wrestling world championships, the first NIRA champion to win a professional championship. Two had coached three years, Todd White of Weatherford College and Coach Kelvin Sharp of West Texas A&M, the other coach with the Ph.D. While a student at Chadron State College in Nebraska, Sharp had finished fifth in the nation twice in team roping. Having two years' experience, WTC coach Greg Rhodes had returned to his alma mater to coach after riding bulls for Coach Doty, then rodeoing at Sul Ross State for Coach Mahoney. Rhodes's six national titles won for WTC by 2003 were Jeff Decker, saddle bronc; Tona Wright, barrel racing; Jill Childers, goat tying; 2000 women's team; Jamie Standifer, all-around; and Houston Hutto, calf roping twice. New Mexico Junior College coach Wayne Smith, a former NIRA contestant, grew up with parents who were both from ranch families. His dad, two brothers, and sister had competed in college rodeo. Smith started announcing college rodeos at age twelve, was the 1999–2000 Southwest Region faculty director, and was elected national faculty president in 2001.

With teams and coaches and rodeo recognized as a college sport on many campuses, a timely idea that was the perfect partner for college rodeo was for colleges and universities to educate people for careers in rodeo or for a lifetime avocation. The PRCA had the successful Wrangler Judging Schools to train judges, which raised the quality of rodeo competition to a professional level and provided career opportunities; however, the judging schools were limited to PRCA members. Almost everyone who is involved in agriculture will some day either help with a 4-H rodeo or their hometown rodeo, so knowing how to produce and manage a rodeo would benefit the sport. It seemed inevitable that some college or university would access the untapped potential offered by adding a Rodeo Management Option to their agriculture programs. Sylvia Mahoney of Vernon College presented to Dr. Susan Couch, Vernon College instructional dean, a rodeo curriculum that included such courses as Management of Facilities and Stock, Rules for Judging Rodeo, and Rodeo Production and Management. Dr. Gary Don Harkey, Vernon College ag instructor, saw the timeliness of the idea and added a Rodeo Management Option to his Farm and Ranch Management degree, which was to be available for the first time during the fall semester 2002; however, the new option was put on hold because of some transferability and territorial issues. Eventually, schools will recognize the numerous career opportunities associated with rodeo and include a rodeo management option in their ag degrees.

Along with competition and education, cowboys' and cowgirls' lives often ran parallel from birth through college. Pam Conner, daughter of James and Mable Conner of Decatur, Texas, and her college roommate Buffy McCarley, daughter of Ronnie and Susie McCarley of Bridgeport, Texas, were born thirteen hours apart in the same hospital in Arlington, Texas, on June 21 and June 22, 1969. Pam said, "Our daddies bulldogged and traveled together for years. My mother had me late one night, and Buffy's parents came to see me. While she was there, Buffy's mother went into labor. Buffy was born early the next morning. When we were a week old, we went to our first rodeo together at Mesquite, Texas. When we went to college, we went as roommates."[35]

If rodeo is one big family, then college rodeo is the mating mecca. Numerous marriages have been initiated at regional rodeos and the college finals. What better place to meet people of like kind than at a regional rodeo where twelve to fifteen colleges and universities send the same cowboys and cowgirls to ten regional rodeos a year. Then, a major national mating meeting occurred at the CNFR. Some of the contestants remarked when the finals moved from Bozeman, Montana, that "now everyone won't get to experience The Cat's Paw." Before that it was Molly Brown's. However, rodeo contestants are like cattle on a trail drive, it doesn't take long for them to find a water hole so that they can mix and mingle and get to know one another better.

College cowboys and cowgirls marry each other much like species are attracted to their own kind, uniting rodeo families nationally and internationally. In 2000 the wedding of Robyn Byars in Vernon, Texas, and Kelly Armstrong of Big Valley, Alberta, Canada, illustrated the national and international connections through which college rodeo had extended and increased the rodeo family. Kelly's best man Colin "Roudy" Bauer of Bunderburg, Australia, had been recruited to rodeo for Vernon Regional Junior College along with others from Montana, New Mexico, Washington, Texas, and Saskatchewan, Canada. They all returned to attend the wedding.

After the weddings, along came the cowkids, and the families proved college rodeo was a family sport. One of the Weber State University champion women's team members Fawn Kennedy Allen's husband Rusty Allen, a senior mechanical engineering student, qualified in four events for the 1997 CNFR: bull riding, saddle bronc, steer wrestling, and calf roping. Both Fawn and Rusty, the 1997 reserve champion all-around cowboy, were athletes and full-time WSU students, which made a full daily schedule for them. Add thirteen-month-old Ashley, and they had a juggling act. Their parents naturally supported the couple's education and rodeo efforts by helping with their grandchild. Rusty's parents had competed for Utah State University. Fawn's family had competed in rodeo, and her sister had worn the Miss Rodeo Utah crown. Members of the WSU teams also helped with Ashley. Coach Roger Johnson said, "It is nice to have a baby in the rodeo club."[36]

The NIRA Alumni reunions reinforced the strong bonds forged during the NIRA years. The alumni had taken their places in society as successful business people and ranchers, who were giving back to rodeo and their communities. Two 1942 Texas A&M rodeo team members and both successful businessmen, J. R. "Shorty" Fuller of Colorado City, Texas, and F. C. "Caddo" Wright of Lubbock, Texas, exemplified lifelong friendships. Wright said, "Shorty and I have talked to each other on the phone at least once a week since we graduated (about fifty years)."[37]

Reunions highlighted another value of college rodeo teams. At the 1998 CNFR both of the 1968 Sam Houston State champion teams of Coach Sonny Sikes returned for a thirty-year reunion. Seven of the nine team members made the reunion in Rapid City, South Dakota, the first teams to be reunited. The women's team members Willie Gregson Little and Kay Steele Campbell along with Tootie Deaton, who competed for SHSU, and the men's team members

Ronnie Williams, Bill Burton, Bob Smith, and Carl Deaton, the 1968 and 1969 steer wrestling champ along with Dan Harris savored the pleasures of friendships and competition.

In January, 2000, NIRA commissioner Tim Corfield, who had successfully guided the NIRA through major areas of growth during his twenty-one years at the helm, reviewed the past and reflected on the future. He said that the NIRA, from its inception, had carried high the banner of academic standards. "NIRA has not allowed a general erosion of academic standards which would discredit the sport," said Corfield. He said that as rodeo contestants progress through the public school system and advance to the college level of rodeo competition, there is a high attrition rate because of the boost in the competitive level in college rodeo. Corfield said, "The addition of the officials seminars and the employment of qualified judges has had a major impact on college rodeo since 1985. ProRodeo benefits because as contestants progress into the next level, they already know the rules and expect the rules to be enforced."[38]

College rodeo still had needed improvements. Commissioner Tim Corfield pointed out some aspects when he said, "The production of college rodeos has not improved as significantly as most would prefer." This has hindered the "pursuit of new sponsors," which "drains a budget" rather than "adds to the scholarship dollars available." The board was developing a "licensed product approach which will allow the NIRA to benefit from the marketing of items bearing the marks that belong to college rodeo." Corfield said that sponsors were being recruited and "a new approach to providing added value to each sponsorship is being pursued by the national board."[39]

The CNFR had hit a snag but had it corrected by CNFR 2001. The CNFR had been in the red since it left Bozeman in 1997. After two in-the-red years at Rapid City, South Dakota, the NIRA had signed a five-year contract in 1999 with Casper, Wyoming. The option-out clause allowed either party to break the contract after three years. If either party opted out, the board would have to deal with a CNFR relocation. A conflict in dates at the Casper Events Center led to an agreement to have CNFR 2000 at the Central Wyoming Indoor Multi-Purpose Sports Facility, which was not finished until May, 2000. Although it was new and indoors, it was not a coliseum, so it lacked the amenities of a coliseum with its 3,460 seats, 2,200 less than the Bozeman coliseum had. Frequent remarks at CNFR 2000 were that it was like attending a roping. However, this was rectified when CNFR 2001 moved back to the Casper Events Center, and state and local sponsors were secured to subsidize expenses. NIRA commissioner Tim Corfield said that sponsorships and ticket sales had "grossed approximately $220,000, with the most heavily attended nights, Friday and Saturday, still to come." The break-even point was $230,000, which it exceeded after the final night. The NIRA announced that Casper would be the CNFR's home for two more years.[40]

As the CNFR recovered, the NIRA hit a political hot spot. When the NIRA commissioner's position, changed to a full-time commissioner from a part-time general manager, was established, it stipulated that the position would be advertised every fourth year. After Tim Corfield served four years as the first commissioner, the position was advertised. After a week of behind the scenes politics at CNFR 2001, the issue made the media. The twelve to ten vote by the board ousted commissioner Tim Corfield. "It's a situation where a few personal agendas swayed the votes of a bunch of students who are leaving college rodeo and who really probably don't understand the impact of what they've done," said Corfield.[41]

The change in leadership created a multitude of questions. McNeese State University coach John Smith replaced Corfield. Smith, who had served as NIRA faculty president and longtime NIRA board member, took office on July 1, 2001. Questions were raised about his running the NIRA office in Walla Walla, Washington, from his position at McNeese in Lake Charles, Louisiana, where he had been for thirty-three years, with his most recent position being department head of the agricultural science department and rodeo coach. He was scheduled to retire from the university in January, 2002, but he would step down as coach and instructor with only administrative services to perform until then. "I'll fly in when needed," Smith said, and the rest of the work would be done "by phone, e-mail, and fax." Issues that the new administration expected to address were "bringing the NIRA budget into the black, increasing sponsorship opportunities, increasing media relations, and adding more continuity to the four regional playoffs, rather than having them run by different managers."[42]

Making a leadership change with an almost evenly divided board raised concerns. The twelve on the board—composed of eleven students and eleven faculty—who voted for John Smith were predominately students. Smith said that the board has "always had an ability to come back and unite and work together. I don't think it will be any different." Casper raised concerns that the

CNFR would go somewhere else.[43] By 2003, the board had united amicably, Smith's plan for running the office was working successfully, and the CNFR was in the black and had signed a five-year contract with Casper.

By 2003 the academic and economic significance of college rodeo was beginning to be recognized. However, the historical and social effects of college rodeo were still in the shadows. Cowboy and rodeo museums and authors of rodeo books tended to focus on early-day rodeo contestants or professional rodeo champions with the more than eighty years of college rodeo going relatively undocumented.

As college rodeo evolved from a show produced by agricultural departments to a college sport, it produced a new level of professional competitor and numerous new career opportunities, even the possibility of new college degrees. College cowboys and cowgirls earned an education and honed their rodeo skills while they socialized with other college-age rodeo contestants across national and international borders. They left college with degrees and desires to compete professionally or on a part-time basis or to give their children the same rodeo opportunities. Rodeo expanded its audience as it became the sport of people who went into many professions. By the end of the twentieth century, college rodeo was using the same judges, the same stock, and produced a national finals rodeo equal to the professional finals. From college rodeo's beginning almost eighty years earlier as a university fund-raiser, it had fostered a way of life that was rooted in the values and mores of the American way of life and in the myth of the cowboy that had captured the mind of the world. The impact of the NIRA and college rodeo on the academic world, on economic development, on rodeo history, on social and cultural directions, and on rodeo itself had been significant, in spite of its obscurity outside of its realm of operation.

First Intercollegiate Rodeo, 1939

First Intercollegiate Rodeo held April 8, 1939
C Bar G Ranch near Victorville, California,
produced by Cal Godshall
The 44 men and 18 women contestants
who competed at the first intercollegiate rodeo:
Information was available only in the
Victor Press, April 7 and 14, 1939.

UNIVERSITY OF CALIFORNIA AT DAVIS:
Carl Stevenson
John Anderson
Rodney Scott
Fred Valenzuela
Dan Smart
Bob O'Neil
Gregory Lougher
Theo Grandora

UC AT DAVIS—WOMEN:
Betty Garvey
June Miller
Cecelia Johnson
Irma Sahm
Barbara Higgins

UNIVERSITY OF SOUTHERN CALIFORNIA:
Bob Haynes
Bill Decker
Verne Ballard
Bob Wildman

Ell Wood
Howard Dennis
Bill Richardson

USC—WOMEN:
Jeanne Godshall
Deborah Abbot
Jane Lykker
Margaret Wolverton

CALIFORNIA POLY AT SAN LUIS OBISPO:
Bud Ross
Jim Blake
Gene Vinyard
Wayne Copely
Lloyd Schmitt
Hilliard Comstock
Les Brown
Craig Tebbe
Carl Miller
Vic Tomei
Boots Austin
Ralph Lyall
Jack Washington
Ed Tomei
Cleoyd Laughlin

UNIVERSITY OF ARIZONA:
Bill Felts
Bob Temple
Bill Bradley

UCLA:
Jim Lau
Meredith Shale

Robert B. Young
Stanley Anderson

UCLA—WOMEN:
Ann Begnall
Tony Lundsborough
Virginia Tegner

OCCIDENTAL:
George Hunter
Barney Mollett

LONG BEACH JUNIOR COLLEGE:
Walt LaRue
Bud Merrill

PASADENA JUNIOR COLLEGE:
Carlton Carver
Harvey Traveller

SAWYERS COLLEGE:
Frank Seeborn

POMONA COLLEGE:
Ann Rivers
Jean Fulford
Patricia Percival
Francilla Abbot
Jane Woolsey

REDLANDS:
Margaret Watson

FIRST INTERCOLLEGIATE MEN'S ALL-AROUND:

Gregory Lougher—Davis 7 1/2 points

Bill Felts—UA 7 points

Bill Richardson—USC 6 1/2 points

Jim Blake—Cal Poly 6 points

BAREBACK AND SADDLE RIDING FOR GIRLS:

1. Pat Percival of Pomona

2. Betty Garvey of Davis

3. Francilla Abbott of Pomona

SADDLE BRONCHO (*sic*) RIDING FOR MEN:

1. Bill Felts of UA

2. Bud Merrill of Long Beach JC

3. Gregory Lougher of Davis

COW-MILKING FOR MEN: WINNING TIME: 30 SECONDS

1. Bill Richardson of USC

2. Jim Blake of Cal Poly

3. Jim Dodds of Davis

PIPE AND NEEDLE RACE:

Francilla Abbott & June Woolsey, Pomona

WOMEN'S POTATO RACE:

Pomona College defeated Davis College

BAREBACK RIDING:

1. Gregory Lougher of Davis

2. Bill Wildman of USC

3. Bill Felts of UA

STEER RIDING:

1. Carl Miller of Cal Poly
2. Dan Smart of Davis
3. Howard Dennis of USC

RESCUE RACE FOR GIRLS:

1. Jean Fulford of Pomona
2. Tony Lundsborough of UCLA
3. Jeanne Godshall of USC

CALF ROPING:

1. Fred Valenzuela of Davis
2. Hilliard Comstock of Cal Poly
3. John Robertson of Pasadena JC

COW-MILKING FOR GIRLS: WINNING TIME 30 SECONDS

1. June Miller of Davis
2. Betty Garvey of Davis
3. Irma Sahm of Davis

TEAM ROPING: WINNING TIME 24 SECONDS

1. Craig Tebbe (Jim Blake, partner) of Cal Poly
2. Bill Richardson (Harvey Traveller, partner) USC

First Meetings to Organize NIRA, 1948–49

First Meeting to Organize on November 6, 1948

Representatives of twelve schools at the Sul Ross rodeo in Alpine, Texas, met to set a plan in motion to organize a national college rodeo organization.

TEXAS:

1. Sul Ross State Teachers College (Sul Ross State University), Alpine, Texas
2. Texas A&M University, Bryan, Texas
3. John Tarleton Agricultural College (Tarleton State University), Stephenville, Texas
4. Texas A&I University (Texas A&M at Kingsville), Kingsville, Texas
5. Texas Tech University, Lubbock, Texas
6. West Texas State College (West Texas A&M University), Canyon, Texas
7. Hardin-Simmons University, Abilene, Texas
8. Uvalde Junior College (Southwest Texas Junior College), Uvalde, Texas

NEW MEXICO:

9. New Mexico A&M (New Mexico State University), Las Cruces, New Mexico
10. University of New Mexico, Albuquerque, New Mexico

COLORADO:

11. Colorado A&M (Colorado State University), Fort Collins, Colorado

OKLAHOMA:

12. Cameron Agricultural College (Cameron University), Lawton, Oklahoma

JANUARY 28–30, 1949, ORGANIZATIONAL MEETING AT DALLAS, TEXAS

13 Official Voting Representatives with 33 Participants
NIRA Officially Organized on January 30, 1949, *voting delegates
Information taken from minutes of the meeting.

1. Abilene Christian College   *Raymond McNutt   Rodeo Club
   Abilene, Texas
   Peggy Powell
2. Baylor University   *David Shurley   Rodeo Club   Waco, Texas
   Barbara Conally
3. Colorado A&M   *Joe Forney   Livestock Club   Ft. Collins,
   Colorado
4. Hardin-Simmons University   *Carl Meyers   Rodeo Club
   Abilene, Texas
   Roy Eckles
5. New Mexico A&M   *Ham Scott   Aggie Club   Las Cruces, New
   Mexico
   Tom Hadley, Punk Hennigan, Daryl Smith, Tee Knox
6. Oklahoma A&M   *Buddy Reger   Rodeo Club   Stillwater,
   Oklahoma
7. Sul Ross State College   *Buster Lindley   SR Rodeo Assn.   Alpine,
   Texas
   Hank Finger, Constitutional Chairman; R. R. Walston
8. Texas A&M   *Charlie D. Rankin   Saddle & Sirloin   College
   Station, Texas
   Jack Kingsbery, Bubba Day, Prince Wood, Bud Hawkins
9. Texas Christian University   *Norman Hughes   TCU Rodeo
   Assn.   Fort Worth, Texas
10. Texas A&I *Frog Adams   A&I Rodeo Club   Kingsville, Texas
    Jack Resh, George Merzbacher, Rip Moore
11. Texas Tech   *H. G. Bedford   Block & Bridle Club   Lubbock,
    Texas
12. University of Arizona   *Jack Thompson   Tucson, Arizona
    Joe Nesbitt

13. University of Wyoming   *George Jim Berger   Laramie, Wyoming
    Bob Laramore, Fran Marsh, Pete Burns

First National NIRA Convention April 15–16, 1949, Shirley-Savoy Hotel, Denver, Colorado

*voting delegates; 15–16, attended both days; 15, attended first day only; 16, attended second day only. Information from the official minutes of the meeting.

*Tommie Bell, Texas Tech College, 15 & 16

*Billy Brown, Oklahoma A&M College, 15

Pete Burns, University of Wyoming, 15 & 16 (voting delegate 16)

*Perry Clay, University of Wyoming, 15 & 16

Eldon Dudley, Oklahoma A&M College, 15

Jim Easley, Texas Tech College, 15

*Hank Finger, Sul Ross State College, 15 & 16

*John L. Finley, Kansas State College, 15 & 16

*Joe W. Forney, Colorado A&M College, 15 & 16

*J. H. Foss, Washington State College, 15 & 16

Bud Halsell, Texas Tech College, 15

Dr. R. S. Jackson, Colorado A&M (Faculty Adviser), 15 & 16

*Bill Jones, University of Wyoming, 15 & 16

*Clint Josey, University of Texas, 15 & 16

*Dick Kelley, New Mexico A&M, 15 & 16

*Garland Kelley, Oklahoma A&M, 15

*Paul H. Kramer, Texas A&M, 15 & 16

*Sid Lanier, Texas A&M, 15 & 16

*Frank Lilley, Colorado A&M, 15 & 16

*Buster Lindley, Sul Ross State, 15 & 16

*Lester Matlock, Arizona State, 15 & 16

*"Mac" McArthur, Cameron Agricultural College, 16

*Thomas O. Morast, Kansas State, 15 & 16

Bob Morris, Texas Tech, 15

Charles D. Rankin, Texas A&M, 15 & 16

*Dale C. Riggins Jr., Arizona State, 15 & 16

Fred B. Widmoyer, Texas Tech (Faculty Adviser), 15

*John Wilson, Texas Tech, 15 & 16

Dale Winders, Texas Tech, 15

*John Woodard, Washington State, 15 & 16

Chuck Baker, University of California (guest), 16

Mary V. MacCaskill, Kansas State College (guest), 15

Jack Owens, University of California (guest), 16

George Payne, University of California (guest), 16

Miss College Rodeo

1949	Jone Pederson	Santa Rosa, Calif., high school student, crowned Queen of the Cow Palace NIRA Rodeo
1957	Karna Jean Thorson	Cal Poly-San Luis Obispo
1958	Patricia Louise McDaniel	Texas Christian University
1963	Nancy Ann Sheldon	Cal Poly-San Luis Obispo
1964	Rebecca Ramsey	Texas Tech University
1965	Carolynn Seay Vietor*	Southwest Texas State University
1966	Marianne Munz Brunson	Texas Tech University
1967	Marcheta McCain	California State-Fresno
1969	Terry Jo Stephens	Montana State University
1970	Luann Corn	Kansas State University
1971	Lorna Stewart	Cal Poly-Pomona
1972	Claudia Barconi	California State-Fresno
1973	Vicki Stewart	California State-Fresno
1974	Ruth Smith	University of Arizona
1975	Cathy Tvedt	Montana State University
1976	Tina Dalton	California State-Fresno
1977	Janet Bignell	Montana State University
1978	Shelly Moore	College of Southern Idaho
1979	Elaine Maronick	Montana State University
1980	Leslyn McLain	Sul Ross State University
1981	Gina Burns	Texas Tech University
1982	Jan Woolery	Tyler Junior College, Texas
1983	Robin Bail	South Dakota State University
1984	Suzie Wilkie	Sul Ross State University
1985	Jill Thurgood	Weber State University, Utah
1986	Chrissy Sparling Neuens*	Cal Poly-San Luis Obispo
1987	Joni James Smith*	College of Southern Idaho

1988	Pamela Benoit	McNeese State University, Louisiana
1989	Kelly Freitag	Kansas State University
1990	Amy Crain	Southwest Texas Jr. College
1991	Nancy Reese	University of Colorado
1992	Angel Antan	Scottsdale Community College

A notice was issued from the NIRA office on February 28, 1992, that the Miss College Rodeo Pageant was discontinued due to lack of financial support. No pageant was held in June, 1992. Miss Angel Antan was crowned in 1991 and finished her year in June, 1992.

*crowned Miss Rodeo America
**Information taken from NIRA newspapers and newsletters

Charter Board of Directors of NIRA Alumni

1991–92 NIRA ALUMNI (NIRAA) CHARTER BOARD OF DIRECTORS (JULY 1, 1991, TO JUNE 30, 1992)

President	Sylvia G. Mahoney	Vernon, Texas
Secretary-Treasurer	Betty Sims Solt	Roswell, New Mexico
Directors:		
Awards/Honors	Bob Clore	Manhattan, Kansas
Media	Paulette Moss	Riverton, Wyoming
Program	Darla Doty	Snyder, Texas
Historical Collection	Evelyn Bruce Kingsbery	Crystal City, Texas
Local Arrangements (2)	Buz Cowdrey	Bozeman, Montana
	Sally Jane Mosby	Bozeman, Montana

Directors of Regions: Grand Canyon and Northwest not filled

Big Sky	Carolynn Vietor	Philipsburg, Montana
Central Plains	Betty Gayle Cooper Ratliff	Durant, Oklahoma
Central Rocky Mt.	Butch Morgan	Colorado Springs, Colorado
Great Plains	Tom Richter	Brookings, South Dakota
Ozark	Bud Young	Coldwater, Mississippi
Rocky Mountain	Shawn Davis	Filer, Idaho
Southern	Charlie Rankin	McAllen, Texas
Southwest	Jo Gregory Knox	Midland, Texas
West Coast	Molly McAuliffe Hepper	Fort Klamath, Oregon
NIRA Student President	K. C. Jones	Las Animas, Colorado
NIRA Faculty President	John Mahoney	Vernon, Texas

First NIRA National Champions and Contestants

1949 INVITATIONAL NATIONAL FINALS RODEO AT COW PALACE, SAN FRANCISCO, APRIL 9–11, 1949

TEAMS:	POINTS
1. Sul Ross State College–Alpine, Texas	345
2. California Poly–San Luis Obispo	300
3. University of Wyoming–Laramie	235
4. New Mexico A&M–Las Cruces	225
5. University of New Mexico–Albuquerque	190
6. Colorado A&M–Fort Collins	165
7. Texas A&M–College Station	110
8. Oklahoma A&M–Stillwater	100
9. Pierce College–Canoga Park, California	70
10. Montana State College–Bozeman	50
11. Arizona State College–Tempe	10
12. Fresno State College–California	No points
13. Kansas State College–Manhattan	No points
14. Texas Tech–Lubbock	No points

ALL-AROUND:

1. Harley May	Sul Ross State	225
2. Cotton Rosser	Cal Poly-SLO	165
3. Dale Stiles	U of Wyoming	155

BAREBACK RIDING: 51 ENTRIES

First Round	Norman McNew	U of New Mexico	40
	Dan Rogers	Pierce College	30
	Buster Lindley	Sul Ross State	20
	Dale Stiles	U of Wyoming	10
Second Round	Harley May	Sul Ross State	40
	Charlie Rankin	Texas A&M	30
	Dale Stiles	U of Wyoming	15
	Dick Hutchinson	Cal Poly-SLO	15
Average	Harley May	Sul Ross State	40
	Norman McNew	U of New Mexico	30
	Dale Stiles	U of Wyoming	20
	Buster Lindley	Sul Ross State	10

TOTAL POINTS IN BAREBACK RIDING:

1. Harley May	Sul Ross State	80
2. Norman McNew	U of New Mexico	70
3. Dale Stiles	U of Wyoming	45
4. Buster Lindley	Sul Ross State	30
5. Dan Rogers	Pierce College	30
6. Charlie Rankin	Texas A&M	30
7. Dick Hutchison	Cal Poly-SLO	15

SADDLE BRONC: 23 ENTRIES

First Round	Dale Stiles	U of Wyoming	40
	Cotton Rosser	Cal Poly-SLO	30
	Harley May	Sul Ross State	20
	Bill Whitney	U of Wyoming	10
Second Round	Bill Whitney	U of Wyoming	40
	Dale Stiles	U of Wyoming	30
	Hank Finger	Sul Ross State	20
	Harley May	Sul Ross State	10
Average	Dale Stiles	U of Wyoming	40

Bill Whitney	U of Wyoming	30
Harley May	Sul Ross State	20
Cotton Rosser	Cal Poly-SLO	10

TOTAL POINTS IN SADDLE BRONC RIDING

1. Dale Stiles	U of Wyoming	110
2. Bill Whitney	U of Wyoming	80
3. Harley May	Sul Ross State	50
4. Cotton Rosser	Cal Poly-SLO	40
5. Hank Finger	Sul Ross State	20

BULL RIDING: 47 ENTRIES

First Round	Billy Bashor	Colorado A&M	40
	Cotton Rosser	Cal Poly-SLO	30
	Earl Guthrie	Texas A&M	20
	Harley May	Sul Ross State	10
Second Round	Bubba Day	Texas A&M	40
	Harley May	Sul Ross State	25
	Harry Hopson	New Mexico A&M	25
	Bud Penland	Pierce College	10
Average	Harley May	Sul Ross State	40
	Bud Penland	Pierce College	30
	Billy Bashor	Colorado A&M	20
	Cotton Rosser	Cal Poly-SLO	10

TOTAL POINTS FOR THE BULL RIDING

1. Harley May	Sul Ross State	75
2. Billy Bashor	Colorado A&M	60
3. Bud Penland	Pierce College	40
4. Cotton Rosser	Cal Poly-SLO	40
5. Bubba Day	Texas A&M	40
6. Harry Hopson	New Mexico A&M	25
7. Earl Guthrie	Texas A&M	20

Calf Roping: 43 entries

				TIME
First Round	Robert Doner	Cal Poly-SLO	40	16.3
	Cotton Rosser	Cal Poly-SLO	30	18.4
	Eldon Dudley	Oklahoma A&M	20	19.2
	Tuffy Cooper	U of New Mexico	10	20.0
Second Round	Eldon Dudley	Oklahoma A&M	40	22.5
	Tuffy Cooper	U of New Mexico	30	23.1
	Richard Thompson	U of New Mexico	20	28.1
	Andrew Cruse	Colorado A&M	10	29.3
Average	Eldon Dudley	Oklahoma A&M	40	41.7
	Tuffy Cooper	U of New Mexico	30	43.1
	Boog Trainham	New Mexico A&M	20	50.6
	Cotton Rosser	Cal Poly-SLO	5	57.3
	Andrew Cruse	Colorado A&M	5	57.3

TOTAL POINTS IN THE CALF ROPING

1. Eldon Dudley	Oklahoma A&M	100	41.7
2. Tuffy Cooper	U of New Mexico	70	43.1
3. Robert Doner	Cal Poly-SLO	40	
4. Cotton Rosser	Cal Poly-SLO	35	57.3
5. Boog Trainham	New Mexico A&M	20	
6. Richard Thompson	U of New Mexico	20	
7. Andrew Cruse	Colorado A&M	15	

Steer Wrestling: 32 entries

First Round	Tom Hadley	New Mexico A&M	40	10.9
	Boog Trainham	New Mexico A&M	30	20.3
	Harley May	Sul Ross State	20	20.5
	Les Pyeatt	Colorado A&M	10	22.6
Second Round	Tom Hadley	New Mexico A&M	40	10.5
	Les Pyeatt	Colorado A&M	30	12.2
	Andrew Cruse	Colorado A&M	20	15.2

	Boog Trainham	New Mexico A&M	10	25.6
Average	Tom Hadley	New Mexico A&M	40	21.4
	Les Pyeatt	Colorado A&M	30	34.8
	Boog Trainham	New Mexico A&M	20	45.9
	Eugene Pedersen	Montana State	10	60.7

TOTAL POINTS IN THE STEER WRESTLING

1. Tom Hadley	New Mexico A&M	120	21.4
2. Les Pyeatt	Colorado A&M	70	34.8
3. Boog Trainham	New Mexico A&M	60	45.9
4/5. Harley May	Sul Ross State	20	
4/5. Andrew Cruse	Colorado A&M	20	
6. Eugene Pedersen	Montana State	10	

WILD COW MILKING: 47 ENTRIES

First Round	Lem Boughner	Cal Poly-SLO	40	33.2
	Tom Andre	Cal Poly-SLO	30	37.4
	James Wood	Texas A&M	20	37.8
	Henry Winter	Cal Poly-SLO	10	38.2
Second Round	Gene Newman	Sul Ross State	40	25.6
	Cotton Rosser	Cal Poly-SLO	30	26.8
	Richard Thompson	U of New Mexico	20	31.5
	Thomas Johnson	Arizona State	10	40.7
Average	Bob Sauke	Montana State	40	170.8
	Gene Newman	Sul Ross State	30	
	Cotton Rosser	Cal Poly-SLO	20	
	Richard Thompson	U of New Mexico	10	

LIST OF 84 CONTESTANTS WHO COMPETED AT THE COW PALACE

*PLACED IN A ROUND OR THE AVERAGE

1. Henry Burns	Arizona State
2. Thomas Johnson*	Arizona State

3. Stuart Jones	Arizona State
4. Don Martin	Arizona State
5. Rusty Steward	Arizona State
6. Calvin Stuart	Arizona State
7. Tom Andre*	Cal Poly-SLO
8. Lem Boughner*	Cal Poly-SLO
9. Robert Doner*	Cal Poly-SLO
10. Dick Hutchison*	Cal Poly-SLO
11. Cotton Rosser*	Cal Poly-SLO
12. Henry Winter*	Cal Poly-SLO
13. Billy Bashor*	Colorado A&M
14. Andrew W. Cruse*	Colorado A&M
15. Tommy Kuiper	Colorado A&M
16. Danny Marioni	Colorado A&M
17. Les Pyeatt*	Colorado A&M
18. Dick Ritchey	Colorado A&M
19. Wilton S. Bools	Fresno State
20. Tommy Gatewood	Fresno State
21. Presley Schmall	Fresno State
22. Francis Springer	Fresno State
23. Jerry Taylor	Fresno State
24. Al Veater	Fresno State
25. Frederick L. Bennett	Kansas State
26. John Finley	Kansas State
27. Dick Jepsen	Kansas State
28. Darold Marlow	Kansas State
29. Bud Nace	Kansas State
30. Willard Phillips	Kansas State
31. Edwin Atkins	Montana State
32. William C. Cornelius	Montana State
33. Charlie Dunning	Montana State
34. Perry Moore	Montana State
35. Eugene Pedersen*	Montana State
36. Bob Sauke*	Montana State
37. Clyde Gossett	New Mexico A&M
38. Tom Hadley*	New Mexico A&M

39. Punk Hennigan	New Mexico A&M
40. Harry Hopson*	New Mexico A&M
41. Ham Scott	New Mexico A&M
42. Boog Trainham*	New Mexico A&M
43. Billy Brown	Oklahoma A&M
44. Eldon Dudley*	Oklahoma A&M
45. A. T. Ferree	Oklahoma A&M
46. Garland Kelley	Oklahoma A&M
47. John Pritchett	Oklahoma A&M
48. Dale Reagan	Oklahoma A&M
49. Dave Clark	Pierce College
50. Dutch Hoffman	Pierce College
51. Bud Penland*	Pierce College
52. Buford "Corky" Randall	Pierce College
53. Rodney Renting	Pierce College
54. Dan Rogers*	Pierce College
55. Hank Finger*	Sul Ross State
56. Charles Hall	Sul Ross State
57. Bub Hull	Sul Ross State
58. Buster Lindley*	Sul Ross State
59. Harley May*	Sul Ross State
60. Gene Newman*	Sul Ross State
61. G. C. Damuth	Texas A&M
62. Bubba Day*	Texas A&M
63. Earl Guthrie*	Texas A&M
64. Charlie D. Rankin*	Texas A&M
65. J. E. Sauls	Texas A&M
66. James P. Wood*	Texas A&M
67. Tommie Bell	Texas Tech
68. Jim Easley	Texas Tech
69. Bud Halsell	Texas Tech
70. Bob Morris	Texas Tech
71. John Wilson	Texas Tech
72. B. F. Yeates	Texas Tech
73. Jack Cargill	U of New Mexico
74. Tuffy Cooper*	U of New Mexico

75. John Daniel	U of New Mexico
76. Jon Frost	U of New Mexico
77. Norman McNew*	U of New Mexico
78. Richard Thompson*	U of New Mexico
79. Pete Dalzell	U of Wyoming
80. John P. Gammon	U of Wyoming
81. Bob Laramore	U of Wyoming
82. Fran Marsh	U of Wyoming
83. Dale Stiles*	U of Wyoming
84. Bill Whitney*	U of Wyoming

Information: finals program and "Recapitulation of Entries and Points Won" NIRA Cow Palace report.

College and University NIRA National Champions

1949–2003 COLLEGE AND UNIVERSITY NATIONAL NIRA TEAM AND EVENT CHAMPIONSHIPS

ARIZONA STATE UNIVERSITY

1957	bull riding	Ken Adams
1966 women's team		
1966	calf roping	Stan Harter
1966	ribbon roping	Stan Harter
1974	goat tying	Pam Simon Sproul

ARKANSAS STATE UNIVERSITY

1976	team roping	Wayne Smith

BACONE COLLEGE, OKLAHOMA

2003	calf roping	Stephen L. Reagor

BLACK HILLS STATE UNIVERSITY, SOUTH DAKOTA

1967	saddle bronc	David Dahl
1969	bull riding	Lonnie Hall
1970	all-around men	Tom Miller
1971	all-around men	Tom Miller
1981	goat tying	Shari Simmons
1984	goat tying	Shari Simmons

BLUE MOUNTAIN COMMUNITY COLLEGE, OREGON

1971	saddle bronc	Everett Jones
1972	calf roping	Danny Torricellas
1972	barrel racing	Becky Fullerton
1979	team roping	Mike Beers

1983	all-around men	Rocky Steagall
1983	bull riding	Rocky Steagall
1984	steer wrestling	Mike Currin
1984	all-around men	John Opie
1986	all-around women	Molly McAuliffe Hepper
1987 men's team		
1987	calf roping	Kelsey Allen Felton
1988	calf roping	Bradley Goodrich
1991	bull riding	Dan Wolfe
1999	saddle bronc	Jerad McFarlane
1999	team roping	Kain Garcia (Matt Funk, Lewis-Clark SC)

BOISE STATE UNIVERSITY, IDAHO

1986	bareback riding	Gary Bret Brogan

BRIGHAM YOUNG UNIVERSITY, UTAH

1964	calf roping	John Fincher
1970	calf roping	Nick Baldwin
1977	breakaway roping	Sherre Stoddard

CAL POLY STATE UNIVERSITY AT SAN LUIS OBISPO, CALIFORNIA

1956	team roping	Monty Roberts
1957	steer wrestling	Monty Roberts
1958	goat tying	Merna Muller
1959	all-around men	Jack Roddy
1959	steer wrestling	Jack Roddy
1959	ribbon roping	Bill Nielson
1960 men's team		
1960	ribbon roping	Bill Nielson
1960	steer wrestling	Riley Freeman
1964	bull riding	C. W. Adams
1965	bull riding	C. W. Adams
1967	bareback riding	Dan Freeman
1967	bull riding	Bobby Berger

1967	barrel racing	Barbara Baer
1969	all-around women	Nancy Robinson Petersen
1969	barrel racing	Barbara Baer
1970 men's team		
1970	ribbon roping	Tom Ferguson
1970	bareback riding	Melvin Dick
1970	saddle bronc	Melvin Dick
1970	goat tying	Sharon Meffan Camarillo
1971 men's team		
1971	calf roping	Jerry Koile
1973 men's team		
1973	steer wrestling	Tom Ferguson
1973	calf roping	Tom Ferguson
1973	breakaway roping	Colleen Semas
1977	calf roping	Chris Lybbert
1981	steer wrestling	John W. Jones Jr.
1982	team roping	Allen Gill
1984	breakaway roping	Wendy Monchamp
1984	team roping	Rocky Carpenter
1985	team roping	Nolan Twisselman
1989 women's team		
1989	barrel racing	Holly Foster
1990	steer wrestling	Dean Wang
1991	all-around women	Julie Adair
1991	goat tying	Julie Adair
1993	steer wrestling	Ross Gomez
1994	steer wrestling	Tyler Keith
2000	bull riding	Thomas Clark
2003	all-around men	Jesse M. Segura

CALIFORNIA STATE UNIVERSITY, FRESNO

1974	all-around men	Dudley Little
1978	steer wrestling	Samuel Edmondson

CASPER COLLEGE, WYOMING

1963 men's team		
1964 men's team		
1964	all-around men	Pink Peterson
1964	bareback riding	Pink Peterson
1964 (tie)	saddle bronc	Pink Peterson (Ned Londo, Lamar College)
1965 men's team		
1965	all-around men	Pink Peterson
1965	bareback riding	Claude Wilson
1966 men's team		
1966	bareback riding	Joe Alexander
1966	saddle bronc	Ivan Daines
1971	ribbon roping	Dave Brock
1978	bull riding	Hank Franzen
1983	saddle bronc	Guy Lenard Shapka

CENTRAL ARIZONA COLLEGE

1978 women's team		
1978	all-around women	Barrie Beach Smith
1978	goat tying	Barrie Beach Smith
1979 women's team		
1979	all-around women	Barrie Beach Smith
1987	all-around men	Roy Cordova
1995	team roping	Whip Lewis (Paul Griemsman, EWC)

CENTRAL WASHINGTON UNIVERSITY

| 1990 | team roping | Clay Ring |

CENTRAL WYOMING COLLEGE

1998	all-around women	Lynn Wiebe
1998	goat tying	Lynn Wiebe
1998	breakaway roping	Lynn Wiebe
2000	bareback riding	Paul Jones

CHADRON STATE COLLEGE, NEBRASKA

1956	calf roping	Don Meter
1978	breakaway roping	Jean Fuchs Poythress
1979	breakaway roping	Kathryn Kennedy
1999	bull riding	William Farrell
2001	bull riding	Dustin Elliott
2002	bull riding	Will Farrell

CISCO COLLEGE, TEXAS

1975	calf roping	Roy Cooper

COLLEGE OF SOUTHERN IDAHO

1979	bull riding	Doyle Parker
1986	saddle bronc	Frank Patrick Norcutt
1987	saddle bronc	Wayne Norcutt
1990	all-around men	Zane Davis
1993	bareback riding	Zane Davis
1993	all-around men	Zane Davis
1996	all-around men	Jason Call
1996 men's team		
2001 men's team		
2001	all-around men	Cody Demers
2001	saddle bronc	Cody Demers
2001	breakaway roping	Kini Wright
2002 men's team		
2002	all-around	Cody Demers

COLORADO STATE UNIVERSITY (A&M)

1954	bareback riding	Bob Schild
1954	saddle bronc	Bob Schild
1954	steer wrestling	John Gee
1954 men's team		
1956	all-around women	Kathlyn "Chickie" Younger Knox
1956	barrel racing	Kathlyn "Chickie" Younger Knox

247

1956	bareback riding	Don Yates
1956	steer wrestling	John Gee
1957	optional race	Teresa Sully
1963 women's team		
1963	all-around women	Leota Hielscher
1963	goat tying	Sally Spencer
1964 women's team		
1966	barrel racing	Cleonne Skinner Steinmiller

DAWSON COMMUNITY COLLEGE, MONTANA

1975	team roping	Phil Luman & Bill Parker
1980	bull riding	Chuck Simonson
1981	bull riding	Chuck Simonson
1981 men's team		
1981	bareback riding	Larry Peabody
1984	bareback riding	William Ward
2001	steer wrestling	Beau Franzen

DICKINSON STATE UNIVERSITY, NORTH DAKOTA

1959	bull riding	Freddie Kist
1980	saddle bronc	Brad Gjermundson
1984	bull riding	Quint McDermand
1994	saddle bronc	Shawn Stroh
1996	saddle bronc	Jeremy Crane
1998	saddle bronc	Jeremy Crane
1999	calf roping	Matt Otto

EASTERN MONTANA COLLEGE

| 1968 | saddle bronc | J. C. Bonine |
| 1969 | saddle bronc | J. C. Bonine |

EASTERN NEW MEXICO UNIVERSITY

| 1967 women's team | | |
| 1968 | all-around women | Donna Kinkead |

1968	barrel racing	Donna Kinkead
1969	men's team	
1970	all-around women	Linda Blackburn Sultemeier
1971	steer wrestling	Ed Wright
1972	breakaway roping	Betty Gayle Cooper Ratliff
1972	women's team	
1974	men's team	
1976	barrel racing	Chris Helker
1981	women's team	
1983	women's team	
1983	all-around women	Anna Crespin Gardner
1983	goat tying	Anna Crespin Gardner

EASTERN OREGON UNIVERSITY

| 1971 | bareback riding | Lee Eddins |

EASTERN WYOMING COLLEGE

| 1986 | goat tying | Shelley Meter |
| 1995 | team roping | Paul Griemsman (Whip Lewis, CAC) |

EASTFIELD COLLEGE, TEXAS

| 1982 | bareback riding | Thom Hickey |

FRANK PHILLIPS COLLEGE, TEXAS

| 2000 | steer wrestling | Joshua Peek |

FORT HAYS STATE UNIVERSITY, KANSAS

| 1973 | barrel racing | Colette Graves |
| 1974 | bareback riding | Jerry Beagley |

FORT SCOTT COMMUNITY COLLEGE, KANSAS

| 1990 | bull riding | Casey Gates |
| 2001 | bareback riding | Clint Evers |

GARDEN CITY COMMUNITY COLLEGE, KANSAS

| 1993 | barrel racing | Marilee McGraw |

HARDIN-SIMMONS UNIVERSITY, TEXAS

1950	bareback riding	James Mickler
1951	bareback riding	James Mickler
1951	steer wrestling	Bill Guest
1952	saddle bronc	Joe Chase
1953	saddle bronc	Joe Chase
1953	bareback riding	Dick Barrett
1953	men's team	
1954	calf roping	Lee Cockrell
1954	team roping	Bill Teague
1954	all-around women	Becky Jo Smith Doom
1955	all-around women	Becky Jo Smith Doom
1955	optional race	Becky Jo Smith Doom
1955	steer wrestling	Gene Frazier

HARTNELL COLLEGE, CALIFORNIA

1981	saddle bronc	Chuck Morris
1982	saddle bronc	Chuck Morris
1983	steer wrestling	Ross Rianda
1983	bareback riding	Stephen Smith Jr.

HILL COLLEGE, TEXAS

1993	bull riding	Philip Elkins
1996	bull riding	Charles Aaron Williams
1998	calf roping	Aaron Adamson
2003	bull riding	Chad Eubank

HOWARD COLLEGE, TEXAS

1975	bull riding	Jack Himes
1977	bareback riding	Jack Lee Himes
1994	team roping	John Folmer (Tye Maben, Texas Tech)

IDAHO STATE UNIVERSITY

1959 (tie)	bareback riding	Dick Henson (Larry O'Neill, U Texas)
1966	all-around men	Dave Hart
1989	goat tying	Patti O'Maley
1992	saddle bronc	Michael Giannini

KANSAS STATE UNIVERSITY

1967	all-around women	Barbara Socolofsky

LAMAR COLLEGE, COLORADO

1964 (tie)	saddle bronc	Ned Londo (Pink Peterson, Casper College)
1975	steer wrestling	Paul Hughes

LABETTE COLLEGE, KANSAS

1981	barrel racing	Kendra Bennett

LEWIS-CLARK STATE COLLEGE, IDAHO

1998 women's team		
1999	team roping	Matt Funk (Kain Garcia, Blue Mt. CC)

LUBBOCK CHRISTIAN UNIVERSITY, TEXAS

1958	bull riding	Don Workman
1960	all-around men	Edd Workman
1960	saddle bronc	Edd Workman
1961	all-around men	Edd Workman
1962	all-around men	Edd Workman
1962	saddle bronc	Edd Workman

MCNEESE STATE UNIVERSITY, LOUISIANA

1955	barrel racing	Kathlyn "Chickie" Younger Knox

1957	men's team	
1957	all-around men	Clyde May
1958	men's team	
1958	bareback riding	Jim Miller
1959	men's team	
1963	bull riding	Nelson Spotts
1985	all-around men	Kent Jude Richard
1987	barrel racing	Holly Foster
1994	barrel racing	Shane Hooks
1995	bareback riding	James Boudreaux
1997	steer wrestling	Gus Ledoux

MESA COMMUNITY COLLEGE, ARIZONA

| 1967 | calf roping | Sherrick Grantham |
| 1967 | bareback riding | J. C. Trujillo |

MILES COMMUNITY COLLEGE, MONTANA

| 1982 | bull riding | Scott Breding |
| 1995 | breakaway roping | Nacona Pauley |

MISSOURI STATE UNIVERSITY

| 1971 | all-around women | Jan Wagner |
| 1971 | breakaway roping | Jan Wagner |

MISSOURI VALLEY COLLEGE

| 2002 | saddle bronc riding | Cody Martin |

MONTANA STATE UNIVERSITY

1949	wild cow milking	Bob Sauke
1958	steer wrestling	Vic Small
1961	all-around women	Sue Burgraff Melaney
1961	steer wrestling	Gary Murphy
1964	goat tying	Karen Coleman Miller
1966	all-around women	Carol O'Rourke Smith
1972	men's team	
1972	bareback riding	Robert Schall

1972		saddle bronc	Jock McDowell
1972		steer wrestling	Lynn Perry
1972		ribbon roping	Dean Perkins
1973		saddle bronc	Jock McDowell
1974		bull riding	Butch Bratsky
1975	men's team		
1975		saddle bronc	Bud Munroe
1978		saddle bronc	David Griffith
1979		saddle bronc	David Griffith
1986	women's team		
1988	men's team		
1988		all-around men	Ken Lensegrav
1988		bareback riding	Ken Lensegrav
1988		bull riding	Rex Phillips
1989		bareback riding	Ken Lensegrav
1990	men's team		
1991	men's team		
1991		all-around men	Shawn Vant
1991		bareback riding	Shawn Vant
1991		saddle bronc	Dan Mortensen
1992		bareback riding	Shawn Vant
1992		goat tying	Lana Tibbetts
1994		all-around men	Jason Jackson
1994		bareback riding	Jason Jackson
1995	men's team		
1995		all-around men	Jason Jackson
1995		bull riding	Jason Jackson

MURRAY STATE COLLEGE, OKLAHOMA

1996	calf roping	Jerome Schneeberger
1997	calf roping	Jerome Schneeberger

NATIONAL AMERICAN UNIVERSITY, SOUTH DAKOTA

1970	steer wrestling	Bob Christopherson
1985	bareback riding	Scott M. Gress
1988	steer wrestling	Cory Ferguson

1997	bareback riding	Erick Delan Blanton
2003	barrel racing	Jessica L. Mueller

NEW MEXICO JUNIOR COLLEGE

2002	breakaway roping	Keli Jo Smith

NEW MEXICO STATE UNIVERSITY (A&M)

1949	steer wrestling	Tom Hadley
1951	calf roping	F. C. Stover
1952	calf roping	F. C. Stover
1952	steer wrestling	Don Driggers
1956	goat tying	Pat Dunigan Marr
1957	all-around women	Betty Sims Solt
1957	barrel racing	Betty Sims Solt
1958	barrel racing	Betty Sims Solt
1958	all-around women	Pat Dunigan Marr
1959	all-around women	Pat Dunigan Marr
1959	calf tying	Pat Dunigan Marr
1961	ribbon roping	Dub Cox
1962 (tie)	calf roping	Dub Cox
		(Bill James, Sul Ross
		State U)
1963	barrel racing	Linda Kinkead
1966	steer wrestling	Leburt Saulsberry
1975 women's team		
1975	all-around women	Jennifer Haynes
1975	breakaway roping	Jennifer Haynes
1975	goat tying	Jennifer Haynes
1976 women's team		
1976	all-around women	Janet Stover Crowson
1976	breakaway roping	Janet Stover Crowson
1976	goat tying	Jennifer Haynes
1977	saddle bronc	Sid Morrow
1983	barrel racing	Tammy King Engle
1987	team roping	Darin B. Simpson
1990	bareback riding	Randy Slaughter

NORTHEASTERN OKLAHOMA A&M COLLEGE

2002	team roping	Colt Braden & Wendall Stanley

NORTHEAST TEXAS COMMUNITY COLLEGE

2003	team roping	Shane B. Powell (Justin L. Lovell, Stephen F. Austin State U)

NORTHERN MONTANA COLLEGE

1962	barrel racing	Lorraine Taylor

NORTHWEST COMMUNITY COLLEGE, WYOMING

1985	bull riding	Clint Branger
2002	bareback riding	Colby Olsen

NORTHWESTERN STATE UNIVERSITY, LOUISIANA

1995	steer wrestling	Chad Hagan

ODESSA COLLEGE, TEXAS

1986	bull riding	Jim Sharp
1987	bull riding	Jim Sharp
1989	men's team	
1989	all-around men	Ty Murray
1989	bull riding	Ty Murray
1989	saddle bronc	Ty Murray
1989	calf roping	Shawn McMullan
1990	calf roping	Shawn McMullan
1992	bull riding	Jerome Davis
1997	bull riding	Ben Duggar
2003	bareback riding	Cimarron L. Gerke

OKLAHOMA STATE UNIVERSITY (A&M)

1949	calf roping	Eldon Dudley
1952	all-around men	Dick Barrett

1952	bareback riding	Dick Barrett
1952	ribbon roping	Dick Barrett
1953	steer wrestling	Don Fedderson
2001 women's team		
2001	barrel racing	Janae Ward
2002	calf roping	Trent Creager

OREGON STATE UNIVERSITY

| 1978 | barrel racing | Julie Doering |

OREGON TECHNICAL COLLEGE

| 1957 | saddle bronc | Bill Duffy |
| 1959 | saddle bronc | Gary Gregg |

PANHANDLE STATE UNIVERSITY, OKLAHOMA

1992	calf roping	Chad David Hiatt
1993	saddle bronc	George Cliff Norris
1994	calf roping	Marty McCloy
1996 (tie)	team roping	Andy Bolton & Benjamin Blue (Buck Brandon Garcia & Joe Verastegui, Southwest Tex. Jr. C)
1997 men's team		
1998 men's team		
1998	steer wrestling	Josh McIntyre
1998	team roping	Brian Dunning & Travis Goad
2000 men's team		
2000	all-around men	Jesse Bail
2001	team roping	Logan Olson & Jett Hillman

PIMA COMMUNITY COLLEGE, ARIZONA

| 1976 | bull riding | Richard Escalante |

RICKS COLLEGE, UTAH

1961	calf roping	Evan Goulding
1971	goat tying	Jeanne Coates
1972	bull riding	Lamar Roche
1973	bull riding	Lamar Roche
1974	steer wrestling	Tom Clyde
2002	barrel racing	McKenzie Miller

SAM HOUSTON STATE UNIVERSITY, TEXAS

1953	calf roping	Sonny Sikes
1953	ribbon roping	Sonny Sikes
1955	all-around men	Ira Akers
1955	bareback riding	Ira Akers
1955	saddle bronc	Ira Akers
1955	bull riding	Ira Akers
1955	calf roping	Sonny Sikes
1955	team roping	Sonny Sikes
1956	all-around men	Ira Akers
1956	saddle bronc	Ira Akers
1956	bull riding	Ira Akers
1956 men's team		
1960	all-around women	Karen Mangum
1960	goat tying	Karen Mangum
1961 women's team		
1961	bull riding	Leo Anderson
1963	saddle bronc	Leo Anderson
1964	ribbon roping	Martin Ruffeno
1965 women's team		
1965	all-around women	Becky Berggren
1965	barrel racing	Becky Berggren
1968 men's team		
1968 women's team		
1968	steer wrestling	Carl Deaton
1969	steer wrestling	Carl Deaton
1969	all-around men	Phil Lyne

1969	calf roping	Phil Lyne
1974 women's team		
1974	all-around	Jimmie Gibbs Munroe
1974	barrel racing	Jimmie Gibbs Munroe
1974	breakaway roping	Cindy Galow
1974	calf roping	Brad McReynolds
1975	barrel racing	Jimmie Gibbs Munroe
1984 women's team		
1984	barrel racing	Lynn McCaffety
1985	steer wrestling	Chip N. Gatlin
1986	barrel racing	Lynn McCaffety
1996	bareback riding	Jason Jeter

SAN JUAN COMMUNITY COLLEGE, NEW MEXICO

| 1996 | goat tying | Renee Wood Byrd |

SCOTTSDALE COMMUNITY COLLEGE, ARIZONA

1986	breakaway roping	Deborah Ann Rogers
1987 women's team		
1987	goat tying	Kelly Harsh
1997	team roping	Cody Mathew Willson (Preston Williams, UNLV)

SHERIDAN COLLEGE, WYOMING

| 1969 | bareback riding | Chris LeDoux |
| 1971 | bull riding | Wally Badgett |

SOUTH DAKOTA STATE UNIVERSITY

1964	barrel racing	Carlee Obervy
1966	bull riding	Don Reichert
1968	bull riding	Don Reichert
1985	breakaway roping	Tammy Wink
1992	team roping	Seth Alan Weishaar
1994	goat tying	Kristie Price

SOUTHEASTERN OKLAHOMA STATE UNIVERSITY

1976	men's team	
1976	all-around men	James D. Ward
1976	bareback riding	James D. Ward
1977	men's team	
1977	bull riding	Jerry Beagley
1978	men's team	
1978	team roping	Olie Smith
1979	men's team	
1979	bareback riding	Jimmy Cleveland
1979	goat tying	Sabrina Pike
1980	men's team	
1980	women's team	
1980	breakaway roping	Sabrina Pike
1981	all-around women	Sabrina Pike
1981	calf roping	Lesley Jenkins
1982	women's team	
1982	all-around women	Sabrina Pike
1982	breakaway roping	Sabrina Pike
1995	women's team	
1995	all-around women	Caryn Standifer Snyder
1995	goat tying	Caryn Standifer Snyder
1996	women's team	
1996	all-around women	Caryn Standifer Snyder
1996	barrel racing	Caryn Standifer Snyder
1997 (tie)	breakaway roping	Caryn Standifer Snyder (Toni Arave, West Hills C, Calif.)

SOUTHERN ARKANSAS UNIVERSITY

1984	all-around women	Nancy Rea
1987	all-around women	Sherry Lynn Rosser
1989	all-around women	Cathy Dennis

SOUTHWESTERN OKLAHOMA STATE UNIVERSITY

1976	steer wrestling	Randy E. Taylor
1979	barrel racing	Bana Perry
1980	bareback riding	Joe Eckert
1985 men's team		
1986	steer wrestling	Marty Shawn Musil
1988 women's team		
1988	breakaway roping	Donelle Kvenild
1989	breakaway roping	Shannon Lord
1991	barrel racing	Annesa Musil
1992 men's team		
1993 men's team		
1993	all-around women	Shelley Johnston
1993	goat tying	Shelley Johnston
1994 women's team		
1994	all-around women	Tori Woodard
1995	calf roping	T. W. Snyder
1998	bareback riding	Davey Shields
1998	bull riding	Corey Navarre
1999 men's team		
2000 (tie)	goat tying	Jennifer Heisman (Lee McKnight, Weber SU)

SOUTHWEST MISSOURI STATE UNIVERSITY

1991	calf roping	Randall Orr
1994	breakaway roping	Leah Moellman

SOUTHWEST TEXAS JUNIOR COLLEGE

1963	calf roping	Richard Walker
1963	ribbon roping	Richard Walker
1965	ribbon roping	Roger Forehand
1996 (tie)	team roping	Buck Brandon Garcia & Joe Verastegui (Andy Bolton & Benjamin Blue, Panhandle State U)

SOUTHWEST TEXAS STATE UNIVERSITY

1960	bull riding	Royce Rodgers
1968	goat tying	Mary Fuller
1968	all-around men	Phil Lyne
1968	calf roping	Phil Lyne
1969	ribbon roping	Jim Jackson
1983	team roping	Billy Dale Haley
1984 men's team		
1985	calf roping	Lanham Mangold

STATE FAIR COMMUNITY COLLEGE, SEDALIA, MISSOURI

1979	all-around men	Joe Peabody

STEPHEN F. AUSTIN STATE UNIVERSITY, TEXAS

2003	team roping	Justin L. Lovell (Shane B. Powell, Northeast Texas CC)

SUL ROSS STATE UNIVERSITY, TEXAS

1949 men's team		
1949	all-around men	Harley May
1949	bareback riding	Harley May
1949	bull riding	Harley May
1950 men's team		
1950	all-around men	Harley May
1950	saddle bronc	Harley May
1950	bull riding	Harley May
1951 men's team		
1951	all-around men	Harley May
1951	saddle bronc	Harley May
1951	all-around women	Jo Gregory Knox
1952 men's team		
1952	bull riding	Johnny Ackel
1953	all-around men	Tex Martin
1953	all-around women	Elisabeth Prude Longbotham

1953	bull riding	Ira Akers
1954	bull riding	Tex Martin
1954	goat tying	Charlotte Martin
1958	saddle bronc	Don Lee Smith
1961 (tie)	calf roping	Bill James (Dub Cox, New Mexico State U)
1961	calf tying	Donna Saul
1962 men's team		
1962 women's team		
1962	bull riding	George Eads
1962	team roping	Bill James
1962	all-around women	Donna Saul
1962	goat tying	Donna Saul
1982 men's team		
1982	all-around men	Cody Lambert
1983 men's team		
1983	breakaway roping	Jayne Gentry
1985 women's team		

TARLETON STATE UNIVERSITY, TEXAS

1967 men's team		
1969 women's team		
1969	goat tying	Angie Watts Averhoff
1969	breakaway roping	Sally Preston
1970 women's team		
1970	barrel racing	Connie Wilkinson Wood
1971 women's team		
1971	barrel racing	Martha Tompkins
1973	bareback riding	Perry Lee
1977	steer wrestling	Steve Fryar
1988	team roping	Kenneth David Key
1999	all-around women	Jennifer Smith
1999	barrel racing	Jennifer Smith
2000	team roping	Kurt Kiehne & Levi Garcia

TEXAS A&M UNIVERSITY

1950	steer wrestling	Bill Hogg
1951	bull riding	Maxie Overstreet
1992	barrel racing	Mindy Morris
2000	barrel racing	Amanda Barrett

2002 women's team

TEXAS A&M AT KINGSVILLE (TEXAS A&I)

1957	team roping	Grady Allen
1957	calf roping	Jack Burkholder
1958	all-around men	Jack Burkholder
1958	ribbon roping	Jack Burkholder
1958	calf roping	Jack Burkholder
1959	calf roping	Jack Burkholder
1960	calf roping	Jack Burkholder

TEXAS TECH UNIVERSITY

1955 men's team

1957	bareback riding	Dave Hopper
1961	bareback riding	John Holt
1965	goat tying	Eileen Cochran
1966	goat tying	Marianne Munz Brunson
1967	goat tying	Marianne Munz Brunson
1984	saddle bronc	Derek Clark
1987	breakaway roping	Karen Cochran Smith
1993	breakaway roping	Lari Dee Guy
1994	team roping	Tye Maben (Wayne Folmer, Howard College)

UNIVERSITY OF ARIZONA

1960	bareback riding	Gerry Bishop
1962	steer wrestling	Sonny Ehr
1963	steer wrestling	Sonny Ehr
1972	goat tying	Wendy Bryan

1973 women's team

1973	goat tying	Wendy Bryan
1978	calf roping	Joe Parsons
1982	goat tying	Linda O'Neal
1983	calf roping	Clay Parsons
1985	goat tying	Kelly Sue Kay

UNIVERSITY OF CENTRAL ARKANSAS

| 1980 | all-around women | Lea Erwin |

UNIVERSITY OF IDAHO

| 1954 | all-around men | Howard Harris |

UNIVERSITY OF MISSOURI AT COLUMBIA

| 1980 | goat tying | Phyllis Crouse |

UNIVERSITY OF MONTANA

1985	all-around women	Lisa Carol Scheffer
1985	barrel racing	Lisa Carol Scheffer
1997	barrel racing	Rachael Myllymaki Sproul
1999	all-around men	Bryant Mikkelson
1999	steer wrestling	Bryant Mikkelson

UNIVERSITY OF NEVADA AT LAS VEGAS

1994	bull riding	Beau Gillespie
1997	all-around men	Preston Williams
1997	team roping	Preston Williams (Cody Mathew Willson, Scottsdale CC)
1998	all-around men	Ross Coleman

1999 women's team

1999	breakaway roping	Stacie Sorensen
2001	all-around women	Suzanne Montero
2001	goat tying	Suzanne Montero
2002	all-around women	Jonlyn Vaccaro

2002	goat tying	Jonlyn Vaccaro
2003	all-around women	Suzanne Montero
2003	goat tying	Suzanne Montero

UNIVERSITY OF NEW MEXICO

1950	calf roping	Dale "Tuffy" Cooper

UNIVERSITY OF SOUTHERN COLORADO

1964	all-around women	Marie Mass
1967	steer wrestling	Butch Myers
1968	ribbon roping	Buddy Draper
1970	bull riding	Doug Wilson
1972	all-around men	Dave Brock
1973	all-around men	Dave Brock
1973	ribbon roping	Dave Brock
1974	ribbon roping	Mike McLaughlin
1976	calf roping	Mike McLaughlin
1978	bareback riding	Jay Himes
1980	team roping	J. D. Yates
1981	team roping	J. D. Yates

UNIVERSITY OF TENNESSEE AT MARTIN

1975	all-around men	Skip Emmett
1975	bareback riding	Skip Emmett
1977	all-around men	Tony Coleman
1981	all-around men	George Mesimer
1985	saddle bronc	Mike Merchant
1987	steer wrestling	Will Cody Matthews
1993	team roping	Frank Graves & Brett Gould

UNIVERSITY OF TEXAS

1959 (tie)	bareback riding	Larry O'Neill (Dick Henson, Idaho SU)

UNIVERSITY OF UTAH

1967	all-around men	A. C. Ekker
1967	ribbon roping	A. C. Ekker

UNIVERSITY OF WISCONSIN AT RIVER FALLS

1977	all-around women	Shelly Haskins Mueller

UNIVERSITY OF WYOMING

1949	saddle bronc	Dale Stiles
1962 men's team		
1962	bareback riding	Fred Wilson
1964	steer wrestling	Frank Shepperson
1965	steer wrestling	J. R. Kvenild
1973	all-around women	Lou Ann Herstead
1981	breakaway roping	Jean Fuchs Poythress
1983	steer wrestling	Chris Hansen
1990 women's team		
1990	all-around women	Jimmi Jo Martin
1990	goat tying	Jimmi Jo Martin
1990	saddle bronc	J. W. Simonson
1991 women's team		
1993 women's team		
1996	steer wrestling	Todd Suhn
1996	breakaway roping	Brenda White
2000	breakaway roping	Amy Shepperson
2003	steer wrestling	Levi C. Wisness

UTAH STATE UNIVERSITY

1965	calf roping	Jack Hannum
1970	breakaway roping	Saundra Curlock Sorensen
1972	all-around women	Linda Munns Miller
1977 women's team		
1977	goat tying	Cindy Coombs Lulloft
1980	barrel racing	Lori McNeil
1982	barrel racing	Lori McNeil

UTAH VALLEY STATE COLLEGE (UTAH VALLEY COMMUNITY COLLEGE)

1990	barrel racing	Elisa Nielsen
1991	team roping	Dustin Durfee
2003	saddle bronc	Lance L. Sagers

VERNON COLLEGE, TEXAS (VERNON REGIONAL JUNIOR COLLEGE)

1991	breakaway roping	Lari Dee Guy
1993	calf roping	Shane Hatch
1994 men's team		
1995	barrel racing	Molly Swanson Powell
2003 men's team		
2003 women's team		
2003	breakaway roping	Jaclyn L. Hobbs

WALLA WALLA COMMUNITY COLLEGE, WASHINGTON

1976	saddle bronc	Randy Dains
1979	calf roping	Dave Smith
1990	barrel racing	Kelli Edwards
1992 women's team		
1992	all-around women	Penny Conforth
1992	breakaway roping	Brenda Mays
2002	steer wrestling	Sam MacKenzie

WASHINGTON STATE UNIVERSITY

1977	team roping	Thomas R. Maycumber

WEBER STATE UNIVERSITY, UTAH

1979	steer wrestling	Lance Robinson
1980	all-around men	Lance Robinson
1980	calf roping	Lance Robinson
1980	steer wrestling	Lance Robinson
1984	calf roping	Kyle Kosoff
1988	goat tying	Lori Kay Hadley
1997 women's team		
1997	all-around women	Kelli Lynn Fowers

1997	goat tying	Kelli Lynn Fowers
2000 (tie)	goat tying	Lee McKnight (Jennifer Heisman, SWOSU)

WESTERN DAKOTA VOCATIONAL TECH

1988	saddle bronc	Eudell Larsen

WESTERN OKLAHOMA STATE COLLEGE

1987	bareback riding	Steve Abernathy

WESTERN TEXAS COLLEGE

1974	saddle bronc	John Gass
1977	barrel racing	Joann Whitehead
1982	calf roping	James Zant
1986	men's team	
1986	calf roping	Keith Hudson
1997	saddle bronc	Jeff Decker
1998	barrel racing	Tona Wright
1999	goat tying	Jill Childers
2000	women's team	
2000	all-around woman	Jamie Standifer
2000	calf roping	Houston Hutto
2001	calf roping	Houston Hutto

WESTERN MONTANA COLLEGE

1961	saddle bronc	Shawn Davis
1963	all-around men	Shawn Davis
1963	bareback riding	Shawn Davis
1989	steer wrestling	Tim Garrison
1991	steer wrestling	Jesse Peterson
1992	steer wrestling	Jesse Peterson
2000	saddle bronc	Jacob Hayworth

WEST HILLS COLLEGE, CALIFORNIA

1986	all-around men	Clay D. Hurst
1986	team roping	Clay D. Hurst
1988	all-around women	Cathy Cagliari
1988	barrel racing	Cathy Cagliari
1989	team roping	Chris Green
1992	all-around men	Casey Minton
1997 (tie)	breakaway roping	Toni Arave
		(Caryn Standifer Snyder,
		SEOSU)

WEST TEXAS A&M (WEST TEXAS STATE UNIVERSITY)

1950	team roping	Earl Reynolds
1951	ribbon roping	Roy Reynolds
1959	barrel racing	Mike Reid Settle
1960	barrel racing	Mike Reid Settle
1961	barrel racing	Mike Reid Settle

NIRA Team Championship Records, 1949–2003

Total team championships	Schools that have won team championships *denotes a two-year college	Total men's teams	Total women's teams	Total event champs	Total team & event champions
9	Sul Ross State U, Tex.	7	2	24	33
9	Southeastern Oklahoma State U	5	4	16	25
7	Sam Houston State U, Tex.	2	5	31	38
7	Montana State U	6	1	28	35
6	Southwestern Oklahoma State U	4	2	14	20
6	Eastern New Mexico U	2	4	8	14
5	Cal Poly-San Luis Obispo	4	1	36	42
4	University of Wyoming	1	3	13	18
4	*Casper C, Wyo.	4	0	12	16
4	Tarleton State U, Tex.	1	3	11	15
3	Colorado State U	1	2	11	14
3	McNeese State U, La.	3	0	8	11
3	Panhandle State U, Okla.	3	0	9	12
3	*C of Southern Idaho	3	0	11	14
3	*Vernon College, Tex.	2	1	4	7
2	New Mexico State U	0	2	25	27
2	*Western Texas College	1	1	9	11
2	*Central Arizona C	0	2	5	7
1	*Blue Mt. CC, Ore.	1	0	14	15
1	Hardin-Simmons U, Tex.	1	0	12	13
1	*Odessa C, Tex.	1	0	10	11
1	Texas Tech University	1	0	9	10
1	U of Arizona	0	1	9	10
1	Weber State U, Utah	0	1	9	10
1	SW Texas State U	1	0	7	8
1	*Dawson CC, Mont.	1	0	7	8
1	Utah State University	0	1	6	7
1	U Nevada-Las Vegas	0	1	11	12
1	*Walla Walla CC, Wash.	0	1	6	7
1	Arizona State University	0	1	4	5
1	*Scottsdale CC, Ariz.	0	1	3	4
1	Oklahoma State U	0	1	7	8
1	Lewis-Clark State C, Idaho	0	1	1	2
1	Texas A&M University	0	1	4	5

NIRA National Champions, 1949–2003

1949 COW PALACE, SAN FRANCISCO, CALIFORNIA, NIRA INVITATIONAL FINALS, FIRST NIRA CHAMPIONS

Men's Team	Sul Ross State College	Alpine, Tex.
Men's All-Around	Harley May	Sul Ross State, Tex.
Bareback Riding	Harley May	Sul Ross State, Tex.
Saddle Bronc	Dale Stiles	U of Wyoming
Bull Riding	Harley May	Sul Ross State, Tex.
Calf Roping	Eldon Dudley	Oklahoma A&M
Steer Wrestling	Tom Hadley	New Mex. A&M
Wild Cow Milking	Bob Sauke	Montana State College

1950 COW PALACE, SAN FRANCISCO, CALIFORNIA, FIRST NIRA CHAMPIONSHIPS BASED ON POINTS WON DURING THE YEAR (1949) AND FINALS RODEO POINTS.

Men's Team	Sul Ross State College	Alpine, Tex.
Men's All-Around	Harley May	Sul Ross State, Tex.
Bareback Riding	James Mickler	Hardin-Simmons U, Tex.
Saddle Bronc Riding	Harley May	Sul Ross State, Tex.
Bull Riding	Harley May	Sul Ross State, Tex.
Calf Roping	Tuffy Cooper	U of New Mex.
Steer Wrestling	Bill Hogg	Texas A&M
Team Roping	Earl Reynolds	West Texas State

1951 FORT WORTH, TEXAS, WILL ROGERS COLISEUM

NIRA championships were based on 1950 points and 1951 finals points. The 1951 champions, from the NIRA newsletter, *The Rigging*, May 1951, and corroborated by the champions themselves, are different from the national records.

Men's Team	Sul Ross State College	Alpine, Tex.
Men's All-Around	Harley May	Sul Ross State, Tex.

Women's All-Around	Jo Gregory Knox	Sul Ross State, Tex.
Bareback Riding	James Mickler	Hardin-Simmons U, Tex.
Saddle Bronc	Harley May	Sul Ross State, Tex.
Bull Riding	Maxie Overstreet	Texas A&M
Calf Roping	F. C. Stover	New Mex. A&M
Steer Wrestling	Bill Guest	Hardin-Simmons U, Tex.
Ribbon Roping	Roy Reynolds	West Texas State College

1952 PORTLAND, OREGON

NIRA championships were based on points for three semesters (spring 1951, fall 1951, and spring 1952 rodeos) and the finals rodeo points. After this year, points won during the fall and spring semesters of each school year and the finals points were used.

Men's Team	Sul Ross State College	Alpine, Tex.
Men's All-Around	Dick Barrett	Oklahoma A&M
Bareback Riding	Dick Barrett	Oklahoma A&M
Saddle Bronc Riding	Joe Chase	Hardin-Simmons U, Tex.
Bull Riding	Johnny Ackel	Sul Ross State, Tex.
Calf Roping	F. C. Stover	New Mex. A&M
Steer Wrestling	Don Driggers	New Mex. A&M
Ribbon Roping	Dick Barrett	Oklahoma A&M

1953 ABILENE, TEXAS, HARDIN-SIMMONS UNIVERSITY

Men's Team	Hardin-Simmons U	Abilene, Tex.
Men's All-Around	Tex Martin	Sul Ross State, Tex.
Women's All-Around	Elisabeth Prude Longbotham	Sul Ross State, Tex.
Bareback Riding	Dick Barrett	Hardin-Simmons U, Tex.
Saddle Bronc Riding	Joe Chase	Hardin-Simmons U, Tex.
Bull Riding	Ira Akers	Sul Ross State, Tex.
Calf Roping	Sonny Sikes	Sam Houston State, Tex.
Steer Wrestling	Don Fedderson	Oklahoma A&M
Ribbon Roping	Sonny Sikes	Sam Houston State, Tex.

1954 LAKE CHARLES, LOUISIANA

Men's Team	Colorado A&M	Fort Collins, Colo.
Men's All-around	Howard Harris	U of Idaho
Women's All-around	Becky Jo Smith Doom	Hardin-Simmons U, Tex.
Bareback Riding	Bob Schild	Colorado A&M
Saddle Bronc Riding	Bob Schild	Colorado A&M
Bull Riding	Tex Martin	Sul Ross State, Tex.
Calf Roping	Lee Cockrell	Hardin-Simmons U, Tex.
Steer Wrestling	John Gee	Colorado A&M
Team Roping	Bill Teague	Hardin-Simmons U, Tex.
Goat Tying	Charlotte Martin	Sul Ross State, Tex.

1955 LAKE CHARLES, LOUISIANA

Men's Team	Texas Tech	Lubbock, Tex.
Men's All-Around	Ira Akers	Sam Houston State, Tex.
Women's All-Around	Becky Jo Smith Doom	Hardin-Simmons U, Tex.
Bareback Riding	Ira Akers	Sam Houston State, Tex.
Saddle Bronc Riding	Ira Akers	Sam Houston State, Tex.
Bull Riding	Ira Akers	Sam Houston State, Tex.
Calf Roping	Sonny Sikes	Sam Houston State, Tex.
Steer Wrestling	Gene Frazier	Hardin-Simmons U, Tex.
Team Roping	Sonny Sikes	Sam Houston State, Tex.
Barrel Racing	Kathlyn Younger Knox	McNeese State, La.
Goat Tying	Becky Jo Smith Doom	Hardin-Simmons U, Tex

1956 COLORADO SPRINGS, COLORADO

Men's Team	Sam Houston State	Huntsville, Tex.
Men's All-Around	Ira Akers	Sam Houston State, Tex.
Women's All-Around	Kathlyn Younger Knox	Colorado A&M
Bareback Riding	Don Yates	Colorado A&M
Saddle Bronc Riding	Ira Akers	Sam Houston State, Tex.
Bull Riding	Ira Akers	Sam Houston State, Tex.
Calf Roping	Don Meter	Chadron State, Nebr.
Steer Wrestling	John Gee	Colorado A&M
Team Roping	Monty Roberts	Cal Poly-SLO
Barrel Racing	Kathlyn Younger Knox	Colorado A&M
Goat Tying	Pat Dunigan Marr	New Mex. A&M

1957 Colorado Springs, Colorado

Men's Team	McNeese State	Lake Charles, La.
Men's All-Around	Clyde May	McNeese State, La.
Women's All-Around	Betty Sims Solt	New Mex. A&M
Bareback Riding	Dave Hopper	Texas Tech
Saddle Bronc Riding	Bill Duffy	Oregon Tech C
Bull Riding	Ken Adams	Arizona State
Calf Roping	Jack Burkholder	Texas A&I
Steer Wrestling	Monty Roberts	Cal Poly-SLO
Team Roping	Grady Allen	Texas A&I
Barrel Racing	Betty Sims Solt	New Mex. A&M
Goat Tying	Teresa Sully	Colorado State U

1958 Colorado Springs, Colorado

Men's Team	McNeese State	Lake Charles, La.
Men's All-Around	Jack Burkholder	Texas A&I
Women's All-Around	Pat Dunigan Marr	New Mex. A&M
Bareback Riding	Jim Miller	McNeese State, La.
Saddle Bronc Riding	Don Lee Smith	Sul Ross State, Tex.
Bull Riding	Don Workman	Lubbock Christian C
Calf Roping	Jack Burkholder	Texas A&I
Steer Wrestling	Vic Small	Montana State
Ribbon Roping	Jack Burkholder	Texas A&I
Barrel Race	Betty Sims Solt	New Mex. A&M
Goat Tying	Merna Muller	Cal Poly-SLO

1959 Klamath Falls, Oregon

Men's Team	McNeese State	Lake Charles, La.
Men's All-Around	Jack Roddy	Cal Poly-SLO
Women's All-Around	Pat Dunigan Marr	New Mexico State C
Bareback Riding (tie)	Dick Henson	Idaho SU
	Larry O'Neill	U of Texas
Saddle Bronc Riding	Gary Gregg	Oregon Technical C
Bull Riding	Freddie Kist	Dickinson SU, N.Dak.
Calf Roping	Jack Burkholder	Texas A&I
Steer Wrestling	Jack Roddy	Cal Poly-SLO

Ribbon Roping	Bill Nielson	Cal Poly-SLO
Barrel Race	Mike Reid Settle	West Texas State
Calf Tying	Pat Dunigan Marr	New Mex. A&M

1960 CLAYTON, NEW MEXICO

During 1960, the NIRA split into two organizations—the American Collegiate Rodeo Association (ACRA) and the parent NIRA. Records are for the NIRA champions only.

Men's team	Cal Poly-SLO	San Luis Obispo, Calif.
Men's All-Around	Edd Workman	Lubbock Christian C
Women's All-Around	Karen Mangum	Sam Houston State, Tex.
Bareback Riding	Gerry Bishop	U of Arizona
Saddle Bronc Riding	Edd Workman	Lubbock Christian C
Bull Riding	Royce Rodgers	Southwest Tex. SU
Calf Roping	Jack Burkholder	Texas A&I
Steer Wrestling	Riley Freeman	Cal Poly-SLO
Ribbon Roping	Bill Nielson	Cal Poly-SLO
Barrel Race	Mike Reid Settle	West Texas SU
Goat Tying	Karen Mangum	Sam Houston State, Tex.

1961 SACRAMENTO, CALIFORNIA

First year to have a women's team champion.

Men's Team	U of Wyoming	Laramie, Wyo.
Women's Team	Sam Houston SU	Huntsville, Tex.
Men's All-Around	Edd Workman	Lubbock Christian C
Women's All-Around	Sue Burgraff Melaney	Montana SU
Bareback Riding	John Holt	Texas Tech U
Saddle Bronc Riding	Shawn Davis	Western Montana C
Bull Riding	Leo Anderson	Sam Houston State, Tex.
Calf Roping	Evan Goulding	Ricks C, Utah
Steer Wrestling	Gary Murphy	Montana SU
Ribbon Roping	Dub Cox	New Mex. SU
Barrel Race	Mike Reid Settle	West Texas SU
Calf Tying	Donna Jean Saul	Sul Ross State, Tex.

1962 LITTLETON, COLORADO

Men's Team	Sul Ross State U	Alpine, Tex.
Women's Team	Sul Ross State U	Alpine, Tex.
Men's All-Around	Edd Workman	Lubbock Christian C
Women's All-Around	Donna Jean Saul	Sul Ross State, Tex.
Bareback Riding	Fred Wilson	U of Wyoming
Saddle Bronc Riding	Edd Workman	Lubbock Christian C
Bull Riding	George Eads	Sul Ross State, Tex.
Calf Roping (tie)	Bill James	Sul Ross State, Tex.
	Dub Cox	New Mex. State
Steer Wrestling	Sonny Ehr	U of Arizona
Ribbon Roping	Bill James	Sul Ross State, Tex.
Barrel Race	Lorraine Taylor	Northern Mont. C
Goat Tying	Donna Jean Saul	Sul Ross State, Tex.

1963 LITTLETON, COLORADO

Men's Team	Casper College	Casper, Wyo.
Women's Team	Colorado State U	Fort Collins, Colo.
Men's All-Around	Shawn Davis	Western Montana C
Women's All-Around	Leota Hielscher	Colorado SU
Bareback Riding	Shawn Davis	Western Montana C
Saddle Bronc Riding	Leo Anderson	Sam Houston State, Tex.
Bull Riding	Nelson Spotts	McNeese SU, La.
Calf Roping	Richard Walker	SW Tex. Jr. C
Steer Wrestling	Sonny Ehr	U of Arizona
Ribbon Roping	Richard Walker	SW Tex. Jr. C
Barrel Race	Linda Kinkead	New Mexico SU
Goat Tying	Sally Spencer	Colorado SU

1964 DOUGLAS, WYOMING

Men's Team	Casper College	Casper, Wyo.
Women's Team	Colorado State	Fort Collins, Colo.
Men's All-Around	Pink Peterson	Casper C, Wyo.
Women's All-Around	Marie Mass Gatlin	U of Southern Colo.
Bareback Riding	Pink Peterson	Casper C, Wyo.
Saddle Bronc Riding (tie)	Ned Londo	Lamar C, Colo.
	Pink Peterson	Casper C, Wyo.

Bull Riding	C. W. Adams	Cal Poly-SLO
Calf Roping	John Fincher	Brigham Young U, Utah
Steer Wrestling	Frank Shepperson	U of Wyoming
Ribbon Roping	Martin Ruffeno	Sam Houston State, Tex.
Barrel Racing	Carlee Obervy	South Dakota SU
Goat Tying	Karen Coleman Miller	Montana SU

1965 Laramie, Wyoming

Men's Team	Casper College	Casper, Wyo.
Women's Team	Sam Houston SU	Huntsville, Tex.
Men's All-Around	Pink Peterson	Casper C, Wyo.
Women's All-Around	Becky Berggren	Sam Houston State, Tex.
Bareback Riding	Claude Wilson	Casper C, Wyo.
Saddle Bronc Riding	Pink Peterson	Casper C, Wyo.
Bull Riding	C. W. Adams	Cal Poly-SLO
Calf Roping	Jack Hannum	Utah SU
Steer Wrestling	J. R. Kvenild	U of Wyo.
Ribbon Roping	Roger Forehand	SW Tex. Jr. C
Barrel Racing	Becky Berggren	Sam Houston State, Tex.
Goat Tying	Eileen Cochran	Texas Tech

1966 Vermillion, South Dakota

Men's Team	Casper College	Casper, Wyo.
Women's Team	Arizona State U	Phoenix, Ariz.
Men's All-Around	Dave Hart	Idaho SU
Women's All-Around	Carol O'Rourke Smith	Montana SU
Bareback Riding	Joe Alexander	Casper C, Wyo.
Saddle Bronc Riding	Ivan Daines	Casper C, Wyo.
Bull Riding	Don Reichert	South Dakota SU
Calf Roping	Stan Harter	Arizona SU
Steer Wrestling	Leburt Saulsberry	New Mexico SU
Ribbon Roping	Stan Harter	Arizona SU
Barrel Racing	Cleonne Skinner Steinmiller	Colorado SU
Goat Tying	Marianne Munz Brunson	Texas Tech

1967 St. George, Utah

Men's Team	Tarleton SU	Stephenville, Tex.
Women's Team	Eastern New Mex. U	Portales, N.Mex.
Men's All-Around	A. C.Ekker	U of Utah
Women's All-Around	Barbara Socolofsky	Kansas SU
Bareback Riding	Dan Freeman	Cal Poly-SLO
Saddle Bronc Riding	David Dahl	Black Hills SU, S.Dak.
Bull Riding	Bobby Berger	Cal Poly-SLO
Calf Roping	Sherrick Grantham	Arizona SU
Steer Wrestling	Butch Meyers	U of Southern Colo.
Ribbon Roping	A. C. Ekker	U of Utah
Barrel Racing	Barbara Baer	Cal Poly-SLO
Goat Tying	Marianne Munz Brunson	Texas Tech

1968 Sacramento, California

Men's Team	Sam Houston SU	Huntsville, Tex.
Women's Team	Sam Houston SU	Huntsville, Tex.
Men's All-Around	Phil Lyne	SW Texas SU
Women's All-Around	Donna Kinkead	Eastern NMU
Bareback Riding	J. C. Trujillo	Mesa C, Ariz.
Saddle Bronc	J. C. Bonine	Eastern Mont. C
Bull Riding	Don Reichert	South Dakota SU
Calf Roping	Phil Lyne	SW Texas SU
Steer Wrestling	Carl Deaton	Sam Houston State, Tex.
Ribbon Roping	Buddy Draper	Southern Colo. SU
Barrel Race	Donna Kinkead	Eastern NMU
Goat Tying	Mary Fuller	SW Texas SU

1969 Deadwood, South Dakota

Men's Team	Eastern New Mex.U	Portales, N.Mex.
Women's Team	Tarleton SU	Stephenville, Tex.
Men's All-Around	Phil Lyne	Sam Houston State, Tex.
Women's All-Around	Nancy Robinson Petersen	Cal Poly-SLO
Bareback Riding	Chris LeDoux	Sheridan C, Wyo.
Saddle Bronc Riding	J. C. Bonine	Eastern Mont. C
Bull Riding	Lonnie Hall	Black Hills SU, S.Dak.
Calf Roping	Phil Lyne	Sam Houston State, Tex.
Steer Wrestling	Carl Deaton	Sam Houston State, Tex.

Ribbon Roping	Jim Jackson	SW Texas SU
Barrel Race	Barbara Baer	Cal Poly-SLO
Goat Tying	Angie Watts Averhoff	Tarleton SU, Tex.
Breakaway Roping	Sally Preston	Tarleton SU, Tex.

1970 BOZEMAN, MONTANA

Men's Team	Cal Poly-SLO	San Luis Obispo, Calif.
Women's Team	Tarleton SU	Stephenville, Texas
Men's All-Around	Tom Miller	Black Hills SU, S.Dak.
Women's All-Around	Linda Blackburn Sultemeier	Eastern NMU
Bareback Riding	Melvin Dick	Cal Poly-SLO
Saddle Bronc Riding	Melvin Dick	Cal Poly-SLO
Bull Riding	Doug Wilson	U of Southern Colo.
Calf Roping	Nick Baldwin	Brigham Young U, Utah
Steer Wrestling	Bob Christopherson	Nat. C Business, S.Dak.
Ribbon Roping	Tom Ferguson	Cal Poly-SLO
Barrel Race	Connie Wilkinson Wood	Tarleton SU, Tex.
Goat Tying	Sharon Meffan Camarillo	Cal Poly-SLO
Breakaway Roping	Saundra Curlock Sorensen	Utah SU

1971 BOZEMAN, MONTANA

Men's Team	Cal Poly-SLO	San Luis Obispo, Calif.
Women's Team	Tarleton SU	Stephenville, Tex.
Men's All-Around	Tom Miller	Black Hills SU, S.Dak.
Women's All-Around	Jan Wagner	Missouri State C
Bareback Riding	Lee Eddins	Eastern Oregon C
Saddle Bronc Riding	Everett Jones	Blue Mt. CC, Ore.
Bull Riding	Wally Badgett	Sheridan C, Wyo.
Calf Roping	Jerry Koile	Cal Poly-SLO
Steer Wrestling	Ed Wright	Eastern NMU
Ribbon Roping	Dave Brock	Casper C, Wyo.
Barrel Racing	Martha Tompkins	Tarleton SU, Tex.
Goat Tying	Jeanne Coates	Ricks C, Utah
Breakaway Roping	Jan Wagner	Missouri State

1972 Bozeman, Montana

Men's Team	Montana SU	Bozeman, Mont.
Women's Team	Eastern NMU	Portales, N.Mex.
Men's All-Around	Dave Brock	U of Southern Colo.
Women's All-Around	Linda Miller Munns	Utah SU
Bareback Riding	Robert Schall	Montana SU
Saddle Bronc	Jock McDowell	Montana SU
Bull Riding	Lamar Roche	Ricks C, Utah
Calf Roping	Danny Torricellas	Blue Mt. CC, Ore.
Steer Wrestling	Lynn Perry	Montana SU
Ribbon Roping	Dean Perkins	Montana SU
Barrel Racing	Becky Fullerton	Blue Mt. CC, Ore.
Goat Tying	Wendy Bryan	U of Arizona
Breakaway Roping	Betty Gayle Cooper Ratliff	Eastern NMU

1973 Bozeman, Montana

Men's Team	Cal Poly-SLO	San Luis Obispo, Calif.
Women's Team	U of Arizona	Tucson, Ariz.
Men's All-Around	Dave Brock	U of Southern Colo.
Women's All-Around	Lou Ann Herstead	U of Wyoming
Bareback Riding	Perry Lee	Tarleton SU, Tex.
Saddle Bronc Riding	Jock McDowell	Montana SU
Bull Riding	Lamar Roche	Ricks C, Utah
Calf Roping	Tom Ferguson	Cal Poly-SLO
Steer Wrestling	Tom Ferguson	Cal Poly-SLO
Ribbon Roping	Dave Brock	U of Southern Colo.
Barrel Racing	Colette Graves Baier	Fort Hays SU, Kans.
Goat Tying	Wendy Bryan	U of Arizona
Breakaway Roping	Colleen Semas	Cal Poly-SLO

1974 Bozeman, Montana

Men's Team	Eastern NMU	Portales, N.Mex.
Women's Team	Sam Houston SU	Huntsville, Tex.
Men's All-Around	Dudley Little	Cal State-Fresno
Women's All-Around	Jimmie Gibbs Munroe	Sam Houston State, Tex.
Bareback Riding	Jerry Beagley	Fort Hays SU, Kans.
Saddle Bronc Riding	John Gass	Western Texas C
Bull Riding	Butch Bratsky	Montana SU

Calf Roping	Brad McReynolds	Sam Houston State, Tex.
Steer Wrestling	Tom Clyde	Ricks C, Utah
Ribbon Roping	Mike McLaughlin	U of Southern Colo.
Barrel Racing	Jimmie Gibbs Munroe	Sam Houston State, Tex.
Goat Tying	Pam Simon Sproul	Arizona State U
Breakaway Roping	Cindy Galow	Sam Houston State, Tex.

1975 BOZEMAN, MONTANA

Men's Team	Montana SU	Bozeman, Mont.
Women's Team	New Mexico SU	Las Cruces, N.Mex.
Men's All-Around	Skip Emmett	U of Tenn.-Martin
Women's All-Around	Jennifer Haynes	New Mexico SU
Bareback Riding	Skip Emmett	U of Tenn.-Martin
Saddle Bronc Riding	Bud Munroe	Montana SU
Bull Riding	Jack Himes	Howard C, Tex.
Calf Roping	Roy Cooper	Cisco Jr. C, Tex.
Steer Wrestling	Paul Hughes	Lamar C, Colo.
Team Roping	Bill Parker	Dawson CC, Mont.
Team Roping	Phil Luman	Dawson CC, Mont.
Barrel Racing	Jimmie Gibbs Munroe	Sam Houston State, Tex.
Goat Tying	Jennifer Haynes	New Mexico SU
Breakaway Roping	Jennifer Haynes	New Mexico SU

1976 BOZEMAN, MONTANA

Men's Team	Southeastern Okla. SU	Durant, Okla.
Women's Team	New Mexico SU	Las Cruces, N.Mex.
Men's All-Around	James D. Ward	SE Okla. SU
Women's All-Around	Janet Stover Crowson	New Mexico SU
Bareback Riding	James D. Ward	SE Okla. SU
Saddle Bronc Riding	Randy Dains	Walla Walla CC
Bull Riding	Richard W. Escalante	Pima CC, Ariz.
Calf Roping	Mike P. McLaughlin	U of Southern Colo.
Steer Wrestling	Randy E. Taylor	SW Okla. SU
Team Roping	Wayne Smith	Arkansas SU-Beebe
	Jack Pearce	Brigham Young U
Barrel Racing	Chris A. Helker	Eastern NMU
Goat Tying	Jennifer Haynes	New Mexico SU
Breakaway Roping	Janet Stover Crowson	New Mexico SU

1977 BOZEMAN, MONTANA

Men's Team	Southeastern Okla. SU	Durant, Okla.
Women's Team	Utah SU	Logan, Utah
Men's All-Around	Tony Coleman	U of Tenn.-Martin
Women's All-Around	Shelly H. Mueller	U of Wisconsin-RF
Bareback Riding	Jack Lee Himes	Howard C, Tex.
Saddle Bronc Riding	J. Sidney Morrow	New Mexico SU
Bull Riding	Jerry Beagley	SE Okla. SU
Calf Roping	Chris Lybbert	Cal Poly-SLO
Steer Wrestling	Steve Fryar	Tarleton SU, Tex.
Team Roping	Thomas Maycumber	Washington SU
Barrel Racing	Joann Whitehead	Western Texas C
Goat Tying	Cindy Coombs Lulloft	Utah SU
Breakaway Roping	Sherre Stoddard	Brigham Young U, Utah

1978 BOZEMAN, MONTANA

Men's Team	Southeastern Okla. SU	Durant, Okla.
Women's Team	Central Ariz. C	Coolidge, Ariz.
Men's All-Around	Hank Franzen	Casper C, Wyo.
Women's All-Around	Barrie Beach Smith	Central Arizona C
Bareback Riding	Jay Himes	U of Southern Colo.
Saddle Bronc Riding	David J. Griffith	Montana SU
Bull Riding	Hank Franzen	Casper C, Wyo.
Calf Roping	Joe Parsons	U of Arizona
Steer Wrestling	Samuel Edmondson	Calif. SU-Fresno
Team Roping	Olie Smith	SE Okla. SU
Barrel Racing	Julie Doering	Oregon SU
Goat Tying	Barrie Beach Smith	Central Arizona C
Breakaway Roping	Jean Fuchs Poythress	Chadron SU, Nebr.

1979 LAKE CHARLES, LOUISIANA

Men's Team	Southeastern Okla. SU	Durant, Okla.
Women's Team	Central Ariz.C	Coolidge, Ariz.
Men's All-Around	Joe Peabody	State Fair CC, Mo.
Women's All-Around	Barrie Beach Smith	Central Arizona C
Bareback Riding	Jimmy A. Cleveland	SE Okla. SU

Saddle Bronc Riding	David J. Griffith	Montana SU
Bull Riding	Doyle Parker	C of Southern Idaho
Calf Roping	Dave P. Smith	Walla Walla CC
Steer Wrestling	Lance K. Robinson	Weber SU, Utah
Team Roping	Mike Beers	Blue Mt. CC, Ore.
Barrel Racing	Bana J. Perry	SW Okla. SU
Goat Tying	Sabrina L. Pike	SE Okla. SU
Breakaway Roping	Kathryn L. Kennedy	Chadron SU, Nebr.

1980 BOZEMAN, MONTANA

Men's Team	Southeastern Okla. SU	Durant, Okla.
Women's Team	Southeastern Okla. SU	Durant, Okla.
Men's All-Around	Lance Robinson	Weber SU, Utah
Women's All-Around	Lea Erwin	U of Central Ark.
Bareback Riding	Joe Eckert	SW Okla. SU
Saddle Bronc Riding	Brad Gjermundson	Dickinson SU, ND
Bull Riding	Chuck Simonson	Dawson CC, Mont.
Calf Roping	Lance Robinson	Weber SU, Utah
Steer Wrestling	Lance Robinson	Weber SU, Utah
Team Roping	J. D. Yates	U of Southern Colo.
Barrel Racing	Lori McNeil	Utah SU
Goat Tying	Phyllis Crouse	U of Missouri-Col.
Breakaway Roping	Sabrina Pike	SE Okla. SU

1981 BOZEMAN, MONTANA

Men's Team	Dawson CC	Glendive, Mont.
Women's Team	Eastern New Mex. U	Portales, N.Mex.
Men's All-Around	George Mesimer	U of Tenn.-Martin
Women's All-Around	Sabrina Pike	SE Okla. SU
Bareback Riding	Larry Peabody	Dawson CC, Mont.
Saddle Bronc Riding	Chuck Morris	Hartnell C, Calif.
Bull Riding	Chuck Simonson	Dawson CC, Mont.
Calf Roping	Lesley Jenkins	SE Okla. SU
Steer Wrestling	John W. Jones Jr.	Cal Poly-SLO
Team Roping	J.D. Yates	U of Southern Colo.
Barrel Racing	Kendra Bennett	Labette C, Kans.
Goat Tying	Shari Simmons	Black Hills SU, S.Dak.
Breakaway Roping	Jean Fuchs Poythress	U of Wyoming

1982 BOZEMAN, MONTANA

Men's Team	Sul Ross SU	Alpine, Tex.
Women's Team	Southeastern Okla. SU	Durant, Okla.
Men's All-Around	Cody Lambert	Sul Ross State, Tex.
Women's All-Around	Sabrina Pike	SE Okla. SU
Bareback Riding	Thom Hickey	Eastfield C, Tex.
Saddle Bronc Riding	Chuck Morris	Hartnell C, Calif.
Bull Riding	Scott Breding	Miles CC, Mont.
Calf Roping	James Zant	Western Texas C
Steer Wrestling	Ross Rianda	Hartnell C, Calif.
Team Roping	Allen Gill	Cal Poly-SLO
Barrel Racing	Lori McNeil	Utah SU
Goat Tying	Linda O'Neal	U of Arizona
Breakaway Roping	Sabrina Pike	SE Okla. SU

1983 BOZEMAN, MONTANA

Men's Team	Sul Ross SU	Alpine, Tex.
Women's Team	Eastern New Mex. U	Portales, N.Mex.
Men's All-Around	Rocky Steagall	Blue Mt. CC, Ore.
Women's All-Around	Anna Crespin Gardner	Eastern NMU
Bareback Riding	Stephen W. Smith Jr.	Hartnell C, Calif.
Saddle Bronc Riding	Guy Lenard Shapka	Casper C, Wyo.
Bull Riding	Rocky Steagall	Blue Mt. CC, Ore.
Calf Roping	Clay H. Parsons	U of Arizona
Steer Wrestling	Chris W. Hansen	U of Wyoming
Team Roping	Billy Dale Haley	Southwest Tex. SU
Barrel Racing	Tammy King Engle	New Mex. SU
Goat Tying	Anna Crespin Gardner	Eastern NMU
Breakaway Roping	Jayne Gentry	Sul Ross State, Tex.

1984 BOZEMAN, MONTANA

Men's Team	Southwest Tex. SU	San Marcos, Tex.
Women's Team	Sam Houston SU	Huntsville, Tex.
Men's All-Around	John Opie	Blue Mt. CC, Ore.
Women's All-Around	Nancy Rea	Southern Ark. U
Bareback Riding	William Ward	Dawson C, Mont.
Saddle Bronc Riding	Derek Clark	Texas Tech

Bull Riding	Quint McDermand	Dickinson SU, N.Dak.
Calf Roping	Kyle Kosoff	Weber SU, Utah
Steer Wrestling	Mike Currin	Blue Mt. CC, Ore.
Team Roping	Rocky Carpenter	Cal Poly-SLO
Barrel Racing	Lynn McCaffety	Sam Houston State, Tex.
Goat Tying	Shari Simmons	Black Hills SU, S.Dak.
Breakaway Roping	Wendy Monchamp	Cal Poly-SLO

1985 BOZEMAN, MONTANA

Men's Team	Southwestern Okla. SU	Weatherford, Okla.
Women's Team	Sul Ross SU	Alpine, Tex.
Men's All-Around	Kent Jude Richard	McNeese SU, La.
Women's All-Around	Lisa Carol Scheffer	U of Montana
Bareback Riding	Scott M. Gress	National C, S.Dak.
Saddle Bronc Riding	Mike Merchant	U of Tenn.-Martin
Bull Riding	Clint Branger	Northwest CC, Wyo.
Calf Roping	Lanham Mangold	Southwest Tex. SU
Steer Wrestling	Chip N. Gatlin	Sam Houston State, Tex.
Team Roping	Nolan Twisselman	Cal Poly-SLO
Barrel Racing	Lisa Scheffer	U of Montana
Breakaway Roping	Tammy Wink	South Dakota SU
Goat Tying	Kelly Sue Kay	U of Arizona

1986 BOZEMAN, MONTANA

Men's Team	Western Texas C	Snyder, Tex.
Women's Team	Montana SU	Bozeman, Mont.
Men's All-Around	Clay D. Hurst	West Hills C, Calif.
Women's All-Around	Molly McAuliffe Hepper	Blue Mt. CC, Ore.
Bareback Riding	Gary Bret Brogan	Boise SU, Idaho
Saddle Bronc Riding	Frank Patrick Norcutt	C of Southern Idaho
Bull Riding	Jim Sharp	Odessa C, Tex.
Calf Roping	Keith Hudson	Western Texas C
Steer Wrestling	Marty Shawn Musil	SW Okla. SU
Team Roping	Clay D. Hurst	West Hills C, Calif.
Barrel Racing	Dana Lynn McCaffety	Sam Houston State, Tex.
Breakaway Roping	Deborah Ann Rogers	Scottsdale CC, Ariz.
Goat Tying	Shelley Dee Meter	Eastern Wyo. C

1987 BOZEMAN, MONTANA

Men's Team	Blue Mountain CC	Pendleton, Ore.
Women's Team	Scottsdale CC	Scottsdale, Ariz.
Men's All-Around	Roy Cordova	Central Arizona C
Women's All-Around	Sherry Lynn Rosser	Southern Ark. U
Bareback Riding	Steve Abernathy	Western Okla. SC
Saddle Bronc Riding	Wayne D. Norcutt	C of Southern Idaho
Bull Riding	Jim Sharp	Odessa C, Tex.
Calf Roping	Kelsey Allen Felton	Blue Mt. CC, Ore.
Team Roping	Darin B. Simpson	New Mex. SU
Steer Wrestling	Will Cody Matthews	U of Tenn.-Martin
Barrel Racing	Holly Foster	McNeese SU, La.
Breakaway Roping	Karen Cochran Smith	Texas Tech
Goat Tying	Kelly Harsh	Scottsdale CC, Ariz.

1988 BOZEMAN, MONTANA

Men's Team	Montana SU	Bozeman, Mont.
Women's Team	Southwestern Okla. SU	Weatherford, Okla.
Men's All-Around	Ken Lensegrav	Montana SU
Women's All-Around	Cathy Cagliari	West Hills C, Calif.
Bareback Riding	Ken Lensegrav	Montana SU
Saddle Bronc Riding	Eudell Larsen	Western Dak. Vo. T
Bull Riding	Rex Phillips	Montana SU
Calf Roping	Bradley Goodrich	Blue Mt. CC, Ore.
Steer Wrestling	Cory Ferguson	National C, S.Dak.
Team Roping	Kenneth David Key	Tarleton SU, Tex.
Barrel Racing	Cathy Cagliari	West Hills C, Calif.
Goat Tying	Lori Kay Hadley	Weber SU, Utah
Breakaway Roping	Donelle Kvenild	SW Okla. SU

1989 LAKE CHARLES, LOUISIANA

Men's Team	Odessa C	Odessa, Tex.
Women's Team	Cal Poly-SLO	San Luis Obispo, Calif.
Men's All-Around	Ty Murray	Odessa C, Tex.
Women's All-Around	Cathy Dennis	Southern Ark. U
Bareback Riding	Ken Lensegrav	Montana SU
Saddle Bronc Riding	Ty Murray	Odessa C, Tex.

Bull Riding	Ty Murray	Odessa C, Tex.
Calf Roping	Shawn McMullan	Odessa C, Tex.
Steer Wrestling	Tim Garrison	Western Montana C
Team Roping	Chris Green	West Hills C, Calif.
Barrel Racing	Holly Foster	Cal Poly-SLO
Goat Tying	Patti J. O'Maley	Idaho SU
Breakaway Roping	Shannon Lord	SW Okla. SU

1990 BOZEMAN, MONTANA

Men's Team	Montana SU	Bozeman, Mont.
Women's Team	U. of Wyoming	Laramie, Wyo.
Men's All-Around	Zane Davis	C of Southern Idaho
Women's All-Around	Jimmi Jo Martin	U of Wyoming
Bareback Riding	Randy Slaughter	New Mex. SU
Saddle Bronc Riding	J. W. Simonson	U of Wyoming
Bull Riding	Casey Gates	Fort Scott CC, Kans.
Calf Roping	Shawn McMullan	Odessa C, Tex.
Steer Wrestling	Dean Wang	Cal Poly-SLO
Team Roping	Clayton Ring	Central Wash. U
Barrel Racing	Elisa Nielsen	Utah Valley CC
Goat Tying	Jimmi Jo Martin	U of Wyoming
Breakaway Roping	Kelli Edwards	Walla Walla CC

1991 BOZEMAN, MONTANA

Men's Team	Montana SU	Bozeman, Mont.
Women's Team	U of Wyoming	Laramie, Wyo.
Men's All-Around	Shawn Vant	Montana SU
Women's All-Around	Julie Adair	Cal Poly-SLO
Bareback Riding	Shawn Vant	Montana SU
Saddle Bronc Riding	Dan Mortensen	Montana SU
Bull Riding	Dan Wolfe	Blue Mt. CC, Ore.
Calf Roping	Randall Orr	SW Missouri SU
Steer Wrestling	Jesse Peterson	Western Montana C
Team Roping	Dustin Durfee	Utah Valley CC
Barrel Racing	Annesa Musil	SW Okla. SU
Goat Tying	Julie Adair	Cal Poly-SLO
Breakaway Roping	Lari Dee Guy	Vernon Reg. JC, Tex.

1992 Bozeman, Montana

Men's Team	Southwestern Okla. SU	Weatherford, Okla.
Women's Team	Walla Walla CC	Walla Walla, Wash.
Men's All-Around	Casey Minton	West Hills C, Calif.
Women's All-Around	Penny Conforth	Walla Walla CC
Bareback Riding	Shawn Vant	Montana SU
Saddle Bronc Riding	Michael Giannini	Idaho SU
Bull Riding	Jerome Davis	Odessa C, Tex.
Calf Roping	Chad David Hiatt	Panhandle SU, Okla.
Steer Wrestling	Jesse Peterson	Western Montana C
Team Roping	Seth Alan Weishaar	South Dakota SU
Barrel Racing	Mindy Morris	Texas A&M
Goat Tying	Lana Tibbetts	Montana SU
Breakaway Roping	Brenda Mays	Walla Walla CC

1993 Bozeman, Montana

All championships starting with 1993 were based on points won at the finals with points awarded for eight places in the two long rounds and averaged; four places in the short round.

Men's Team	Southwestern Okla. SU	Weatherford, Okla.
Women's Team	U of Wyoming	Laramie, Wyo.
Men's All-Around	Zane Davis	C of Southern Idaho
Women's All-Around	Shelley Johnston	SW Okla. SU
Bareback Riding	Zane Davis	C of Southern Idaho
Saddle Bronc Riding	George Cliff Norris	Panhandle SU, Okla.
Bull Riding	Philip Elkins	Hill C, Tex.
Calf Roping	Shane Hatch	Vernon Reg. JC, Tex.
Steer Wrestling	Ross Gomez	Cal Poly-SLO
Team Roping	Frank Graves	U of Tenn.-Martin
	Brett Gould	U of Tenn.-Martin
Barrel Racing	Marilee McGraw	Garden City CC, Kans.
Goat Tying	Shelley Johnston	SW Okla. SU
Breakaway Roping	Lari Dee Guy	Texas Tech

1994 BOZEMAN, MONTANA

Men's Team	Vernon Regional Jr. C	Vernon, Tex.
Women's Team	Southwestern Okla. SU	Weatherford, Okla.
Men's All-Around	Jason Jackson	Montana SU
Women's All-Around	Tori Woodard	SW Okla. SU
Bareback Riding	Jason Jackson	Montana SU
Saddle Bronc Riding	Shawn Stroh	Dickinson SU, N.Dak.
Bull Riding	Beau Gillespie	U of Nev.-LV
Calf Roping	Marty McCloy	Panhandle SU, Okla.
Steer Wrestling	Tyler Keith	Cal Poly-SLO
Team Roping	Tye Maben	Texas Tech U
	John Folmer	Howard C, Tex.
Barrel Racing	Shane Hooks	McNeese SU, La.
Goat Tying	Kristie Price	South Dakota SU
Breakaway Roping	Leah Moellman	SW Missouri SU

1995 BOZEMAN, MONTANA

Men's Team	Montana SU	Bozeman, Mont.
Women's Team	Southeastern Okla. SU	Durant, Okla.
Men's All-Around	Jason Jackson	Montana SU
Women's All-Around	Caryn Standifer Snyder	SE Okla. SU
Bareback Riding	James Boudreaux	McNeese SU, La.
Saddle Bronc Riding	Paul Sandal	Sheridan C, Wyo.
Bull Riding	Jason Jackson	Montana SU
Calf Roping	Thomas W. Snyder	SW Okla. SU
Steer Wrestling	James Chad Hagan	NWSU, La.
Team Roping	Whip Lewis	Central Arizona C
	Paul Griemsman	Eastern Wyo. C
Barrel Racing	Molly Swanson Powell	Vernon Reg. JC, Tex.
Goat Tying	Caryn Standifer Snyder	SE Okla. SU
Breakaway Roping	Nacona Pauley	Miles CC, Mont.

1996 BOZEMAN, MONTANA

Men's Team	C of Southern Idaho	Twin Falls, Idaho
Women's Team	Southeastern Okla. SU	Durant, Okla.
Men's All-Around	Jason Call	C of Southern Idaho
Women's All-Around	Caryn Standifer Snyder	SE Okla. SU

Bareback Riding	Jason Jeter	Sam Houston State, Tex.
Saddle Bronc Riding	Jeremy Crane	Dickinson SU, N.Dak.
Bull Riding	Charles Aaron Williams	Hill C, Tex.
Calf Roping	Jerome Schneeberger	Murray SC, Okla.
Steer Wrestling	Todd Suhn	U of Wyoming
Team Roping (tie)	Andy Bolton	Panhandle SU, Okla.
	Benjamin Blue	Panhandle SU, Okla.
	Buck Brandon Garcia	Southwest Tex. Jr. C
	Joe Verastegui	Southwest Tex. Jr. C
Barrel Racing	Caryn Standifer Snyder	SE Okla. SU
Goat Tying	Renee Wood Byrd	San Juan CC, N.Mex.
Breakaway Roping	Brenda White	U of Wyoming

1997 Rapid City, South Dakota

Men's Team	Panhandle SU	Goodwell, Okla.
Women's Team	Weber SU	Ogden, Utah
Men's All-Around	Preston Williams	U of Nev.-LV
Women's All-Around	Kelli Fowers Tolbert	Weber SU, Utah
Bareback Riding	Erick Delan Blanton	National C, S.Dak.
Saddle Bronc Riding	Jeff Decker	Western Texas C
Bull Riding	Ben Duggar	Odessa C, Tex.
Calf Roping	Jerome Schneeberger	Murray SC, Okla.
Steer Wrestling	Gus Ledoux	McNeese SU, La.
Team Roping	Cody Mathew Willson	Scottsdale CC, Ariz.
	Preston Williams	U of Nev.-LV
Barrel Racing	Rachael Myllmaki Sproul	U of Montana
Goat Tying	Kelli Fowers Tolbert	Weber SU, Utah
Breakaway Roping (tie)	Toni Jo Arave	West Hills C, Calif.
	Caryn Standifer Snyder	SW Okla. SU

1998 Rapid City, South Dakota

A third long round was added with top 12 in short round.

Men's Team	Panhandle SU	Goodwell, Okla.
Women's Team	Lewis-Clark SC	Lewiston, Idaho
Men's All-Around	Ross Coleman	U of Nev.-LV
Women's All-Around	Lynn Wiebe	Central Wy. C
Bareback Riding	Davey Shields	SW Okla. SU

Saddle Bronc Riding	Jeremy Crane	Dickinson SU, N.Dak.
Bull Riding	Corey Navarre	SW Okla. SU
Calf Roping	Aaron Adamson	Hill C, Tex.
Steer Wrestling	Josh McIntyre	Panhandle SU, Okla.
Team Roping	Brian Dunning	Panhandle SU, Okla.
	Travis Goad	Panhandle SU, Okla.
Barrel Racing	Tona Wright	Western Texas C
Goat Tying	Lynn Wiebe	Central Wyo. C
Breakaway Roping	Lynn Wiebe	Central Wyo. C

1999 Casper, Wyoming

Men's Team	Southwestern Okla. SU	Weatherford, Okla.
Women's Team	U of Nevada-Las Vegas	Las Vegas, Nev.
Men's All-Around	Bryant Mikkelson	U of Montana
Women's All-Around	Jennifer Smith	Tarleton SU, Tex.
Bareback Riding	Jacob Hayworth	Western Montana C
Saddle Bronc Riding	Jerad McFarlane	Blue Mt. CC, Ore.
Bull Riding	William Farrell	Chadron SU, Nebr.
Calf Roping	Matthew Otto	Dickinson SU, N.Dak.
Steer Wrestling	Bryant Mikkelson	U of Montana
Team Roping	Matt Funk	Lewis-Clark SC, Idaho
	Kain Garcia	Blue Mt. CC, Ore.
Barrel Racing	Jennifer Smith	Tarleton SU, Tex.
Goat Tying	Jill Childers	Western Texas C
Breakaway Roping	Stacie Sorensen	U of Nev.-LV

2000 Casper, Wyoming

Men's Team	Panhandle SU	Goodwell, Okla.
Women's Team	Western Texas College	Snyder, Tex.
Men's All-Around	Jesse Bail	Panhandle SU, Okla.
Women's All-Around	Jamie Standifer	Western Texas C
Bareback Riding	Paul Jones	Central Wyo. C
Saddle Bronc Riding	Jacob Hayworth	Western Montana C
Bull Riding	Thomas Clark	Cal Poly-SLO
Calf Roping	Houston Hutto	Western Texas C
Steer Wrestling	Joshua Peek	Frank Phillips C, Tex.
Team Roping	Kurt Kiehne	Tarleton SU, Tex.
	Levi Garcia	Tarleton SU, Tex.

Barrel Racing	Amanda Barrett	Texas A&M
Goat Tying (tie)	Jennifer Heisman	SW Okla. SU
	Lee McKnight	Weber SU, Utah
Breakaway Roping	Amy Shepperson	U of Wyoming

2001 Casper, Wyoming

Men's Team	C of Southern Idaho	Twin Falls, Idaho
Women's Team	Oklahoma State University	Stillwater, Okla.
Men's All-Around	Cody Demers	C of Southern Idaho
Women's All-Around	Suzanne Montero	U of Nev.-LV
Bareback Riding	Clint Evers	Fort Scott CC, Kans.
Saddle Bronc Riding	Cody Demers	C of Southern Idaho
Bull Riding	Dustin Elliott	Chadron State U, Nebr.
Calf Roping	Houston Hutto	Western Texas C
Steer Wrestling	Beau Franzen	Dawson CC, Mont.
Team Roping	Logan Olson	Panhandle SU, Okla.
	Jett Hillman	Panhandle SU, Okla.
Barrel Racing	Janae Ward	Okla. State U
Goat Tying	Suzanne Montero	U of Nev.-LV
Breakaway Roping	Kini Wright	C of Southern Idaho

2002 Casper, Wyoming

Men's Team	C of Southern Idaho	Twin Falls, Idaho
Women's Team	Texas A&M University	College Station, Tex.
Men's All-Around	Cody Demers	C of Southern Idaho
Women's All-Around	Jonlyn Vaccaro	U of Nev.-LV
Bareback Riding	Colby Olsen	Northwest College, Wyo.
Saddle Bronc Riding	Cody Martin	Missouri Valley College
Bull Riding	Will Farrell	Chadron State College
Calf Roping	Trent Creager	Okla. State U
Steer Wrestling	Sam MacKenzie	Walla Walla CC, Wash.
Team Roping	Colt Braden	Northeastern Okla. A&M
	Wendell Stanley	Northeastern Okla. A&M
Barrel Racing	McKenzie Miller	Ricks College, Idaho
Goat Tying	Jonlyn Vaccaro	U of Nev.-LV
Breakaway Roping	Keli Smith	New Mexico Jr. College

2003 CASPER, WYOMING

Men's Team	Vernon College	Vernon, Texas
Women's Team	Vernon College	Vernon, Texas
Men's All-Around	Jesse M. Segura	Cal Poly-SLO
Women's All-Around	Suzanne F. Montero	U of Nevada-LV
Bareback Riding	Cimarron L. Gerke	Odessa C, Tex.
Saddle Bronc Riding	Lance L. Sagers	Utah Valley SC
Bull Riding	Chad Eubank	Hill C, Tex.
Calf Roping	Stephen L. Reagor	Bacone C, Okla.
Steer Wrestling	Levi C. Wisness	U of Wyoming
Team Roping	Justin L. Lovell	Stephen F. Austin SU
	Shane B. Powell	Northeast Texas CC
Barrel Racing	Jessica L. Mueller	NationalAmer.U, S.Dak.
Goat Tying	Suzanne F. Montero	U of Nevada-LV
Breakaway Roping	Jaclyn L. Hobbs	Vernon College, Tex.

Notes

CHAPTER 1

1. Elmer Kelton, "Intercollegiate Rodeo Association," *Persimmon Hill* 8 (winter, 1974): 33.
2. Kristine Fredriksson, *American Rodeo: From Buffalo Bill to Big Business,* 4, 10, 140.
3. Clifford D. Westermeier, *Man, Beast, Dust: The Story of Rodeo,* 40.
4. Fredriksson, *American Rodeo,* 57.
5. Ibid., 67.
6. Westermeier, *Man, Beast, Dust,* 432.
7. Fredriksson, *American Rodeo,* 88.
8. Westermeier, *Man, Beast, Dust,* 351–53.
9. Fredriksson, *American Rodeo,* 67.
10. Ibid., 65, 69.
11. Ibid., 65.
12. Ibid., 65, 70.
13. Ibid., 73, 78.
14. Teresa Jordan, *Cowgirls: Women of the American West,* 189.
15. Mary Lou LeCompte, *Cowgirls of the Rodeo: Pioneer Professional Athletes,* 40.
16. Michael Allen, *Rodeo Cowboys in the North American Imagination,* 24.
17. LeCompte, *Cowgirls of the Rodeo,* 144.
18. Richard W. Slatta, *The Cowboy Encyclopedia,* 22.
19. Allen, *Rodeo Cowboys in the North American Imagination,* 24.
20. John Bascom, letter to NIRA Secretary-Manager Tim Corfield, Walla Walla, Washington, May 14, 1993.
21. Fern Sawyer, interview with author, Childress, Texas, June 5, 1993.
22. "A&M Rodeo to Be a Novelty Livestock Show," *The Battalion,* Texas A&M newspaper, November 5, 1920.
23. "Novelty Show a Big Success," *The Battalion,* Texas A&M newspaper, November 27, 1919.
24. Ed Knocke, "For Old Times' Sake," *Dallas Morning News,* January 20, 1999.
25. Ibid.
26. "Annual Rodeo Friday Night Great Success," *The Battalion,* Texas A&M newspaper, October 27, 1922.
27. "Large Crowd Attends Annual Rodeo," *The Battalion,* Texas A&M newspaper, November 12, 1924.
28. *1927 Longhorn,* Texas A&M Yearbook.
29. *The Wrangler,* Colorado State University newspaper, April 1, 1996.
30. William "Bill" Felts, letter to author, November 24, 1989.

31. University of Arizona rodeo programs, 1938, 1939, 1940.

32. David Nasaw, *The Chief: The Life of William Randolph Hearst,* 279–80.

33. Jeanne Godshall, Studio City, California, telephone interview with author, September 12, 1994.

34. Jean Campbell DeBlasis, Victorville, California, telephone interview with author, 1994.

35. Ann Rivers, Victorville, California, telephone interview with author, 1994.

36. "World's First Intercollegiate Rodeo Ready for Saturday's Thrills, Spills at Rancho," *The Victor Press,* April 7, 1939.

37. Ibid.

38. "Desert Sage Says," *The Victor Press,* April 7, 1939.

39. "World's First," *The Victor Press,* April 7, 1939.

40. Ibid.

41. Jim Lau, interview with author, Bozeman, Montana, June 5, 1989.

42. "College Students Attend First Rodeo," *The Victor Press,* April 14, 1939.

43. "Felts, Arizona Entry Wins Honors at Godshall Collegiate Rodeo April 8," newspaper article clipping, n.d.

44. Jocelyn McAlpine, "Rodeo . . . University Style," newspaper clipping, n.d.

45. "College Rodeo Provides Fast Program Here," University of Arizona, n.d.

46. "Campus Waddies to Risk Necks in Bulldogging Ferocious Rodeo Bovines," University of Arizona, newspaper clipping, 1940.

47. "University of Arizona Spectacular Show Sunday," newspaper clipping, 1940.

48. Hyde Merritt, "Cussin' and Discussin'," *Bi-Weekly Rodeo News,* December 18, 1948.

49. J. R. "Shorty" Fuller, interview with author, Bozeman, Montana, June 19, 1993.

50. Giles Lee, interview with author, Hobbs, New Mexico, February 10, 1987, and February 6, 1990.

51. Lee interview.

52. Ibid.

53. Ibid.

54. Ibid.

55. Ibid.

56. Ibid.

57. Ibid.

58. Mary Ellen Chandler Kimball, interview with author, Alpine, Texas, September 7, 1986.

59. "Local Man India Rodeo Director," clipped newspaper photo with caption, July 29, 1945.

60. Bob Frazer, letter to Charlie Rankin, McAllen, Texas, May 8, 1992.

61. Cecil Jones, interview with author, Las Vegas, Nevada, December 11, 1986.

62. *University of Arizona Rodeo,* program, 1947.

63. *Hardin-Simmons Rodeo,* program, April 27–28, 1950.

64. "Montana's First College Rodeo?" *College Rodeo,* November, 1982.

65. Matthew J. Wald, *MSU Rodeo: 1947–1989,* unpublished manuscript.

66. Lee interview.

67. Jack Longbotham, interview with author, Abilene, Texas, April 24, 1987.

68. Allen, *Rodeo Cowboys in the North American Imagination,* 200.

CHAPTER 2

1. Charlie Rankin, telephone interview with author, McAllen, Texas, August 3, 1988.

2. Charlie Rankin, letter to Morton J. O'Brien, Tucson, Arizona, June 9, 1949.

3. Doyle Stout, "Sul Ross News Release," December 8, 1947.

4. *SRSU Bar SR Bar History of the Organization,* pamphlet, 1947.

5. Murry H. Fly, letter to Doug Fernandes, Alpine, Texas, October 25, 1948.

6. Mary Ellen Chandler Kimball, interview with author, Alpine, Texas, September 7, 1986.

7. Hank Finger, "Autobiography," Bar SR Bar Rodeo Association, n.d.

8. "Report on the Meeting Held by Representatives from Twelve Colleges to Discuss Forming a National Intercollegiate Rodeo Association," n.d.

9. Rankin interview.

10. "Colleges May Organize," *Bi-Weekly Rodeo News,* December 18, 1948.

11. "New Blood for the Rodeo Business: College Students are Getting Interested," *The Buckboard,* January, 1949.

12. "As Heard over the Mike," *The Buckboard,* 1949.

13. Hyde Merritt, "Cussin' and Discussin'," *Bi-Weekly Rodeo News,* December 18, 1948.

14. Charlie Rankin, letter to Morton J. O'Brien, Tucson, Arizona, June 9, 1949.

15. Evelyn Bruce [Kingsbery], "National Intercollegiate Rodeo Association," *Hoofs and Horns,* December, 1949.

16. Rankin letter to O'Brien.

17. Hank Finger, letter to Toots Mansfield, Big Spring, Texas, February 21, 1949.

18. Rankin interview.

19. NIRA Constitution, 1949.

20. Bill Brady, letter to Sul Ross Rodeo Club, Alpine, Texas, January 7, 1949.

21. Matthew J. Wald, *MSU Rodeo: 1947–1989,* unpublished manuscript.

22. Hank Finger, letter to University of Texas Varsity Rodeo Club, Austin, Texas, March 15, 1949.

23. Hank Finger, letter to Charlie Rankin, College Station, Texas, March 24, 1949.

24. NIRA Constitution, Bylaws, Section I, 1949.

25. Ibid.

26. Ibid.

27. Ibid.

28. "Charlie Rankin: The First President," *Chats,* for the National Association of Farm Broadcasters, April 1995.

29. Timi Kramer, letter to Evelyn Bruce Kingsbery, Alpine, Texas, September 29, 1949.

30. Charlie Rankin, letter to Hank Finger, Alpine, Texas, February 4, 1949.

31. Hyde Merritt, letter to Charlie Rankin, College Station, Texas, n.d.

32. Charlie Rankin, letter to H. G. Bedford, Lubbock, Texas, February 28, 1949.

33. Jerry Armstrong, "Picked Up in the Rodeo Arena," *Western Horseman,* June 1949, 41.

34. Charlie Rankin, letter to Claude B. Mullins, Halletsville, Texas, June 9, 1949.

35. Charlie Rankin, letter to Joe Fornay, Fort Collins, Colorado, June 9, 1949.

36. Charlie Rankin, letter to Red Clark, Canoga Park, California, March 16, 1949.

37. Charlie Rankin, letter to Ham Scott, State College, New Mexico, March 11, 1949.

38. *California Aggie College of Agriculture,* newspaper, March 31, 1949.

39. Kyle Partain, "NFR First Takes Root at 1958 Meeting," *ProRodeo Sports News,* January 14, 1998, 26.

40. Harley May, interview with author, Las Vegas, Nevada, December 12, 1986.

41. *Richmond* (California) *Independent,* newspaper article, n.d., 1949.

42. Dale Stiles, interview with author, Bozeman, Montana, June 20, 1987.

43. *Hutchison Kansas Record,* newspaper article, April 8, 1949.

44. *San Francisco Bulletin,* newspaper article, April 11, 1949.

45. *San Francisco Examiner,* newspaper article, April 10, 1949.

46. Carl L. Garrison, letter to Hank Finger, Alpine, Texas, April 21, 1949.

47. Modesto, California, newspaper article, April 11, 1949.

48. Susan Goldsmith, "Corky Randall," newspaper article, n.d.

49. Tibba McMullan, letter to Evelyn Bruce Kingsbery, Alpine, Texas, 1949.

50. Texas Tech, letter to Evelyn Bruce Kingsbery, Alpine, Texas, October 22, 1949.

51. Clyde Gordon Jr., letter to Evelyn Bruce Kingsbery, Alpine, Texas, November 3, 1949.

52. James Mickler, letter to Evelyn Bruce Kingsbery, Alpine, Texas, November 8, 1949.

53. Maxie Overstreet, letter to Evelyn Bruce Kingsbery, Alpine, Texas, n.d.

54. Evelyn Bruce Kingsbery, letter to Charlie Rankin, College Station, Texas, April 21, 1949.

55. "Evelyn Bruce Selected NIRA Publicity Director," n.d.

56. Chuck King, letter to Evelyn Bruce Kingsbery, Alpine, Texas, September, 1949.

57. Ethel "Ma" Hopkins, letter to Evelyn Bruce Kingsbery, Alpine, Texas, October 5, 1949.

58. Jack Kingsbery and Evelyn Bruce Kingsbery, interview with author, Uvalde, Texas, March 24, 1989.

59. Hank Finger, letter to Charlie Rankin, College Station, Texas, November 19, 1949.

60. Jo Gregory Knox, letter to Charlie Rankin, College Station, Texas, November 15, 1949.

61. J. H. Foss, letter to Evelyn Bruce Kingsbery, Alpine, Texas, November 21, 1949.

62. Joe Koller, letter to Evelyn Bruce Kingsbery, Alpine, Texas, November 26, 1949.

63. Charlie Rankin, letter to Evelyn Bruce Kingsbery, Alpine, Texas, December 8, 1949.

64. J. Ben Dow, letter to Charlie Rankin, College Station, Texas, n.d., 1949.

65. J. H. Foss, letter to Evelyn Bruce Kingsbery, Alpine, Texas, August 1, 1949.

CHAPTER 3

1. Hyde Merritt, "Just Whittlin'," *Western Horseman,* March 1950, 5.

2. "Minutes of the NIRA Convention," Denver, Colorado, January 2–3, 1950.

3. Evelyn Bruce Kingsbery, letter to Chuck King, Billings, Montana, December 8, 1949.

4. Charlie Rankin, telephone interview with author, McAllen, Texas, August 3, 1988.

5. Garnet Rose Kotkin, letter to Harley May, Alpine, Texas, n.d.

6. "Minutes of the NIRA Convention," December 5, 1950.

7. "Talk from Back of the Chute," *The Rigging,* NIRA newsletter, 3, and "Hank Finger, Alpine Chamber of Commerce Manager, Killed," *Standard Times,* Del Rio, December 17, 1950.

8. "Meet Our President," *The Rigging,* NIRA newsletter, May, 1951, 15.

9. "NIRA Convention," *The Rigging,* NIRA newsletter, March, 1951, 12.

10. "Intercollegiate Rodeo Now Numbers 43 Teams Across U.S.," *The Oregonian,* June 12, 1952.

11. "Education Helps, Says College Rodeo Cowboy," *The Oregonian,* June 12, 1952.

12. "NIRA and RCA Have Agreement for Collegians," newspaper clipping, Abilene, Texas, March 1952.

13. Alvin G. Davis, interview with author, Lubbock, Texas, October 24, 1986.

14. "Notice for Old and Prospective New Member Clubs of the NIRA," Flyer, n.d.

15. "Hoss Inman," obituary, from Virginia Inman, Lamar, Colorado, August 26, 1993.

16. "College Rodeo Stars to Appear Here during Fiesta in Championship Finals," *The San Antonian,* Texas newspaper, January 28, 1950.

17. Charlie Rankin, typed note clipped to "College Rodeo Stars to Appear during Fiesta in Championship Finals," *The San Antonian,* January 28, 1950, newspaper article, NIRA Alumni archives.

18. Howard Harris, letter to editor of *The Buckboard,* RCA newspaper, n.d.

19. Article II, Section IV, NIRA Constitution, Rules, and Bylaws, 1951, 2.

20. Harley May, letter to Guy Weadick, Calgary, Alberta, Canada, March 8, 1951.

21. Guy Weadick, letter to Harley May, Alpine, Texas, May 12, 1951.

22. Mike Cervi, "How to Produce a Collegiate Rodeo," booklet, 1958.

23. NIRA column, *Rodeo News,* March 11, 1950.

24. Evelyn Bruce Kingsbery, letter to James Cathey, Fort Worth, Texas, 1950.

25. Chuck King, editor of the *Bi-Weekly Rodeo News,* May 6, 1950.

26. Mary Ann Reed, letter to Harley May, Alpine, Texas, May 26, 1951.

27. Alvin and Barbara Davis, *Rodeo Roundup,* April–May, 1957.

28. Jean Muir, "Cowboys on Campus," *Saturday Evening Post,* February 10, 1951, 141.

29. Jean Muir, letter to Harley May, Alpine, Texas, April 11, 1951.

30. Muir, "Cowboys," 141.

31. "Minutes of the NIRA Convention," Albuquerque, New Mexico, January, 1951.

32. "Notice to All Clubs," *The Rigging,* March 1951, 15.

33. Bill Brock, letter to Bill Guest and carbon to four regional directors and Harley May, Abilene, Texas, April 22, 1951.

34. "NIRA Convention 1955," *Rigging Bag,* April 1955, 3.

35. F. C. Stover, letter to Betty Sims Solt, Roswell, New Mexico, June 3, 1996.

36. *The Rigging Bag,* published by Sam Houston State Teachers College, Huntsville, Texas, April 23, 1955, 3.

37. "Jim Deutsch Top NIRA Bull Rider," *The South Texas* 28 (April 11, 1953): 1.

38. Bob McKeller, "Poly Cowpokes Swamp Visiting Dirt Eaters in Two-Day Rodeo," *El Paso Mustang,* Cal Poly, San Luis Obispo, California, May 25, 1951.

39. Garnet Rose Kotkin, letter to Harley May, Alpine, Texas, January 10, 1951.

40. Garnet Rose Kotkin, letter to Harley May, Alpine, Texas, January 22, 1951.

41. Jo Gregory Knox, interview with author, Tarzan, Texas, April 16, 1987.

42. "Cowgirls in the NIRA Finals," photocopy of page from a rodeo program, 5.

43. *The Rigging Bag,* photo caption, published by Sam Houston State Teachers College, Huntsville, Texas, April 23, 1955, 2.

44. Elisabeth Prude Longbotham, interview with author, Abilene, Texas, April 24, 1987.

45. Betty Sims Solt, interview with author, Roswell, New Mexico, July 22, 1987.

46. Pat Dunigan Marr, interview with author, Bozeman, Montana, June 20, 1992.

47. "Queen of the 1957 NIRA Finals," *National Intercollegiate Rodeo Championship Finals,* souvenir program, Colorado Springs, Colorado, June 13–16, 1957.

48. "Queen of the 1958 NIRA Finals," *NIRA Championship Finals,* souvenir program, Colorado Springs, Colorado, June 12–15, 1958.

49. Becky Jo Smith Doom, interview with author, Jal, New Mexico, March 1, 1988.

50. "Talk from Back of the Chutes," *The Rigging,* NIRA newsletter, May, 1951, 3.

51. Jerry Armstrong, "Picked Up in the Rodeo Arena," *Western Horseman,* June 1950, 21.

52. "Final Standings for 1950," *The Rigging,* NIRA newsletter, 1950, 5.

53. Armstrong, "Picked Up," June, 1950, 21, 38, 40.

54. "Cow Palace Results—Revised," two typed pages, May 3, 1950.

55. "Black List (Individuals)," *The Rigging,* NIRA newsletter, 1950, 4.

56. "Ride 'em cowboys," photo caption, *Daily Palo Alto Times,* March 19, 1951, 14.

57. Jerry Armstrong, "Picked Up in the Rodeo Arena," *Western Horseman,* May 1951, 20.

58. "College Rodeo," *Time,* May 21, 1951, n.p.

59. George B. Dolan, "Sul Ross Gets Rodeo Trophy for Keeps after Third Straight Victory," *Fort Worth Star Telegram,* May, 1951.

60. "Noted Cowboy Will Judge College Rodeo," newspaper clipping, Fort Worth, Texas, May 5, 1951.

61. "Texans Take Top Spot in Rodeo, Oklahoman Collegian Solo Winner," *The Oregonian,* June 15, 1952.

62. *National Intercollegiate Rodeo Finals,* program, Portland, Oregon, 1952.

63. Alvin G. Davis, "The National Intercollegiate Rodeo Finals," *The Horse Lover's Magazine,* 1953, 10.

64. NIRA Finals, program, Abilene, Texas, 1953.

65. Bob Schild, interview with author, Bozeman, Montana, June 18, 1994.

66. Howard Harris, interview with author, Vernon, Texas, May 18, 1994.

67. Monty Roberts, interview with author, Bozeman, Montana, June 15, 1996.

68. Jack Burkholder, letter to author, Vernon, Texas, May 26, 1993.

69. Tim Corfield, letter to Ross F. Caton, Alba, Texas, July 21, 1999.

70. C. O. Schoonover, letter to Charles Bowman, Bozeman, Montana, June 12, 1959.

71. Charles Bowman, letter to Hoss Inman and James Heath, Lamar, Colorado, November 9, 1959.

72. "Minutes of the NIRA Convention," Albany Hotel, Denver, Colorado, January 2–3, 1950, 12.

73. Bowman, letter to Inman and Heath, November 9, 1959.

74. Ibid.

75. Hoss Inman, letter to Dale Stiles, Casper College, Casper, Wyoming, November 17, 1959.

76. "Minutes of the Rocky Mountain Faculty Rodeo Conference," Casper College, Casper, Wyoming, December 18, 1959, 3.

77. "Minutes of the RMFRC," December 18, 1959, 4.

78. Ibid., 5.

CHAPTER 4

1. "Report on the NIRA Board Meeting," January 10–11, 1960.

2. NIRA Convention Minutes, 1960.

3. Ibid.

4. Dale Hewson, letter to Jim Moore, University of Wyoming, no month, 1960.

5. Dale Stiles, letter to Charles Bowman, Montana State College, no month, 1960.

6. Charles Bowman, letter to Dale Stiles, Casper College, no month, 1960.

7. *ACRA Newsletter,* April, 1960.

8. Agenda, NIRA Board Meeting, 1960.

9. Sonny Sikes, interview with author, Bozeman, Montana, June 17, 1986.

10. NIRA Board Minutes, 1964.

11. NIRA Board Minutes, 1967.

12. "1962 National Intercollegiate Rodeo Finals," ABC *Wide World of Sports,* September 8, 1962.

13. "NIRA Rodeo Reaches Big Payoff," *The Laramie Daily Boomerang,* July 10, 1965.

14. "Teams Claim National Honor," *SR Rodeo,* July 15, 1962.

15. "The 1967 National Intercollegiate Rodeo Finals," program, St. George, Utah, June 27–July 1, 1967.

16. *NIRA Rodeo Finals,* program, 1967.

17. Del Higham, "Report of Public Relations Activities," All NIRA Executive Board Members, *Memorandum,* January 10, 1969.

18. Del Higham, "All Club Advisers," *Memorandum,* March 10, 1969.

19. Del Higham, "Public Relations Activities," All NIRA Executive Board members, *Memorandum,* May 9, 1969.

20. Irving M. Munn, letter to Sonny Sikes, Huntsville, Texas, April 9, 1965.

21. Bud Purdy, letter to W. A. Harris, University of Wyoming, Laramie, Wyoming, November 16, 1965.

22. W. A. Harris, letter to Bud Purdy, Montana State University, Bozeman, Montana, November 8, 1965.

23. *NIRA Rodeo Finals,* program, 1967.

24. NIRA Constitution, Bylaws, and Rules, 1967–68.

25. "NIRA Executive Board Meeting," NIRA Minutes, June 26, 1967.

26. Ibid.

27. "Montana State Rodeo Results," NIRA Newsletter, May 12, 1961.

28. Shawn Davis, interview with author, Bozeman, Montana, June 17, 1986.

29. "NIRA Rodeo Reaches Big Payoff," *The Laramie Daily Boomerang,* July 10, 1965.

30. "TSC Wins National Rodeo," *Stephenville Daily Empire,* July 9, 1967.

31. Jim Fain, "College Rodeo National Finals," *Western Horseman,* 1967, 21.

32. Ibid.

33. "Minutes of NIRA Executive Board Meeting," Sacramento, California, July 1–3, 1968.

34. "Linderman Award," *PRCA Media Guide 2000,* 220.

35. David G. Brown, *Gold Buckle Dreams: The Rodeo Life of Chris LeDoux,* 224–29.

36. Jean Mead, "Wyoming's Singing Cowboy," *Empire Magazine* in *Denver Post,* November 8, 1981, n.p.

37. "NIRA Executive Board Minutes," June 26, 1967.

38. "NIRA Board Minutes," Sacramento, California, July 1, 1968.

39. *Sul Ross State University Rodeo,* program, Alpine, Texas, May 13–15, 1965.

40. Marianne Munz Brunson, interview with author, Bozeman, Montana, June 15, 1997.

41. "Texas Western College Rodeo Results, March 27–29, 1961," NIRA Newsletter, May 12, 1961.

42. Mary Fuller, interview with author, Bozeman, Montana, June 20, 1998.

43. Randy Magers, interview with author, Odessa, Texas, March 13, 1993.

CHAPTER 5

1. Harlan Schott, letter to author, Vernon, Texas, July 14, 1998.

2. "Fact or Fiction," *Rodeo Collegian,* February 15–March 15, 1976, 1, 4.

3. "NIRA Board Minutes," December 15, 1974, 7.

4. "Rattling the Gate," *Rodeo Collegian,* final edition, 1976, 2.

5. "Riding Herd on Rodeo Results—On a Computer," *College National Finals Rodeo,* program, 1973, n.p.

6. Van J. Rigby Jr., letter to Southwest Region Faculty Advisers, Students, and Directors, n.d.

7. Randy Witte, "Walt Garrison, Still a Cowboy," *Western Horseman,* April 1991, 18–19, 21–24.

8. "U.S. Tobacco Offers NIRA $74,000 Dip," *Rodeo Collegian,* sample edition, 1975, 4, 16.

9. "NIRA Hall of Fame to be Established," *College Rodeo News,* January 1977, 1.

10. "Regional Awards Created by Director," *Rodeo Collegian,* sample edition, 1975, 13.

11. Bob Clore, interview with author, Bozeman, Montana, June 20, 1987.

12. "1972 College National Finals Rodeo," *Rodeo Collegian,* 1972, 13.

13. "Bob Miller," *Rodeo Collegian,* 1974, 44.

14. "Highlights from the Oklahoma City Board Meeting," *Rodeo Collegian,* January 15–February 15, 1976, 12.

15. "Summary of Winter Board Meeting 1976," *College Rodeo News,* January 1977, n.p.

16. "Board Meeting Highlights," *Rodeo Collegian,* October 15–November 15, 1975, 16.

17. "Summary of Winter Board Meeting 1976," *College Rodeo News,* January, 1977, n.p.

18. "Stock Contractors for the CNFR Have Been Announced," NIRA Newsletter, May 2, 1975.

19. "RCA Professional Rodeo Judging Seminar," NIRA Newsletter, February 21, 1975.

20. Sonny Sikes, letter to NIRA Executive Board, December 6, 1978.

21. Pat Hamilton, interview with author, Bozeman, Montana, June 20, 1987.

22. Ibid.

23. "Corfield's catching up with NIRA," *The World of Rodeo,* September 1979.

24. NIRA Alumni Reunion video, 1994.

25. Del Higham, "Editor's Page," *Rodeo Collegian,* 1973, 3.

26. Jay Murphey, "UTM Paves Rodeo Road of Success," *The Collegiate Arena,* May 1998.

27. "1977 College National Finals Rodeo," *Rodeo Collegian,* NIRA Annual, 1977, 14.

28. "Champion Steer Wrestler, Steve D. Fryar," *Rodeo Souvenir,* 1977.

29. "Champion Team Roper, Thomas R. Maycumber," *Rodeo Souvenir,* 1977.

30. "Champion Bareback Rider, Jack Lee Himes," *Rodeo Souvenir,* 1977.

31. "Champion Barrel Racer, D. Joann Whitehead," *Rodeo Souvenir,* 1977.

32. Suzi Stevko, "He's Come a Long Way," *The World of Rodeo,* September, 1979, 11.

33. *PWRA/WPRA Official Reference Guide,* vol. 8, 1991, 5, 36.

34. "Horsemanship and Rodeo," Southeastern Oklahoma State University pamphlet, n.d.

35. "All-Around Cowgirl, Shelly Haskins Mueller," *Rodeo Souvenir,* 1977.

36. "Champion Breakaway Roper, Sherre J. Stoddard," *Rodeo Souvenir,* 1977.

37. Dr. Sam A. Monticello, "Notice to CNFR Contestants," *The World of Rodeo,* April, 1979, 13.

CHAPTER 6

1. Patricia H. Moree, "Finals Are Not Minor Undertaking for MSU and Its Partners," *The World of Rodeo,* June, 1980, 18.

2. Jack Tanner, "Springer Started a Mutual Love Affair between the NIRA and U.S. Tobacco," *The World of Rodeo,* October, 1980, 10.

3. Jack Tanner, "Miller, Glossen Growing with the NIRA," *The World of Rodeo,* October, 1980, 11.

4. "NIRA Board Minutes," December 7, 1986.

5. CNFR, program, 1986.

6. Patricia H. Moree, "He's Making the CNFR Bigger and Better," *The World of Rodeo,* May, 1981, 14.

7. "Summer Board Meeting Minutes," NIRA, 1983–84.

8. "NIRA Board Minutes," June 26, 1985.

9. Ibid.

10. "Davis Named New Manager for '84 College Finals Rodeo," *College National Finals Rodeo* edition, *Bozeman Daily Chronicle,* June 18, 1984, A8.

11. "NIRA Board Minutes," Las Vegas, Nevada, December, 1988.

12. "NIRA Board Minutes," Las Vegas, Nevada, December 5–6, 1987.

13. "NIRA Board Minutes," June 18, 1986.

14. "Minutes," December, 1988.

15. NIRA Bylaws, Article VIII, 3B (2) rule, 1980.

16. "NIRA Board Minutes," winter 1982.

17. Steve Fleming, "Cryer Fills PRCA Commissioner's Position," *ProRodeo Sports News,* December, 1987, 5.

18. *ProRodeo Special News Release,* October 22, 1986.

19. Molly McAuliffe Hepper, interview with author, Bozeman, Montana, June 16, 1989.

20. Bob Doty, interview with author, Stephenville, Texas, May 3, 1987.

21. Ibid.

22. Carl Hill, "SEOSU Marks Return of CNFR to Bozeman with a Remarkable Double Team Victory," *The World of Rodeo,* July, 1980, 5–6.

23. Patricia H. Moree, "CNFR, National Champs Decided at Bozeman," *The World of Rodeo,* July, 1981, 5.

24. Cathy Cagliari, interview with author, Bozeman, Montana, June 21, 1988.

25. Cathy Dennis, interview with author, Bozeman, Montana, June 16, 1989.

26. Clay Robinson, interview with author, Bozeman, Montana, June 21, 1991.

27. Jack Tanner, "There Was No Stopping Robinson," *The World of Rodeo,* July, 1980, 7.

28. Ibid.

29. "Dawson College Suspension Announced at Bozeman Finals," *The World of Rodeo,* July, 1981, 8.

30. Kendra Santos, "Professional Bull Riders," *Western Horseman,* September, 1995, 110.

31. Ed Knocke, "PBR Enjoying the Ride," *Dallas Morning News,* March 18, 1999.

32. CNFR, program, 1985.

33. "Plane Crash Kills 4 PRCA Cowboys," PRCA News Release, July 3, 1990.

34. Ruth Rudner, "Rodeo Days at the Old College Corral," *Wall Street Journal,* August 28, 1987.

35. Dave Lensegrav, interview with author, Bozeman, Montana, June 16, 1989.

36. Ty Murray, interview with author, Bozeman, Montana, June 16, 1989.

37. Shawn McMullan, interview with author, Lubbock, Texas, November 11, 1990.

38. Jim Watkins, interview with author, Stephenville, Texas, May 2, 1987.

39. Ibid.

40. Murray interview.

41. Gordon Clark, interview with author, Bozeman, Montana, June 16, 1988.

42. Harry Vold, interview with author, Bozeman, Montana, June 18, 1986.

43. Tim Corfield, interview with author, Bozeman, Montana, June 17, 1989.

CHAPTER 7

1. Molly McAuliffe Hepper, interview with author, Bozeman, Montana, June 16, 1990.

2. McAuliffe Hepper interview.

3. Tim Corfield, "Challenge of Change," *The Collegiate Arena,* October, 1996, 9.

4. Tyler Keith, "From the NIRA Student President—His Views on CNFR Qualification Rule Change," letter to the editor, *Cowboy's Digest,* March 15, 1995, C9.

5. "CNFR Qualification Rule Change Deleted after January Ballot," *Cowboy's Digest,* March 15, 1995, 1, C4.

6. Ibid.

7. Kay Lynn Beard, "NIRA Faculty President Looking Forward to Keen Competition at the 1996 CNFR," *The Collegiate Arena,* premier issue, June 3, 1996, 3.

8. "Gender Equity," NIRA information sheet for CNFR, 1996.

9. Bud Young, interview with author, Bozeman, Montana, June 20, 1989.

10. Shawn Davis, interview with author, Bozeman, Montana, June 15, 1996.

11. Michael Finkel, "Rasslin' with Hard Times," *Sports Illustrated,* 1993.

12. John Larick, interview with author, Bozeman, Montana, June 19, 1993.

13. Article III, Articles of Incorporation, National Intercollegiate Rodeo Foundation, Inc. 1994.

14. Masahiro Kitamura, interview with author, Bozeman, Montana, June 15, 1991.

15. Randy Magers, interview with author, Odessa, Texas, March 14, 1993.

16. "No More NIRA Queen Pageant," *NIRA News,* April, 1992, 6.

17. Zane Davis, interview with author, Bozeman, Montana, June 16, 1990.

18. Zane Davis, interview with author, Bozeman, Montana, June 19, 1993.

19. Shawn Davis, interview with author, Bozeman, Montana, June 19, 1993.

20. Davis interview, June 15, 1996.

21. John Larick, interview with author, Bozeman, Montana, June 16, 1990.

22. Shawn Vant, interview with author, Bozeman, Montana, June 22, 1991.

23. Dan Mortensen, interview with author, Bozeman, Montana, June 15, 1991.

24. "Injured Bull Rider Jerome Davis Making Miracle Strides," *Cowboy's Digest,* June 15, 1999, 1, 11.

25. Cliff Norris, interview with author, Bozeman, Montana, June 19, 1993.

26. Philip Elkins, interview with author, Bozeman, Montana, June 19, 1993.

27. Beau Gillespie, interview with author, Bozeman, Montana, June 18, 1994.

28. Marty McCloy, interview with author, Bozeman, Montana, June 18, 1994.

29. Whip Griemsman, interview with author, Bozeman, Montana, June 17, 1995.

30. Davis interview, June 15, 1996.

31. Jeremy Crane, interview with author, Bozeman, Montana, June 15, 1996.

32. Aaron Williams, interview with author, Bozeman, Montana, June 15, 1996.

33. Elisa Nielsen, interview with author, Bozeman, Montana, June 16, 1990.

34. Jimmi Jo Martin, interview with author, Bozeman, Montana, June 16, 1990.

35. Julie Adair, interview with author, Bozeman, Montana, June 22, 1991.

36. Lari Dee Guy, interview with author, Vernon, Texas, January 4, 1991.

37. Shelley Johnston, interview with author, Bozeman, Montana, June 19, 1993.

CHAPTER 8

1. "Meet the Press," *Daily at the College National Finals Rodeo* in *Tri-State Livestock News,* June 1, 1997, 2.

2. "National Intercollegiate Rodeo Association Current Rule Changes," NIRA Winter Board Meeting, December 11, 1998; *The Collegiate Arena,* February, 1999, 22.

3. Ibid.

4. Susan Kanode, "Walt Garrison Top Hand Award Honors Program Founder," United States Tobacco News Release, Casper, Wyoming, 1999.

5. Susan Kanode, "Scholarship Award Program Passes $4 Million Mark," U.S. Smokeless Tobacco Company Scholarship Awards Program News Release, June, 2001.

6. "Meet Ed Mayberry, Miles City, Mont." *Daily at the College National Finals Rodeo* in *Tri-State Livestock News,* June 8, 1997, 15.

7. William O. "Doc" Beazley, interview with author, Abilene, Texas, April 27, 1991.

8. Sarah Neely, "PRCA's Terri Greer to Attend '97 CNFR," *The Collegiate Arena,* May, 1997, 22.

9. Commissioner Tim Corfield, "NIRA Negotiates CNFR in Bozeman, Sponsor Commitments," *The Collegiate Arena,* October, 1998, 5.

10. Ibid.

11. "Casper, Wyoming, Here We Come!" *The Collegiate Arena,* January, 1999, 7.

12. "Tom Parker: Casper College 'Tradition' Helps Bring College National Finals to Wyoming," *The Collegiate Arena,* January, 1999, 7.

13. Pamela Vaull Starr, "1998 College National Finals Rodeo: Some Goals Grasped . . . Some Dreams Dashed," *Tri-State Livestock News,* June 27, 1998, B9.

14. Bryant Mikkelson, interview with author, Bozeman, Montana, June 19, 1999.

15. Tim Corfield, "2000 State of the NIRA Address," *The Collegiate Arena,* January, 2001, 5.

16. Ibid.

17. Tim Corfield, "New Playoff Series Announced," *The Collegiate Arena,* July, 2000, 5.

18. "The Senate Concurrent Resolution No. 67," adopted by both the Senate and House of the State of Texas and signed by Governor George W. Bush, April 26, 1999.

19. Kolt Dowdy, interview with author, Vernon, Texas, May 1, 1995.

20. Travis Griffin, interview with author, Vernon, Texas, May 2, 1995.

21. Kirby Berry, interview with author, Vernon, Texas, May 4, 1995.

22. Colin "Roudy" Bauer, interview with author, Vernon, Texas, May 4, 1995.

23. Dowdy interview.

24. Shane Hatch, interview with author, Vernon, Texas, May 5, 1995.

25. Ibid.

26. Dowdy interview.

27. Bauer interview.

28. Dowdy interview.

29. Berry interview.

30. Doug Fennell, interview with author, Vernon, Texas, May 2, 1995.

31. Hatch interview.

32. Dowdy interview.

33. Brian Steinberg, "California Tradition Ends as Rodeo Unable to Wrangle Funds from College," *Community College Week,* May 5, 1997.

34. Baxter Black, "The College Rodeo Team," *The Collegiate Arena,* May, 1998, 7.

35. Pam Conner, interview with author, Vernon, Texas, April 28, 1990.

36. "Allen's Have Time for Rodeo Success, Family," *The Collegiate Arena,* July, 1997, 4.

37. F. C. "Caddo" Wright, interview with author, Lubbock, Texas, May 31, 1990.

38. "Rodeo 2000: Commissioner Corfield State of the NIRA Address," *The Collegiate Arena,* January, 2000, 8.

39. Ibid.

40. Ron Gullberg, "Board Ousts Corfield," *Casper Star Tribune,* June 16, 2001, A14.

41. Ibid., 1.

42. Ibid., A14.

43. Ibid.

Bibliography

BOOKS

Allen, Michael. *Rodeo Cowboys in the North American Imagination.* Reno: University of Nevada Press, 1998.

Brown, David G. *Gold Buckle Dreams: The Rodeo Life of Chris LeDoux.* Greybull, Wyo.: Wolverine Gallery, 1986.

Fredriksson, Kristine. *American Rodeo: From Buffalo Bill to Big Business.* College Station: Texas A&M University Press, 1985.

Jordan, Teresa. *Cowgirls: Women of the American West.* New York: Anchor Press, 1982.

LeCompte, Mary Lou. *Cowgirls of the Rodeo: Pioneer Professional Athletes.* Urbana: University of Illinois Press, 1993.

Nasaw, David. *The Chief: The Life of William Randolph Hearst.* Boston: Houghton Mifflin, 2000.

Slatta, Richard W. *The Cowboy Encyclopedia.* New York: W.W. Norton, 1994.

Westermeier, Clifford D. *Man, Beast, Dust: The Story of Rodeo.* Lincoln: University of Nebraska Press, 1947.

MAGAZINES, NEWSPAPERS, PAMPHLETS

"1962 National Intercollegiate Rodeo Finals." ABC *Wide World of Sports,* September 8, 1962.

"1972 College National Finals Rodeo." *Rodeo Collegian.* 1972.

"1977 College National Finals Rodeo." *Rodeo Collegian.* NIRA Annual, 1977.

ACRA Newsletter, April, 1960.

"Allen's Have Time for Rodeo Success, Family." *The Collegiate Arena,* July, 1997.

"A&M Rodeo to Be a Novelty Livestock Show." *The Battalion,* Texas A&M newspaper, November 5, 1920.

"Annual Rodeo Friday Night Great Success." *The Battalion,* Texas A&M newspaper, October 27, 1922.

Armstrong, Jerry. "Picked Up in the Rodeo Arena." *Western Horseman,* June, 1949.

———. "Picked Up in the Rodeo Arena." *Western Horseman,* June, 1950.

———. "Picked Up in the Rodeo Arena." *Western Horseman,* May, 1951.

"As Heard Over the Mike." *The Buckboard,* n.a. 1949.

Beard, Kay Lynn. "NIRA Faculty President Looking Forward to Keen Competition at the 1996 CNFR." *The Collegiate Arena,* premier issue, June 3, 1996.

Black, Baxter. "The College Rodeo Team." *The Collegiate Arena,* May, 1998.

"Black List (Individuals)." *The Rigging,* NIRA newsletter, 1950.

"Board Meeting Highlights." *Rodeo Collegian,* October 15–November 15, 1975.

"Bob Miller." *Rodeo Collegian,* 1974.

Bruce [Kingsbery], Evelyn. "National Intercollegiate Rodeo Association." *Hoofs and Horns,* December, 1949.

California Aggie College of Agriculture. Newspaper. March 31, 1949.

"Campus Waddies to Risk Necks in Bulldogging Ferocious Rodeo Bovines." University of Arizona, newspaper clipping, 1940.

"Casper, Wyoming, Here We Come!" *The Collegiate Arena,* January, 1999.

Cervi, Mike. "How to Produce a Collegiate Rodeo." Booklet. 1958.

"Charlie Rankin: The First President." *Chats,* for the National Association of Farm Broadcasters, April, 1995.

"CNFR Qualification Rule Change Deleted after January Ballot." *Cowboy's Digest,* March 15, 1995.

"College Rodeo." *Time,* May 21, 1951.

"College Rodeo Provides Fast Program Here," University of Arizona, n.d.

"College Rodeo Stars to Appear Here during Fiesta in Championship Finals." Texas newspaper. *The San Antonian,* January 28, 1950.

"Colleges May Organize." *Bi-Weekly Rodeo News,* December 18, 1948.

"College Students Attend First Rodeo." *The Victor Press* (Victorville, California), April 14, 1939.

Corfield, Tim. "Challenge of Change." *The Collegiate Arena,* October, 1996.

———. "NIRA Negotiates CNFR in Bozeman, Sponsor Commitments." *The Collegiate Arena,* October, 1998.

———. "New Playoff Series Announced." *The Collegiate Arena,* July, 2000.

———. "2000 State of the NIRA Address." *The Collegiate Arena,* January, 2001.

"Corfield's Catching up with NIRA." *The World of Rodeo,* September, 1979.

"Cowgirls in the NIRA Finals." Photocopy of page 5 from a rodeo program.

"Cow Palace Results—Revised." Two typed pages. May 3, 1950.

Davis, Alvin and Barbara. *Rodeo Roundup,* April-May, 1957.

Davis, Alvin G. "The National Intercollegiate Rodeo Finals." *The Horse Lover's Magazine,* 1953.

"Davis Named New Manager for '84 College Finals Rodeo." *College National Finals Rodeo.* Edition. *Bozeman Daily Chronicle,* June 18, 1984.

"Dawson College Suspension Announced at Bozeman Finals." *The World of Rodeo,* July, 1981.

"Desert Sage Says." *The Victor Press* [Victorville, Calif.], April 7, 1939.

Dolan, George B. "Sul Ross Gets Rodeo Trophy for Keeps after Third Straight Victory." *Fort Worth Star Telegram,* May, 1951.

"Education Helps, Says College Rodeo Cowboy." *The Oregonian,* June 12, 1952.

"Evelyn Bruce Selected NIRA Publicity Director." n.d.

"Fact or Fiction." *Rodeo Collegian,* February 15–March 15, 1976.

Fain, Jim. "College Rodeo National Finals." *Western Horseman,* 1967.

"Felts, Arizona Entry Wins Honors at Godshall Collegiate Rodeo April 8." Newspaper clipping, n.d.

"Final Standings for 1950." *The Rigging*, NIRA newsletter, 1950.

Finger, Hank. "Autobiography." Bar SR Bar Rodeo Association. n.d.

Finkel, Michael. "Rasslin' With Hard Times." *Sports Illustrated*, 1993.

Fleming, Steve. "Cryer Fills PRCA Commissioner's Position." *ProRodeo Sports News*, December, 1987.

"Gender Equity." NIRA information sheet for CNFR. 1996.

Goldsmith, Susan. "Corky Randal." Newspaper article. n.d.

Gullberg, Ron. "Board Ousts Corfield." *Casper Star Tribune*, June 16, 2001.

"Hank Finger, Alpine Chamber of Commerce Manager, Killed." *Standard Times*, Del Rio, Texas, December 17, 1950.

Higham, Del. "Report of Public Relations Activities." All NIRA Executive Board Members. *Memorandum*, January 10, 1969.

———. "All Club Advisers." All NIRA Executive Board members. *Memorandum*, March 10, 1969.

———. "Public Relations Activities." All NIRA Executive Board members. *Memorandum*, May 9, 1969.

———. "Editor's Page." *Rodeo Collegian*, 1973.

"Highlights from the Oklahoma City Board Meeting." *Rodeo Collegian*, January 15–February 15, 1976.

Hill, Carl. "SEOSU Marks Return of CNFR to Bozeman with a Remarkable Double Team Victory." *The World of Rodeo*, July, 1980.

"Horsemanship and Rodeo." Southeastern Oklahoma State University. Pamphlet, n.d.

"Hoss Inman." Obituary from Virginia Inman. Lamar, Colorado, August 26, 1993.

Hutchison Kansas Record. Newspaper article. April 8, 1949.

"Injured Bull Rider Jerome Davis Making Miracle Strides." *Cowboy's Digest*, June 15, 1999.

"Intercollegiate Rodeo Now Numbers 43 Teams Across U.S." *The Oregonian*, June 12, 1952.

"Jim Deutsch Top NIRA Bull Rider." *The South Texas* 28 (April 11, 1953): 1.

Kanode, Susan. "Walt Garrison Top Hand Award Honors Program Founder." United States Tobacco News Release, Casper, Wyoming, 1999.

———. "Scholarship Award Program Passes $4 Million Mark." U.S. Smokeless Tobacco Company Scholarship Awards Program News Release, June, 2001.

Keith, Tyler. "From the NIRA Student President—His Views on CNFR Qualification Rule Change." Letter to the editor. *Cowboy's Digest*, March 15, 1995, C9.

Kelton, Elmer. "Intercollegiate Rodeo Association." *Persimmon Hill* 8 (winter, 1974): 33–43.

King, Chuck. Editor of the *Bi-Weekly Rodeo News.* May 6, 1950.

Knocke, Ed. "For Old Times' Sake." *Dallas Morning News*, January 20, 1999.

———. "PBR Enjoying the Ride." *Dallas Morning News*, March 18, 1999.

"Large Crowd Attends Annual Rodeo." *The Battalion*, Texas A&M newspaper, November 12, 1924.

"Local Man India Rodeo Director." Newspaper photo with caption clipping. July 29, 1945.

McAlpine, Jocelyn. "Rodeo . . . University Style," newspaper clipping, n.d.

McKeller, Bob. "Poly Cowpokes Swamp Visiting Dirt Eaters in Two-Day Rodeo." *El Paso Mustang,* Cal Poly, San Luis Obispo, California, May 25, 1951.

Mead, Jean. "Wyoming's Singing Cowboy." *Empire Magazine* in *Denver Post,* November 8, 1981.

"Meet Ed Mayberry, Miles City, Mont." *Daily at the College National Finals Rodeo* in *Tri-State Livestock News,* June 8, 1997.

"Meet Our President." *The Rigging,* NIRA newsletter, May, 1951.

"Meet the Press." *Daily at the College National Finals Rodeo* in *Tri-State Livestock News,* June 1, 1997.

Merritt, Hyde. "Cussin' and Discussin'." *Bi-Weekly Rodeo News,* December 18, 1948.

———. "Just Whittlin'." *Western Horseman,* March, 1950.

Modesto, California. Newspaper article clipping. April 11, 1949.

"Montana's First College Rodeo?" *College Rodeo,* November, 1982.

"Montana State Rodeo Results." NIRA Newsletter. May 12, 1961.

Monticello, Dr. Sam A. "Notice to CNFR Contestants." *The World of Rodeo,* April, 1979.

Moree, Patricia H. "Finals Are Not Minor Undertaking for MSU and Its Partners." *The World of Rodeo,* June, 1980.

———. "He's Making the CNFR Bigger and Better." *The World of Rodeo,* May, 1981.

———. "CNFR, National Champs Decided at Bozeman." *The World of Rodeo,* July, 1981.

Muir, Jean. "Cowboys on Campus." *Saturday Evening Post,* February 10, 1951.

Murphey, Jay. "UTM Paves Rodeo Road of Success." *The Collegiate Arena,* May, 1998.

"National Intercollegiate Rodeo Association Current Rule Changes." NIRA Winter Board Meeting, December 11, 1998. *The Collegiate Arena,* February, 1999.

Neely, Sarah. "PRCA's Terri Greer to Attend '97 CNFR." *The Collegiate Arena,* May, 1997.

"New Blood for the Rodeo Business: College Students are Getting Interested." *The Buckboard,* January, 1949.

"NIRA and RCA Have Agreement for Collegians." Newspaper clipping. Abilene, Texas, March, 1952.

NIRA column. *Rodeo News,* March 11, 1950.

"NIRA Convention." *The Rigging,* NIRA newsletter, March, 1951.

"NIRA Convention 1955." *Rigging Bag,* April, 1955.

"NIRA Hall of Fame to Be Established." *College Rodeo News,* January, 1977.

NIRA Newsletter. December, 1950.

"NIRA Rodeo Reaches Big Payoff." *The Laramie Daily Boomerang,* July 10, 1995.

"NIRA Stars in National Finals Rodeo." *Rodeo Collegian,* November 15–December 15, 1975.

"No More NIRA Queen Pageant." *NIRA News,* April, 1992.

"Noted Cowboy Will Judge College Rodeo." Newspaper clipping. Fort Worth, Texas, May 5, 1951.

"Notice for Old and Prospective New Member Clubs of the NIRA." Flyer, n.d.

"Notice to All Clubs." *The Rigging,* March 1951.

"Novelty Show a Big Success." *The Battalion,* Texas A&M newspaper, November 27, 1919.

Partain, Kyle. "NFR First Takes Root at 1958 Meeting." *ProRodeo Sports News,* January 14, 1998.

"Plane Crash Kills 4 PRCA Cowboys." PRCA News Release, July 3, 1990.

ProRodeo Special News Release, October 22, 1986.

"Queen of the 1957 NIRA Finals." *National Intercollegiate Rodeo Championship Finals.* Souvenir program. Colorado Springs, Colorado. June 13–16, 1957.

"Queen of the 1958 NIRA Finals." *NIRA Championship Finals.* Souvenir program. Colorado Springs, Colorado, June 12–15, 1958.

Rankin, Charlie. Typed note clipped to "College Rodeo Stars to Appear during Fiesta in Championship Finals." *The San Antonian,* January 28, 1950. Newspaper article. NIRA Alumni archives.

"Rattling the Gate." *Rodeo Collegian.* Final edition. 1976.

"RCA Professional Rodeo Judging Seminar." NIRA Newsletter, February 21, 1975.

"Regional Awards Created by Director." *Rodeo Collegian.* Sample edition. 1975.

"Report on the Meeting Held by Representatives from Twelve Colleges to Discuss Forming a National Intercollegiate Rodeo Association," n.d.

Richmond (California) *Independent.* Newspaper article clipping, n.d., 1949.

"Ride 'em cowboys." Photo caption. *Daily Palo Alto Times,* March 19, 1951.

The Rigging Bag, published by Sam Houston State Teachers College, Huntsville, Texas, April 23, 1955.

"Rodeo 2000: Commissioner Corfield State of the NIRA Address." *The Collegiate Arena,* January, 2000.

Rudner, Ruth. "Rodeo Days at the Old College Corral." *Wall Street Journal,* August 28, 1987.

San Francisco Bulletin. Newspaper article clipping. April 11, 1949.

San Francisco Examiner. Newspaper article clipping. April 10, 1949.

Santos, Kendra. "Professional Bull Riders." *Western Horseman,* September, 1995.

"The Senate Concurrent Resolution No. 67." Adopted by both the Senate and House of the State of Texas and signed by Governor George W. Bush. April 26, 1999.

SRSU Bar SR Bar History of the Organization. Pamphlet. 1947.

Starr, Pamela Vaull. "1998 College National Finals Rodeo: Some Goals Grasped . . . Some Dreams Dashed." *Tri-State Livestock News,* June 27, 1998.

Steinberg, Brian. "California Tradition Ends as Rodeo Unable to Wrangle Funds from College." *Community College Week,* May 5, 1997.

Stevko, Suzi. "He's Come a Long Way." *The World of Rodeo,* September, 1979.

"Stock Contractors for the CNFR Have Been Announced." NIRA Newsletter, May 2, 1975.

Stout, Doyle. "Sul Ross News Release." December 8, 1947.

"Summary of Winter Board Meeting 1976." *College Rodeo News,* January, 1977.

"Talk from Back of the Chutes." *The Rigging,* NIRA newsletter, 1950.

"Talk from Back of the Chutes." *The Rigging,* NIRA newsletter, May, 1951.

Tanner, Jack. "There Was No Stopping Robinson." *The World of Rodeo,* July, 1980.

———. "Springer Started a Mutual Love Affair between the NIRA and U.S. Tobacco." *The World of Rodeo,* October, 1980.

———. "Miller, Glossen Growing with the NIRA." *The World of Rodeo,* October, 1980.

"Teams Claim National Honor." *SR Rodeo,* July 15, 1962.

"Texans Take Top Spot in Rodeo, Oklahoman Collegian Solo Winner." *The Oregonian,* June 15, 1952.

"Texas Western College Rodeo Results, March 27–29, 1961." NIRA Newsletter, May 12, 1961.

"Tom Parker: Casper College 'Tradition' Helps Bring College National Finals to Wyoming." *The Collegiate Arena,* January, 1999.

"TSC Wins National Rodeo." *Stephenville Daily Empire,* July 9, 1967.

"University of Arizona Spectacular Show Sunday." Newspaper clipping, 1940.

"U.S. Tobacco Offers NIRA $74,000 Dip." *Rodeo Collegian.* Sample edition. 1975.

Wald, Matthew J. *MSU Rodeo: 1947–1989.* Unpublished manuscript. NIRA Alumni archives.

Witte, Randy. "Walt Garrison, Still a Cowboy." *Western Horseman,* April, 1991.

"World's First Intercollegiate Rodeo Ready for Saturday's Thrills, Spills at Rancho." *The Victor Press* (Victorville, California), April 7, 1939.

The Wrangler, Colorado State University newspaper, April 1, 1996.

CORRESPONDENCE

Bascom, John. Letter to Tim Corfield. Walla Walla, Washington. May 14, 1993.

Bowman, Charles. Letter to Hoss Inman and James Heath. Lamar, Colorado. November 9, 1959.

———. Letter to Dale Stiles. Casper, Wyoming. 1960.

Brady, Bill. Letter to Sul Ross Rodeo Club. Alpine, Texas. January 7, 1949.

Brock, Bill. Letter to Bill Guest and carbon to four regional directors and Harley May. Abilene, Texas. April 22, 1951.

Burkholder, Jack. Letter to author. Vernon, Texas. May 26, 1993.

Corfield, Tim. Letter to Ross F. Caton. Alba, Texas. July 19, 1999.

Dow, J. Ben. Letter to Charlie Rankin. College Station, Texas. n.d., 1949.

Felts, William "Bill." Letter to author. Vernon, Texas. November 24, 1989.

Finger, Hank. Letter to Toots Mansfield. Big Spring, Texas. February 21, 1949.

———. Letter to University of Texas Varsity Rodeo Club. Austin, Texas. March 15, 1949.

———. Letter to Charlie Rankin. College Station, Texas. March 24, 1949.

———. Letter to Charlie Rankin. College Station, Texas. November 19, 1949.

Fly, Murry H. Letter to Doug Fernandes. Alpine, Texas. October 25, 1948.

Foss, J. H. Letter to Evelyn Bruce Kingsbery. Alpine, Texas. August 1, 1949.

———. Letter to Evelyn Bruce Kingsbery. Alpine, Texas. November 21, 1949.

Frazer, Bob. Letter to Charlie Rankin. McAllen, Texas. May 8, 1992.

Garrison, Carl L. Letter to Hank Finger. Alpine, Texas. April 21, 1949.

Gordon Jr., Clyde. Letter to Evelyn Bruce Kingsbery. Alpine, Texas. November 3, 1949.

Harris, Howard. Letter to editor of *The Buckboard.* RCA newspaper. n.d.

Harris, W. A. Letter to Bud Purdy. Bozeman, Montana. November 8, 1965.

Hewson, Dale. Letter to Jim Moore. University of Wyoming. 1960.

Hopkins, Ethel "Ma." Letter to Evelyn Bruce Kingsbery. Alpine, Texas. October 5, 1949.

Inman, Hoss. Letter to Dale Stiles. Casper, Wyoming. November 17, 1959.

King, Chuck. Letter to Evelyn Bruce Kingsbery. Alpine, Texas. Sept. 1949.

Kingsbery, Evelyn Bruce. Letter to Charlie Rankin. College Station, Texas. April 21, 1949.

———. Letter to Chuck King. Billings, Montana. December 8, 1949.

———. Letter to James Cathey. Fort Worth, Texas. 1950.

Knox, Jo Gregory. Letter to Charlie Rankin. College Station, Texas. November 15, 1949.

Koller, Joe. Letter to Evelyn Bruce Kingsbery. Alpine, Texas. November 26, 1949.

Kotkin, Garnet Rose. Letter to Harley May. Alpine, Texas. n.d.

———. Letter to Harley May. Alpine, Texas. January 10, 1951.

———. Letter to Harley May. Alpine, Texas. January 22, 1951.

Kramer, Timi. Letter to Evelyn Bruce Kingsbery, Alpine, Texas. September 29, 1949.

May, Harley. Letter to Guy Weadick. Calgary, Alberta, Canada. March 8, 1951.

McMullan, Tibba. Letter to Evelyn Bruce Kingsbery. Alpine, Texas. 1949.

Merritt, Hyde. Letter to Charlie Rankin. College Station, Texas. n.d.

Mickler, James. Letter to Evelyn Bruce Kingsbery. Alpine, Texas. November 8, 1949.

Muir, Jean. Letter to Harley May. Alpine, Texas. April 11, 1951.

Munn, Irving M. Letter to Sonny Sikes. Huntsville, Texas. April 9, 1965.

Overstreet, Maxie. Letter to Evelyn Bruce Kingsbery. Alpine, Texas. n.d.

Purdy, Bud. Letter to W. A. Harris. Laramie, Wyoming. November 16, 1965.

Rankin, Charlie. Letter to Hank Finger. Alpine, Texas. February 4, 1949.

———. Letter to H. G. Bedford. Lubbock, Texas. February 28, 1949.

———. Letter to Ham Scott. State College, New Mexico. March 11, 1949.

———. Letter to Red Clark. Canoga Park, California. March 16, 1949.

———. Letter to Claude B. Mullins. Halletsville, Texas. June 9, 1949.

———. Letter to Joe Fornay. Fort Collins, Colorado. June 9, 1949.

———. Letter to Morton J. O'Brien. Tucson, Arizona. June 9, 1949.

———. Letter to Evelyn Bruce Kingsbery. Alpine, Texas. December 8, 1949.

Reed, Mary Ann. Letter to Harley May. Alpine, Texas. May 26, 1951.

Rigby Jr., Van J. Letter to Southwest Region Faculty Advisers, Students, and Directors. n.d.

Schoonover, C. O. Letter to Charles Bowman. Bozeman, Montana. June 12, 1959.

Schott, Harlan. Letter to author. Vernon, Texas. July 14, 1998.

Sikes, Sonny. Letter to NIRA Executive Board. December 6, 1978.

Stiles, Dale. Letter to Charles Bowman. Montana State College. 1960.

Stover, F. C. Letter to Betty Sims Solt. Roswell, New Mexico. June 3, 1996.

Texas Tech. Letter to Evelyn Bruce Kingsbery. Alpine, Texas. October 22, 1949.

Weadick, Guy. Letter to Harley May. Alpine, Texas. May 12, 1951.

INTERVIEWS

Adair, Julie. Interview with author. Bozeman, Montana. June 22, 1991.

Backstrom, Ellen. Interview with author. Bozeman, Montana. June 18, 1986.

Bauer, Colin "Roudy." Interview with author. Vernon, Texas. May 4, 1995.

Beazley, William O. "Doc." Interview with author. Abilene, Texas. April 27, 1991.

Berry, Kirby. Interview with author. Vernon, Texas. May 4, 1995.

Brunson, Marianne Munz. Interview with author. Bozeman, Montana. June 15, 1997.

Cagliari, Cathy. Interview with author. Bozeman, Montana. June 21, 1988.

Clark, Gordon. Interview with author. Bozeman, Montana. June 16, 1988.

Clore, Bob. Interview with author. Bozeman, Montana. June 20, 1987.

Connor, Pam. Interview with author. Vernon, Texas. April 28, 1990.

Corfield, Tim. Interview with author. Bozeman, Montana. June 17, 1989.

Crane, Jeremy. Interview with author. Bozeman, Montana. June 15, 1996.

Davis, Alvin G. Interview with author. Lubbock, Texas. October 24, 1986.

Davis, Shawn. Interview with author. Bozeman, Montana. June 17, 1986, June 19, 1993, and
    June 15, 1996.

Davis, Zane. Interview with author. Bozeman, Montana. June 16, 1990, and June 19, 1993.

DeBlasis, Jean Campbell. Telephone interview with author. Victorville, California. 1994.

Dennis, Cathy. Interview with author. Bozeman, Montana. June 16, 1989.

Doom, Becky Jo Smith. Interview with author. Jal, New Mexico. March 1, 1988.

Doty, Bob. Interview with author. Stephenville, Texas. May 3, 1987.

Dowdy, Kolt. Interview with author. Vernon, Texas. May 1, 1995.

Elkins, Philip. Interview with author. Bozeman, Montana. June 19, 1993.

Fennell, Doug. Interview with author. Vernon, Texas. May 2, 1995.

Fuller, J. R. "Shorty." Interview with author. Bozeman, Montana. June 19, 1993.

Fuller, Mary. Interview with author. Bozeman, Montana. June 20, 1998.

Gillespie, Beau. Interview with author. Bozeman, Montana. June 18, 1994.

Godshall, Jeanne. Studio City, California. Telephone interview with author. September 12,
    1994.

Griemsman, Whip. Interview with author. Bozeman, Montana. June 17, 1995.

Griffin, Travis. Interview with author. Vernon, Texas. May 2, 1995.

Guy, Lari Dee. Interview with author. Vernon, Texas. January 4, 1991.

Hamilton, Pat. Interview with author. Bozeman, Montana. June 20, 1987.

Harris, Howard. Interview with author. Vernon, Texas. May 18, 1994.

Hatch, Shane. Interview with author. Vernon, Texas. May 5, 1995.

Hepper, Molly McAuliffe. Interview with author. Bozeman, Montana. June 16, 1989, and
    June 16, 1990.

Johnston, Shelley. Interview with author. Bozeman, Montana. June 19, 1993.

Jones, Cecil. Interview with author. Las Vegas, Nevada. December 11, 1986.

Kimball, Mary Ellen Chandler. Interview with author. Alpine, Texas. September 7, 1986.

Kingsbery, Jack, and Evelyn Bruce. Interview with author. Uvalde, Texas. March 24, 1989.

Kitamura, Masahiro. Interview with author. Bozeman, Montana. June 15, 1991.

Knox, Jo Gregory. Interview with author. Tarzan, Texas. April 16, 1987.

Larick, John. Interview with author. Bozeman, Montana. June 16, 1990, and June 19, 1993.

Lau, Jim. Interview with author. Bozeman, Montana. June 5, 1989.

Lee, Giles. Interview with author. Hobbs, New Mexico. February 10, 1987, and February 6, 1990.

Lensegrav, Dave. Interview with author. Bozeman, Montana. June 16, 1989.

Longbotham, Elisabeth Prude. Interview with author. Abilene, Texas. April 24, 1987.

Longbotham, Jack. Interview with author. Abilene, Texas. April 24, 1987.

Magers, Randy. Interview with author. Odessa, Texas. March 13, 1993.

Marr, Pat Dunigan. Interview with author. Bozeman, Montana. June 20, 1992.

Martin, Jimmi Jo. Interview with author. Bozeman, Montana. June 16, 1990.

May, Harley. Interview with author. Las Vegas, Nevada. December 12, 1986.

McCloy, Marty. Interview with author. Bozeman, Montana. June 18, 1994.

McMullan, Shawn. Interview with author. Lubbock, Texas. November 11, 1990.

Mikkelson, Bryant. Interview with author. Bozeman, Montana. June 19, 1999.

Mortensen, Dan. Interview with author. Bozeman, Montana. June 15, 1991.

Murray, Ty. Interview with author. Bozeman, Montana. June 16, 1989.

Nielsen, Elisa. Interview with author. Bozeman, Montana. June 16, 1990.

Norris, Cliff. Interview with author. Bozeman, Montana. June 19, 1993.

Rankin, Charlie. Telephone interview with author. McAllen, Texas. August 3, 1988.

Rivers, Ann. Telephone interview with author. Victorville, California. 1994.

Roberts, Monty. Interview with author. Bozeman, Montana. June 15, 1996.

Robinson, Clay. Interview with the author. Bozeman, Montana. June 21, 1991.

Sawyer, Fern. Interview with author. Childress, Texas. June 5, 1993.

Schild, Bob. Interview with author. Bozeman, Montana. June 18, 1994.

Sikes, Sonny. Interview with author. Bozeman, Montana. June 17, 1986.

Solt, Betty Sims. Interview with author. Roswell, New Mexico. July 22, 1987.

Stiles, Dale. Interview with author. Bozeman, Montana. June 20, 1987.

Vant, Shawn. Interview with author. Bozeman, Montana. June 22, 1991.

Vold, Harry. Interview with author. Bozeman, Montana. June 18, 1986.

Watkins, Jim. Interview with author. Stephenville, Texas. May 2, 1987.

Williams, Aaron. Interview with author. Bozeman, Montana. June 15, 1996.

Wright, F. C. "Caddo." Interview with author. Lubbock, Texas. May 31, 1990.

Young, Bud. Interview with author. Bozeman, Montana. June 20, 1989.

BIBLIOGRAPHY

NIRA Bylaws and Minutes, Rodeo Programs, Yearbooks, Video

Agenda. NIRA Board Meeting. 1960.

Articles of Incorporation. National Intercollegiate Rodeo Foundation, Inc. 1994.

CNFR. Program. 1973. 1985. 1986.

Hardin-Simmons Rodeo. Program. April 27–28, 1950.

"Minutes of the NIRA Convention." January 2–3, 1950. December 5, 1950.

"Minutes of the Rocky Mountain Faculty Rodeo Conference." Casper College. Casper, Wyoming. December 18, 1959.

National Intercollegiate Rodeo Finals. Program. 1952. 1953. 1967.

NIRA Alumni Reunion video. 1994.

NIRA Board Minutes. January 10–11, 1960. 1964.

NIRA Board Minutes. Summer. 1967. 1968. 1983–84. 1985. 1986.

NIRA Board Minutes. Winter. 1974. 1982. 1986. 1987. 1988.

NIRA Constitution. 1949, 1951, 1967–68, 1980.

NIRA Convention Minutes. 1960.

PRCA Media Guide 2000.

PWRA/WPRA Official Reference Guide. 1991.

Rodeo Souvenir. 1977.

Sul Ross State University Rodeo. Program. May 13–15, 1965.

Texas A&M Yearbook. *1927 Longhorn.*

University of Arizona rodeo programs. 1938. 1939. 1940. 1947.

Index

Southern Region, 31, 58

Southwestern Exposition & Livestock Show & Rodeo, 9

Southwestern Oklahoma State University, 175, 212

Southwestern Oklahoma State University, NIRA finals: during the 1970s, 283, 285; during the 1980s, 149, 150, 159, 285, 287–89; during the 1990s, 181, 183, 189, 190, 205, 207, 289–93; during the early 2000s, 294; summarized, 260, 271

Southwest Missouri State University, NIRA finals, 260, 289, 291

Southwest Region, 57–58, 108–109

Southwest Texas Junior College (Uvalde Junior College): NIRA administrative activities, 227; NIRA finals, 103, 158, 187, 232, 260, 278–79, 292

Southwest Texas State University, NIRA finals: during the 1960s, 96, 231, 277, 280; during the 1980s, 159, 286–87; summarized, 261, 271

Spencer, Sally, 102, 248, 278

Spires, Bill, 14, 15

Sponsor Contests, 14

sponsors. See scholarships

Sports in Action, 85

Spotts, Nelson, 252, 278

Springer, Francis, 240

Springer, Red, 109, 110, 134–35

Springer, Ty, 158

Sproul, Pam Simon, 131, 243, 283

Sproul, Rachael Myllmaki, 202, 264, 292

St. George, Utah, NIRA finals, 85, 94–95, 280

Standifer, Jamie, 203, 215, 268

Standifer Snyder, Caryn, 148, 190–91, 202, 259, 269, 291–92

Stanley, Marion, 68

Stanley, Wendall, 255

State Fair Community College, NIRA finals, 124, 261, 284

Steagall, Rocky, 157, 244, 286

steer riding, Victorville rodeo, 225

steer roping, women's beginnings, 7

steer wrestling, NIRA champions listed: in 1949, 238–39, 273; during the 1950s, 273–77; during the 1960s, 277–81; during the 1970s, 281–85; during the 1980s, 285–89; during the 1990s, 289–93; during the early 2000s, 293–95. See also National Intercollegiate Rodeo Association (NIRA), championship finals

steer wrestling, photos, 118

Steiner, Tommy, 67

Steinmiller, Cleonne Skinner, 102, 248, 279

Stephen F. Austin State University, NIRA finals, 261, 295

Stephens, Terry Jo, 85, 231

Stevens, Kelly, 189

Stevenson, Carl, 221

Steward, Rusty, 240

Stewart, Lorna, 231

Stewart, Vicki, 231

Stiles, Dale: ACRA leadership, 78, 81–82; as coach, 34, 91–94, 93; NIRA finals, 36, 38, 40, 235–37, 242, 266, 273; NIRA leadership, 77

Stiles, Roger, 93

Still, Perry, 52

stock contracting: during the 1970s, 113, 115; during the 1980s, 134, 139; during the 1990s, 177, 196, 199

Stoddard, Sherre J., 130–31, 244, 284

Stone, Jeff, 109

Stover, F. C., 15, 20, 58, 67, 130, 254, 274

Stover Crowson, Janet, 130

Stricklin, Jack, 18–19

Stroh, Shawn, 248, 291

Stroud, Bill, 59, 65

Stuart, Calvin, 240

Stubbs, Frank, 9